TRADITIONS OF WAR

Traditions of War

OCCUPATION, RESISTANCE, AND THE LAW

KARMA NABULSI

OXFORD

UNIVERSITY PRESS

OXFORD
UNIVERSITY PRESS

Great Clarendon Street, Oxford OX2 6DP
Oxford University Press is a department of the University of Oxford.
It furthers the University's objective of excellence in research, scholarship,
and education by publishing worldwide in

Oxford New York

Athens Auckland Bangkok Bogotá Buenos Aires Calcutta
Cape Town Chennai Dar es Salaam Delhi Florence Hong Kong Istanbul
Karachi Kuala Lumpur Madrid Melbourne Mexico City Mumbai
Nairobi Paris São Paulo Singapore Taipei Tokyo Toronto Warsaw

and associated companies in Berlin Ibadan

Published in the United States
by Oxford University Press Inc., New York

British Library Cataloguing in Publication Data
Data available

Library of Congress Cataloging in Publication Data
Nabulsi, Karma.
Traditions of war: occupation, resistance, and the law/Karma Nabulsi.
Includes bibliographical references.
1. War (International law)—History. 2. Combatants and noncombatants
(International law)—History. 3. War (International law)—Philosophy. I. Title
JZ6387.N33 1999 341.6—dc21 99-15995

ISBN 0-19-829407-7

1 3 5 7 9 10 8 6 4 2

Typeset by Best-set Typesetter Ltd., Hong Kong
Printed in Great Britain
on acid-free paper by
Biddles Ltd
Guildford and King's Lynn

Vincent Wright,
Natus ad gloriam.

ACKNOWLEDGEMENTS

I know that this work was only possible because I was perched upon the shoulders of a veritable peoples' army; like all true peoples' armies, it was made up of individuals who willingly volunteered their energies, each of whom made a vital contribution. As all military theorists know, victories are achieved due to a variety of factors. In my case five were crucial: technical, financial, intellectual, moral, and spiritual.

As to the first, many thanks to the disciplined and expert troop of librarians at the Bibliothèque Nationale, the Archives Nationales, the Bibliothèque Polonaise (Adam Mickiewitz), the Bibliothèque Historique de la Ville de Paris, and the Conseil d'État (all in Paris), and to Robert Thiery of the Bibliothèque d'Études Rousseauistes in Montmorency; M. Christian Peri of the Centre de Recherches Corses in Corte; the International Committee of the Red Cross, the Institut Henri Dunant, and the Bibliothèque Publique de la Ville de Génève, all in Geneva; the Bodleian Law Library, and the Codrington in Oxford. I would like especially to thank the librarians in the Upper Reading Room of the Bodleian: David Busby, Helen Rogers, and Vera Ryhajilo who never faltered despite being buried under a bombardment of requests. I would also like to thank the archivists of the foreign ministries of France, Belgium, the United States, and Great Britain in Nantes, Brussels, Washington, DC, and Kew. Many individuals gave documents that proved invaluable; Professor Geoffrey Best supplied handwritten annotations on Brussels, as well as his very own notes on this work in its previous incarnation as a D.Phil.; Colin Lucas generously permitted the pillage of his libraries, both at King's Mound and Balliol; Professor Adam Roberts came up with numerous obscure texts and a comprehensive bibliography on military occupation and resistance, and Professor Ian Clark was unfailingly encouraging and supportive both during and after the examination of my D.Phil. I had a technical ops team whose work in the arts of translation was phenomenal: first of all a heartfelt thanks to Michal Myck of St Peter's College, who represents the finest of Polish traditions of peace, and whose work at the National Library in Warsaw gave me both Tadeusz Kosciuszko and Karol Stolzman. *Sono grata a* Dr Federico Varese and Luca Nunziata, both of Nuffield College, for the Italian translations of the legendary Carlo Bianco, count of St Jorioz (Freddie also offered helpful words of encouragement on the concluding quotation). I am grateful to the National Museum of Wroclaw for the transparency of Artur Grottger's work 'Wojna'. My sincere thanks to Nannerl Keohane for giving me my own copy of her inspiring *Philosophy and the State in France*, which has proved a trusty code-breaking manual for approaching the minefields of the history of thought. Most of all I would like to thank my editor, Dominic Byatt, who has been clever, tough, helpful, wise, and encouraging in exactly the combination required for a first-time author. And he has been extremely patient as well. Amanda Watkins has shown supreme efficiency and much kindness, as has my copy-editor, Edwin Pritchard, who also demonstrated enormous fortitude of character when confronted with my singular grammar. Finally, a huge thanks to Frank Pert, who has now become the family indexer, for such a magnificent job.

As to the second factor, the true quarter-master general who made the entire campaign possible was Yassir Arafat, first by letting me take what turned into a rather extended leave from official duties, secondly for generously furnishing the means to do so, and, finally, for providing me with such a remarkable political education for so many years. In the last few years there also appeared (from the heavens) a legion of friends and family members sporting deeply-cut pockets. First to descend from the skies was (alphabetically) David Astor; rapidly followed by Ian Gilmour, Bob Himoff, Hikmat Nabulsi, Hayat and Peter Palumbo, the Earl and Countess of Portsmouth, and Wafiq Said. The generous *per diem* given to the Palestinian negotiating team in Washington in 1991–3 allowed for several archival trips. The Politics Fellows of St John's, Worcester, and Oriel all provided teaching lecturerships at a crucial stage in my transition from political practitioner to scholar; the Master and Fellows of St Peter's (particular thanks to Gavin Williams), in electing me to a College Lectureship in Politics, provided a model community in which to be one. The Cyril Foster Fund provided the means for a first raid into the archives of Ajaccio, Bastia, and Corte on the famous liberty trail of Pasquale Paoli. Lastly, the Warden and Fellows of Nuffield College, in electing me to a Research Fellowship, conferred upon me the pleasure of revising the last chapter of this book on an extremely powerful computer, and the most sociable environment in which to work.

For intellectual guidance I was blessed with a fearless army of individuals, all armed with particularly fine-toothed combs. They descended upon the blotchy tangle of my confused strategic plan, managing to tease out the worst snarls with great gentleness and humour. All remaining clumps are the result of my obstinacy. First thanks to Adam Roberts, who encouraged and guided this work when it was a thesis and I was at Balliol. Secondly grateful thanks to Martha Dewell, Robert Gildea, Roger Griffin, Ruth Harris and Iain Pears, Marc Stears, Harriet Vyner, Ngaire Woods, Andrew Walter, and especially Sudhir Hazareesingh for reading various drafts more carefully than I wrote them (and especially the restraint shown by the latter individual, who continually reined back his immaculate sense of style when he clearly wanted to bring a sharp set of shears to the entire proceedings). Thanks to Isaiah Berlin for reading the chapter on martialism, making several helpful comments, and laughing in all the right places; and to Quentin Skinner for reading my republicans with such care, for his many pertinent and illuminating comments, and for constantly encouraging me in my next project (which has helped me to finish this one); thanks also to Robert Wokler for his attentive reading and helpful comments on J. J. Rousseau, and generously sharing his extensive knowledge of both the man and his work. For one brief year, I was blessed with the incredible event of Natalie Zemon Davis, and am eternally grateful for all the inspiring discussions about everything. When I was just starting my research, Nabil Shaath indulged my new passion by allowing chunks of my archival findings to be incorporated into the official Palestinian documents at Washington, to be read (to my delight and their dismay) across the negotiating table in the direction of our interlocutors.

For moral support, I had the truest band of citizens to encourage me in my new campaign: Ahmed Khalidi, Avi Shlaim, Annie Portsmouth, Bella Freud, Bridget Gilchrist, Flora McEwen Mason, Gwyn Daniel, James Fox, Jerry Cohen, Julia Cameron, Julia Hore, Harriet Vyner, Laila Nabulsi, Lynn Welchman, Mary Ellen Lowe, Michael Freeden, Munib el Masri, Ngaire Woods, Satya, Thara, and Sandy Hazareesingh. In these last days, Marc Stears has demonstrated that republican virtue is alive and well in academe; in the first days, Alan Montefiore, Joseph Raz, and Edward Said all did so as well. I would like also to thank Noam Chomsky who (by reminding me to choose my battles with great care), helped me to cross from the public to private sphere whence I discovered this new world. And, of course, and most importantly (again), Shunu, with whom I have the good fortune to share it. As is by now clear, I have thanked enough people to be able fairly to spread the blame around for any mistakes contained in the text: however, any remaining surely belong to me.

As for the last factor; it is the one which I know informs my work and all aspects of my life to this day: my companions-in-arms of those scorching summer days before, during, and after the battle and siege of Beirut of 1982. Such was the giving of themselves with a nonchalance and style, good humour and simplicity of spirit, that it continues to illuminate the way I live to this moment. It is to them, especially to those who fell *sur le chemin*, that I dedicate this work:

'Ora e Sempre'

K. N.

Nuffield College
21 December 1998

CONTENTS

Introduction

This story is about wars and military occupation, and the ideas underlying them. The search for these ideas will be carried out in the domain
of the laws of war, a body of rules which seeks to regulate the practices
of war and those permitted to fight in it. This will be done by addressing the challenge posed by a particular principle in the modern laws
of war: the distinction between combatant and non-combatant. This
concept has been recognized as the fundamental principle upon which
the entire notion of 'humanity in warfare' rests; equally it has been
acknowledged as the most fragile. The forces which underpinned this
distinction (more precisely, a distinction between the lawful and unlawful combatant) will be explored by presenting three ideologies, each
representing a distinct political tradition of war. These traditions were
rooted in incommensurable conceptions of the good life, and the overall
argument of this work is that this incommensurability lay at the source
of the failure fully to resolve the problem of distinction between lawful
and unlawful combatants between 1874 and 1949.

This book will make use of concepts and methods borrowed from a
range of intellectual disciplines: political thought, history, and international theory. In terms of the first, political theory will be used to analyse
the premises upon which different ideologies of war were constructed,
and how far they cohered. Historical examples will be relied upon to
ground these intellectual constructs in the practices of war in the
modern European experience. Finally, this work will situate itself within
the field of 'classical' traditions of international theory, examining the
influence of key thinkers on war such as Machiavelli, Grotius, and
Rousseau. However, it differs from this orthodox approach in two ways.
First, it is not seeking to ascertain the 'true' meaning of their philosophies, but rather with how their political thoughts were interpreted and
shaped by later generations. Finally, this influence is not restricted to
abstract theorists and philosophers: this work is centrally concerned
with paradigms constructed by practitioners of war, both professional
and civilian.

The first three chapters of the book lay out the differing contexts through which this dilemma in the laws of war can be viewed; political and diplomatic, social, and intellectual. The narrative begins by summarizing the diplomatic history of the conferences at Brussels in 1874, the Hague in 1899 and 1907, and at Geneva in 1949. While the negotiations of the laws of war proved successful in many respects, they consistently failed to agree on a common understanding of a lawful combatant. The second chapter illustrates the social history of army occupation in Europe and resistance to it (from the Napoleonic period to the Franco-Prussian war), and places these diplomatic failures in their broader social and political context. A range of intellectual approaches to the laws of war and war itself are explored in the third chapter, and their relative methodological value assessed.

After these accounts, the three traditions of war will be presented in successive chapters. First to be introduced will be the martial tradition. Its properties will initially be contrasted with realism in order to highlight its distinct values and characteristics. How this ideology operated in practice will then be shown by the development of the tradition in Britain, chosen above all because it is normally seen as exempt from such 'illiberal' values. Chapter 5 will be devoted to the Grotian tradition of war, in many senses the most dominant, in that its core principles lay at the heart of the very project of the laws of war. Although related to it, this paradigm is distinct from what is commonly known as the Grotian tradition in international relations. The republican tradition will be represented partially through the writings of Jean Jacques Rousseau, who, along with Pasquale Paoli and Tadeusz Kosciuszko, advanced a unified system of the republican good life and war in conjunction with the laws of war. The way in which this tradition developed in the nineteenth century will then be depicted.

The traditions presented here are emblematic in a number of ways. They came to life and were embedded in situations of wars of conquest, military occupation, and foreign rule. It was exclusively in such conditions that martialists set forth the justifying claims for their actions; republicans constructed their theories of popular sovereignty and practices of insurrectionary war; and Grotians attempted to provide guidelines which would distinguish civilians from soldiers. Since these traditions only functioned in these types of conflict, this work will not be concerned with the types of war which were limited to professional armies (such as the First World War). Equally, the emphasis here is on a particular type of military occupation, driven by the imperatives of conquest and domination. Although legally obsolete in Europe during the period with which this book is concerned, the practices of expansion, conquest, and foreign rule remained. Besides resting on these temporal and spatial foundations, these traditions all operated within a wide range of social and institutional settings. They could be defined by ideologues and pamphleteers, adopted by political groups, flourish in narrow technical communities or in broad political cultures, or even embody the core values of a particular institution such as the army, as will be seen in Chapter 4.

As ideological constructs, these traditions had five essential features. Central to their identity were a number of myths about man, society, war, liberty, patriotism, and nationalism. The precise nature of these myths will be explored in the last three chapters. Arising out of these myths were singular ideological discourses, with all their associated attributes, notably a common language, a similar set of questions, and identically defined goals. They were also traditions in a literal sense, in that their arguments were conducted not only synchronically but also diachronically. In other words, the aims and objectives of each tradition were defined within generations, as well as transmitted across them. In this movement across time, the core characteristics of the traditions sometimes came to be modified. Thus, between the mid-nineteenth and mid-twentieth centuries the Grotian tradition underwent quite radical transformations. During the same period, the martialists retained their core values, but the locus of their implementation shifted considerably. The republicans, finally, developed two distinct political strands during the nineteenth century.

Last but not least, what defined these ideologies as traditions was that they interacted not only amongst themselves, but with each other. In books and newspapers, at barricades, over conference floors, across geographical boundaries (and especially where these boundaries had dissolved), successive generations of martialists, Grotians, and republicans insulted, confronted, and captivated each other. And it is the story of this common engagement which will unfold in this narrative.

1

The Modern Laws of War
from 1874 to 1949

The general project of the modern laws of war was driven by the ambition to introduce internationally recognized legal conventions into the practice of war itself. This goal was to be achieved by codifying existing customs and practices of armies, with the aim of mitigating, standardizing, and thus stabilizing the conduct of war. As a French military jurist explained: 'Our goal here is to humanize war, by which we mean that it must be regularized.' This was because guerilla war, while 'constituting a doubtful benefit and efficiency', constituted 'a certain atrocity'; it was the 'most terrible aggravation of war'.[1] The foundation of the modern laws of war was based on the concept of *jus in bello* (the laws of war), and the exclusion of *jus ad bellum* (principles of just war).[2]

In the second half of the nineteenth century some progress was made on the regulation of war. By 1874 the European powers had agreed upon two international conventions, the Geneva Convention on Prisoners of War of 1864, inspired by Henri Dunant's book (and his subsequent lobbying of the Swiss government), *Un souvenir de Solférino*, an eye-witness account of extreme suffering endured by wounded soldiers on the field during the Austro-Italian war,[3] and the St Petersburg Declaration of 1868.[4] Still unresolved were the lawful practices of

[1] A. Brenet, *La France et l'Allemagne devant le droit international pendant les opérations militaires de la guerre de 1870–71* (Paris: A. Rousseau, 1902), 26.
[2] For a clear legal exposition on the difficulties in reconciling (or indeed keeping separate) these two strands of law, see C. Greenwood, 'The Relationship between Jus ad Bellum and Jus in Bello', *Review of International Studies*, 9 (1983), 221–34.
[3] See T. E. Holland, 'A Lecture on the Brussels Conference of 1874, and other Diplomatic Attempts to Mitigate the Rigours of Warfare', *Lectures 1874–84* (Oxford: Oxford University Press, 1886), 5–7. See also Henri Dunant's classic *Un souvenir de Solférino* (Geneva: Éditions l'Âge d'Homme, 1969).
[4] The St Petersburg declaration, which is directed at 'Renouncing the use, in time of war, of explosive projectiles under 400 grammes in weight' contains the famous statement of principle: 'the only legitimate object which States should endeavour to accomplish during war is to weaken the forces of the enemy state'. A. Roberts and R. Guelff, *Documents on the Laws of War* (Oxford: Clarendon Press, 1989), 30–1.

armies on land, and the difficulties these caused, notably the distinction between combatant and non-combatant and the rights and duties of occupying powers and occupied inhabitants.[5] The one existing national codification, the Lieber Code,[6] introduced a set of legal guidelines at the time of the civil war in the United States, and provided the basis for a draft text presented to the various delegations which gathered at Brussels in the summer of 1874.[7]

This conference, which took place against the express wishes of Bismarck, was little more in origin than a careless scheme devised by royal families. This emerges clearly from the diplomatic archives of the period. The French ambassador to London explained to his government what underlay its apparent sinister designs. The Belgian diplomat, the Comte de Derby (who was to represent his country at the forthcoming conference), had told him that on receiving the invitation to attend from the Cabinet Office at St Petersburg, he, too, had first believed it to have originated from the German government, 'admitting to me that he had feared that it was a manœuvre of Prince Bismarck to incite a quarrel with France, but that he had been immediately reassured that he should have no doubt that the Chancellor of the Empire was not only a stranger to the project but deeply opposed to it. It was, he was informed "a personal inspiration of Emperor Alexander, who had devised it directly with Emperor William during the illness and absence of Prince Bismarck, and had obtained William's agreement on the matter. Upon his return, the Prince could not manage to get the old Emperor to go back on his word".'[8] Indeed, it is clear from the archives that very few diplomats wanted the gathering to take place at all. The French ambassador in Berne reported home that 'the Germans say it has nothing to do with them. Austria has no instructions, but thinks humanitarian projects utterly stupid. Holland, Sweden, and Belgium all don't want it— *no one* wants this conference.'[9] The French Ambassador in Vienna recounted to his Ministry: 'Great incertitude and complete confusion

[5] Doris Graber, *The Development of the Law of Belligerent Occupation 1863–1914: A Historical Survey* (New York: Columbia University Press, 1949), 13–36.

[6] *Instructions for the Government Armies in the Field, issued as General Orders No. 100 of 24 April 1863*. For more details on the Lieber Code see Richard Baxter's 'Le Premier Effort moderne de codification du droit de la guerre: Francis Lieber et l'Ordonnance no. 100', *Revue internationale de la Croix Rouge* (April–May 1963).

[7] 'Actes de la Conférence Réunie à Bruxelles, du 27 juillet au 27 août 1874, pour régler les lois et coutumes de la guerre' (hereafter 'Actes'), *Nouveau Recueil général de traités*, iv (1879–80), 15.

[8] La Rochefoucauld, in London, to the French Minister of Foreign Affairs, 26 June 1874. Brussels, Légations Fond A 25, Archives du Quai d'Orsay, Nantes.

[9] Ambassador Laboulaye, 23 July 1874. Brussels, Légations Fond A 25.

reigns over everything concerning this international conference. The Russian government launched this affair without first consulting the powers who are to take part. Nothing has been organised, no President designated. The Emperor's government has had to address itself to his Majesty the Emperor of Russia in order to obtain the relevant information. This information has yet to arrive.'[10] So there was much uncertainty about the nature and purpose of the Brussels Conference. Furthermore, many countries were convinced that this was a meeting that would benefit some much more than others.

Lesser powers, with Britain and France on their side, had no ambition to see the Prussian army's occupation practices of 1870–1 codified into international law, while even Bismarck could see little advantage in such a development. As A. J. P. Taylor noted on Bismarck's policy at this time: 'after 1870, his diplomacy was aimed at the preservation of the newly established *status quo*. "Immobility" and "restraint" were the key objectives of this policy . . . Bismarck's fundamental objectives were to secure agreements with both Austria and Russia.' German war ambitions were, in fact, more suited to an uncodified customary 'might is right' philosophy, which the Chancellor had no desire to see challenged in a public arena.[11]

The smaller powers' fears were confirmed by the Russian draft of the convention circulated to delegates in the summer of 1874. The legal norms proposed so obviously favoured occupying forces that this text became known in European ministries as the 'The Code of Conquest'. The British representative in Brussels, Savile Lumley, described the widespread response to the project in a letter to Lord Derby as a 'general feeling of uneasiness . . . created by the consideration of [Russia's] propositions, which have been aptly designated as the "Code of Conquest".'[12] The French Ambassador to the Court of St James was more candid in his description of the draft text:

First we were astonished by the development of the project itself, prematurely announced . . . and when we became enlightened as to the propositions themselves, we have remarked that all the measures seem calculated to guarantee conquering armies the advantages of their organization and their invading marching masses, and, on the other hand, to diminish the means of defence of

[10] 7 June 1874. Brussels, Légations Fond A 25.
[11] For the wider political tensions, see J. de Breucker's 'La Déclaration de Bruxelles de 1874 concernant les lois et coutumes de la guerre', *Chroniques de politique étrangère*, 27/1 (1974), 1; also A. J. P. Taylor, *The Struggle for Mastery in Europe* (Oxford: Oxford University Press, 1971), 135.
[12] 7 July 1874. FO 83/481, Foreign Office Archives, Public Record Office (PRO).

populations surprised by such an invasion. It is, in truth, a code of conquest rather than one of defence.[13]

It was the Results of the Franco-Prussian War of 1870–1 that fundamentally reaffirmed the tenet that force equalled law, and so disturbed the French diplomats cited above, illustrating that the right of conquest was still a legitimate feature of the international system. The state system of the period was highly Vattelian: international law was seen as an exclusive tool of governments, and indeed states were regarded as the only recognized actors in the international system. But the relationship among these states was clearly ordered: empires remained the dominant political norm, and the hierarchical role they enjoyed within the Concert of Europe meant that their interests were always given priority. In the case of the Brussels Project, there was thus a 'striking resemblance' between the Russian draft's stipulation on armies in the field and the Prussian view, a point noted by the French diplomat Laboulaye at Berne. Speaking of the agent of Prussia at the conference, the renowned international lawyer Bluntschli: 'The German sympathies have not prevented one from remarking, with a certain alarm, the striking resemblance between the Project and book VIII of *The International Law of War* by Mr Bluntschli.' He added, somewhat disingenuously, 'one could almost say that the one is a copy of the other.'[14] In addition, the Russian jurist de Martens admitted that he conceived the Brussels project with the central purpose of serving the particular needs of his imperial army: 'at the very moment when obligatory military service is on the way to being introduced here the need to settle, in law, the rights and duties of troops has become an absolute imperative.' This strictly hierarchical conception of international society was also in evidence during negotiations, where there was no equality in the decision-making process among the European states invited—lesser powers had little real negotiating ability.[15]

Once the Brussels conference had begun it was clear that the Prussian representative, General Voigt-Rhetz, and his legal firepower, Bluntschli, did not suffer from the lesser powers' skittishness about the

[13] La Rochefoucauld to the Minister of Foreign Affairs, 26 June 1874. Brussels, Légations Fond A 25.

[14] 23 July 1874. Brussels, Légations Fond A 25.

[15] Baron Lambermont, the Belgian host, noted how all the diplomats invited were terrified not to 'compromise' themselves with the great powers, but nonetheless could not absent themselves from the conference: 'Saturday, Sunday and Monday I successively received all the delegations. Except for the Russians and the Germans . . . all are vague, all perplexed, all desperate not to compromise themselves.' 29 July 1874. Dossier B. 7484, Archives of the Ministry of Foreign Affairs, Brussels.

aims of project. A Belgian delegate, Lambermont evocatively captured their bullish confidence when he described, in his diary, how they appeared to treat the entire Conference as a battlefield: 'Long conversation with General Voigt-Rhetz. Germans do conferences as they do war; they send an army corps. The noble General believes he has come to make a real treaty.'[16] And, showing much less indulgence towards their lawyer, he commented: 'At any rate the arrival of Bluntschli is getting on the nerves of Count Chotek and most of the other delegates. We expect endless harangues and tirades . . . one senses it is understood in Berlin that the Russian project harmonised extremely well with Prussian practices.'[17]

In the end, the Brussels Conference broke up after a month of debates without any clear agreement, except for a draft 'Brussels Declaration', which disgruntled jurists immediately began to pick over. That the outcome was always likely to be a 'shipwreck' was apparent to nearly all European parties concerned.[18] But two important groups seemed unaware of the possibility of failure: the personal representatives and jurists of the Russian and German emperors, and the assorted publicists on the laws of war in Britain and the Continent, who pressured their respective governments to convene it in the first place. As the French minister at Versailles complained: 'It appeared obvious to me that we could not decline the invitation to participate in the project's deliberations, especially on a subject which current publicists have kept, without cease, in the public eye.'[19]

Undeterred by the failure of Brussels, these jurists took up the torch within the portals of the recently formed Institute of International Law, writing and rewriting drafts of a possible legal code at various international gatherings. The text they produced became known as the 'Oxford Manual' of 1880, which most countries ignored.[20] This

[16] Lambermont told of the Russian delegate threatening this view: 'Jomini told me that if the minor States don't fall in line, the entire treaty could well be signed between the four great military Powers of the Continent—Is this a serious idea? A means of intimidation?', ibid.

[17] Baron Lambermont, 26 July 1874, ibid.

[18] Holland described the controversy over the question of a distinction between lawful and unlawful combatant as the reef that 'shipwrecked' the Brussels conference, *Lectures*, 5. See Graber, *The Development of the Law of Belligerent Occupation*, 24–6. Lord Derby's report on the Brussels Conference gives an in-depth explanation on the reasons Britain and others would not sign the treaty. *British and Foreign State Papers 1873–4* (1881), lxv. 1014–111.

[19] Baron Baude, French Minister, Versailles, 16 June 1874. Brussels, Légations Fond A 25.

[20] On the founding of the Institute see, J. Scott (ed. and trans.), *Resolutions of the Institute of International Law* (New York: Oxford University Press, 1916); P. Bordwell, *The*

was, however, less vexing than the loud, official repudiation of the Manual by others, who took the opportunity to insult its authors and dispute the legitimacy of the entire enterprise. Although it had been Bluntschli who had worked so tirelessly to get the text accepted by jurists of other European nations, it was he that received a total (and public) humiliation from his own Prussian superiors, Von Hartmann and Von Moltke in their public response to his efforts. Von Hartmann wrote the official reply of the Prussian Ministry of War to the proposal for a 'Codification of the Laws of War' of 1880, entitled *Military Necessities and Humanity* which confirmed the army's preference for uncodified law in absolute terms. He wrote: 'the expression "civilised warfare", used by Bluntschli, seems hardly intelligible; for war destroys this very equilibrium . . . If military authority recognises duties it is because it imposes them upon itself in full sovereignty. It will never consider itself subject to outside compulsion. *Absolute military action in time of war is an indispensable condition of military success.*' Indeed, Hartmann refuted the whole notion of laws of war themselves, criticizing lawyers like Bluntschli 'whose aim was to produce an evolution of the means of war in a direction completely opposite to the nature and the objects of every war'.[21] But there was worse in store for Herr Bluntschli. Von Moltke, the military hero of Prussia, used the opportunity to compose his now infamous exposition on war and peace: 'Perpetual peace', he wrote to Bluntschli, 'is a dream, and it is not even a beautiful dream: war forms part of the universal order constituted by God. In war are displayed the most noble virtues, courage and abnegation, fidelity to duty, and the spirit of sacrifice which will hazard life itself; without war humanity would sink into materialism.'[22]

The next set of negotiations on the laws of war took place at The Hague in the summer of 1899. The Hague was one of a series of grand international 'peace' treaties envisioned by diplomats and politicians

Law of War between Belligerents: A History and Commentary (London: Stevens & Sons, 1908), 100. On the work of the Institute in preparing a manual based on the final draft at Brussels, see G. Rolin-Jacquemyns, 'Institut de Droit International: Travaux préliminaires à la session de la Haye, 1874–1875', *Revue de droit international et législation comparée*, 7 (1875). The only country to adopt 'the Manual' was Argentina. See Graber, *The Development of the Law of Belligerent Occupation*, 30.

[21] J. Von Hartmann, *Kriegsbrauch im Landkriege*, cited in J. Morgan (ed.), *The German War Book* (London: John Murray, 1915), 33. Emphasis in text.

[22] H. Von Moltke, in a letter to M. Bluntschli, the international lawyer, in 1880. From C. Andler's *Frightfulness in Theory and Practice* (London: T. Fisher Unwin, 1913), 46. See also H. Holborn, 'The Prusso-German School: Moltke and the Rise of the German General Staff', in P. Paret, G. Craig, and F. Gilbert (eds.), *The Makers of Modern Strategy* (Princeton: Princeton University Press, 1986), 354.

from various corners of the world to resolve such vexing issues as world disarmament and international arbitration.[23] The international atmosphere was radically different. As one lawyer was later to rhapsodize almost idiotically:

> To listen to the diplomatic wisdom of veteran statesmen like Baron de Staal, Count Nigra, and Lord Pauncefote; to hear the profoundest problems of International Law debated thoroughly and most brilliantly by authorities like de Martens, Asser, Descamps, Lammasch, and Zorn; to observe the notable idealism of Baron d'Estournelles, the sound judgement of M. de Basily and Jonkheer van Karnebeek, and the unerring prudence of Switzerland's efficient representative, M. Odier,—and finally, to watch the perfection of decision and tact in the firm but most amiable management of all these various elements by the chairman, M. Bourgeois,—all this would in itself be of sufficient general interest to deserve an enduring record.[24]

Still, the underlying fissures remained. As Ian Clark noted, at the Hague Conference: 'these efforts were little more than a faint descant in a diplomatic melody dominated by another mood'.[25] There were also several strands of broadly divergent political ideologies which gave support to the general notions of disarmament and peace; the peace internationalists, organizations promoting the economic values of free trade, institutes such as Nobel's which offered a peace prize as from 1897, and the more rarefied Institute of International Law of 1873.[26] At the Hague Conference in 1899, the American delegation invited all delegates to pay tribute to the influence of Hugo Grotius over their deliberations on the laws of war. In a distinctly religious ceremony at his grave, speeches were made in his honour, and on his tomb was laid a wreath made of laurel leaves of 'silver with berries of gold' on one side and an 'oak branch with silver leaves and gold acorns' on the other. As one proud lawyer recounted: 'it seemed peculiarly appropriate that

[23] Sixteen Latin American countries attended as well as Siam, China, Mexico, Japan, together with the influential presence of the United States: although the concern with the laws of war was predominantly European, The Hague was not, as its predecessor conference, a purely European affair. See W. Hull, *The Two Hague Conferences and their Contributions to International Law* (Boston: Ginn & Co., 1908), 10–17.

[24] G. F. W. Holls, *The Peace Conference at the Hague and its Bearing on International Law* (New York: Macmillan, 1900), 172–3. See also J. Hayward, 'The Official Social Philosophy of the French Third Republic: Léon Bourgeois and Solidarism', *International Review of Social History*, 6 (1961), 19–48.

[25] I. Clark, *The Hierarchy of States: Reform and Resistance in the International Order* (Cambridge: Cambridge University Press, 1980), 144.

[26] For a background of the aims and infrastructures of the broader peace movements in Europe at the time, see the comprehensive study by Sandy Cooper, *Patriotic Pacifism: Waging War on War in Europe 1815–1914* (Oxford: Oxford University Press, 1991).

the American delegation . . . should recall with gratitude the founder of international law, and the instigator, if not the initiator, of the Conference'.[27] However, as will be shown in Chapter 5, behind this legal cult engrossed in the beatification of Grotius lay a turbulent tale of plagiarism and bullying by the Russian delegation.

As at Brussels, it was the Russian Emperor who gave the impetus for the conferences. And also, as in 1874, it was Feodor Martens, the Russian jurist, who justified his Emperor's motivations (and in the same breath vindicated his own actions at The Hague):

Since 1874, the relations between European powers have changed a great deal: many of the prejudices which, in 1874, dominated the society of civilized nations, were replaced by a more just and more enlightened appreciation of political and social aspirations. The apprehension of becoming victim of an unjust and unprovoked invasion by a great power was replaced by the sentiments of mutual confidence and national security. All . . . have been penetrated by the conviction that Russia, in proposing the revision of the laws and customs of war of 1874, had in mind to compile neither a 'code of invasion', nor to bring weak nations into a 'regime of defeat'. This general conviction guaranteed the success of the discussion of the peace conference which should bring about a satisfactory result.[28]

Although it was the growing realization of the dangers of Europe's rapid over-militarization which pushed nervous statesmen to the table, rather than the desire to regulate the manner in which wars were fought, a convention entitled *The Laws and Customs of War on Land* (known as the Hague Regulations) nonetheless emerged from the first round of discussions. It omitted the majority of troublesome issues which had wrecked the Brussels Conference of 1874.[29] Also, in spite of an article which restricted the customary method of collective penalties against civilian populations in the Hague Regulations, Oppenheim noted in his *International Law* that the Hague Convention

---

[27] James Scott, *The Hague Peace Conferences of 1899 and 1907* (Baltimore: Johns Hopkins University Press, 1909), 185.

[28] *La Paix et la guerre* (Paris: Arthur Rousseau, 1901), 121. As Geoffrey Best noted, the writings of Martens offered a peculiar mix of rationalism and imperial militarism; he was not espousing equality as a political concept, merely a juridical one. *Humanity in Warfare* (London: Methuen, 1983), 163–4.

[29] However, as one Montague Burton Professor duly noted, in spite of the commonly held reputation of The Hague as a 'failed' disarmament conference, in 1899 it produced two important multilateral treaties and three prohibitory declarations. Adam Roberts, 'Land Warfare: From the Hague to Nuremberg', in M. Howard, G. J. Andreopoulos, and M. R. Shulman (eds.), *The Laws of War: Constraints on Warfare in the Western World* (New Haven: Yale University Press, 1994), 123.

does not at all prevent reprisals on the part of belligerents occupying enemy territory. In case acts of illegitimate warfare are committed by enemy individuals not belonging to the armed forces, reprisals may be resorted to, although practically innocent civilians are thereby punished for illegal acts for which they are neither legally nor morally responsible—for instance, when a village is burned by way of reprisals for a treacherous attack on enemy soldiers committed there by some unknown individuals. Nor does this new rule prevent the occupant from taking hostages.[30]

Following the Hague conferences and the First World War, there was an acceleration in the pace of international legal codification. The 1929 Geneva Convention on Prisoners of War constituted a great advance from the previous regulations, but still failed to raise the question of civilians who resisted occupation and whether they should be granted the privileges of belligerency (POW status).[31] Equally, the efforts in the 1930s of the International Committee of the Red Cross (ICRC) to persuade the major powers to sign a convention protecting civilians proved fruitless.[32] However, two other international treaties of the era also bore indirectly on the laws of war: the Covenant of the League of Nations and the Kellogg–Briand Pact (1928). Both were informed by the liberal internationalist view that war could be eradicated through enlightened diplomacy and collective action.[33] Also directly influencing the Geneva negotiations in 1949 were the various national and international positions on war crimes during and after the Second World War. For example, one of the most important legal precedents was the 1942 *London Declaration of War Crimes*, issued at the height of the war by the Allies, which proclaimed hostage-taking and other

[30] Article 50: 'No general penalty, pecuniary or otherwise, can be inflicted on the population on account of the acts of individuals for which it cannot be regarded as jointly or severally responsible'. L. Oppenheim, *International Law* (London: Longman, 1912), i. 175–6; Howard et al. *The Laws of War*, 56.

[31] Articles 77 and 79, 'Geneva Convention of July 27, 1929, Relative to the Treatment of Prisoners of War', *Handbook of the International Red Cross*, iv (Geneva: ICRC/IRCS, 1951), 90–1. Although the International Committee of the Red Cross had been responsible for authoring and revising several conventions on the sick and wounded in wartime, this was the first time a participatory role was assigned to the ICRC in a humanitarian capacity during conflict. See Dominique Junod's fascinating account of the subsequent tensions in developing this role in *The Imperilled Red Cross and the Palestine-Eretz Israel Conflict: 1945–1952* (London: Kegan Paul International, 1996), 11.

[32] See Hilaire McCoubray, *International Humanitarian Law: The Regulation of Armed Conflicts* (Aldershot: Dartmouth Publishing, 1990), 144.

[33] On both moral and legal restraints on war derived from such types of international legislation see G. Draper, 'The Ethical and Juridical Status of Constraints in War', *Military Law and Law of War Review*, 55 (1972), 169–86.

customary occupying army practices a war crime.[34] This gave an enormous impetus to states to create a legal convention which would actually reflect this politically inspired stance, in particular the Nuremberg Trials of 1946, and the Universal Declaration of Human Rights of 1948.[35]

A final set of negotiations resulted in the four Geneva Conventions of 1949, which covered different aspects of the limitations on war.[36] By 1949 the international system had been profoundly transformed by a number of events, of which the most momentous was the Second World War. As the Franco-Prussian War cast a spell over the Brussels Conference in 1874, so memories of the events of the early 1940s were still fresh in the minds of delegates at Geneva in 1949. The state system had also changed significantly. Empire, with all its political, social, and cultural ramifications was much less the prevailing norm in the European states system than had been the case at Brussels and The Hague. The British were the one delegation which seemed unaware of these changes in the international system. They were clearly still guided by a hierarchical conception of international order, and took positions at Geneva which isolated them. For example, the British attempt at introducing non-democratic procedures at Geneva was a resounding failure. Sir Eric Beckett of the FCO had instructed his representatives:

[34] 'Declaration of War Crimes, adopted by the Inter-Allied Conference at St. James's Palace on January 13, 1942', cited in G. Schwarzenberger, *International Law and Totalitarian Lawlessness* (London: Stevens, 1943), 140, 147–8. On the complex legal issues surrounding hostage-taking in occupied territory, see E. Hammer, and M. Salvin's seminal: 'The Taking of Hostages in Theory and Practice', *American Journal of International Law*, 38 (1944); A. Kuhn, 'The Execution of Hostages', *American Journal of International Law*, 36 (1942); and Lord Wright, 'The Killing of Hostages as a War Crime', *American Journal of International Law*, 25 (1946).

[35] For the task of creating (with accompanying difficulties) the legal foundations for the Nuremberg trials, see S. Paulson, 'Classic Legal Positivism at Nuremberg', *Philosophy and Public Affairs*, 4/2 (1975); for the influence of the principles of the League and Kellogg–Briand on Nuremberg, see Quincy Wright's typically virtuoso 'The Law of the Nuremberg Trials', *American Journal of International Law*, 40 (1947), and 'Legal Positivism and the Nuremberg Judgement', *American Journal of International Law*, 42 (1948); and see also M. E. Bathurst, 'The United Nations War Crimes Commission', *American Journal of International Law*, 39 (1945), 565–70.

[36] The four 1949 Geneva Conventions are: 'The Amelioration of the Wounded and Sick Armed Forces in the Field'; 'The Amelioration of the Condition of Wounded, Sick, and Shipwrecked Members of Armed Forces at Sea'; 'The Treatment of Prisoners of War'; and 'The Convention for the Protection of Civilians in Times of War'. The Geneva conventions of 12 Aug. 1949 (Geneva: International Committee of the Red Cross, 1949). See G. Cahen-Salvador, 'Protéger les civils', *Hommes et mondes*, 67 (Feb. 1952); P. de la Pradelle, *La Conférence diplomatique et les nouvelles Conventions de Genève du 12 août 1949* (Paris: Éditions Internationales, 1951), 44–139.

But I think our view is it really does not matter, indeed it is rather a good thing, if small countries are not represented at all of the meetings of every commission. They really cannot contribute much to the discussions and it is rather a good thing if they do not vote too much on matters [for] which really their views have not very great importance.[37]

However, decision-making processes had become somewhat more transparent, rendering negotiating positions more responsive to popular opinion. Not two weeks after the instructions from Beckett to dismiss the smaller countries, the British tried a new tack and reported its success at their morning meetings:

At the meeting last week we discussed the question of contacts with members of the smaller delegations. It was agreed that it may well be profitable to cultivate these people [*sic*] ... The idea is that we should make a concerted and special effort to get to know the members of these small delegations.[38]

Also, significantly, democratic and pluralist norms had developed within the differing departments of state which made up individual delegations. Accordingly, the French diplomat from the Quai d'Orsay, Lamarle, or the Conseil d'État representative, the well-known jurist Cahen-Salvador, were restrained in their decision-making capabilities by representatives of prisoner of war and resistance organizations who were part of the French delegation. Indeed, an extraordinary two-year battle had taken place at the Ministry of *Anciens Combattants* between 1947 and 1949, where Lamarle and Cahen-Salvador had fortnightly (or sometimes even weekly) meetings with representatives of each of the various resistance groups in France to formulate a common position at Geneva.[39] So too, the British War Office delegate, Colonel William Gardner, was severely marginalized at Geneva by both the pro-resistance atmosphere, and, more effectively, by members of his own delegation from the Home and Foreign Offices. A Minister reported confidentially:

Miss Gutteridge has written a personal letter to me from Geneva. It appears quite clearly from her letter that she is unhappy about the representation of the U.K. Delegation on Committee III which is considering the Civilians Convention. She does not explain in detail the issues which are at stake (although I gather they relate to security). It seems that the U.K. attitude is too rigid and legalistic and as a result our Delegation is being viewed with increasing dis-

---

[37] 26 Apr. 1949. FO 369/4149.
[38] Beau Rivage Hotel, 9 May 1949. FO 369/4149.
[39] Fonds Union Internationale, 290, Archives du Quai d'Orsay, Nantes.

favour not only by foreign Delegations but also some of the Commonwealth Delegations.[40]

A further complicating factor was the arrival on the scene of the socialist camp. The Soviet Union and its allies' views of international law provided much discomfort to many. As one bitter British delegate wrote home:

> We knew beforehand that we should have trouble with the 'idealist' countries such as Mexico and others like France who had been occupied in the recent war; but we had hoped that the Soviet Union and the majority of the Satellites would boycott the Conference. This, however, has not happened as the Soviet Delegation has not *only* sent a Delegation but *also* insisted that Byelo Russia and Ukraine should be represented.[41]

The consequences of this new international correlation of forces was that it provided the backbone for a series of measures which introduced some limitations on the actions of occupying armies. However, although comprehensive, the Geneva Conventions still did not provide a clear solution to the central problem of the distinction between lawful and unlawful combatant.

THE LEGAL CONTROVERSY

The challenge of formulating the distinction between lawful and un-lawful combatant drove most aspects of the legal controversy at conferences between 1874 and 1949. As Otto Von Glahn most helpfully pointed out,

> the question of the right of the people in an occupied territory to rise in arms against the belligerent occupant is corollary to the obedience requirement, whether the latter is imposed as a legal duty or by the power of the successful invader. Few problems connected with belligerent occupation have given rise to as much bitter debate and acrimonious protests.[42]

[40] Gardner attempted to preserve the right of the British army to take hostages, and had a secret meeting (behind the backs of the rest of his delegation), with the ICRC official at Geneva on this. Letter to Sir Eric Becket, 11 May 1949. FO 369/4149.

[41] Alexander to Kemball, 30 Apr. 1949. FO 369/4149; emphasis in text.

[42] O. Von Glahn, *The Occupation of Enemy Territory* (Minneapolis: University of Minnesota Press, 1965), 480. Jean Pictet, introduction and legal commentary: *The Geneva Conventions of 12 August 1949: Commentary*, 4 (Geneva: ICRC, 1960). For an analysis of the legal difficulties outstanding after the Geneva Conventions were negotiated, see what has by now become the classic legal starting point in the literature: R. Baxter, 'So Called "Unprivileged Belligerency": Spies, Guerrillas, and Saboteurs', *British Yearbook of International Law*, 28 (1951), 323–45.

The first problem was the definition of occupation, and hinged on the precise conditions necessary for its legal commencement. For invading armies, the sooner an overrun territory was declared occupied, the more rapidly they were recognized as occupying powers.[43] In the opinion of occupying armies, simply tacking a poster to a tree was sufficient to declare that a military occupation had begun in that area and was the only condition needed to require the complete passivity of the population.[44] Others, however, believed a large number of conditions had to be met; not only did the local population first have to be completely subdued, but also for an occupation to continue, it needed to be maintained by force. The object of stipulating such exacting conditions was tactical: the further a state of occupation could be delayed, the longer citizens had a right to bear arms in defence of their country.[45]

The second problem was the question of legitimate combatants. Indeed, as one legal historian noted, at the 1949 diplomatic Conference, the 'question of the definition of combatants, and above all of partisans', was 'designated' by Max Huber, the President of the ICRC, 'as the "point explosif" of the entire system of the Geneva Conventions'.[46] In the traditional laws of war, only professional soldiers were granted belligerent status. This historical privilege was created to serve what Michael Howard rather sharply (and accurately) described as 'the parasitic warrior-aristocracy'.[47] Accordingly, all civilians who participated in hostilities were considered outlaws, and, in the chilling words of the draft Russian text at Brussels in 1874, were to be 'delivered to justice'.[48] In contrast, those contesting this legal norm argued that all

[43] Sir Graham Bower, 'The Nation in Arms: Combatants and Non-Combatants', *Transactions of the Grotius Society*, iv (London: Grotius Society, 1919), 75.

[44] The Dana edition of Wheaton's *International Law* asserted that occupation actually changed the 'political status' of the inhabitants (London: G. G. Wilson, 1889), 469; likewise Birkhimer declared that once people lived under the Occupying Power's rule and received the 'benefits' of his law, they owed him a duty of obedience termed allegiance. W. Birkhimer, *Military Government and Martial Law* (Washington, DC, 1892), 3.

[45] An in-depth legal debate on the accepted conditions for military occupation can be found in *Revue de droit international et législation comparée*, 8 (1875–6), where jurists of the Institute of International Law attempted to address the flaws in the Brussels Draft through an extensive questionnaire. On contemporary typologies of military occupation, see Adam Roberts, 'What is a Military Occupation?', *British Journal of International Law*, 55 (1984), 249–305.

[46] M. Veuthey, *Guérrillas et droit humanitaire* (Geneva: International Committee of the Red Cross, 1976), 193.

[47] 'Temperamenta Belli: Can War be Controlled?', in *Restraints on War* (Oxford: Oxford University Press, 1979).

[48] 'Actes', 223–4, and Appendix, 302.

citizens who bore arms for the nation were legitimate combatants.[49] Equally controversial was the issue of prisoners of war. Small countries sought to have all armed defenders protected from reprisals if captured (as professional soldiers already were).[50] A further debate centred on the concept of *levée en masse*. As the famed legal scholar Droop dryly put it:

All that can be learnt from the precedents of Napoleon's wars is that each belligerent, when invaded, appealed to the peasantry to rise and expel the invader, without caring how much they suffered, provided they did some harm to the enemy; but whenever the same nation became in its turn an invader it did not scruple to treat the enemy's peasants as brigands.[51]

The larger powers sought to have the conditions for a legitimate uprising restricted in several ways, above all by requiring its necessary organization under military command. It was also to be limited both temporally and spatially, in that it was to be launched only at the moment of an invasion, and occur only in territories not yet subjected to occupation.[52]

The final set of legal issues centred around the question of permitted army methods in occupied territories, such as reprisals, levies, and requisitions.[53] The first of these, reprisals, was a customary method used by armies to punish illegal acts by the inhabitants of occupied

[49] See M. Clarke, T. Glynn, and A. Rogers, 'Combatants and Prisoner of War Status', in M. Meyer (ed.), *Armed Conflict and the New Law: Aspects of the 1977 Geneva Protocols and the 1981 Weapons Convention* (London: British Institute of International and Comparative Law, 1989), 111; see also C. Rousseau, *Le Droit de conflit armé* (Paris: A. Pedone, 1983), 72.

[50] See A. Rosas, *The Legal Status of Prisoners of War: A Study in International Humanitarian Law Applicable in Armed Conflicts* (Helsinki: Helsinki Academia Scientiarum Fernica, 1976).

[51] H. Droop, 'On the Relations between an Invading Army and the Inhabitants, and the Conditions under which Irregular Troops are Entitled to the Same Treatment as Regular Soldiers', *Transactions of the Grotius Society* (London: Wildy, 1871), 722. This example was used by Droop to argue for an international conference to regulate the laws of war. The best legal work on this general subject remains James Spaight's *War Rights on Land* (London: Macmillan, 1911), see 51–3.

[52] 'La restriction la plus importante résulte de la double limitation dans l'espace et dans le temps', H. Meyrowitz, 'Le Statut des saboteurs dans le droit de la guerre', *Revue de droit pénal et droit de la guerre*, 5 (1966), 144.

[53] For a broad survey of these methods in the nineteenth century see J. Bray, *L'Occupation militaire en temps de guerre* (Paris: A. Rousseau, 1900), 154, 181–3, 191; see also F. Morgenstern, 'The Validity of the Acts of the Belligerent Occupant', *British Yearbook of International Law*, 28 (1951), 291–322.

territories.[54] Those who argued for the rights of armies wanted to maintain and consolidate the practice; those who campaigned for the rights
of resistance advocated its complete abolition; and finally, those who saw
themselves as introducing a degree of 'humanity in warfare' desired to
mitigate the practice. Occupying armies typically used levies and requisitions as further methods of punishment and opinion was deeply
divided over their appropriate use.[55] As might have been expected,
armies and occupying states insisted upon a free hand in their application, while representatives of nations likely to be invaded argued they
should be used more sparingly.

All delegates (whether setting out the legal claims for civilians or for
armies availed), themselves of a range of examples which they claimed
had been in use throughout the late eighteenth century and up to 1874,
the first Brussels conference. In the most heated exchanges at the three
sets of conferences, the veracity of many of these historical examples
were disputed by the warring delegates, and became a major source of
animosity. The next chapter will explore some of the social history of
war in nineteenth-century Europe. In particular, it will examine the
range of army practices under occupation, and the effect they had on
civilian life.

[54] For an overview of nineteenth- and early twentieth-century practices see the comprehensive work by Fritz Kalshoven, *Belligerent Reprisals* (Leyden: Sijthoff, 1971).
[55] On the effects of pillage, as well as requisitions and levies as customary methods
of reprisal see E. Stowell, 'Military Reprisals and the Sanctions of the Laws of War',
American Journal of International Law, 36 (1942), 642–4.

2

Occupying Armies and Civilian Populations in Nineteenth-Century Europe

The events of the Second World War have traditionally been seen as a landmark in the history of conflict. The introduction of dangerous new features in warfare (from ideologies to weapons of mass destruction) is conventionally seen to justify the creation of an entirely new military paradigm: 'total war'. This view has many adherents, from political and legal historians to authorities on war.[1] In particular, its hold upon the literature of the laws of war is powerful. This literature establishes that the catastrophic results of 'total war' were the primary factor behind the introduction of the new civilians' convention in 1949, which was designed to protect civilians the better in wartime. The character of war, it was argued, had radically changed from the 'traditional' conflict between two professional armies in the field. It was thus claimed that, as a new set of norms had been created between 1939 and 1945, a new set of laws were needed to reflect them. The British delegate at Geneva, Joyce Gutteridge, cited five new factors which 'blur the distinction between combatant and non-combatant', and provided the impetus for the 1949 civilians convention.[2] The jurist W. Ford expressed this representative view:

Hardly a century ago war was a matter involving but small numbers of people. The situation changed when national consciousness and democracy began to develop. Since then the number of people affected by war has constantly increased so the important dividing line between combatants and non-combatants laid down in the law of war has gradually become blurred . . . Wars are developing into struggles between the masses. Sir Winston Churchill said

---

[1] See P. Calvocoressi, and G. Wint, *Total War: The Causes and Courses of the Second World War* (London: Penguin Press, 1972). On the concept of total war, see P. Masson, *Une guerre totale 1939–1945: stratégies, moyens, controverses* (Paris: Pluriel, 1990), 13; H. Michel, *La Seconde Guerre mondiale* (Paris: Presses Universitaires de France, 1972), 5.

[2] J. Gutteridge, 'The Geneva Conventions of 1949', *British Yearbook of International Law*, 26 (1949), 294–325.

'When democracy forced itself upon the battlefield war ceased to be a gentle-man's game'.[3]

Two factors were seen to be key to the advent of total war and the subsequent international legislation at Geneva in 1949: first the methods used by the Axis armies of occupation, in particular those of the Nazi regime. The British legal historian G. Draper summarized this common interpretation of the origins of the Civilians' Convention: 'it reflects in a particularly vivid manner the experience of the Second World War. One lesson from this experience was that war crimes caused more loss of life than military operations'; he goes on to illustrate: 'it is known that a figure of some four million were killed by gassing in Auschwitz . . . These figures do not include those killed by shooting, hanging, flogging . . . Over and above these enormities, large numbers were killed as hostages under the "100 to 1" order.'[4] Another factor in the origins of the Civilians' Conventions was seen to be the introduction of large-scale resistance as a new feature of war. War historian Masson noted that in the years before, during, and after the First World War military strate-gists did not concern themselves with methods of guerrilla warfare at the military academies nor in military literature: 'The interest is however minor. The guerrilla does not feature in the programmes of the military academies [in Europe]. It does not provoke any serious study . . . The debates of the period bore essentially upon the potentials of tanks and aircraft, on the offensive–defensive dialectic. The marxists, which may come as a surprise, only accorded a limited interest to the guerrilla as well.'[5] However, the practices of armies and civilians under occupation which were foremost on the minds of delegates at Geneva had much older antecedents than the Second World War. As will be detailed in some depth in the following three chapters, vibrant doctrines of con-quest and occupation already existed in the nineteenth century, and were themselves competing with equally powerful ideologies of resis-tance. The purpose of this chapter is to offer an empirical introduction and counterpoint to these doctrines, by focusing in particular on two sets of practices in nineteenth-century Europe: those of occupying armies and those of civilians in occupied territory.

[3] W. Ford, 'Resistance Movements and International Law', being extracts from the *International Review of the Red Cross*, Geneva (Oct., Nov., Dec. 1967, Jan. 1968), 43.
[4] G. Draper, *The Red Cross Conventions* (London: Stevens, 1958), 26.
[5] P. Masson, *Une guerre totale*, 314–15; M. Heller, *La Machine et les rouages: la for-mation de l'homme sovietique* (Paris: Calmann-Lévy, 1985), especially 97–111. This is not to minimize the terrible and deliberate new policies of the Third Reich, namely the exter-mination camps. But there were many features in common with nineteenth-century European military occupations.

Contrary to Ford's assertion, resistance to occupation was a widespread phenomenon in nineteenth-century Europe. Indeed, it was often driven not by intellectuals or political and administrative elites, but by localized groups of civilians acting autonomously (and sometimes spontaneously) on the basis of a distinct set of patriotic inspirations. In this chapter the different types of civilian response to occupation in the continental wars of the nineteenth century will be explored. Civilian actions will be shown to have been prompted by a range of concerns: some were immediate practical responses to the presence of occupying powers, others were inspired by a more complex set of principles and values. After analysing these reactions—ranging from active collaboration to substantive acts of military resistance—the social, political, and religious cultures which prompted them will be explored.

The story begins, however, by looking at the reverse side of the coin: the behaviour of occupying armies towards civilian populations in the nineteenth century. Two aspects of this conduct will be illustrated. First will be shown the range of military actions and policies which directly affected the livelihood of local inhabitants, such as pillage, taxes, and requisitioning. Secondly, some of the methods used by occupying armies to enforce and maintain a distinction between combatants and noncombatants will be described. These methods were highly coercive and often repressive in nature: they included the execution of those suspected of involvement in resistance activities, reprisals such as hostage-taking, as well as collective punishments against civilian populations for rebellious acts by individuals and groups.

ARMIES OF OCCUPATION IN NINETEENTH-CENTURY EUROPE

1. For every offence punish someone; the guilty if possible, but someone.
2. Better a hundred innocent should suffer than one guilty man escape.
3. When in doubt shoot the prisoner.

These are the three great principles of invaders' law; and they proceed naturally from the fact that the invader has to deal with a population unanimously opposed to him.[6]

---

[6] H. Edwards, *The Germans in France: Notes on the Method and Conduct of the Invasion, the Relations between Invaders and Invaded, and the Modern Usages of War* (London: E. Stanford, n.d.), 286.

The first part of this chapter will examine the two types of practices pursued by occupying armies in the nineteenth century, both of which had important implications for the inhabitants whose territory came under military rule. The first policies to be examined are of a more general kind, often an inevitable outcome of the arrival of an occupying army: the exaction of levies to support the occupation, the imposition of taxes, billeting and requisitions (of a temporary or more permanent character), and acts of looting and pillaging. The second set had a more direct bearing on the negotiations at the conferences at Brussels and The Hague: the methods used to impose a distinction between legitimate and illegitimate combatants. The primary weapon in the legal and military arsenal of invading and occupying troops was the custom of reprisals. This tool was applied in several ways; it could have either a pecuniary and physical nature, and could be enforced collectively or individually. This last method, the use of force against the population, was a customary, if highly contentious, practice of occupying armies throughout the nineteenth century.

PILLAGING, LOOTING, REQUISITIONS, AND BILLETING

Napoleon wrote to his brother Joseph, when, after the latter ascended the throne of Naples, the inhabitants of lower Italy made various attempts at revolt in 1806:

The security of your dominion depends on how you behave in the conquered province. Burn down a dozen places which are not willing to submit themselves. Of course, not until you have first looted them; my soldiers must not be allowed to go away with their hands empty.[7]

Officially, of course, Napoleon rejected this practice. The French historian Tarlé commented on this unofficial policy by noting that, within a week of crossing the Russian frontiers, Napoleon had signed a strict order to arrest all soldiers caught in the act of looting or marauding, to try them by court martial, and to shoot them in the event of conviction. He added: 'but even the frequent executions did not stop the plunder ... In no Napoleonic war with the exception of the Italian campaign ... had the troops looted so unceremoniously and so thoroughly devastated an occupied territory.'[8] Memoirs by soldiers serving in occupa-

---

[7] J. Morgan, *The German Warbook: Being 'The Usages of War on Land' Issued by the Great General Staff of the German Army* (London: John Murray, 1915), 121.

[8] E. Tarlé, *Napoleon's Invasion of Russia: 1812* (London: George Allen & Unwin, 1942), 78.

tion forces during this period tended not to dwell on the brutal customs of pillaging and looting. And when they are mentioned, it is rarely without a justifying entreaty to the reader. For example, after describing an incident of looting during the Napoleonic campaign, an officer explained his actions: 'we found ourselves in enemy territory and it seemed to us that everything belonged to us by right of conquest, a right hallowed by time', adding, 'however abominable and monstrous it may be'.[9] A somewhat infamous exception where soldiers are seen to brag about this type of action is recovated, from the Dutch provinces: 'in Aachen a newspaper reported French generals boasting of "leaving the inhabitants only their eyes, so they could weep" '.[10] Concerning the practice of looting in particular, there is ample documentation to demonstrate that occupying troops often began their rule by seeking their own financial advancement. In his detailed account of the mechanics of occupation under Napoleonic rule, Stuart Woolf set out the consequences of viewing occupied lands as enemy territory: 'first the military commander felt free to requisition and exact what (at the least) he judged necessary to supply his army, and (at the worst) he believed could be extorted for his soldiers, his suppliers, his government' and, he continued, 'last but not least, himself'.[11] The higher echelons in the military blamed such practices on bureaucratic disorder, which forced soldiers on the front line to behave in such fashion:

We had no kind of administrative organization to deal with requisitions; we had to live as best we could, and off the resources of the region in which we found ourselves—resources which were soon exhausted, especially as the armies had crossed and recrossed this territory several times. One can imagine all the disorder which then ensued, for the commanding officers had other things to worry about than taking care of administration—they were incapable of doing it anyway. At the same time, one can imagine the distress of the army; it could exist only by plundering. . . . Another consequence was the destruction of all bonds of discipline throughout the ranks of the army.[12]

So wrote a Napoleonic marshal when looking back over his experiences of commanding occupying French troops in the late eighteenth and early nineteenth century. Naturally, his concerns were primarily with the effects of pillaging and looting on the army, rather than on the civilian

[9] Gen. J.-F. Boulart, *Mémoires militaires sur les guerres de la République et de l'Empire* (Paris: Librairie Illustrée, 1892), 10–11.

[10] Simon Schama, *Patriots and Liberators: Revolution in the Netherlands 1780–1813* (New York: Knopf, 1977), 11.

[11] S. Woolf, *Napoleon's Integration of Europe* (London: Routledge, 1991), 45.

[12] *Mémoires du Maréchal-Général Soult, Duc de Dalmatie* (Paris: N. H. Soult, 1854), 264.

population. However, most commentators who had experienced the effect of troops were more candid about the consequences for the inhabitants themselves. During the occupation of part of France by Russian troops after the Napoleonic defeat, a local writer explained: 'In the attacks and counter-attacks, the cossacks and the Asian cavalry who went before them inspired a veritable terror', as they rode up and down the countryside which the French troops had come to abandon: 'torturing the inhabitants to discover their hidden provisions and family treasures, looking above all for alcohol and never hesitating to rape girls and women.' He concluded: 'one fled to find refuge in the woods'.[13] Another local historian described the appetites of occupying forces as vicious: 'they wanted the ruin, the devastation, the desolation and the destruction to complete their demented task of pillage. They shattered doors and windows, panes of glass, hacked down panelling, . . . ripped up tiles, burnt barns and haystacks, destroyed shrines, vineyards, broke up implements and tools, and threw into the gutter the phials and glass jars of the pharmacists'.[14] And a contemporary historian, looking back on the effects this pillage and looting must have had on the populace (in early nineteenth-century Italy) wrote: 'Equally typical was the looting, rape, and vandalism they suffered at the hands of the French soldiers . . . To those on the receiving end, an incursion by these unpaid, unfed, undisciplined hordes seemed to be not liberation but an "invasion of barbarians", with the sole object of pillaging and looting.'[15]

The sack of Cordoba is a sobering illustration of the effect occupation troops could have on entering a heavily populated area: 'The Cordovans had closed their gates, but it was rather for the purpose of gaining time for a formal surrender than with any intention of resisting.' Nevertheless the city was sacked 'from cellar to garret'. Whenever there was the least resistance: 'they slew off whole households: but they were rather intent on pillage and rape than on murder. Dupont's undisciplined conscripts broke their ranks and ran amok through the streets, firing into the windows and battering down doors.'[16] These practices of pillaging and looting were in themselves often sufficient to turn a population which was merely hostile to violent opposition. In this context the practice of billeting, financially supporting the enemy in one's own

[13] M. Blancpain, *La Vie quotidienne dans la France du Nord sous les Occupations: 1814–1944* (Paris: Hachette, 1983), 21.

[14] Dubois, ibid. 22.

[15] T. C. W. Blanning, *The French Revolution in Germany: Occupation and Resistance in the Rhineland 1792–1802* (Oxford: Clarendon Press, 1983), 148.

[16] C. Oman, *History of the Peninsular War* (Oxford: Clarendon Press, 1902), i. 130.

home, also frequently produced desperate reactions. Below is just one example of several of these types of accounts culled by T. C. W. Blanning in his meticulous study of the occupation of the Rhineland at the end of the eighteenth century:

From 4 November until 6 December I was allocated a French major, together with his wife and two servants; he behaved outrageously, threatening to send me 25 sick common soldiers if I did not supply him with victuals; then came General Poncet and *fourteen* servants who proceeded to vandalise my house; I had to keep him supplied throughout his eight-week stay, which meant that every day I was feeding between one and two dozen people at my table.[17]

During the Prussian occupation of France in 1870–1, a Rouen newspaper's account of one peasant's attempts to preserve himself and his larder provided a vivid illustration of the dilemmas of billeting:

The peasants were even accused of keeping back for the Prussians, whose orders they did not dare disobey, the provisions they withheld from their own countrymen; and it is a fact that, on one occasion, in a village between Le Havre and Fécamp, a number of *mobiles*, who entered a farmhouse at night, only succeeded in getting supper by pretending to be Prussians. When, as quickly happened, the innocent deception was discovered, the farmer, who was not afraid of his own countrymen, wished to take the supper away, but was not allowed to do so.[18]

In their distress, local inhabitants often turned upon their own leaders. An Englishman abroad witnessed such an event during the Franco-Prussian War: 'at Charly, near Nanteuil, I heard an announcement publicly read to the effect that the mayor and municipal council, in consequence of the unjustifiable attacks made upon them in connection with the billeting of soldiers, were anxious to resign'.[19]

The policies of plunder and looting underwent a refinement in the eighteenth and early nineteenth centuries. Armies still took what they wanted, but it was no longer called looting, but rather became known as *requisitioning* and *collections*. Historically, the right to ask for requisitions and contributions evolved after the eighteenth century when occupied communities, instead of being subjected to pillage and sacking, were permitted to 'buy immunity for their property by furnishing the occupant with specified goods and paying specified sums to him'.[20] Two important distinctions separated these practices from the more dubious

---

[17] Blanning, *The French Revolution in Germany*, 90–1.
[18] Edwards, *The Germans in France*, 279.   [19] Ibid. 217.
[20] Graber, *The Development of the Law of Belligerent Occupation*, 217.

customs practised hitherto by occupying armies. The first was that a comprehensive inventory of supplies which were needed or desired had to be made. As one general put it: 'and in order to fend off the always brutal requisitions it was necessary to give, so that I could prevent them from taking; and it was necessary that things be brought to me, so that I not be forced to have them fetched'.[21] However, the establishment of this new system for obtaining goods did not in any way restrict or limit the demands. As the legal publicist Spaight rhetorically asked: 'What may be requisitioned? Practically everything under the sun ... Mr Sutherland Edwards says he knows of a bootjack having been requisitioned, and at La Besace, he found a requisition for six eggs.'[22] The second innovation was the requirement that the occupied populace be given a receipt for the goods taken, in order to make claims for compensation to their own government once the war was over. As one writer declared, the onus was on the inhabitant to obtain a written receipt from the occupying forces:

Commanding officers in actual warfare do not ask permission of landowners to make use of the land as a battle field ... ; nor will the objection by fashionable watering places, that military manœuvres interfere with summer visitors, receive any attention from the commander of the invading army ... the seizure of all kinds of transport; horses, motor-cars, motor-boats, carts, bicycles, carriages, tramcars, balloons, aeroplanes, river pleasure-steamers, canal-barges, and so forth—all may be seized by the occupant ... In all these cases the persons from whom articles are taken *should obtain receipts*, so that they may have evidence on which to base their claims for compensation when the war is over ... requisitions are to be paid for ... in ready money ... if payment is not made [the commander] *must give receipts* for whatever he takes.[23]

But as the historian Geoffrey Best observed, this was a practice which usually left the inhabitants destitute, with a sheaf of papers (if they had been bold enough to demand them) as their only consolation.[24] Even more daunting for populations were contributions levied on whole com-

[21] Général Baron Dieudonné-Adrienne Thiébault, *Mémoires* (Paris: E. Plon, Nourrit et Cie., 1893–5), iv. 355.
[22] Spaight, *War Rights on Land*, 402.
[23] A. Higgins, *Non-Combatants and the War* (Oxford: Oxford University Press, 1914), 23–4; emphasis added. Graber noted that the German lawyer Loening, discussing the Prussian occupation of Alsace in 1870–1, imposed responsibility for obtaining requisition receipts 'on the people, rather than obligating the occupier to issue them routinely': *The Development of the Law of Belligerent Occupation*, 217. Loening, however, makes no mention in his article of the actual success rate for obtaining these slips. 'L'Administration du gouvernement général de l'Alsace durant la guerre de 1870–71', *Revue de droit international et législation comparée*, 4 (1872).
[24] G. Best, *War and Law since 1945* (Oxford: Clarendon Press, 1994), 35.

munities, especially if they did not have the necessary provisions to supply occupying troops. And the means used to gather requisitions could be somewhat brusque: 'How can levying of requisitions and contributions be enforced? The German plan in 1870–1 was to increase the amount demanded'; if it were not immediately forthcoming and 'if the inhabitants still proved recalcitrant, to bombard and burn the town or village'.[25]

It was the collection of fines on towns and districts which provided an excellent illustration of the methods an occupying army applied to enforce a distinction between combatant and non-combatant. The exclusive aim of the earlier practices outlined was to service the occupying army, although these customs in themselves gave lie to the claim that civilians who did not participate in hostilities were exempted from the effects of war. Collective fines (*amendes*), which were usually listed under requisitions in military manuals of the nineteenth century, were a tool used to punish the civilian population for criminal acts committed by one or more of its members. Such practices, whereby groups of people were punished (albeit fiscally rather than physically) for acts carried out by individuals had enough similarities with the more controversial policy of reprisals for certain states to recommend placing collective fines under the category of reprisals. Collective fines were imposed for the same reasons as reprisals. Their central purpose had two elements: retribution and the repression of the occupied populace.

REPRISALS

The legal definition of a reprisal could at first appear deceptively uncomplicated. Below is a general description by a specialist of the laws of war: 'a reprisal is by its nature a *prima facie* illegal act which is undertaken as a response to some unlawful act committed by another party which may be said thereby to have "moved the legal goal posts".'[26] Another, more advanced classification of reprisals comes closer to defining their true object in the laws of war: 'Reprisals are acts of victimization or vengeance by a belligerent directed against a group of civilians, prisoners of war or other persons *hors de combat,* in response to an attack by persons of unprivileged status or by persons not

---

[25] Spaight, *War Rights on Land*, 406.
[26] McCoubrey, *International Humanitarian Law*, 150.

immediately connected with the regular forces of the army.'[27] Both these definitions of reprisals accurately describe different aspects of the mechanism, yet do not seek to understand the underlying motives of belligerent reprisals. Once these are established, it becomes clear that the principles and practices behind reprisals were different in occupied territories than in other areas of war. The cardinal point to establish, and which underpinned reprisals between two belligerents, was the precise character of the actors. In the words of the Dutch jurist Kalshoven, 'an act . . . constitutes a reprisal when, firstly, both the actor and the addressee of the act are States or other entities enjoying a degree of international respectability'. Accordingly, its purpose is to 'coerce the addressee to change its policy and bring it into line with the requirements of international law, be it in respect of the past, the present or the future'.[28] As Kalshoven noted further, there was a strong retaliatory character to reprisals, which raised the issue of the precise object of such actions. If retaliation was carried out against an enemy state, then it was classified as a 'true reprisal'. Accordingly, the occupying army would be charged with inflicting belligerent reprisals on the populace in order to affect actions by its members—for the express purpose of bringing about a 'change of policy in the authorities'.[29]

However, in the case of military occupation, it was understood that local authorities had neither the means nor the power to control hostile acts by individuals among the general populace. As was shown earlier in this chapter, although local authorities often called for resistance by civilians, it was clear that such acts could rarely be *prevented* by public officials even when they tried. In one circular published during the Franco-Prussian War, the Mayor of Dijon appealed to his constituents:

It happened recently that the guards were insulted by stones being thrown at them. All guards received the order that, if similar circumstances were to present themselves, they were to use their arms and fire. The Mayor urged his citizens to abstain from all acts of aggression against German soldiers, and above all against guards, as the results could create dangerous situations.[30]

Thus, the various types of reprisals engaged in by occupying armies of the nineteenth century had a dual purpose: they had both a deterrent and a punitive nature. These important but complex features for occu-

---

[27] Ingrid Detter de Lupis, *The Law of War* (Cambridge: Cambridge University Press, 1987), 255.
[28] Kalshoven, *Belligerent Reprisals*, 33.   [29] Ibid. 37.
[30] A. Brullé, *Les Murailles dijonnaises pendant la guerre 1870–1871* (Dijon: Imp. Darantiere, 1875), 198.

piers and occupied were outlined by Kalshoven in depth, and are therefore worth quoting in full:

such retaliatory measures against an occupied population not aiming to effect a change of policy of responsible authorities do not, like reprisals properly speaking, act as sanctions in the international legal order. Rather, their object will be (in the most favourable case) to protect the vital interests of the occupant, and the occupation régime which is the juridical expression of these interests, against potentially harmful activities on the part of unknown members of the population. This is to say that the basis of such measures can only be sought in the principle of military necessity: the same principle, that is, which lies at the root not only of the other means at the disposal of an occupant for the maintenance of the occupation régime (such as punishment of the actual perpetrators of hostile acts, and internment of suspected persons), but indeed of the whole occupant's powers in respect of the occupied territory and its inhabitants. In other words, a requirement for such measures would be that they could with reasonable certainty expect the measure to have a deterrent effect on those unknown individuals likely to commit further infractions of the occupation régime. This is tantamount to saying that there must exist a definite relationship between those individual persons (and their activities) and the population as a collectivity—the same relation of 'collective responsibility', in fact, as discussed above from the angle of responsibility for acts already committed.[31]

From the above it can be concluded that there were two justifications for the use of reprisals by an occupying force against the population. The first stipulated that all hostile acts of the population were illegal, while the second claimed the principle of military necessity. With regard to the first condition which necessitated outlawing the belligerency of occupied inhabitants (whether organized or individual), this was the most consistent position taken by occupying armies in the nineteenth century. As the very perspicacious historian Mougenot noted: 'Whether it was an officer like Marbot, or a non-combatant like Larrey, a Frenchman like Thiébault, or a foreigner like Napier, a Marshal like Jourdan, or a soldier like Wagré, who spoke Spanish', civilians are 'always designated as insurgents. The same term is employed in proclamations and other official documents.' But it is often replaced by a more 'energetic expression, and generals' ministers, functionaries, *memorialistes*, historians even, described the defenders of Spanish independence as bandits or brigands'. He concluded that this policy of categorization actually permitted the invaders to have recourse to much more 'energetic

---

[31] *Belligerent Reprisals*, 40.

procedures, which constituted nothing more, for the vast majority of cases, than simple reprisals'.[32]

All the commentators in Mougenot's recital concurred in their bias towards the army (as in the case of Napier), or on the side of the French (all the others cited). Pelissier remarked: 'The diverse participants in the conflict attribute the glory of the victory diversely. The English reduce as much as they can the part taken by their Spanish allies', and added: 'in reality the Spanish war, both on the side of the Spanish as well as that of the invaders, was a veritable chaos'.[33] Legally, however, when civilians' behaviour had been determined 'criminal' by the army, the population in question (and this included civilians who had not participated in any 'criminal' or hostile activity) could be punished with the weapon of reprisals.

The second prerequisite, which appealed to the principle of military necessity, had a long and somewhat troubled history in the theory and practice of the laws of war. The doctrine was based, according to a legal analyst, on a distinction between necessity and custom: 'Between *Kriegraison* (the "reason" or "necessity" or "convenience" of war), and *Kriegsmanier* (custom of war); the latter binding on a belligerent in the ordinary circumstances, the former overruling it in special circumstances, where necessary either for escaping military danger, or for attaining military success.'[34]

All military occupiers defended their actions against civilians according to the first of the justifications cited above, the protection of their troops. Napier forcefully declared that 'All armies have the incontestable right to defend themselves when they are engaged in hostilities. An insurrection of armed peasants is military anarchy,' and, in these circumstances 'men cannot be restricted in the customs of regular war. This is why, no matter the apparent injustice' one cannot give quarter to 'armed peasants, and the right to burn their villages must rest on the principle of necessity'.[35] Likewise, Marbot believed that for the French

[32] R. Mougenot, *Des pratiques de la guerre continentale durant le Premier Empire* (Paris: Librairie Militaire R. Chapelot et Cie., 1903), 376.

[33] 'Les Libéraux "Patriotes" Espagnols devant les contradictions de la Guerre d'Indépendance', in P. Viallanaix and J. Ehrard (eds.), *La Bataille, l'armée, la gloire 1745–1871* (Paris: Clermont-Ferrand II, 1985), 261. Walter Laqueur remarked: 'the attitude of the British Commanders toward the guerrillas was ambiguous. Wellington hardly ever mentioned them in his dispatches, Napier wrote that these "undisciplined bands" had been as dangerous to their own country as the enemy'. *Guerrilla: A Historical and Critical Study* (London: Weidenfeld & Nicholson, 1977), 39.

[34] J. Stone, *Legal Controls of International Conflict: A Treatise on the Dynamics of Disputes and War-Law* (London: Stevens, 1959), 352.

[35] Mougenot, *Des pratiques de la guerre continentale*, 377.

in Spain, as well as for soldiers at war anywhere, 'All means are permitted against those who revolt' and the best means of defence was to
'put the town to torch and shoot constantly upon the inhabitants in
order to prevent them from putting the fire out'.[36]

The undisputed founders of this doctrine were the Prussians, who
tended to emphasize the imperative of military success in their employment of reprisals.[37] When discussing the practice of hostage-taking, the
German army handbook explains: 'Herein lies its justification [of
hostage-taking] under the laws of war, but still more in the fact that it
proved completely successful.' The text, however, went on to confirm that
the more usual justification, self-defence, was also an important part of
the doctrine of military necessity. Yet in the full passage of the text, it is
taken even further out of the realm of right, and proclaimed as an honourable and even virtuous obligation: 'To protect oneself against attack
and injuries from the inhabitants and to employ ruthlessly the necessary
means of defence and intimidation is obviously not only a right but
indeed *a duty* of the staff of the army.' The handbook goes on to conclude:
'the ordinary law in this matter generally will not suffice, it must be sup-
plemented by the law of the enemy's might.'[38] A German lawyer, writing
at the time of the Prussian occupation of France in 1870 in an official
French publication, added a final (somewhat unscholarly) defence to the
two reasons already cited above: 'We have done nothing except what is
required by both duty and necessity, and, in any event, we have not done
the tenth of what the French would have in the same cirumstances.'[39]

But it was not only Prussians who had a tendency to regard reprisals
as a sacred duty. A French general, writing on the futility of attempting
to outlaw reprisals stated with resignation (and under a pseudonym):
'this terrible right has always been exercised against an enemy that will
not respect the customs of war, or who takes recourse to forbidden measures.' He added that reprisals would simply 'never disappear, because
the laws of war are the laws of necessity, and it will always be necessary
to repress acts of treachery, of bad faith and of vengeance'.[40]

[36] General Marbot, *Mémoires* (Paris: E. Plon Nourrit et Cie., 1880), iii. 382.
[37] The German devotion to the legal concept of military necessity was construed by
one author to be a result of the evolution of their domestic law on self-defence. See P.
Weiden, *Necessity in International Law* (London: Transactions of the Grotius Society,
1939), 105–31.
[38] Morgan, *The German War Book*, 120; emphasis in text.
[39] 'Moniteur officiel du gouvernement général du nord de la France de la préfecture
de Seine-et-Oise', *Journal quotidien* (Seine-et-Oise, 1871, 15 Jan.).
[40] General 'T' (Brialmont), *Angleterre et les Petits États* (Brussels: C. Muquardt,
Librairie Militaire, 1875), 65.

It is difficult to judge the effectiveness of reprisals precisely because their underlying purpose was obscured by problems of definition. Reprisals were purportedly administered when there had been a violation of the laws of war. Yet, as can be seen from the examples given by Mougenot, accusing civilians of such illegal acts did not in itself amount to a universally agreed proof of criminality. As he noted, the line of 'demarcation between brigands and true partisans is difficult to establish, and confusion is easy: the *guérilleros* requisition, bands pillage, insufficient distinction'. This does not permit 'the French to separate defenders of the land with highway robbers'.[41]

Many of the guerrillas in the war against Napoleon wore military badges of some sort and took orders from a commander. Yet, once they were called insurgents or 'révoltés', in Marbot's terms, their actions could be deemed to contravene the laws of war, and reprisals could ensue. And, without an independent authority to rule on such issues, it was usually the case that the occupier had a clear field in determining when a violation occurred. When occupying powers actually went through the motions of a legal trial for inhabitants suspected of criminal activities, the practice was as follows: 'the principle of throwing the *onus* of proving his innocence on the accused appears unjust and cruel, but it is a necessary principle of martial law justice. The occupant's interest is to secure the maintenance of order and compliance with his martial law regulations, and he cannot, under war conditions be expected to adhere scrupulously to the rule of abstract justice which forbids the presumption of anyone's guilt and which regards with horror the punishing of an innocent person.' Accordingly, 'vicarious punishment is the very soul of *reprisals* and reprisals are still, unfortunately, a living part of martial justice'.[42] This could give birth, as Kalshoven dryly put it, to an 'unsatisfactory situation'.[43] For example, in the occupation of France in 1870:

the Germans issued a proclamation under which French combatants, not possessing the distinguishing marks considered by their enemy to be necessary, were to be liable to the penalty of death, and in cases in which it was not inflicted were to be condemned to a penal servitude for ten years, and to be kept in Germany until the expiration of the sentence. The whole question by what kind of marks combatants should be indicated, and to what degree such marks should be conspicuous, *was at that time an open one*; if inadequate marks were

[41] Mougenot, *Des pratiques de la guerre continentale*, 52–3.
[42] Spaight, *War Rights on Land*, 349–50. The chapter itself is entitled: 'Under Martial Law the Guilt of the Accused is Assumed'.
[43] Kalshoven, *Belligerent Reprisals*, 41.

used, they would be used in the vast majority of instances under the direction or the permission of the national authorities; and the individual would as a rule be innocent of any intention to violate the laws of war.[44]

A further factor to be taken into consideration was the danger that reprisals, far from re-establishing an occupying power's control, could actually engender further hostile acts by the populace. In a long article on the legal aspects of the Franco-Prussian War, the jurist Rolin-Jacquemyns, for example, was adamant in rejecting the principle of military necessity as the basis for reprisals, and advanced the opinion that in fact they encouraged further resistance. In an analysis of a German army proclamation which assigned culpability for individual acts to entire communities, and setting out the punishments warranted by such infractions, he wrote (in a kinder mood than in his other work):

> But this proclamation goes even further, in some of its parts. It tends to transform municipal magistrates of the invaded country into agents, if not spies of the invading army. And it allows the terrible sanction of burning, or of bombarding all houses and villages 'that have given shelter to francs-tireurs, without letting the mayor know.' And the mayor and the inhabitants must not remain absolutely neutral and passive. They must still call out the enemy troops against their own citizens under penalty, if they hesitate, of bringing the punishment of fire upon their entire village. Thus non-resistance and non-denunciation are transformed into acts of complicity. We do not hesitate to say that, to our eyes, there is no military necessity that could justify laws like these. Indeed, experience has shown that, in times of war as in times of peace, repression pushed past a certain limit, far from intimidating populations, does more to exasperate them, and give to even the most fearful a force derived from despair.[45]

Reprisals were thus controversial for a number of reasons: their legal applicability, their principles, and their effects.[46] Yet they remained the most frequently used method of enforcing the distinction between lawful and unlawful combatant. Having established the principles and purposes in the usage of reprisals by occupying armies in nineteenth-century Europe, this chapter will proceed with one example of the vast range and types of reprisals routinely employed by occupying powers: hostage-taking.

---

[44] W. Hall, *A Treatise on International Law* (Oxford: Oxford University Press, 1924), 496. Emphasis added.

[45] G. Rolin-Jacquemyns, 'Essai complémentaire sur la Guerre Franco-Allemande dans ses rapports avec le droit international', *Revue de droit international et législation comparée*, 3 (1871), 515.

[46] See P. de Waxel, *L'Armée d'invasion et la population: leurs rapports pendant la Guerre étudiés au point de vue du droit des gens naturel* (Leipzig: Krueger, 1874), 96–104.

HOSTAGE-TAKING

The policy of hostage-taking was applied in a number of ways. It was commonly used to guarantee the payment of fines. Not only did Hall agree with this method, but Prussian troops, not overly concerned about whether they were operating under the martial law of occupation, regularly practised this policy in Normandy, according to a British journalist who witnessed the following during the Franco-Prussian War: 'They might come back at any moment, and in the case of proved disobedience during their absence, levy contributions and carry away hostages. For it was not in occupied territory alone that hostages were seized. Indeed it was, above all, in districts theoretically but not practically occupied that they were taken.' Edwards gave an example of an incident in Neufchâtel, 'halfway between Dieppe and Amiens—in the midst of a large district in theoretically occupied country—the mayor and his adjunct were both made prisoners for having allowed the arrest of some provisions dealers engaged in supplying the Prussian army'. He concluded that 'as a general rule, where a fine was not paid, the two chief officials were kept in custody, or under surveillance, until the money was forthcoming'.[47]

Still more common was the use of hostages to deter civilians from hostile activity. This was a system defined by Spaight as 'prophylactic reprisals', deployed not to punish violations of the laws of war, but in order to prevent them. Such practices were widespread in Napoleon's campaigns at the beginning of the nineteenth century: 'for insurance' remarked Mougenot, 'the invader often took hostages; in Spain above all, to contain the population and prevent *guérillas'* attacks', it was often ordered that local 'notables, churchmen, members of the *juntes*, individuals designated or chosen in turn and in pairs' remain constantly under supervision of the guards, and, 'at the first shot of gunfire, are killed'.[48] Again, however, hostage-taking of this kind in Spain provoked the 'unsatisfactory situation', deplored by Kalshoven, of provoking counter-reprisals. This example concerns an incident in the province of Biscaye in 1810:

In September General Drouet d'Erlon took over supreme command of the provinces of the north of Spain. After attempting to put down the insurrectionary movement, he ordered the arrest of fathers, mothers, brothers and

---

[47] *The Germans in France*, 268. Hall explains: 'hostages are sometimes seized by way of precaution in order to guarantee the maintenance of order in occupied territory.' *A Treatise on International Law*, 565.

[48] *Des pratiques de la guerre continentale*, 356.

sometimes grandparents of the head of guerrilla bands, and locked them up in prisons. Also, he ordered those monks and priests who encouraged their compatriots to take up arms to be locked up immediately. These strict measures were followed by swift reprisals. On the 14th of October, at noon, 'le Manchot' penetrated the Elorrio with some of his band, kidnapped the daughter of the municipal magistrate, and announced that if the French did not promptly release his mother imprisoned in Bilbao, he would keep the young girl as hostage and destroy the town.[49]

Occupiers sometimes threatened hostage-taking for activities which by no stretch of the imagination could be conceived as injurious to their vital interests. After marching a detachment of French prisoners of war through the town in front of its inhabitants, one Prussian officer told the mayor and municipal council officials of Château Thierry in 1870:

When the prisoners were passing, I heard, as soon as my back was turned, such words as '*brigand*', '*bandit*', pronounced. These insults came, for the most part, from women, so I said nothing; but if ever again offensive names are applied to me by a man, I shall do what I have a right to do—I shall reply with my hand. Please inform your fellow-citizens of my determination, and remember moreover, that if you cannot induce them to remain more quiet, I shall be obliged to take hostages from among the municipal council.[50]

The most infamous case of hostage-taking in the nineteenth century took place during the Franco-Prussian War and was one of the instances where, noted Hall in a typical understatement, a 'belligerent is sometimes drawn by the convenience of intimidation into acts which are clearly in excess of his rights'.[51] There are many written accounts of the incident, and the version given below seems the most authoritative. It concerns two French corps of voluntary engineers, known as the 'Wild Boars of the Ardennes' and 'The Railway Destroyers', largely composed of artisans of all classes. They carried picks, crowbars, mining tools, hatchets, powder petards and cases, and were skilled at pulling up rails, blowing up bridges, felling trees, and mining roads. Following their various successes, the Germans ordered the seizure of hostages. They ordered that all trains should

be accompanied by inhabitants who are well known and generally respected, and who shall be placed upon the locomotive, so that it may be known that every accident caused by the hostility of the inhabitants will, in the first place,

---

[49] E. Martin, *La Gendarmerie française en Espagne et en Portugal* (Paris: Imprimerie-Librairie Léautey, 1898), 139.
[50] Edwards, *The Germans in France*, 217.
[51] *A Treatise on International Law*, 565.

injure their countrymen. At Nancy the first hostage was the venerable President of the Court of Appeal, M. Leclair; another notable citizen who was 'invited' to go travelling was the Procureur-General Isard, who, escorted by two Prussian gendarmes, had to mount the tender and travel to Lunéville, where his colleagues in that town took his place. The President of the Chamber of Commerce, a judge, and a barrister also occupied in turn the post of danger.[52]

The German proclamation read: 'railways having been frequently damaged, the trains shall be accompanied by well known and respected persons inhabiting the towns or other localities in the neighbourhood of the lines'. It stated that they 'shall be placed upon the engine, so that it may be understood that in every accident caused by the hostility of the inhabitants, their compatriots will be the first to suffer'. They added that the competent civil and military authorities together with the railway companies and 'the *etappen* commandants will organise a service of hostages to accompany the trains'.[53]

TYPES OF CIVILIAN BEHAVIOUR:
1. OBEDIENCE TO THE OCCUPIER

Military occupation negated dialogue.[54]

The first type of civilian conduct towards an occupying army comes loosely under the term 'obedience'. The nature and duty of obedience was open to a multitude of legal interpretations by different traditions within the laws of war. In its ideal-typical form, 'passive' obedience represented the unconditional acceptance of the superior force of the occupying power. According to this paradigm the occupied people conceded the imposition of foreign rule. In the rosy and somewhat utopian view of Vattel, he argued that 'war is carried on by regular troops; the people, the peasants, the citizens, take no part in it, and generally have nothing to fear from the sword of the enemy.' This is, however, 'provided the inhabitants submit to him who is master of the country, pay the contributions imposed, and refrain from all hostilities'. If they can manage all this, 'they live in as perfect tranquillity as if they were friends: they even continue in possession of what belongs to them.' Indeed, Vattel believed that 'the country people come freely to the camp to sell their

[52] H. Hozier, *The Franco-Prussian War: Its Causes, Incidents, and Consequences* (London: MacKenzie, 1876), ii. 90.
[53] 'Order of the Civil Governor of Rheims', cited in Hall, *A Treatise on International Law*, 566. [54] Woolf, *Napoleon's Integration of Europe*, 53.

provisions, and are protected, as far as possible, from the calamities of war'. He also added that the 'troops alone carry on the war and the rest of the people remain at peace'.[55]

This ideal type bore little resemblance to the reality of military occupations in eighteenth- and nineteenth-century Europe. In so far as it represented any actual occurrences, it evoked the peasants' tendency to act as suppliers of occupation forces. It was also obviously true that normal civilian life tended to be less disturbed when armies were passing through a district or province than when they remained in a fixed location. But Vattel's notion of the possibility of a rigid separation of military conflict from civilian life was unrealistic in at least three ways: it overestimated the extent of civilian subservience to military occupation; significantly overplayed the scope for 'normal' life in times of occupation; and, finally, failed to identify the problems which civilians consistently encountered even when they pledged public allegiance to their new military overlords.

In real life, civilian obedience to occupation took a variety of forms. One common response merely sought to appease the occupier, and was a direct response to his presence in the locality. It was difficult to ignore troops if they were quartered in one's village or house, as to disobey would have immediate and negative consequences. Accordingly, a more active type of obedience, often pre-emptive in intention, was also widespread. As one local official (the President of the Appeal Court of Colmar), noted in France during the Franco-Prussian War of 1870–1: 'Our houses are packed with Prussians to feed . . . they give us nothing much to complain of, outside of the bitter lament of having to submit to foreigners.'[56]

But obedience could often develop beyond an inert and passive duty. It could become a clear and active form of political association with the occupying power. In his *Letter to Prince Metternich*, the Marquis Wieloposki, formerly Polish envoy in London and a supporter of the same Prince, offered the Polish nation to Tsar Nicholas, using these words:

'We come to hand ourselves to you, as the most magnanimous of our adversaries. We were yours, as subjects, by the right of partition, in our fear not weighing the oaths you compelled us to swear. To-day you are winning a new title to authority. We submit to you as free men, voluntarily, and you become our Lord by the Grace of God.'[57]

[55] E. Vattel, *The Law of Nations* (Washington: Carnegie Institute, 1916), 318.
[56] S. Audoin-Rouzeau, *1870: la France dans la Guerre* (Paris: Armand Colin, 1989), 262.
[57] M. Dziewanowski, '1848 and the Hotel Lambert', *Slavonic and East European Review*, 26 (1948), 361–2.

Another Polish example was Stanislaw-Szczesny Potocki (1751–1805), who in the aftermath of the Third Partition declared: 'Poles should abandon all memory of their fatherland; I am a Russian forever!'[58] The memoirs of General Paul Thiébault, who played a leading role in Napoleon's continental campaigns, provide a rich (if not completely reliable) source of evidence for this type of behaviour. Wherever he went, there appeared to be great joy, celebration and festivities—despite the fact that fierce resistance took place in many other regions occupied by French troops. Here, Thiébault described the sense of gratitude of the Spanish population at the time of his departure—a feeling which could have been prompted by considerations other than those he imputed:

The Spanish render to me justice. They offered me a protective guard when Balestreros was approaching with 17,000 men of the town of Burgos which was defended by a garrison composed of only 250 sick men. They demonstrated their sadness and regret when I left my second government . . . and wrote this down in a letter, in which the civil and ecclesiastical authorities thanked me for my humane and impartial administration'.[59]

When he left Fulde in Germany, this humane and impartial administrator received as a souvenir from the members of the provisional local government a sword with the following inscription: 'To General Thiébault from the country of the Fulde with appreciation'. In the words of the fortunate recipient of local gratitude: 'the day of departure, an enormous crowd gathered in the streets of the town and regretfully bid a final farewell to the benevolent administration'.[60] Collaboration could also lead to the artistic celebration of the virtues of the occupant. In Hamburg, for example, where French occupation imposed serious hardships on the population, 'several senators of the town, touched by the efforts of General Thiébault to render less painful the rigours of invasion, requested from him the authorization to commission his portrait in order to conserve the image of a man whose humanity and correctness had touched them all'.[61] Another French soldier wrote that by 1809 Vienna was for the occupying French troops 'a sojourn of pleasantries and festivals' where 'victory seemed to open all the doors of the palace to us'.[62]

[58]   Norman Davies, *A Short History of Poland* (Oxford: Clarendon Press, 1981), 180.
[59]   *Mémoires*, 291–9.
[60]   Ibid. 67–8. See also his *Journal des opérations militaires et administratives du Blocus de Gênes*, 2 vols. (Paris: J. Corréard, 1846–7).
[61]   Mougenot, *Des pratiques de la guerre continentale*, 155.
[62]   H. D'Espinchal, *Souvenirs militaires 1792–1814* (Paris: Masson et Boyer, 1904), i. 283, 291.

This type of tribute to the forces of military occupation in nineteenth-century Europe had much of its origin in the class structures of the period. The upper and middle classes, as well as the clergy, often identified and associated with the political and ideological authority of a foreign military power. However, the clergy could also be, on occasion, a force to be reckoned with by foreign troops, and their role in inciting insurrection against the occupying powers will be shown in a later section examining cases of resistance by civilians in the Spanish War against Napoleon's troops. However, in the main, at a time when loyalties to the nation and the state were frequently undercut by local particularisms as well as transnational allegiances based on class and religion, local elites often displayed a flexible tendency to affiliate with whatever ruling power was available, a position which was sometimes reinforced by ideological considerations. During the Franco-Prussian War, the hatred of subversive ideologies often led to the view that the occupier could save France from the 'red peril'. But this view could be even more perilous to those who held it, as a local nobleman of Haute-faye (Dordogne) found to his cost. Suspected of being in cahoots with the Prussians, he was lynched and then burnt alive by a peasant mob.[63] Arthur de Gobineau's view was perhaps another, more extreme example of this attitude, but many of his opinions of the Prussians and the population's relationship to the invading army were no doubt representative. As the mayor of the village of Tyre during the Prussian occupation, he was well placed to document its effects. In a letter to their daughter, his wife expressed their common view that 'we have no fear of the Prussians . . . we are much more tormented by the reds, who are intolerably rude'.[64]

Gobineau, like many of the French aristocracy at the time, believed the *franc-tireurs* who resisted the Prussian occupation were not patriots, but merely a 'boisterous band as much without honour and without conscience as without talent or strength'.[65] He respected the Prussians for the same reasons for which, seventy years earlier, he believed they had respected French troops on their soil: 'Every nation has a distinctive trait, an impulsion which it follows by preference. That which characterizes the German is obedience.'[66] However, he suffered the same gradual disenchantment with the occupier as the Germans did when they eventually began to turn against Napoleon's troops. Indeed, acceptance of occupation was frequently a function of local correlations

---

[63] The story is recounted in J. Villefranche, *Curés et Prussiens* (Paris: Bourg, 1877), 49.
[64] A. de Gobineau, *Ce qui est arrivé à la France en 1870* (Paris: Klincksieck, 1970), 67.
[65] Ibid. 72.
[66] L. Lévy-Bruhl, *L'Allemagne depuis Leibnitz* (Paris: Hachette, 1890), 163.

of forces. Writing about the French continental wars of the First Empire, Mougenot asserted that the French occupation was 'docilely accepted in Germany, as long as it was an expression of force'; when the French power declined, it no longer appeared legitimate, and the Germans 'violated their alliance and rose against the French'.[67]

This also illustrates an important political aspiration among the upper and middle classes: their need for legitimacy and their strong desire for order. A notable exception was the first Polish insurrection of 1830–1, which was directed by and involved the nobility to a remarkable extent. Furthermore, the peasants did not participate as much as they were to in 1861, fearing the same treatment under either regime. As Beauvois rather sweepingly commented on *their* behaviour: 'As for the illiterate peasants, everyone knows that they remained passive, seeing the insurrection as simply an affair of nobles.'[68] Occupying powers of the nineteenth century relied on these sentiments to reinforce the basis of their legitimate authority, and many in the upper classes concurred with Napier's view that 'an insurrection is military anarchy'.[69]

Describing the local willingness to serve the French in the early years of the Napoleonic occupation, Coignet marvelled at the German capacity for order, efficiency, and fatalism: 'long live our good Germans, so full of resignation, who never did abandon their homes'. He gave a graphic description of one scene he had witnessed, which clearly supported his cultural stereotype of German national character:

I saw a postmaster killed in his house by a Frenchman, and his house serving as the ambulance. He was on his deathbed, while his daughter and wife searched for linen to attend to our wounded. They said, 'It is the will of God'.[70]

It should be noted that much of the obedience described in these accounts was based on fear. And even the active collaboration of the upper and middle classes was in part also prompted by the possibility of losing power and influence. In the case of Spain and Russia at the beginning of the nineteenth century, this apprehension was exacerbated by the subversive effect of arming the peasantry, coupled with the revolutionary rhetoric of the invader. Many Russian aristocrats feared for

---

[67] *Des pratiques de la guerre continentale*, 390.

[68] See J. Skowronek, 'Insurrection polonaise de 1830: révolution ou nationalisme?', and the discussion that followed with D. Beauvois in *Pologne: l'insurrection de 1830–1831 et sa réception en Europe: actes du colloque* (Lille: Université de Lille, 1982), 213.

[69] W. Napier, *A Narrative of the Peninsular Campaign 1807–1814* (London: Bickers & Son, 1889), ii. 205.

[70] A. Coignet, *Les Cahiers du Capitaine Coignet, 1799–1815* (Paris: Hachette, 1883), 130.

their lives not from the occupant, but from their own countrymen. Tarlé remarked that there was 'definite evidence as early as 1805–7, and at the beginning of the invasion of 1812' of this. There were 'rumours associating Napoleon with dreams of emancipation circulated among the Russian peasantry (above all, among servants and near the cities)'. Tarlé also mentions much talk of 'a letter Napoleon had allegedly sent to the Tsar, warning him that until he liberated the peasants, there would be war and no peace'.[71] Although the case of the Russian peasantry against Napoleon was one of the strongest examples of fierce resistance to occupation, the aristocracy were unable to predict whether their own people would target the French or themselves. In the words of Pozdeyev, a Russian landowner: 'The French are spreading everywhere, preaching freedom for the peasants, so you may expect a general uprising . . . you may expect a general insurrection against the Tsar and the nobles and their stewards . . . All you can do is keep quiet and await the general massacre.'[72]

Indeed, sometimes such apocalyptic visions were realized. Many Russian nobles provided themselves with French soldiers for their own self-defence as soon as they came under Napoleonic occupation. The ability to inspire fear (or, as it was better known, 'terror') was the primary method used by occupation forces to exert control over an occupied people and their territory. In the case of active collaboration (in Russia or Prussia) D'Espinchal noted that one could find 'with the vanquished both the amenities and the benefits of hospitality, indeed a superabundance of virtues that do the Prussians proud, if fear isn't the reason'.[73]

POLITICAL ACTS OF RESISTANCE

> Be quite clear in your calculations, that two weeks earlier or later
> you will have an uprising. It always happens in a conquered
> country.[74]

We have looked at instances in which inhabitants were obedient to occupying armies, either passively or actively; the present section will examine the vast array of actions considered by occupiers to be illegal.

---

[71] *Napoleon's Invasion of Russia*, 184.   [72] Ibid. 195.

[73] *Souvenirs militaires*, 339.

[74] Napoléon Bonaparte, *Correspondance de L'Empéreur Napoléon Ier* (Paris: Panckoucke, 1857–69), 12, 911.

First to be considered are non-violent political acts of resistance, both individual and collective.

At the beginning of the nineteenth century, political power, and, as a result, political participation, was restricted to a small class of people. Overt political activity, especially in the early part of the century was limited to towns, and conducted by the literate classes. Political activity is a term used here to describe such actions as writing or publishing articles hostile or considered inflammatory to the occupant in journals and newspapers; holding unapproved town meetings; voting; convening, participating in, or leading public demonstrations or riots. But there were other activities which came into play only under military occupation, and which were also regarded as eminently political. These were non-violent protests, directed against occupation by foreign troops. Peasants living in isolated hamlets could be as guilty as groups meeting in cellars in large cities; in the case of the peasant, passing on to his own government information concerning the occupying army's movements, size, and location; hiding escaped prisoners of war; feeding partisans or simply remaining silent about their whereabouts—all these were deemed to be as criminal as physically killing a soldier, and the risks were as extreme. Describing events in the Franco-Prussian War, Lt. Col. Amédée Brenet related: 'Such was the exasperation of the Prussians in the midst of this unjust war that they even shot the inhabitants of the farm of Gressey because they had received and fed francs-tireurs'.[75] Surprisingly, given the hazardous nature of these non-violent acts of political resistance (in the nineteenth century, the customary punishment for any of these offences was immediate execution), many peasants and burghers who could not or would not raise a weapon nonetheless managed to make their position towards the occupation clear.[76] In fact, for peasants and merchants to hide or burn their own crops and stores was doubly precarious. For not only were they depriving themselves of their own sustenance, but such actions were illegal, and occupying armies could kill anyone found resorting to them. Often, however, the soldiers could not find the perpetrators, as a captain of the gendarmerie in Spain explained:

The General Abbé left Pampelune on the 22nd of March (1806) in order to forage in the neighbouring valleys, in the hope of finding grain, and in order to augment his provisions. Upon hearing of the arrival of the French,

---

[75] *La France et l'Allemagne devant le droit international*, 33.

[76] Many examples can be found in J. B. Jourdan, *Mémoires militaires du Maréchal Jourdan, Guerre d'Espagne* (Paris: Flammarion, 1899), 110–11, 230, 318–20.

the inhabitants of the villages fled, having first hidden all their possessions.[77]

In a letter to Voronstov after the Napoleonic occupation of Moscow, Count Rostopchin wrote that 'everywhere the people manifested an extraordinary national spirit. They destroyed their own property rather than yield it to the enemy.'[78] In Poland, during the campaign of 1806–7, local inhabitants fled leaving the hungry French and Russian troops to find deserted farms.[79] These actions were replicated all over Europe. The wholesale destruction of their provisions, mills, and houses was followed by the abandonment of entire towns. Coimbre, Viseu, and Villafranca were among examples facing the baffled Napoleonic armies.[80] The ease with which an entire people could adopt a 'scorched earth' policy and migrate with speed across a country was described by Delagrave as a customary response of the Portuguese people to a series of invasions which stretched back to Julius Caesar.[81] In areas of Alsace and Lorraine, where there were strong feelings against the German occupiers in 1870, official notices were torn down, occupation functionaries threatened and assaulted, isolated sentries were fired upon, and acts of sabotage were carried out. In Mulhouse the populace saluted the passage of French prisoners of war through the town by lining the streets and singing the 'Marseillaise' whilst shouting 'à bas la Prusse!'[82]

The most significant element affecting the participation of civilians in the occupations and invasions of nineteenth-century Europe was the extraordinary political change precipitated by the effects of Napoleonic principles. Stuart Woolf's analysis was that even before the French armies moved in, 'the states they subverted were in a condition of crisis that rendered them vulnerable'. From the 'Austrian Empire to the Dutch United Provinces, from Bourbon Naples and Spain to the Swiss Confederation', the rulers of these *ancien régime* states were 'confronted by social tensions which all too easily coagulated around the

---

[77] Martin, *La Gendarmerie française en Espagne*, 259.

[78] Tarlé, *Napoleon's Invasion of Russia*, 196.

[79] François Pils, *Journal de marche du Grenadier Pils 1804–1814* (Paris: P. Ollendorff, 1895), 39.

[80] Marbot, *Mémoires*, ii. 358, 383; D.-C. Parquin, *Souvenirs et campagnes d'un Vieux Soldat de l'Empire 1803–1814* (Paris: Berger-Levraut, 1892), 101; A. Delagrave, *Mémoires du Col. Delagrave, campagne du Portugal 1810–11* (Paris: C. Delagrave, 1902), 87–8.

[81] *Campagne du Portugal*, 71.

[82] Audoin-Rouzeau, *1870: la France dans la Guerre*, 269. The double irony of the populace singing the 'Marseillaise' as a sign of rejection of the Prussian occupation was the fact that it had been banned under the Second Empire. E. Weber, 'Who Sang the Marseillaise?', *My France* (Cambridge: Harvard University Press, 1991), 92–103.

ossified political and administrative structures they upheld or tried to reform.'[83] As noted earlier, the mere rumour of the Emperor's impending visit was sufficient to threaten vulnerable social and political structures, such as existed in Spain and Italy. The arrival of his troops heralded the dawn of a new political order, where rulers had suddenly to depend on their lowliest serfs to maintain their increasingly shaky thrones. By the time of the Franco-Prussian War in 1870, three-quarters of a century of national wars of invasion and liberation had legitimized a far wider participation in the political sphere through the role played by the common people in resisting foreign occupations. However, these actions did not always immediately bear fruit, nor directly benefit those who sacrificed themselves for the greater cause of the Fatherland, as can be seen in the following example from Russia:

Nikolai Ivanovich Turgenev and others of the Decembrist generation have shown that the Russian peasants, after the expulsion of the enemy from Russia, thought that by their heroic struggle against Napoleon they had 'earned their freedom' and that they would receive it from the Tsar. They received not their freedom, but instead a single line in Alexander's manifesto of 1814, in which the Tsar 'most graciously' thanked all classes and granted them various privileges. This single line ran: 'The peasants, our loyal people, will be recompensed by God'.[84]

However, changes did occur. There were popular insurrections in Belgium in 1798, Naples in 1799 and 1806, Spain in 1808, the Netherlands in 1811–12, and Russia in 1812–14; as Robert Gildea remarked: 'confronted by these popular movements, the social élites were given a choice. Either they could join the popular movements or rather take them over in order to control them, or they could collaborate with the occupying power in order to suppress the insurrection.'[85] Bold new codes of political conduct emerged under the pressures of invasion and the threat of rebellion. In 1813 the Prussian Emperor found himself suddenly dependent on the indulgence, and more crucially, the political participation of 'the people' (a social category which he had hitherto deemed deeply subversive).

In Prussia for the first time, the sovereign spoke without intermediary 'to his people'. The necessity in the end chased away the old etiquette. The moment was supreme, the word of Frédéric-Guillaume was simple and manly . . . he said

[83] *Napoleon's Integration of Europe*, 81.
[84] Tarlé, *Napoleon's Invasion of Russia*, 193.
[85] R. Gildea, *Barricades and Borders: Europe 1800–1914* (Oxford: Oxford University Press, 1987), 53.

'This is a decisive struggle for either an honourable peace or a glorious death'. The Prussian spoke in a language unknown since the time of the French Revolution. In his mouth, the rights of people were of interest to sovereigns. They armed the people with the principles of Liberty, Equality, to throw them at Napoleon.[86]

For civilians there was, legally and in practice, no real distinction between non-violent political behaviour and violent resistance. In Poland, Russia officially banned the wearing of mourning clothes as a repressive measure during the 1861–3 insurrection. Breaking this rule had terrible consequences for individuals under martial law. Edwards, the British journalist that later was to cover the Franco-Prussian War, describes the Russian thinking behind the act, and its tragi-comic effects:

'It was time to put an end to this masquerade' says the correspondent of a Russian journal; but the fact is, the true masquerade has only just begun; for you may now see persons who are grieving for their nearest relations dressed as though they had no such loss to deplore, a funeral looking (if it were not for the coffin) like a shabby wedding procession, and women crying their eyes out at a secretly ordered service for the dead, attired in all the colours of the rainbow . . . For brothers, fathers and husbands mourning may, it is true, still be worn, but not without carrying a permit, which any policeman may cause to be produced as often as he thinks fit. I find, too, that those who have lost relations in the insurrection do not consider it advisable to call attention to the Government to the fact.[87]

In the first place, the army did not distinguish between the legality of the two. The historian Norman Davies makes this very point about Poland under the three empires: 'In Tsarist Russia, or in the Austria of Metternich, and to a lesser extent in Bismarck's Prussia, the authorities made no distinction between different degrees of resistance, nor between the different methods employed.' Indeed, they had absolutely no concept of a 'legal opposition', let alone of 'non-violent' resistance. 'Rather, the absolutist empires demanded absolute obedience, and any form of resistance met with the same implacable reaction. If the Poles could not all be professional insurrectionaries, therefore, they were nearly all suspected of latent treason.'[88] Secondly, and more crucially, as political positions and ambitions were the exclusive prerogative of the upper and middle strata of society, either type of activity was often

---

[86] E. Charras, *Histoire de la guerre de 1813 en Allemagne* (Paris: Armand le Chevalier, 1870), 2–3, 218.

[87] H. Edwards, *The Private History of a Polish Insurrection: From Official and Unofficial Sources* (London: Saunders, Otley, & Co., 1865), 212–13.

[88] *A Short History of Poland*, 183.

classed as subversive by their own governments. An additional problem
here is the paucity of sources. Most writings on occupation in nineteenth-century Europe suffer from a general lack of written sources
concerning civilians under occupation, except those which focused on
organized guerrilla groups or mass uprisings. The nineteenth-century
historian Tarlé explained his own difficulties in this area: 'Unfortunately
the records concerning [political] activity are very incomplete', as
'official historiography had long neglected to collect and verify material concerning the National War, almost exclusively dwelling on the
actions of the regular army and the partisans'. He found that 'after the
witnesses died out, it became difficult to obtain authentic data'.[89] This
could suggest that very little political resistance was actually occurring
in occupied lands outside of actions taken by specific partisan groups.
Perhaps because the effects were less tangible on the operations of war,
the motivations of merchants who destroyed their stores and peasants
who preferred to burn their crops have never been systematically
explored. However, an examination of campaign diaries, memoirs of
participating soldiers, original archival sources, and other publications
of the time point to widespread instances of non-violent and violent
popular resistance. In Germany in 1813, a French soldier described the
mood and actions of a people united in attempting to do whatever was
necessary to expel the occupier:

Beyond the enormous sacrifices asked, offered, and accomplished—with an
incomparable ardour—the populations added still more. On all sides committees were formed that provoked patriotic gifts, and affluent gifts at that. Some
gave cash, others silver, and yet others gave cloth of differing kinds. Some here
donated horses and beasts of burden, over there gave grain and fodder. Women
brought their jewellery, their wedding rings even, and received in exchange a
medal of iron which had engraved upon it: 'I Gave Gold for Iron, 1813'; souvenirs that were religiously kept on the mantelpiece at home.[90]

The next section will continue to explore the types of response to the
occupier that arose in the nineteenth century, turning to examine armed
acts of resistance.

ARMED ACTS OF RESISTANCE

From the beginning of the nineteenth century it is relatively easy to find
examples of individual, organized, or indeed spontaneous armed resis-

---

[89] Tarlé, *Napoleon's Invasion of Russia*, 252.
[90] Charras, *Histoire de la guerre de 1813 en Allemagne*, 213.

tance to occupation troops. When Soult invaded Portugal in 1809, several French sources noted that, in many of the villages they entered, there were collective acts of resistance, regardless of gender (and they seemed to find this touching as they killed them):

> In the beginning, the well-to-do peasants shut and barricaded their houses, and fired at our troops from the windows, until the moment when their doors could be broken down, and they were massacred. Their resistance was individual; each was killed in defending the entryway into their village, of his house . . . I saw during this period young and beautiful women shoot at us and receive in turn the death-blow without retreating . . . Some men and even women tried to defend the entrance to the village but this was unsuccessful. I pointed out a young woman to Marshal Soult who, lying dead, was clearly still extremely beautiful; she was lying near one of these resisters and had his rifle and cartridges beside her: she defended herself until the final moment.[91]

In 1814, in Alsace-Lorraine, many peasants refused to be incorporated into the local or regional garrison, but declared themselves ready to fight, on their own, in defence of their hearths and homes. Accordingly, in Montereau and Troyes they threw tiles and furniture from the roofs and ramparts of the towns, and shot at invading soldiers from behind their shutters. There were several independent accounts of solitary farmers descending upon an unfortunate soldier with pitchforks.[92] And in Spain, it appeared to the French as the norm rather than the exception to find inhabitants resisting spontaneously:

> Since the entry of our troops into the Peninsula, each Spaniard is persuaded that he would accomplish a great patriotic act by killing a Frenchman, so that our soldiers, in all circumstances, and especially during long marches, worry about everything—even about women and children. For example on the 5th of June, a mounted policeman named Crouzet, believing he had absolutely nothing to fear from the peasants working at the side of the road, dropped back for a moment from the convoy. Eventually, concerned by his absence, his companions went back to look for him. They found only a corpse; the unfortunate had had his throat cut from ear to ear by these inoffensive looking agricultural labourers.[93]

In France in 1870, although the generic term *franc-tireur* was used to describe citizens resisting the Prussian invasion, whether singly or in groups, the Prussians often remarked that most peasants appeared to have rifles by their sides, and were actually prepared to use them if they happened upon a soldier:

---

[91] *Mémoires militaires du Maréchal Jourdan*, 176.
[92] Gen. Saint-Chamans, *Mémoires 1802–1832* (Paris: E. Plon Nourrit et Cie., 1896), 119, 128. 305; A. Chuquet, *L'Alsace en 1814* (Paris: Plon-Nourrit, 1900), 326–30.
[93] Martin, *La Gendarmerie française en Espagne et en Portugal*, 105.

At all distances and in every country house, our horsemen would be assailed with gunfire. At their approach, the worker would throw down his shovel, and pick up his weapon and begin to fire. Each house was actually a little fortress, each man in peasant dress a *franc-tireur*. It was only by a draconian severity that it was finally possible to put an end to this treacherous and infamous manner of waging war, and to eventually give satisfaction to our troops.[94]

On the question of the reliability of sources, two points need to be mentioned here, both of which become particularly apparent in the course and aftermath of the Franco-Prussian War. Both sides had a need to embellish and exaggerate acts of resistance by *franc-tireurs*. The French did so during the course of the war because they were attempting to encourage yet further resistance (and in some books written after the war in order to rewrite history), the Prussians because they were already coming under fire for the repressive measures they were taking against civilians. Yet it was when the inhabitants organized themselves in bands, or groups, that the sources become far more abundant. Eyewitness reports, from campaign diaries to local histories, give an account of the structures of various organizations, the types of people involved, and the degree of success of partisan activities. The next section will look at organized forms of armed resistance by the populace.

ORGANIZED ACTS OF RESISTANCE: GUERRILLAS AND *FRANC-TIREURS*

The development of partisan fighting had less to do with the progress of the 'science' of this new type of combat than with the social and cultural characteristics of occupied people.[95] The nature of the response to occupation varied enormously in terms of means and methods, intensity, and the extent of politicization. The war in Spain, for example, was highly organized on a regional level by local juntas:

At the start of the war, once people had taken the decision to rush to the defence of Spain, each town had its own junta; a short time later, *juntes provençales* were constituted, which gave a greater cohesion to the *guérillas*,

---

[94] Citation from *Le Journal officiel de L'État-Major prussien*, in Brenet, *La France et l'Allemagne devant le droit international*, 29.

[95] Francis Lieber's article on guerrilla parties was the first extensive (if highly prejudiced) legal account. 'Guerrilla Parties, considered with reference to the Laws and Usages of War', *Miscellaneous Writings* (Philadelphia: Lippincott & Co., 1881), ii. 277–92.

and allowed them to unite upon a common goal. This itself well proves that the war in Spain was a popular one, as the first bands were formed of peasants, artisans, rough workers . . . at the exclusion of the wealthy and the nobility. The chiefs of the *guérillas* were for the most part of obscure origin, veritable patriots, who fought without ambition for a cause they considered sacred.[96]

The military juntas in Spain took their responsibilities seriously, describing tactics of resistance in several pamphlets. In an early manifesto, published in May 1808, the central junta in Seville set out the general strategy: a constant partisan war, which, as the pamphlet said, is 'the system that suits us: we must harass and ravage the enemy armies' by a series of measures including 'withholding victuals, destroying bridges, raising entrenchments in advantageous positions, and taking similar measures'. This is seen as a merely pragmatic military strategy, as 'the locale of Spain, its multitudinous mountains, and even the distribution of its provinces, all invite us to find great success in this type of warfare'.[97] The Prussian assembly at Königsberg instructed the populace, in a similar vein, as to how to respond to the French troops in the edict which raised the *Landsturm* (guerrilla units) and *Landwehr* (*levée en masse*). They also legislated appropriate behaviour under occupation: 'Dans les villes occupées par l'ennemi, les bals, les fêtes, les mariages même sont interdits.'[98]

The Spanish guerrillas succeeded both in demolishing French troops, and in displaying an almost mythical heroism and single-mindedness in the cause of their freedom. Four years after the French had entered Spain, and were occupying large parts of Russia, a young Russian soldier-poet named Denis Davydov called for an imitative response—a war '*à la guérilla*' in Russia. Although given only 180 men by his sceptical superior, Davydov and his troops initiated a powerful and highly effective guerrilla campaign against the French. He was among the few who organized a coherent strategy of partisan warfare, and he kept a diary of his experiences. His journal was reprinted at the height of the 'Great Patriotic War' against the Germans nearly 150 years later.[99] Indeed, such was the similarity between Davydov's methods and those used by his Soviet descendants in 1941, that it was believed his journal

[96] Martin, *La Gendarmerie française en Espagne et en Portugal*, 122. A recent and detailed history of the military strategy employed by the French and the Spanish guerrillas can be found in D. Alexander's *Rod of Iron: French Counter Insurgency Policy in Aragon during the Peninsular War* (Wilmington: Scholarly Resources, 1985).
[97] C. Clerc, *Guerre d'Espagne, Capitulation de Baylen* (Paris: A. Fontemoing, 1903), 77.
[98] Charras, *Histoire de la guerre de 1813 en Allemagne*, 216.
[99] D. Davydov, *Essai sur la Guerre des Partisans*, trans. R. Polignac (Paris: J. Corréord, 1841).

could equally have been an accurate account of Russian partisans' methods during the Second World War:

I distributed among the peasants the rifles and cartridges taken from the enemy and urged them to defend their property. I also gave them instructions on how to deal with bands of marauders outnumbering them. Receive them with friendliness, offer them whatever you have to eat and, especially, to drink with a deep bow, because they do not know Russian and will understand gestures better than words. Put those who are intoxicated to sleep and when you are sure that they are really sleeping, rush for their arms and carry out what God has commanded you to do to the enemies of the Christian Church and of your native land. After exterminating them, bury the bodies in some inaccessible place . . . Now go and tell your neighbours what I have just told you.'[100]

Although the battle against the French was called by the Spanish the 'little war' (literally *guerrilla*), a certain Marquisito's band swelled to 4,300 men in 1812, and some even grew to 8,000—more in keeping with the size of a professional army battalion. While some of these guerrillas were highly coordinated, others functioned much more spontaneously, forming and disintegrating according to circumstance.[101] These erratic and fluid qualities raised two difficulties in establishing clear military demarcations of the guerrilla fighters in Spain (and elsewhere) for occupying armies. The first problem was the annoying elasticity of their status. Unencumbered by the strait-jacket of military institutionalism, civilians could one day be armed fighters, and another, simple toiling Vattelian peasants. The second difficulty lay in establishing the veracity of reports on their conduct, given the unconcealed hostility and prejudice of most accounts, particularly those of the occupation forces themselves. On the question of the legal status of guerrilla fighters, Mougenot noted:

The *guérilleros* can be the object of a double classification: in the first instance one can separate permanent corps, more or less organized, sometimes even equipped with—often dissimilar—uniforms, from bands constituted temporarily by the inhabitants of a region, who, at the approach of the French or for some other reason, constitute themselves—or rather they improvise. This is done without any distinctive sign, without military chiefs, following the local clergy, a municipal magistrate or a simple peasant. Then, once the special task for which they had come together had been accomplished, they lay down their arms and return to their daily occupations. We can yet further distinguish

---

[100] D. Davydov, 'Partisans against Napoleon', *Behind the Lines: Twenty-eight Stories of Irregular Warfare* (London: Cassel & Co., 1956), 12.
[101] See especially Martin's *La Gendarmerie française en Espagne et en Portugal* on these points from p. 48 on.

guérillas from the operations they conduct which are their central, if not sole purpose, who often, under the cover of fanatical patriotism, they pillage their compatriots more than they actually attack the enemy. In one case as with the other, this distinction should not be considered as absolutely set. There is often confusion, and if one considers the Peninsular War in its entirety, one could venture that there could be found at the same time admirable patriots as well as highway robbers, partially organized partisans and badly armed peasants.[102]

Of the hostility and prejudice shown by writers in military journals to guerrillas there are many examples. Sutherland Edwards, an English journalist who, as noted earlier, had covered both the Polish insurrection of 1861–3 and the Franco-Prussian War, argued against taking military accounts seriously. He explained that, during the insurrection in Poland, things were not quite what the Russians had claimed:

As to the general conduct of the contending forces in the field, that of the insurgents . . . has been incomparably better than that of the Russians . . . Any foreigner who was in any of the country districts in Poland during the insurrection, will, I am sure, admit that he would a thousand times rather have fallen in with a band of insurgents than with a party of Russian soldiers, and this general feeling on the subject is better evidence than any number of real or pretended facts on either side.[103]

Guerrilla activities drew heavily on the assistance and benevolence of the local inhabitants. Such goodwill often required some official encouragement. During the Franco-Prussian War, the *Préfet* of the Côte d'Or issued the following enticing circular to his subordinates:

The country is not asking that you assemble yourselves in levied masses, nor that you fight the enemy openly. It asks only that each morning, three or four resolute men from amongst you quit the village and choose a good position from where they can fire on the Prussians without running any risk to themselves. One should, above all, aim at enemy cavalry, and, having acquired their horses, take them directly to the *canton* headquarters. I take it upon myself to here declare recompensation, and, if ever you are killed, your heroic deaths will be published in all the provincial papers as well as in the *Journal Officiel*.[104]

There were numerous instances of heroic popular resistance during the Franco-Prussian War, but also of complete passivity. A historian of the war concluded that generalizations were difficult to come by, since 'the behaviour of civilian populations was not more homogeneous by the end of the invasion than it was at the start'. After an exhaustive trawl

---

[102] *Des pratiques de la guerre continentale durant le Premier Empire*, 50.
[103] *The Private History of a Polish Insurrection*, 202–3.
[104] *Les Mémoires de Bismarck*, ed. Busch (Paris: Fasquelle, 1898), i. 239.

of national and departmental archives, it was clear that, until the armistice, 'the enemy was accepted without resistance in certain localities, and repelled with much vigour in others.' Even further, with the same region, attitudes could be completely opposing from one town or village to another.[105]

LEVÉE EN MASSE AND OTHER ASSORTED INSURRECTIONS

A distinct type of resistance (which was to come under legal classification as from 1874) was the collective uprising *levée en masse*. Although the scope of the concept was later to be truncated by diplomats, its actual practice by civilians during this period was far less controllable. Uprisings, revolts, and insurrections against occupying forces were commonplace occurrences throughout occupied territory.[106]

The *levée en masse* was a phenomenon which governments both instigated and encouraged in defence of their country as an essential weapon to repel an armed invader, and they were often not too concerned about the means that the peasantry and townspeople used to carry it out. They were equally unconcerned about the type of people they invited to participate in these collective uprisings. Kluber's definition of the classification of desirable participants was all inclusive: 'the fighters commanded to rise in the defence of the patrie, by virtue of a *levée en masse*' are subjects who, on the 'express or assumed orders of the government, take only the defence of their area'. For example the inhabitants of 'a town, or of a fortress, given that defence is their sole aim; that is, their taking of arms is purely for defensive purposes'.[107]

Governments threatened with occupation (or already subjected to it) tended to be rather more rigorous in defining what they expected of their civilian populations. However, in Spain, the local junta appeared actively to seek out criminals, as French military policeman and historian Martin was quick to point out: 'In a bando, or edict dated 29th of May, the junta of Seville decreed the arming of all men between the

---

[105] Audoin-Rouzeau, *1870: La France dans la Guerre*, 262.

[106] As shown in Chapter 6, the most famous insurrectionary nation of the nineteenth century was Poland. See, for example, Marion Kukiel's, 'Les Origines de la stratégie et de la tactique des insurrections polonaises au XVIIIe et au XIXe siècle', *Revue internationale d'histoire militaire*, 3 (1952); Norman Davies, *God's Playground: A History of Poland* (Oxford: Clarendon Press, 1981), ii; and I. Pradzynski, *Mémoire historique et militaire sur la guerre en Pologne en 1831* (Paris: Nien, 1840).

[107] J. Kluber, *Droits des gens modernes de l'Europe* (Paris: Guillaumin, 1861), 383–6.

ages of 16 and 60. More interesting is the edict of the next day, which called "under the flag" all "deserters, contrabandeers not charged with theft, asssassination, treachery".'[108] But they also often spelled out what could happen to those who chose to remain uninvolved. A Portuguese proclamation of 1808 made this absolutely clear:

that all adult males, without exception, be armed with a long pike of six or seven feet, or with whatever other arms that can be procured. That in all the cities and towns, the entrances to the streets should be strongly barricaded, in order that the inhabitants can organize to defend themselves once the enemy presents itself. . . . that all persons that refuse to come to the defence of the country will be punished with death, as well as those who lend assistance to the enemy; that every village that does not defend itself against the enemy shall be burnt and razed to the ground.[109]

The term *levée en masse* covered at least three fundamentally distinct classes of event. First, it described an official organization of civilians by the legitimate government, army, or wartime regional authority. The men were usually conscripted and registered under some form of official authority, whether at the local, regional, or national level. The most cited example of this type of *levée* in the military and legal texts was the institutionalizing of the Prussian *Landwehr* and *Landsturm*, established after an act of parliament:

At the approach of the enemy, the masses of the Landsturm should bring all the inhabitants of the village with their animals and their possessions . . . Each citizen is bound to oppose the orders of the enemy and their execution no matter what they may be, to defend themselves and to prevent the enemy's ambitions by all possible means. In case of convening the Landwehr, combat is a necessity, a legitimate means of defence, which authorizes all means. Those most bold and decisive are the best, as who serves in the most efficient manner a just and a sacred cause.[110]

Although the *Landsturm* was the most commonly cited example of this kind in the literature of the laws of war, a much more comprehensive model (with accompanying literature on insurrectionary warfare) was that of nineteenth-century Poland.[111] Napoleon, too, was particularly fond of this manner of raising an army, especially when his military fortunes began to falter. Among his relentless and increasingly

---

[108] *La Gendarmerie française en Espagne et en Portugal*, 75–7.
[109] *Mémoires militaires du Maréchal Jourdan*, 115.
[110] J. de Guelle, *Précis des lois de la guerre: la guerre continentale*, (Paris: G. Pedone-Lauriel, 1881), 28.
[111] See W. Rudzka, 'Studies on the Polish Insurrectionary Government in 1863–4', *Antemurale, VII–VIII, 1863–1963* (Rome, 1963).

manic orders at the end of his reign one finds a decree issued in 1814, which proclaimed a *levée en masse* and ordered the creation of regional committees, consisting of two or three civilian or military members, whose task was to oversee the formation and recruitment of partisans. The decree also declared as traitor any official or civilian who might inhibit this effort.[112] At the end of March he gave the following orders to General Defrance: 'create an insurgency with the inhabitants of the Meuse and the Moselle, ring the tocsin everywhere, arrest the commanders, the enemy convoys, their couriers,' not forgetting to 'completely reorganize the administration of the country'.[113] Or, as one Napoleonic proclamation uttered menacingly after instructing the populace to rise against occupying soldiers: 'The voice of the Emperor calls you, it is that of the exterminating angel.'[114]

These demands for a collective uprising by the populace, with their increasing threats of deadly reprisals, had only a limited success. With his characteristic lucidity, the Emperor himself offered an explanation: 'How can a general rising take place in a country where the revolution has killed the priests and nobles, and I have killed the revolution?'[115]

Much more dangerous to invading or occupying soldiers were what were described as 'insurrections' or 'rebellions': spontaneous uprisings of an occupied people, most often without any official sanction whatsoever. These sorts of uprisings were invariably characterized as criminal, subversive as they were both to the authority of the occupying power and the government which had surrendered its power. Yet the literature often described these sorts of insurrections, or *levées*, according to their end result; like Hobbes, they tended to support the right of rebellion only if it proved successful.[116] Only then, retrospectively, could representations of previous rulers be cast in a negative light. Accordingly, the success of the Spanish insurrections against the French also led to the description of the occupation as a particularly brutish one (except by Napier who remained consistently hostile to the Spanish). In contrast, chronicles of rebellions with limited achievements tended to fault the

[112] H. Houssaye, *La Patrie guerrière* (Paris: Perrin et Cie, 1913), 14.
[113] *Correspondance de Napoléon*, ed. C.-L. Panckouke, xxvii (Paris: C.-L. Panckouke, 1819), 193, 289, 301.
[114] Proclamation published by Roe, Strasbourg on 26 Mar. 1814, cited in Houssaye, *La Patrie guerrière*, 54–5.
[115] *Correspondance de Napoléon*, xxvi. 156.
[116] An interesting study of this question is by G. Geamanu's *La Résistance à l'oppression et le droit de l'insurrection* (Paris: Domat-Monchrestien, 1933), 278–9, and especially the chapter entitled 'La Certitude du Triomphe'.

participants rather than the occupying troops. In order to understand the character and depth of these types of uprisings it is necessary to explore more thoroughly the ideological underpinnings of this sort of response. Accordingly, the next sections will look at the ideas and values which prompted civilian responses to invasion and occupation.

THE IDEOLOGIES OF RESISTANCE

> Que toutes les communes se lèvent. Que toutes les campagnes pren-
> nent feu! Que toutes les forêts s'emplissent de voix tonnants . . .
> Levez vous! levez vous! Organisons l'effrayante bataille de la
> Patrie![117]

The dominant view among current historians of occupation in the late eighteenth and early nineteenth centuries is to deny the existence of any aggregate character to acts of resistance. Indeed, in a chapter entitled 'The Illusion of Nationalism', Robert Gildea rejects the notion that nationalism played any significant role in popular responses to invasions. He asserted instead that it was predominantly financial oppression which propelled country people to react against occupation forces, believing that although 'French forces of occupation triggered off large and hostile popular insurrections', these should 'not be seen as genuinely nationalistic. They were peasant revolts' of a very traditional kind against 'billeting and plunder, the requisition of foodstuffs, horses, and equipment, taxation and reparation payments, and above all against the conscription of men into Napoleon's armies'.[118]

However, as seen earlier in this chapter the groups which fought Napoleonic troops were largely inspired by nationalist and patriotic sentiments, which were often mediated by the metaphysics of religion. The question, however, is how these phenomena should be conceptualized. A common approach has been to examine the development of such norms by merely focusing on their intellectual articulation. More crucial, however, is the question of what social forces underlay the emergence of ideas of nationalism and patriotism. In an absorbing study of eighteenth and early nineteenth-century patriotism in Britain, Linda Colley demonstrates how a sense of identity in Britain was forged as a result of the threat of invasion, although it began as a defensive reaction: 'the prime incentive to volunteer was not camaraderie, or

---

[117] Victor Hugo, cited in Houssaye, *La Patrie guerrière*, 368.
[118] Gildea, *Barricades and Borders*, 53.

aggression, or greed, or the fear of seeming less a man, but quite simply invasion'.[119] The claim here is that it was the phenomenon of occupation itself which often played a decisive role in the development of these ideologies, and that resistance to occupation could significantly assist the articulation of national and political identities. In an illuminating study of the Spanish War, Pelissier argued persuasively that patriotic mobilization was greater among the popular classes: 'let us say that the people were perhaps less subtle, and had a more brutal and spontaneous conception of patriotism: in the streets of Madrid, on the Second of May, only the unsavoury elements were to be found. The well heeled were at home or at their balconies. Alaca Galiano [a future leader], what is he doing? His mother had banned him from going out.'[120] Often, the origins of the development of national consciousness in nineteenth-century Europe is ascribed to the intelligentsia. Yet such doctrines would not have gained a popular foothold if the brute realities of occupation had not inspired their awakening in the broader populace. As a historian of the French Revolution noted, 'there is much to be said' for the view that 'in so far as the French Revolution strengthened the idea of nationalism', it did so less by the 'positive promotion of the idea of popular sovereignty ... than by awakening a sense of community among the oppressed,' or, even more importantly 'reinvigorating it where it already existed'.[121]

Much has been written on the influence of philosophers and thinkers of the nineteenth century on the development of ideologies of patriotism and nationalism. Less well documented is the influence of popular insurrections and rebellions on the way these doctrines were formulated.[122] Indeed, these influences are systematically marginalized in orthodox writings on the period, which give thinkers and pamphleteers exclusive credit for influencing events. As Lévy-Brühl rather pompously (and erroneously) declared about Germany: 'Sans Kant, pas de guerre d'indépendance.'[123] In a similar vein, Isaiah Berlin, when writing on nationalism, presents thinkers as shrewd and

[119] L. Colley, *Britons: Forging the Nation 1707–1837* (New Haven: Princeton University Press, 1992), 308–19.
[120] 'Les Libéraux "Patriotes" espagnols devant les contradictions de la Guerre d'Indépendance', 261–2.
[121] J. Roberts, *The French Revolution* (Oxford: Oxford University Press, 1978), 129.
[122] For a more recent study, see B. Moore's *Social Origins of Dictatorship and Democracy* (London: Penguin, 1991), especially part 3, ch. 9, 'Peasants and Revolution', 453–84.
[123] *L'Allemagne depuis Leibnitz*, 269. However, quoting the statesman Stein, he does limit his premiss to the German case: 'Les écrits agissent sur les Allemands plus que sur les autres peuples', 313.

prescient deities, awakening drowsy peoples: 'florid and emotive prose was used by Herder, Burke, Fichte, Michelet, and after them sundry awakeners of the national souls of their dormant peoples in the Slav provinces of the Austrian or Turkish empires or the oppressed nationalities ruled by the tsar; and then throughout the world'.[124] Fichte's call to fight or perish in his *Discourse to the German Nation* was seen to be seminal in the creation of a unified Germany: 'in the overwhelming public grief, the idea of Germany was born, and would never be erased. It was a philosopher who articulated it first.'[125] The German poets, Körner, Schenckendorf, Rückert, Uhland, Henri de Kleist were said to be inspired by him rather than by the experiences of Napoleonic occupation.[126]

It may well have been the case that Fichte was the first to formulate the idea of German unity in an expressive and coherent doctrine. However, there is no doubt that he was, to a very significant extent, articulating an already existing body of ideas and sentiments which were common currency in the streets and salons of the occupied German states. Furthermore these ideas had acquired their social meaning and force in the course of patriotic confrontations with the French occupiers. It is thus manifest that German nationalism and especially patriotism, far from being a pure product of idealist philosophy, owed its vitality and perhaps even its genesis to the catalysing force unleashed by the encounter between occupier and occupied.

The next sections will provide examples of ideologies of resistance based on religion, nationalism, and patriotism. We shall see how these ideas emerged from populations confronting foreign troops, provided the inspiration to intellectuals and thinkers, and finally, how statesmen, clerics, and writers attempted to manipulate or influence inhabitants under occupation by championing these forces.

RELIGION AS A SOURCE OF RESISTANCE

Commentators on the causes of various popular revolts against occupation in the nineteenth century often evoke the impetus and power of

---

[124] I. Berlin, *Against the Current* (Oxford: Clarendon Press), 1991, 343. Later, however, he concluded that nationalism could be the result of a 'wound inflicted on the collective feeling of society'. 347.

[125] Lévy-Bruhl, *L'Allemagne depuis Leibnitz*, 267.

[126] Mougenot, *Des pratiques de la guerre continentale durant le Premier Empire*, 202.

religion, but without a clear sense of its constitutive elements or the extent of its power. Religious affiliation could represent a powerful source of nationalist mobilization, for the clergy already played a central role in public and private life; as the historian Blanning pointed out, for example, in Germany, 'not only in matters of religion but in every sphere of human activity the presence of clergy was obtrusive'. He lists: in 'the economic as tithe-lord, landlord, employer, and customer; in the social as educator, censor, organiser of welfare, and distributor of charity; in the political as administrator and even ruler', as some of the relevant spheres of influence.[127] One French observer at the time of the Peninsular War narrowed down the inspiration for popular resistance to two central elements:

If the war was merely *nationalist*, already one would be found in exceptional and less favourable conditions than in Germany or in Austria where they were *political*; so finally the rights of man and the natural law traditions between civilised nations had to be respected. No, the war in Spain was at the same time *national* and *religious*.[128]

Yet Napoleon unwisely believed, in Spain in particular, that religious institutions and values were mere exploitative instruments used by the nobility to keep the populace in poverty and servitude. He declared on invading Spain: 'I shall write upon my banner the words *Liberty, Freedom from Superstition, the Destruction of the Nobility*, and I shall be received as I was in Italy, and all the classes that have national spirit will be on my side.'[129] Although he was to a large extent correct about the way religion was exploited by the ruling classes, he misunderstood both religion's adaptive power and the extent to which it was, certainly in the early part of the century, a crucible for many emerging ideologies. Religious ideas and values were successfully used by the local clergy to appeal to the sentiments of justice and morality, national autonomy, and political accountability of the peasantry. In Germany, for example, religious passion provided an impetus for political participation by a vast number of illiterate civilians fighting Napoleon's troops: 'it was not religion alone', wrote a French historian, 'that inspired among the peasants such raging bellicosity, but the spirit of liberty in all its meanings; in religious as well as in civic life.'[130]

---

[127] *The French Revolution in Germany*, 207.

[128] Clerc, *Guerre d'Espagne, Capitulation de Baylen*, 52.

[129] A. S. Grant and H. W. V. Temperley, *Europe in the Nineteenth Century: 1789–1914* (London: Longman, 1929), 145.

[130] A. N. Rambaud, *La Domination française en Allemagne: l'Allemagne sous Napoléon I, 1804–1811* (Paris: Perrin, 1874), 323.

French campaign veterans often wrote of priests inciting the population in Spain, Russia, Italy, and Austria, and even organizing the local military resistance. Of the numerous instances of this highly politicized and militant role of the clergy, the following example is from eyewitnesses:

In Italy, it is the clergy more than the nobility who push the inhabitants to unite with the Austrians against the French. In 1814, for example, during a battle that took place on the 15th of April under the walls of the city, the archbishop of Plaisance (who had been in contact for quite some time with the Austrians), made sure to let them know the movements of the French troops by sounding the church bells in a pre-arranged warning system.[131]

As illustrated in the above example, both Austria and Germany's resistance to Napoleon relied heavily on religious values and concepts; likewise Spain's *guerrilla* war demonstrated clear elements of a political struggle underpinned by religious doctrine. Occupiers clearly believed that religious leaders were often their most hardened opponents. A Napoleonic military proclamation acknowledged the possibility of encountering hostile priests:

Generals marching against villages must take all the necessary force of repression against all those found with arms on their person, such as setting fire to them, and having them shot. All the priests, the nobles that have remained in the rebel communes shall be arrested as hostages and sent to France . . . All villages who sound the tocsin as warning shall be burnt on the spot.[132]

Priests were crucial in encouraging resistance in the name of faith, the motherland, and the *patrie* in Italy, Portugal, Spain, Austria, and Russia; they used every available means to disseminate these ideas. One of these means was the use of songs and ditties; this one from Russia was just one of many popular at that time: 'Whence does Napoleon originate? From sin. What are the French? Former Christians who have now become heretics. Is it a sin to put a Frenchman to death? No, my father, we gain a place in heaven by killing one of these heretic dogs.'[133] Further, religion was not only a receptacle for newly emerging ideologies, but these ideologies could become the receptacle of new religions.

[131] A. Dedem de Gelder, *Un Général hollandais sous le Premier Empire: mémoires* (Paris: Plon-Nourrit, 1900), 382.
[132] Proclamation announced for Lombardy at the end of the 18th century, cited in Edwards, *The Germans in France*, 286. As shown earlier, he was not unaware of the role the clergy played in resistance.
[133] S. Blaze, *La Vie militaire sous le Premier Empire: mœurs de garnison, du bivouac ou de la caserne* (Paris: Librairie Illustrée, 1888), 22–3.

THE INFLUENCE OF NATIONALISM AND PATRIOTISM

In writings on the emergence of nationalism and patriotism in the nineteenth century, the two concepts are often not adequately distinguished. Without entering into the substance of the debate, the term nationalism should be used to denote forms of linguistic, territorial, cultural, and ethnic attachments. Patriotism, on the other hand, represents a civic virtue based on identification with a distinct system of political values.[134] The sentiment of patriotism, it should be stressed, is compatible with a wide range of social, political, and intellectual positions, ranging from royalist and Catholic to socialist, conservative, and liberal.

As previously stated, it is one-dimensional to view the emergence of these concepts exclusively from the perspective of the elite, as a transmission from the middle-class intelligentsia to the broader populace. It is more fruitful to regard the phenomenon as a cross-fertilization, in which elites influenced civil society, but where social norms and aspirations also determined the intellectual doctrines of nationalism and patriotism. As Mazzini noted: 'ideas grow quickly when watered by the blood of martyrs'.[135] Papantoniou remarked that massacres and sieges in Greece were inspiring in Paris: 'After the massacres of Chios, there was great enthusiasm for the exploits of Canaris, of Miaoulis, of Botzaris' and that the emotion that was 'provoked by the fall of Missalonghi inspired poems, recitations, tableaux, lithographies, and theatrical works'. The name Missolonghi was even 'given to a liquour: "Liquour of the Brave Greeks"'.[136]

The arrival of Napoleonic troops across Europe engendered as well as spread powerful notions of nationalism and patriotism. Mougenot described how, in the course of 1809, in Germany as in Spain, there appeared a new element: 'patriotic enthusiasm reignited the vanquished peoples, national fanaticism' armed those hitherto resigned to their fate and 'drew them from their torpor'. He noted that although it was in the armies that one could witness the 'most consistent and coherent expression of the sentiment' of patriotism, one found in the 'broad masses of

---

[134] For a discussion see M. Viroli, *For Love of Country: An Essay on Patriotism and Nationalism* (Oxford: Clarendon Press, 1995). For a theoretical discussion of some of the current liberal understandings of patriotism see the similarly entitled J. Cohen and M. Nussbaum (eds.), *For Love of Country: Debating the Limits of Patriotism* (Boston: Beacon Press, 1996).

[135] G. Mazzini, *Life and Writings of Mazzini* (London: Smith, Elder & Co. Cornhill, 1864), i, 32.

[136] N. Papantoniou, *L'Indépendance grecque dans la faïence française du 19e siècle*, ed. A. Amandry (Athens: Nafplion/Fondation Ethnographique du Peloponnese 1982), 20–1.

people the most lively expression of these passions'. The Dolomites, and the Spanish *sierras*, served 'both as a refuge and a rampart to these new ideas: illiterate peasants for the most part, they were protagonists struggling for a sacred concept'.[137]

As noted earlier, according to some views, it was the poets who aroused the people to patriotism. In other instances the reverse was argued: it was believed that the patriotic behaviour of the people served to inspire the poets. 'La poésie et la guerre offrit aussi des ressources nouvelles . . . les sentiments patriotiques de la population ont immédiatement inspiré certain poètes.'[138] Both these versions may have been accurate. Here, as in most of the nineteenth century, nationalist sentiment appealed to such diverse notions as country, God, the army, the monarchy, the peasantry, nature, and even mountains. Equally, patriotism incorporated many vague notions about sovereignty, sacrifice, and heroism.[139] Yet tens of thousands were apparently willing to risk their lives for such an incoherent cluster of ideas. As the literature on resistance was to show, this mythology rested on a number of simple but forceful notions that did not necessarily cohere, but were in equal parts romantic and glorious. As one analyst also noted, the writing was often of indifferent quality:

More than just 'war literature', this was a literature of war adventures; more than soldiers, we see in the *francs-tireurs* familiar friendly characters, people in combat, and the transformation of the civilian into warrior seemed to please the authors more than the war itself. Technical accounts are sparse. Often it is a necessary vengeance that . . . creates the *franc-tireur*. Very often as well, the *francs-tireurs* rise spontaneously against the invader, inspired by patriotism . . . one can see that the merits in these works of fiction are not literary, but social; that indeed, their interest resides in their readers and not the authors, and that they rely, in the main, upon the attention of a public rather more than upon the creative power of the writers.[140]

The Spanish junta leaders appealed all at once to both nationalism and patriotism, sovereignty, king and country, warning that if the French succeeded in conquering Spain, all 'would be lost: sovereign, monarchy, property, liberty, independence, and religion' accordingly, in their eyes

[137] *Des pratiques de la guerre continentale durant le Premier Empire*, 185–6.
[138] J. Schlutter, *La Poésie de la Guerre de Revanche* (Paris: Heilbronn, 1878), 55.
[139] For an interesting study of this issue, see M. Colin, 'Mythes et figures de l'héroïsme militaire dans l'éducation patriotique des jeunes Italiens (1860–1900)', *Mythes et figures de l'héroïsme militaire dans l'Italie du Risorgimento* (Caen: Université de Caen, 1982), 143–59. For three very distinct ideological articulations of patriotism, see chs. 4–6.
[140] Claude Digeon, *La Crise allemande de la pensée française 1870–1914* (Paris: Presses Universitaires de France, 1959), 67.

it was necessary to 'sacrifice our lives and our possessions to the defence of the king and country'; and rather than choosing 'to become slaves, we must fight them and die like heros. The Spanish are the same people they have always been, and France—and Europe itself—will see that we are not less strong nor less brave than our illustrious ancestors.'[141]

The concept of risking all for patriotic freedom was set out at the start of the invasion of Spain and before a lengthy experience of French occupation. The experience of occupation often directly inspired intellectuals' theories of liberty and freedom, as well as spread these ideas within a community.[142] Mazzini, for example, wrote about the direct effect an occupying army had on his development as a political activist. After fleeing an Austrian army which suppressed a democratic constitution in his native Italy, he met the conspirators of the Piedmont uprising of 1821, and wrote of his changed feelings: 'for the first time on that day, there was vaguely presented to my mind, I will not say the thought of country and liberty, but the thought that it was possible, and therefore a duty, to fight for the freedom of one's country'.[143]

The events of the 1830s in Poland and Italy were to inspire great writings from all over Europe. Of the authors of the banned Constitution of Naples Byron wrote that they were 'proscribed for having dreamt of liberty'.[144] The plight of the Greeks, five years earlier, had had an effect on others besides Byron:

Another appeal, addressed to the women of Paris (12th of March 1826) had an enormous response. From the start, sixty ladies divided the town of Paris . . . armed with a diploma that bore the symbol of the Philhellenic Committee (with the head of Athena as emblem stamped upon it) . . . Street by street, from shops to attics, knocking on all doors, wealthy and poor: '*Français!* Donations for the noble sons of Greece! Give a little gold to buy arms!'[145]

It has been seen that both the inhabitants who resisted occupation and invasion, and the intelligentsia before and after these events, helped to forge and formulate modern images of nationalism and patriotism.[146]

---

[141] Martin, *La Gendarmerie française en Espagne et en Portugal*, 77.

[142] The Russians were in particular stimulated by the Spanish model. It was often used as an example by Leo Tolstoy's character Pierre Bezukhov in *War and Peace*, who was apparently inspired by the Russian guerrilla leader Davydov. Polish theorists and practitioners also cited the Spanish case when formulating strategy.

[143] G. Mazzini, *Life and Writings of Mazzini*, i. 2–3.

[144] Leslie Marchand, *Byron: A Portrait* (London: John Murray, 1971), 116.

[145] Anne Martin-Fugier, *La Vie élégante ou la formation du Tout-Paris 1815–1848* (Paris: Fayard, 1990), 159–60.

[146] The normative effect of insurrections throughout Europe on its society is now beginning to be examined in academic literature. For a fascinating study of the influence

Yet the development of these notions—nationalism in particular—was said to have a fatal effect on the project of the laws of war. Many writers believed nationalism destabilized the professional method of waging war (soldier to soldier) and turned it instead into an atrocious 'war between peoples':

Henceforth, besides States, there will be nations; in each state, the army will be nothing but the essence of nation in arms; outside the state, members of the same nation will know how to understand each other, to arm themselves and to unite. The consequence will be that wars will take place between peoples, and they will be terrible, implacable, and cruel conflicts.[147]

However, this prophecy rested on a misconception. In many cases, wars of occupation and invasion were not strictly between two enemy peoples, but generally between a professional army and a population it sought to subdue. As one nineteenth-century military commentator, General Thiébault, wryly noted, in the 'war between peoples', it was the troops that had to take care:

in peoples' wars, troops must be seen in as few places as possible, given that the mere sight of a single soldier of the invading army causes a hundred men from the invaded country to rise; and, accordingly, troops must be deployed only to suppress.[148]

CONCLUSION

This chapter has surveyed the three-cornered relationship among civilian populations, official representatives of their state, and occupying armies in nineteenth-century Europe. It has shown that these relationships were complex, and thus not easily reducible to simple formulae. However, six broad sets of conclusions stand out.

First, the phenomenon of occupation itself was far more fluid and dynamic than simple legal and political classifications would allow. Occupation was not always the benign and clinical experience projected

and relationship between the Russian Decembrists and the Greek resistance see *Les Relations gréco-russes pendant la domination turque et la Guerre d'Indépendance grecque* (Thessalonica: Institute for Balkan Studies, 1981), especially I. Dostian's 'L'Attitude de la société russe face au mouvement de libération national grec', 63–86 and Papantoniou's, *L'Indépendance grecque*; Beauvois, *Pologne: l'insurrection de 1830–1831: sa réception en Europe: actes du colloque*; and L. Migliorini, 'L'Héroïsme militaire dans l'Italie après Napoléon', in Viallaneix and Ehrard, *La Bataille, l'armée, la gloire 1745–1871*.

[147] Mougenot, *Des pratiques de la guerre continentale*, 184.
[148] *Mémoires*, 460.

by war propagandists, nor the absolute chaos and savagery which humanitarians highlighted. In the same region, a town or village could be burnt to the ground, while in the next valley, relations between occupier and occupied could remain entirely cordial. Yet what deserves to be underlined is the sheer opaqueness of the nature of occupation. With the arrival of an invading and occupying force, all the rules of normal social and political intercourse were suspended. However, what filled this vacuum was unclear to both sides. Occupation was often as confusing to the soldiers as to the civilians who faced them.

Another conclusion is that civilians responded in a variety of ways to invasion and occupation. According to the Vattelian ideal type, civilians were not only supremely passive, but were even able to maintain the customs of normal everyday life. According to the opposite ideal type, civilians down to the last chicken rose *en masse* to confront the conquering foreign hordes. As one might expect, neither paradigm captured the complex reality on the ground. The reality was that civilian populations were sometimes passive, yet they were also capable of a wide range of hostile reactions to military occupation. These responses differed in form, intensity, scope, and duration, largely because the character of occupation was, as noted above, inherently unpredictable.

Third, the inspirations for hostile civilian responses were diverse. In some areas local populations rallied to the banner of resistance raised by thinkers, priests, or local notables. In other areas challenges to military occupation were both spontaneous and autonomous of local elites. Indeed, on many occasions, occupied populations resisted in spite of the collaborationist instincts of their local leaders. These differences are hard to explain, particularly as they occurred over a broad period of time and a multitude of countries. One hypothesis is that the degree of local autonomy was directly proportionate to the intensity of class conflict in a locality. The advent of foreign occupation often acted as a catalyst, unleashing underlying conflicts which had been simmering within those societies. From this it is also clear that social responses to occupation cannot be explained or understood exclusively through the perspective of interstate conflict. Existing social, political, and religious cultures could have a powerful structuring effect on the character and eventual outcome of an occupation.

Although occupation has been shown to contain many uncertainties, its experiences unearthed a consistent body of practices by the army and by civilians. The history of nineteenth-century occupation revealed a rigorous and systematic set of instruments designed to maintain absolute control over land and people, and a consistent set of practices rejecting it. The doctrinal and prudential justifications of the repressive measures adopted by occupying armies were threefold. Self-defence and deterrence provided the least objectionable grounds for the use of force against civilian populations. More commonly, however, reprisals and collective punishment were practised on the overarching justification provided by the concept of 'military necessity'.

The features which have been analysed in this chapter can in some senses be seen as the practical manifestations of the three ideologies of war which are to follow in the last three chapters. Occupying armies were largely driven by the martial imperative, which gave their rule moral underpinnings. In the Grotian scheme of things, legitimate authority was more important than either liberty or patriotism; indeed, what the 'middle way' can mean under military occupation is clear. However, acts of patriotic resistance were captured most accurately by republican values. Civilians under occupation were confronted with a loss of freedom, autonomy, and national sovereignty, and forced to accept foreign rule. Under these conditions (as will be seen in Chapter 6 to follow), it was the republican paradigm, with its core values of individual liberty and national sovereignty, which most accurately encapsulated the response to this loss.

Finally, and to return to the point with which this chapter began, it has been clearly shown that both the devastation of occupation and heroism of resistance were central features of European politics long before the Second World War. In particular, the phenomena of mass civilian resistance to military occupation did not await the exactions of the Third Reich and their collaborators across Europe. Indeed, no less than hostage-taking or reprisals, civilian resistance was a 'custom' of war, which could take its place alongside other 'customs' such as collaboration, which is currently presented by contemporary historians as rather more the norm in the Second World War, especially in Western Europe.

3

The Conceptualization of War and
the Value of Political Traditions

The failure of the laws of war to resolve the problem of distinguishing between lawful and unlawful combatants provided the starting point for this project. As previous chapters have illustrated, there existed at all levels a profound disagreement as to the classes of people who were permitted to engage in political violence in times of war. This was apparent in legal textbooks, in military manuals, at over seventy-five years of diplomatic conferences, and most sharply on the battlefields and in the towns and villages of occupied Europe in the late eighteenth, nineteenth, and early twentieth centuries. By narrowing the scope of inquiry to only one aspect of the laws of war, the early chapters have also shown that there were strong normative elements to this lack of accord. The remainder of this book will argue that these normative elements were expressions of profound ideological clashes among three contending philosophies of war: martial, Grotian, and republican. From a methodological perspective, the explanation for the failed attempt to construct a distinction between lawful and unlawful combatant will be seen to lie in incommensurable normative frameworks of war, rather than in the specialized analytical tools of legal theory, diplomatic and archival history, and international relations theory.[1] This chapter will first assess both the intellectual contributions and limitations of the latter approaches, before defining three distinct traditions of war, and highlighting their explanatory value.

THE LITERATURE OF THE LAWS OF WAR
AND LEGAL HISTORIES

The first—and most obvious—place to begin the search for an adequate explanation of the problem of distinction must be the traditional

[1] As Ian Clark noted, underlying the military theory of distinction are political philosophies and differing conceptual frameworks. *Waging War: A Philosophical Introduction* (Oxford: Clarendon Press, 1988), 84.

literature concerning the laws of war. There is certainly no shortage of material to draw upon; this abundance, as it happens, is a large part of the problem. Jurists composing legal theories (with their accompanying histories) have offered meticulous interpretations of the tensions and incoherences within the legal texts themselves; historians have reconstructed the political, institutional, and normative contexts within which the laws of war were formulated; and diplomats have left copious archival records of the *Sturm und Drang* which lay beneath the terse formulations of legal subcommittees. Although illuminating and often fascinating, these accounts have one common feature: they have tended to be more interested in the broad successes of the enterprise of the laws of war than in their flaws. However, as stated above, this work is more concerned with explaining the reasons for a specific failure, rather than celebrating the successes of the laws of war in general.

At the same time, archival, legal, and historical sources have provided invaluable building blocks for constructing the normative paradigms which will provide the framework for the remainder of this book. Ample evidence of the existence of different normative views of war may be found in the voluminous archival material left by diplomats and statesmen, much of which has been consulted. The private papers of a Belgian baron, the diplomatic reports sent home from the conference frontline, and indeed, anguished confidential letters to ministers, have revealed profound dissensions amongst and between states on the distinction between lawful and unlawful combatant. But these writings are in the main advisory rather than didactic. They are not overly concerned with first principles, but rather with the achievement of specific objectives derived from them. In short, these writings are informed by normative views and ideological principles, but these are rarely articulated explicitly.

The legal literature presents a similar duality. International lawyers have produced comprehensive accounts and commentaries of the laws of war, both in terms of its practices and underlying purposes. This literature often displays the excellent qualities which typify the legal tradition: precision, elegance, intellectual consistency and rigour, and comprehensiveness. But many of these very qualities prevent an understanding of the ideological underpinnings of the laws of war. In the first place, this literature is written by those who believe deeply in the general project of *jus in bello*; and hence dwelling on its flaws and failures is seen as overly morbid, if not downright destructive. Furthermore, approaches to legal codification tend to be framed within the parameters of states' interests, with the value-laden assumption that these inter-

ests were reconcilable. This emphasis on states and the notion of consensus dismisses the importance of ideologies which not only cut across
narrowly defined national interests, but were ultimately incompatible.
The domination of the literature by jurists also produces a hegemonic
discourse with particular characteristics: overly technical and formalistic, its rational language becomes exclusive to its own terms of
reference, thus rendering an understanding of its foundations near
impossible.[2] This is all the more problematic precisely because while
their language claimed to be ideologically neutral, their authors most
emphatically were not. Indeed, it will emerge that the legal tradition
played a central role not only in shaping the general framework of the
laws of war, but also in excluding all views, principles, and actors who
threatened its vision.[3]

The history of the laws of war has been definitively written.[4] Indeed,
for the purposes of this book, the historical approach has served four
essential functions: illumination, contextualization, demystification, and
conceptualization. The variety of its sources have highlighted the mul-
tiplicity of factors which went into the making of the modern laws of
war. Situating the laws of war within historical contexts has brought out
the influence of normative forces upon their construction.[5] Most importantly, however, historical analysis has broken into the sacred cloisters
of the legal order; it has shown that its careful rituals and holy texts

[2] For a lawyer's critique, see J. Boyle, 'Ideals and Things: International Legal Scholarship and the Prison-house of Language', *Harvard International Law Journal*, 26/2 (1985),
327–59. For an interesting overview of this issue in the examination of different legal cultures in domestic law, see David Nelkin 'Disclosing/Invoking Legal Culture: An Introduction', in *Social and Legal Studies*, 4 (1995), 435–52.

[3] A notable exception was the distinguished French republican lawyer Charles Lucas,
a member of the Institute of International Law, and its sole dissenting voice. His works
include *La Conférence internationale de Bruxelles sur les lois et coutumes de guerre* (Paris:
A. Durand, 1874); *Les Actes de la Conférence de Bruxelles considérés au double point de
vue de la civilisation de la guerre et de la codification graduelle du droit des gens* (Orléans:
E. Colas, 1875); *Civilisation de la guerre, observations sur les lois de la guerre et l'arbitrage international* (Paris: Cotillon, 1881); *Rapport verbal de M. Charles Lucas sur 'Le
Droit de la guerre' de M. Der Beer Poortugael* (Orléans: Colas, n.d.); *Rapport verbal de
M. Charles Lucas sur 'Le Précis des lois de la guerre sur terre' par M. le capitaine Guelle*
(Orléans: E. Colas, n.d.); *Compte-rendu sur le 'Traité de droit international public,
européen et américain, suivant les progrès de la science et de la pratique contemporaines'
par M. Pradier-Fodéré* (Orléans: P. Girardot, 1880).

[4] The two central works are by G. Best, *Humanity in Warfare* (London: Methuen,
1983), and the more recent *War and Law since 1945* (Oxford: Clarendon Press, 1994).

[5] The most comprehensive legal history of the late nineteenth century is without question Doris Graber's *The Development of the Law of Belligerent Occupation*. For a useful
account of the Brussels Conference using archival sources see J. de Breucker, 'La Déclaration de Bruxelles de 1874 concernant les lois et coutumes de la guerre', *Chroniques
de politique étrangère*, 27/1 (1974).

often concealed as much as they revealed. Finally, in identifying the main intellectual influences on the modern laws of war, the empirical approach has helped to set out the paradigms which will form the basis of this argument. Yet because of the sheer scale of the project of the laws of war, its general history is too broad to offer a specific methodological focus for the single debate with which this work will be concerned.

INTERNATIONAL RELATIONS APPROACHES

Given the shortcomings of the legal and historical approaches, theoretical constructs in international thought might appear to provide a better starting point. The most influential general paradigm in international relations theory is the English School's distinction between 'realist', 'rationalist', and 'revolutionist' conceptions.[6] Of the three, realism initially appears as the most promising concept for explaining war, as power and violence are among the values it regards as inherent in international life. Indeed, realism currently remains the most fashionable category for thinking about war in international theory.[7] However, realist concepts are inadequate for several reasons which may be briefly summarized. First, the account that realists (or those seeking to explain realist thought) give of war provides a metatheory of conflict in which all states are treated as identical units from an analytical point of view. Such accounts are notorious for underplaying—or ignoring altogether—the influence of sociological features such as those outlined in previous chapters, as well as the role (or mere existence) of different classes of individuals whose actions initiate, sustain, or help to conclude a war. As is already clear by now, the problem of distinction between lawful and unlawful combatants was not one created and maintained by states alone, although it was incumbent on states' representatives to seek a solution to the problem at international conferences.

Another difficulty with using realism to explain the problem of distinction is its definition of the nature of war itself. Beyond the account it gives of war as a phenomenon reduced to interstate conflict, the realist understanding of war (domestic or international) is based upon a par-

---

[6] For the classic three-way division in international relations theory, see M. Wight, *International Theory: The Three Traditions* (London: Leicester University Press, 1991).

[7] Most recent is Michael W. Doyle's *Ways of War and Peace* (London: W.W. Norton & Co., 1997), where the emphasis is on realist thought. The chapters on liberalism etc. focus on economy and values other than war. See 41–195.

ticularly crude view of both agency and human nature itself. In recent years there have been, of course, international theorists who have advanced more sophisticated versions of realism. However, these more complex formulations have not been accompanied by equally sophisticated typologies of realist war, but remain marred by reductivist political and psychological tendencies.[8] Accordingly, these realists cannot help to think through the basic question of why its different actors could hold such differing notions of the genesis, nature, and very purpose of war.

Finally, and most importantly, realist writers are wedded to an unhelpfully rigid distinction between domestic and international politics. Realist thought sees peace as necessary to the good life. Indeed Hobbes, the patron saint of realism, is claimed to be motivated entirely by an urgent quest for a peaceful political order. In this sense, the attainment of peace *is* the achievement of the good life. Yet for realism, these two objectives, peace and the good life, are attainable only at the domestic level. Accordingly its concern with war is incidental, and not intrinsic.[9] On the international plane, furthermore, notions of the good life appear irrelevant—hence Martin Wight's classic description of international relations theory as the 'theory of survival'.[10] However, it will emerge in subsequent chapters that the three ideologies of wars' formulations of the good life drew heavily from domestic political concepts, and that these notions of the good life also carried into their understanding of international order. The conceptual poverty of the realist view of international order will thus appear in all its starkness.

The Grotian approach will be the object of close scrutiny in a later chapter, and will therefore not be discussed further here. Within the three-cornered system of the 'English School', the only conception which stipulates both the desirability and possibility of the good life at domestic and international levels is the 'revolutionist' branch (also

---

[8] In *Ways of War* Doyle attempts to create a more sophisticated realism whilst maintaining that the term itself still has some useful meaning in his chapters on Thucydides, Machiavelli, Hobbes, and Rousseau entitled 'Complex Realism', 'Fundamental Realism', 'Structural Realism', and 'Constitutional Realism'. See also J. Nye and R. Keohane's definition of 'Complex Realism' in *Power and Interdependence* (Boston: Little Brown, 1989); Peter Gellman's 'Hans J. Morgenthau and the Legacy of Political Realism', *Review of International Studies*, 14/4 (1988); and Steven Forde, 'Varieties of Realism: Thucydides and Machiavelli', *Journal of Politics*, 54/2 (1992).

[9] On this interpretation see T. Nardin, *Law, Morality, and the Relations of States* (New Jersey: Princeton University Press, 1983).

[10] M. Wight, 'Why is there no international theory?', in H. Butterfield and M. Wight (eds.), *Diplomatic Investigations: Essays on the Theories of International Politics* (London: Allen & Unwin, 1966), 33.

known as 'Kantian'). Its most positive feature is its inherent propensity to look inside the state for the factors conducive to international peace or war—in contrast with the realists' focus on the state as a closed and invariable 'unit' of decision-making power. However, there are several reasons why this third school is also not helpful for explaining the problem of maintaining a distinction between combatant and non-combatant.

First, and more specifically, 'Kantian' approaches are typically driven by the search for peace, making them heuristically unsuitable for analysing political philosophies exclusively concerned with the practice of war. More generally, it is clear that Kantian approaches are essentially prescriptive, and are thus better suited to those seeking to engage in normative theorizing rather than social and political explanation. For the purposes of this inquiry, however, a theory is needed which will actually illuminate and make sense of the real practices of war in nineteenth-century Europe.[11] Another problem with the label of 'Kantianism' is its excessive elasticity, and in particular its crude conflation of the differing endeavours of crusading revolutionaries, Marxists, Kantians, and liberals under the same conceptual umbrella. It is true that the one factor which unites the different components of this third school is the desire for structural change. Yet one of the classes of individuals examined earlier, civilians under occupation, cannot be categorized in this manner. Indeed, the evidence shows that they were driven by a wide range of goals and by often conflicting ideologies and sentiments, including nationalism, religion, patriotism, on occasion freedom, but more simply (and more often) fear. Even more apparent was that many of those who underwent occupation did not desire political or institutional change at all. Rather, their primary concern was a return to the *status quo ante bellum*—which could mean the restoration of a reactionary monarchy (as in Spain in the early nineteenth century). Likewise, another class of actors, occupying armies, could not be seen uniformly as either Kantian, liberal, or revolutionary—although they did on occasion aspire to radical structural change. This conceptual confusion partly explains why international relations theorists attempting to make sense of concepts such as patriotism have sometimes created rather incongruous juxtapositions, uniting such 'patriotic founders' as Churchill, Roosevelt, de

---

[11] For a history of 'Kantianism' in international relations, see F. H. Hinsley, *Power and the Pursuit of Peace* (Cambridge: Cambridge University Press, 1963). For more recent interpretations, see A. Hurrell, 'Kant and the Kantian Paradigm in International Relations', *Review of International Studies*, 16/3 (1990); H. Williams and K. Booth, 'Kant: Theorist beyond Limit', in I. Clark and I. Neumann (eds.), *Classical Theories of International Relations* (London: Macmillan, 1996), 74–95.

Gaulle, Ho Chi Minh, and Mandela in the same strand of the 'funda-mentalist realist' school, or—even more surprisingly—conjoining Rousseau and Henry Kissinger as the standard-bearers of another.[12] Such approaches, clouded as they are by methodological and intellectual confusion, thus have little to offer to an enterprise seeking to explain the world views of the different actors involved in occupation and resistance in post-Enlightenment Europe.

More generally, these traditional international relations typologies are heuristically insufficient to describe, let alone explain, the complexities of the social, legal, and diplomatic histories of wars of empire, occupation, and resistance in continental Europe in the nineteenth century. This is also because these typologies are insensitive to the internal structure of ideologies, in particular to their internal ordering of values. For example, all Kantians may believe in the necessity and desirability of peace, but some would regard democracy as its most important precondition, while others would see it emerging primarily from a moral imperative, and others still as a consequence of substantive commercial interactions among states. All these views may be equally 'Kantian', but they are formulated with a different ordering of core values. In its examination of different traditions of war, this book will attempt to define the internal components of their respective ideologies—allowing for a more subtle and discriminating analysis of related patterns of thought. A further advantage of this approach is that it will enable a better understanding of how and why these internal values could change and develop over time—another important dimension of ideological change about which classical theorists of international relations are notoriously silent.

More specific conceptualizations are offered in the historical and theoretical literature on war and peace. Among historians, few have equalled the range and depth of Michael Howard's scholarship, which has covered almost every conceivable topic, from military doctrines and tactics of strategic deception to the cultural and societal dimensions of war.[13] Although his works are always insightful, however, their perspective is too elevated to give a consistent account of the specific patterns of thought with which this work is concerned.

---

[12] Doyle, *Ways of War*, 102, 151. The latter school is called 'constitutional realism'.

[13] A few selections from his *œuvre* are: *Soldiers and Governments: Nine Studies in Civilian–Military Relations* (London: Eyre & Spottiswood, 1957); *Grand Strategy: The History of World War II* (London: HMSO, 1972); *The Franco-Prussian War: The German Invasion of France 1870–1871* (London: Methuen, 1981); *Clausewitz* (Oxford: Oxford University Press, 1983); *War and the Liberal Conscience* (Oxford: Oxford University Press, 1989); *The Lessons of History* (Oxford: Clarendon Press, 1991).

Moral philosophers and theorists of war have provided stimulus and disappointment in equal measures. A classic of the first genre is Michael Walzer's *Just and Unjust Wars: A Moral Argument with Historical Illustrations*, which offers a wealth of examples of how warring states and societies have treated each other from ancient times up to the modern age. Sadly, however, Walzer fails to deliver the promised moral argument when it comes to defining how belligerents ought to treat each other. The problem lies in his unwillingness to spell out the basic philosophical premises of his moral argument. As he baldly states in his introduction: 'I am not going to expound morally from the ground up. Were I to begin with the foundations, I would probably never get beyond them; in any case, I am by no means sure what the foundations are.'[14] The absence of foundational principles thus vitiates his work's relevance to the conceptualization of ideological traditions of war, which rely (above all) upon discrete ethical foundations.[15] But even if Walzer had succeeded in constructing his moral foundations, his contribution to any discussion of the philosophical underpinnings of war would have been extremely limited. Walzer's work is embedded in a particular liberal tradition within which much of normative political theory today is constructed, whereas (as will become manifest in subsequent chapters) liberalism of any branch was by no means the only—or for that matter even the principal—broad ideology which informed nineteenth-century practices of occupation and resistance.[16] If, however, broader and more comparative traditions of moral thought are reflected in this type of literature, they tend to articulate the intellectual project of establishing the ethics of war by a priori reasoning rather than through discussion of concrete historical examples.[17] Yet earlier chapters have shown that, in order to explain the problem of distinction, we need to know how those choices *were* actually made, and what theories and values went into constructing the different traditions of war which informed these choices. In this context mention should be made of Martin Ceadel's

---

[14] M. Walzer, *Just and Unjust Wars* (New York: Basic Books, 1992), xxxiv.

[15] Although Walzer invites the reader, on p. 259, to engage in 'a morally important fantasy' with him, sadly this is insufficient for the nature of this inquiry. Another rigorous critique of this method (and of Walzer's reliance on utilitarianism) can be found in Terry Nardin's *Law, Morality, and the Relations of States*, 297–304. See also the 1997 issue of *Ethics and International Affairs*.

[16] Hedley Bull also remarks with some common sense the effect of Walzer's self-denying ordinance about foundations: 'his message is actually addressed only to the limited circle of those who share his outlook'. 'Recapturing the Just War for Political Theory', *World Politics*, 31/4 (1979), 599.

[17] Terry Nardin, Introduction, *The Ethics of War and Peace: Religious and Secular Perspectives* (Princeton: Princeton University Press, 1996), 3.

Thinking about Peace and War, the most prominent modern work in the taxonomical analysis of war, which also stakes out its ambitions and method early on. Its proclaimed purpose, inscribed in the opening sentence of the book, is to offer a 'guide' to the way in which 'war prevention, the twentieth century's most urgent issue . . . is discussed'.[18] This goal is in direct conflict with the principal object of the book, which is to define war not as an antithesis of peace, but as possessing coherent traditions of practice and patterns of thought in its own right.

While the disciplines of international law, history, international relations, and moral philosophy have been useful in isolating the terrain needing to be explored, it is clear that they cannot offer a coherent conceptual basis for this work. The irresolvable foundational problem in the modern laws of war, it will be remembered, was the clear separation between lawful and unlawful combatants. The challenge of maintaining this distinction arose in a particular place (continental Europe), historical and political context (the nineteenth and twentieth centuries), and under specific circumstances (wars of foreign rule, invasion, and occupation). It was from this crucible that the three distinct articulations of war presented in this book emerged. Hence the recurrence of such themes as conquest, resistance, obedience, patriotism, sovereignty, and independence in their ideological discourse.

TRADITIONS OF WAR

Before presenting these paradigms in full, some sense of how the notion of 'tradition' will be deployed here must be given. The study of comparative patterns of thought has always been central to the endeavours of the 'English school' in international relations, and, in recent years, traditions have been the object of renewed attention across a wide range of disciplines.[19] In the opening chapter of the latest collection of studies on classical thinkers, for example, Ian Clark defined the prevailing understanding of traditions of international thought, and also evaluated their heuristic potential. What emerges from his analysis is that traditions are typically constructed in relation to the problematic of

---

[18] M. Ceadel, *Thinking about Peace and War* (Oxford: Oxford University Press, 1989), 1.

[19] See the comprehensive survey by T. Dunne, 'Mythology or Methodology? Traditions in International Relations', *Review of International Studies*, 19 (1993), 305–18. The most recent collection is Clark and Neumann's *Classical Theories of International Relations*. See also T. Nardin and D. Mapel (eds.), *Traditions of International Ethics* (Cambridge: Cambridge University Press, 1992).

'international society'.[20] In this sense, their inquiries are driven by either the potential or the actuality of an international good life. Absent from these endeavours, however, are historical patterns of thought about war. From the normative perspective of 'international society', this absence needs little justification. Indeed it helps explain why so little attention has been paid to traditions of war: its occurrence appears to express the breakdown of the order and cohesion deemed essential to 'international society', and the attempt to construct 'traditions' of war would seem a regressive step from this creative intellectual enterprise. Likewise normative political theorists have tended to engage in discussions of war whilst remaining firmly within a particular ideological tradition, as noted earlier in the case of Walzer. Where political theorists have traced the historical itineraries of variants of 'liberalism' or 'republicanism' (which could be seen to foreshadow two of the traditions of war in this work), they have done so by concentrating exclusively on the theory of the good life within the state.[21] This approach excludes thinking about war in two important ways. Liberalism and republicanism are thought to be political philosophies concerned exclusively with peace; from this perspective, ideologies concerned with war appear as either atavistic or revolutionary—but in either case as irrelevant. Furthermore, these theoretical constructs nearly always assume a republican or liberal state already in existence, and have set about to examine the values of particular groups within that political community. What might prove more insightful, however, is an account of the values of republican communities who were forging their state by using political violence, or even of liberals who were attempting (through war) to resist this emerging republican polity on the basis of an adhesion to the liberal notion of order in nineteenth-century empires.

In this sense this project purports to be engaged in a similar enterprise to theorists constructing traditions of the good life in domestic politics and international society. Its distinctiveness rests in the fact that the common integrative component of the three traditions presented here is the phenomenon of war, which will be seen to unite individuals and groups within traditions as well as across them, much in the same way as the notions of law, sociability, ethics, and integrative institutions bind together individuals and groups in domestic and international

[20] See also John Rawls's lectures in S. Shute and S. Hurley (eds.), *On Human Rights: The Oxford Amnesty Lectures 1993* (New York: Basic Books, 1995).
[21] An exception is Nicholas Onuf's *The Republican Legacy in International Thought* (Cambridge: Cambridge University Press, 1998). Although it addresses many issues relating to republicanism and the international order, it excludes notions of republican war.

society. It will also become manifest that notions of the good life were integral to the ideologies of conflict—in other words war and political violence were not isolated or marginal concepts, but were central to the operation of their respective political traditions. Three traditions will therefore be at the centre of this argument: the martial, which posited war as a natural conduit for the fulfilment of man's destiny; the Grotian, which believed that prudential limits could be imposed upon its conduct, and the republican, which viewed war as a political conflict between professional armies and citizens. These traditions were comprehensive, in that their particular notions of war were inextricably intertwined in ideological notions of the good life. These conceptions of war were rooted in post-Enlightenment European political culture, and the traditions to which they gave rise significantly influenced European political thought and practice from the late eighteenth to the early twentieth centuries. This influence was visible not only horizontally—from the shores of the Atlantic to the steppes of Russia—but also vertically, encompassing the elevated thoughts of intellectuals all the way down to the political practices of humble villagers.

The term 'martialism' defines an ideology and a political tradition which glorified war and military conquest. Martialism can be crudely summarized as the view that war is both the supreme instrument and the ultimate realization of all human endeavour. Its core values of liberty and patriotism and also its central myths on the nature of man all perceived the role of war as central. It was a doctrine which manifested itself most emphatically in the practices of conquest and foreign rule. Indeed, it could be said that martialism constituted the political philosophy of occupying armies. In this sense, its precepts were entirely favourable to the practices of occupation, and strongly hostile to all manifestations of resistance to its moral and political authority. The most crucial aspect of this ideology was that war was a natural force, which could not be codified or restrained.

The Grotian tradition's objective in the mid to late nineteenth century was the opposite of the martial, namely to codify war; but by so doing it achieved a similar end, which was to favour conquering armies. The Grotian tradition of war developed in a particular manner from the 1860s to 1949 in the context of the framing of the laws of war. It is the most dominant tradition, in that its core principles lay at the very heart of the project of the laws of war. This tradition drew heavily on the writings of Hugo Grotius (1583–1645). Although devoting some effort to justifying private wars, the thrust of his writings was to concentrate the legitimate recourse to war in public hands. This core objective was also successfully pursued by Grotius's self-styled disciples. At the heart of the nineteenth- and early twentieth-century Grotian system was an essential dichotomy between the rights of states and armies on the one hand, and the position of ordinary members of society on the other. The important values of their tradition was law, order, power, and the sovereignty of the state. As the Grotian tradition was 'index-linked' to legitimate power, its central ambition was to limit the rights of belligerency to a particular class of participant (the soldier), and to exclude all others from the right to become actively involved in political violence in times of war.

The final tradition which was to emerge is the republican. Wars of empire and of foreign occupation occurred in Europe throughout the nineteenth and twentieth centuries, and it was the republican response to this predicament which directed this tradition's trajectory. In particular, this ideological paradigm evolved through a specific political understanding of the nature of war and conquest. Republican thought and practice emerged as a direct result of the quest for independence and political autonomy, and developed subsequently into a distinct doctrine of patriotism. Its ideological content borrowed heavily from the writings of Jean Jacques Rousseau, but also from the ideas and more importantly, the practices of such figures as Pasquale Paoli and Tadeusz Kosciuszko in the late eighteenth century. The main features of republican war were liberty and equality, individual and national self-reliance, patriotism and public-spiritedness (and the importance of education to arouse these virtues), and a notion of just war *combined with* justice in war.

THE EXPLANATORY VALUE OF TRADITIONS

Using the concept of a tradition of war to explain the failure to agree on the distinction between combatant and non-combatant offers significant advantages over the competing paradigms and intellectual approaches discussed above. In the first place, the construction of traditions of war will introduce a sustained ideational dimension to the problem of distinction—the three philosophies of war reveal both the scale and the extent of normative disagreements over the issue of combatant status in the laws of war and indeed the larger issue of war itself. More crucially, these constructs illustrate that disagreements were based on philosophical principles rather than narrowly conceived and particularistic state interests. Also, these ideational disputes were not restricted merely to diplomats and lawyers, but between guerrillas and soldiers, subjects and their rulers, and, at a more abstract level, between rival conceptions of war among classical political thinkers. Indeed, traditions of war will allow for a fruitful revisitation of classical texts in a number of ways. For example, they enable a connection to be established between certain classical texts and diplomatic practice. Thus both Francis Lieber and Fedor Martens, who were founders of the modern laws of war, wrote constantly about how Grotius' example as well as his writings inspired and motivated them during their careers. Secondly, traditions of war enable the establishment of a link between classical texts and military practice—as will be illustrated, republicans of the 1830s onwards often referred to concepts of just war as espoused by J. J. Rousseau. But it is not only the case that these texts informed concrete practices. It will be a central argument of the second half of this book that these practices on the ground helped to shape the theories themselves. To cite a specific case, Rousseau's political writings were partially informed by the example of Corsican resistance to Genoese rule. More broadly, understanding concrete practices that drew upon classical texts will shed a different—and perhaps more illuminating—light on these texts themselves. Indeed it will become apparent that a number of misconceptions and delusions can be dispelled in this manner. Contrary to the common view, for example, Rousseau was not the founder of the modern distinction between lawful and unlawful combatant, but held a completely different position on the issue. Focusing on the relationship between textual discourses and political practices also shows that the same body of writings can be interpreted in strikingly different ways by different generations within the same ideological tradition, as will be demonstrated in the contrast between late nineteenth-century conservative Grotian lawyers and their more progressive twentieth-century successors. This point has even broader implications. Delineating distinct traditions of war can bring out the plurality of understandings of a single classical text, such as Clausewitz's *On War*, which has been interpreted in radically different ways according to the interpreter's particular ideological affiliations.

Traditions of war also have the advantage of carrying the explanation of the inability to resolve the distinction beyond the conference floor and into the social and political realm. The failure to resolve the distinction between combatant and non-combatant was thus not merely a problem of state representatives, lawyers, and publicists. It is a reflection of the varying problems of conducting war itself—in theory but also in practice, and particularly in its impact upon local state institutions, occupying armies, and civilian populations on the ground. Indeed, it demonstrates that the successive international conferences of 1874, 1899, and 1949 did not represent the locus of the problem, but one could almost say, were epiphenomenal to it.

In methodological terms, traditions of war will be constructed by drawing from intellectual history, political science, sociological analysis, and moral philosophy. This interdisciplinary approach is not an indiscriminate display of eclecticism for its own sake, but a necessary combination for a more authentic and systematic analysis. In the literature with which this work is concerned, these modern disciplinary distinctions had not yet appeared, and indeed it has been demonstrated that in isolation they cannot provide a valid account of the failure of the modern laws of war. An example of the utility of drawing from different disciplines is the issue of civic and political resistance to occupation in nineteenth-century Europe. Grotian lawyers consistently argued that no such customary practice had occurred, but, outside the legal textbooks, a wealth of memoir literature and archival documents attest to the contrary. So, the social history of occupation not only reveals the existence of a custom of resistance among civilian populations, but also helps to uncover the prejudices and biases which underlay the Grotian posture of discursive neutrality and political objectivity.

Finally, traditions of war allow for the treatment of patterns of thought and practice both within and across time. The synchronic approach helps us to analyse how a particular type of discourse operated within and between those adhering to a distinct ideology, and how both the goals and principles of a particular tradition were forged by debate amongst its members, as well as among conflicting traditions. Different generations of republicans argued among themselves, but also against martialist and Grotian advocates over the long period time with which this book is concerned. The conferences themselves spanned a seventy-year period, while the examples on the ground ranged from the Napoleonic wars until the Second World War—nearly 150 years. But behind this ebb and flow there was much steadiness. Indeed when viewed from within the framework of the book's three traditions, it will emerge that patterns of thought on war remained surprisingly consistent over time, however much the actors themselves may have changed.

4

High Priests of the Temple of Janus:
The Martial Tradition of War

INTRODUCTION

At the conferences on the laws of war, the most powerful (and certainly the noisiest) voice on the question of a distinction between lawful and unlawful combatant was the martial. This voice easily drowned out all others at Brussels in 1874. It was equally pitched at The Hague in 1899, and was still going strong, although definitely more beleaguered, at Geneva half a century later. The main object of this chapter is to present martialism, the political tradition behind that voice. This intellectual paradigm contained a political and philosophical set of assumptions, the importance of which has been consistently undervalued in the literature on war. The second claim here is that this ideology has been unnecessarily conflated into the broader analytical category of 'realism', resulting in a failure to draw out both the specific traits of realism and the distinct properties of martialist thinking. Once the key differences between these two concepts have been identified and illustrated, the influence of martialist thinking on a particular set of conceptions and practices of war which emerged in Britain during the second half of the nineteenth century can be demonstrated.

The term 'martialism' will be used throughout this chapter to define an ideology which glorified war and military conquest. The more commonly used 'militarism', which generally encompasses this ideology, suffers from a number of drawbacks both in its definition and its taxonomy, and, accordingly, its use has been excluded. The first reason that using militarism is inappropriate is because the term itself is ideologically tainted: it arose as part of a general nineteenth-century liberal critique of war and has retained highly pejorative connotations ever since.[1] Secondly, its traditional history has overemphasized its Prussian roots. Blanning has succinctly described the dangers of this approach, which

---

[1] For a chronological development of the use of the term 'militarism' see V. Berghahn, *Militarism: The History of an International Debate* (London: Berg Publishers, 1981).

tends to demonize Prussian history as a 'ghastly amalgam of barrack-room, lunatic asylum and sweatshop'.[2] This leads to a further difficulty with the conventional classification, in that it is in the main too narrow: its origins are generally ascribed to authoritarian and conservative roots on the Continent in a way which excludes martialist doctrines such as imperialism, as well as its locus in countries such as Britain.[3] In some other respects, however, the term is also too broad to be useful; according to one military historian, almost anybody who supports war at some point can be called a militarist.[4] Finally, the term focuses primarily on institutions such as the army, or on institutional structures and individuals from political elites; whereas the martialist tradition (in particular in Britain) relied heavily on more popular expression for its ideological underpinnings.[5]

Martialism can be simply defined as the view that war is both the supreme instrument and the ultimate realization of all human endeavour. It was a doctrine which manifested itself most emphatically in the practices of conquest and foreign rule. Indeed, it could be said that martialism constituted the political philosophy of occupying armies. In this sense, its precepts were entirely favourable to the practices of occupation, and strongly hostile to all manifestations of resistance to its moral and political authority. The body of writing and, especially, practice which advanced this position has been systematically neglected as an

---

[2] T. Blanning, 'The Death and Transformation of Prussia', *History Journal*, 29/2 (1986), 447. A common interpretation which locates the origins of militarism in Germany can be seen in A. Vagts, *A History of Militarism* (London: Hollis & Carter, 1959), 409. See also K. Werner, 'L'Attitude devant la guerre dans l'Allemagne de 1900', in *1914: les psychoses de guerre?* (Rouen: Publications de l'Université de Rouen, 1985), 18; M. Smith, *Militarism and Statecraft* (New York: Knickerbocker Press, 1918), 221–2; N. Angell, *Prussianism and its Destruction* (London: Heinemann, 1914), 2, 7.

[3] Indeed, it has been argued that this ideology cannot be said to exist in Britain during the nineteenth century, simply because philosophers were not writing about it. See J. Burrow's *Evolution and Society: A Study in Victorian Social Theory* (Cambridge: Cambridge University Press, 1968), 261–2. See also M. Ceadel, *Thinking about Peace and War*, 21.

[4] As Michael Howard noted: ' "Militarism", like "Fascism" has become a term of such general illiterate abuse that the scholar must use it with care. ' *War in European History* (Oxford: Oxford University Press, 1976), 110.

[5] See H. Morgenthau, *Politics among Nations* (New York: A. Knopf, 1973), 162. A position more useful for tracing the martial tradition outlined in this chapter is held by J. MacKenzie, who argues that the martial spirit of the mid to late nineteenth century in Britain was 'not to be found in official documents or in the products of the "official mind" of imperialism. It is to be found in the surrounding culture.' *Popular Imperialism and the Military: 1850–1950* (Manchester: Manchester University Press, 1992), 109. See, for example, his *Propaganda and Empire: Imperialism and Popular Culture in Britain* (Manchester: Manchester University Press, 1984).

approach to thinking about theories of war and peace. In this chapter, the essential components of martialism will be outlined through a number of its core values and themes. Martialists had a distinct conception of human nature, the state, liberty, and nationalism, and all these characteristics found their ultimate fulfilment in the unrestrained glorification of war. This perspective differed radically from the core values of realist writers; in this sense, it is suggested that realism should be regarded in aspects as the antithesis of martialism, and not (as many writers of international theory seem to hold) as its corollary. However, although the two patterns of thought will be compared in the following sections, it is important to note that martialism was a much looser cluster of ideas and values than realism. Realism offers a relatively straightforward paradigm comprised of certain canonical texts and principles. Martialism itself was not a rigorous intellectual doctrine, being in essence as it was an approach to action, movement, and anti-rationalism. Further, martialism as a tradition, and the ideology *within* that tradition as it developed over the period of the structuring of the laws of war 1874–1949 had distinct strands both in Europe and outside it (i.e. Japan). This is partly because martialism itself emphasized the expanding nation as a core value; national particularistics became distinctive ideological values for each strand, separating German patterns of thought from French or British ones. Martialist thought and practice can be recognized as belonging to what Phillippe Burrin called 'the same magnetic field' by its similiar approach to war, conquest, and the very purpose of standing armies in the life of the state. It was organized within a much looser framework of ideas which—unlike most other nineteenth-century doctrines—did not rely on a particular literary canon, but (as will be illustrated below in the case of Machiavelli) had a similar 'take' on certain authors and sometimes even that author's purpose. Martialism emphasized similar values, such as heroism, glory, patriotism, and violence, but in a thoroughly different way from, for example, the broader republican tradition's discursive involvement with these principles.

THE LIMITATIONS OF REALISM IN EXPLAINING MARTIALISM

Attempts to identify the sources of the 'realist' school of philosophers immediately run into three problems. The first is what might be called a problem of conceptualization: the creation of an artificial divide between 'realism' and 'idealism' combined with an attempt to force writers into one or the other category.[6] 'Realists' are typically presented as sober, empirical, and prudent thinkers who concerned themselves primarily with power and security. 'Idealists', in contrast, are depicted as exuberant, impractical, daring visionaries whose theories rarely engaged with reality.[7] In so far as they are seen to conform to its core precepts, thinkers such as Machiavelli and Clausewitz are stereotyped as 'realists', with the clear implication that their thinking was devoid of 'idealist' or visionary elements.[8] Conversely, a writer such as Rousseau is categorized by some as a 'realist', and by others as an 'idealist'.[9] Such dichotomies are signally misleading. Realism and idealism were not necessarily mutually exclusive, but could often embody different facets of the same philosopher's thought. With an author like Machiavelli, this dualism has produced strikingly divergent interpretations of his thought. Seen through realist lenses, the Florentine writer appears as a cynical, methodical, and calculating servant of the interests of his state.[10] For some martialist writers, however, the same Machiavelli was an expansive, violent, and passionate advocate of the virtues of war. The point here is not to settle which of these conflicting images is 'true', but to underline that both may well capture important insights into the complexity of Machiavelli's political thought. And it is precisely such forms of intellectual complexity which are a priori excluded from consideration if analytical categories are confined to the sterile dichotomy between 'realism' and 'idealism'. Indeed, what will be shown here is how particular writers participated in the creation of a tradition of war through the very manner in which they consistently interpreted certain classical thinkers. These martial writers were emphatically *not* tracing the idea of *raison d'état*, liberty, or engaged in a study of republican institutions in Renaissance Florence; but rather saw themselves as participating in a process of recovering and affirming what they believed were

---

[6] This is persuasively argued by Raymond Aron, 'Idéalisme et réalisme', in *Paix et guerre entre les nations* (Paris: Calmann-Lévy, 1962), 567–96; see also J. Herz, *Political Realism and Political Idealism* (Chicago: Chicago University Press, 1951).

[7] H. Bull, 'Introduction', in M. Wight, *System of States* (London: Leicester University Press, 1977), 8–9.

[8] See R. Aron, *Penser la guerre, Clausewitz: l'âge européen* (Paris: Gallimard, 1976).

[9] S. Hoffmann, 'Rousseau on War and Peace', *American Political Science Review*, 57 (1963).

[10] For this traditional realist view see H. Butterfield, *The Statecraft of Machiavelli* (London: G. Bell, 1944); R. Aron, *Machiavelle et les tyrannies modernes* (Paris: Gallimard, 1993); M. Smith, *Realist Thought from Weber to Kissinger* (London: Louisiana State University Press, 1986), 10–12.

Machiavelli's 'real' views on war (and which happen to reflect their own).[11] This process of recovery was not an intellectual tracing of chronological thought like that engaged in by historians of ideas, however. It was to capture a particular significance and understanding of the role of war in political life.

Following on from this point, it can be seen that another difficulty with realism lies in its interpretative distortions and limitations. Here, we are in some senses dealing with 'truth' (in as much as it might be seen to exist in questions of intellectual history), through trying to understand the ideological purposes to which the writings of classical authors may be subjected. In much of the literature on most of the 'realist' philosophers on war and peace, the very essence of their writings is often concealed, with their bolder, harsher, and more atavistic principles reinterpreted and salvaged so that they may serve the particular ideological priorities of modern realist writers. This metamorphosis has created a body of 'realist' literature in which its philosophers' most fundamental principles have been stripped of many of their unpleasant and dangerous implications.[12] Accordingly, we are left with a homogenized corpus of writing that leads directly to twentieth-century notions of *raison d'état* and balance of power, often at the expense of a proper understanding of the harsher features of their philosophy of war and military conquest.

A final shortcoming of realism can be described as the problem of exclusion. Those who have not been salvaged or rehabilitated by the realist project (such as de Maistre), or whose writings are too multifarious to be subjected to such an endeavour (such as Carlyle), are diminished and marginalized. They are at best cast into the purgatorial category of 'isolated' thinkers, or at worst altogether excluded from consideration. By presenting these writers afresh through illustrating how they were used by practitioners of the nineteenth-century war, and incorporating them within the traditions of martialism and the code of conquest, we will be able to see certain aspects of their work far more precisely, and think more comfortably about that most uncomfortable of philosophies, 'War as Destiny'.

---

[11] The classic narrative which traces both Machiavelli's thought and Florentine republicanism can be found in J. Pocock, *The Machiavellian Moment: Florentine Political Thought and the Atlantic Republican Tradition* (Princeton: Princeton University Press, 1975); but see also—and especially—vol. i of Q. Skinner's *The Foundations of Modern Political Thought* (Cambridge: Cambridge University Press, 1978), and his *Machiavelli* (Oxford: Oxford University Press, 1981).
[12] For example, the assertion that 'Machiavelli ... was not Machiavellian', G. Mattingly, *Renaissance Diplomacy* (Baltimore: Baltimore University Press, 1964), 35.

As a heuristic device for grasping the philosophy and practice of war and military occupation, the concept of realism is therefore both necessary and insufficient. It is necessary in that its categories do indeed capture important features of classical and modern thought about the nature of war. But it is insufficient because some writers classed as 'realist', as well as theorists tracing realism, have tended to oversimplify, distort, and exclude many specific components of the theory of martialism. In order to make this clear, this chapter will contrast realist and martialist views on a range of core concepts and values: human nature, the state, liberty, nationalism, and war. This comparison will bring out the existence of two separate and distinct traditions: a realist paradigm, which sees war as a necessary evil, and a martialist code, which sees military conflict as a necessary virtue.

THE NATURE OF MAN IN THE REALIST TRADITION

Human nature in the realist tradition of international relations has three essential components which sets it apart from the martialist approach. The first feature is a starkly pessimistic conception of man's nature. As one theorist described realist thought: 'In its most basic outline, the realist picture of the world begins with a pessimistic view of human nature. Evil is inevitably a part of all of us which no social arrangement can eradicate: men and women are not perfectible.'[13] Hobbes, the patron saint of the realists, is seen to have constructed an image of man who was fundamentally flawed and driven by a 'restless power'. Hobbes's description in *Leviathan* emphasizes conflict: 'so that in the nature of man, we find three principall causes of quarrell. First, Competition; Secondly Diffidence; Thirdly, Glory.'[14] It was this 'diffidence', man's fear, which most realists latch onto as the cornerstone of Hobbes's vision of human nature. Niebuhr echoed this view of man's nature being driven by fear: 'Man is insecure and involved in natural contingency; he seeks to overcome his insecurity by a will to power which overreaches the limits . . . Man is ignorant and involved in the limitations of his finite mind; but he pretends he is not limited.'[15] This distinctive characteristic lay the foundation

---

[13] Smith, *Realist Thought from Weber to Kissinger*, 1.
[14] Ed. R. Tuck (Cambridge: Cambridge University Press, 1996), 89.
[15] *The Nature and Destiny of Man: A Christian Interpretation* (New York: Charles Scribner's Sons, 1941), i. 178.

of the entire realist political theory of the state: man behaved immorally, fought with his fellow-men, needed to be constrained and subordinated to a powerful ruler, all because of his overriding search for peace and security.

The second property of the realist perspective was the assertion that man was a profoundly dualistic creature, possessing a rational awareness of his condition but trapped by its awful passions. Thus man resided 'partly in the Passions, partly in his Reason'.[16] This dualism influenced his intellectual faculties, which could not entirely control his destructive instincts. Man was thus a passionate creature, fearful and quarrelsome in equal measures: 'From the same it proceedeth, that men give different names, to one and the same thing, from the difference of their own passions: As they that approve a private opinion, call it Opinion; but they that mislike it, Hæresie: and yet hæresie signifies no more than private opinion; but has onely a greater tincture of choler.'[17] So, in the realist view, there could be no transcendental moral principles, independent of social reality. It was not in man's nature to be moral, it was only society that made him sensitive to ethical considerations. Realist thinkers focus on this unethical nature by citing both Hobbes and Machiavelli to shore up their claim. *Leviathan* is a main source for this view: 'the notions of Right and Wrong, Justice and Injustice have [in nature] no place ... Justice and Injustice are none of the Faculties neither of the Body, nor Mind. If they were, they might be in a man that were alone in the world, as well as his Senses, and Passions. They are Qualities, that relate to men in Society, not in Solitude.'[18] A slightly different tack is taken by other realists. Michael Walzer, for example, strongly approves of the rejection of moral guidelines for leaders expressed in Machiavelli's *Prince*, but on condition. He requires, additionally, an 'inward life' from these leaders—some idea that they have, at least, *thought* about the immorality of their actions: 'we ... want to know; above all, we want a record of their anguish'.[19] So, for some modern realists like Walzer, morally unacceptable behaviour such as murder is acceptable in leaders if they do not overly delight in it. As we shall later see in the martial interpretation of Machiavelli, the virtue is in the violent act itself.

Finally, for realists, not only was man a sorry mess of conflicting passions, endowed with a rational mind, but this rationality afforded him the capacity to be grimly aware of the terrible condition of the world.

---

[16] Hobbes, *Leviathan*, 90.   [17] Ibid. 74.   [18] Ibid. 90.
[19] M. Walzer, 'Political Action: The Problem of Dirty Hands', in M. Cohen et al. (eds.), *War and Moral Responsibility* (Princeton: Princeton University Press, 1974), 78.

Most realists rely upon Hobbes's own evocative description of the conditions of man in the state of nature where there was 'no Knowledge of the face of the Earth, no account of Time, no Arts; no Letters; no Society; and which is worst of all, continuall feare and danger of violent death; And the life of man, solitary, poore, nasty, brutish, and short'.[20] This was by no means an ideal situation. Hence the Hobbesian advocacy of a Leviathan which offered security and order at the expense of liberty. Particular to Hobbes and the realist tradition was this essentially pessimistic identification of anarchy and violence as essential features of the human condition: 'l'homme est naturellement dangereux à l'homme'.[21] In sum, the realist tradition painted a picture of human nature dominated by confusion, anger, aggression, and fear—to which Christian realists such as Niebuhr and Morgenthau added sin and depravity—'the tragic presence of evil in all political action'.[22] This latter strand of realist thought highlighted not only Hobbes's characterization of man's fear, but also an egotistical and corrupt search for glory.[23] These were not merely characteristics of individuals, but pervaded the entire sphere of public and private relations in society.

THE NATURE OF MAN IN THE MARTIALIST TRADITION

The nature of man in the martialist tradition was depicted in distinctly different terms. In contrast to the realist, the martialist did not regard man's nature as irreversibly flawed. Man might wrestle with inherent contradictions, but these were now part of an organic harmony. Aggression was not a flaw in human character, as argued by realists, but its primordial and virtuous manifestation. The thrusting spirit of man was an essential and crucial aspect of his martial nature. Martialists tended to regard the different facets of man's character as interdependent; human qualities could not in their view be appreciated in isolation from one another. Furthermore, these qualities were judged by the extent to which they conformed to the paradigm set by nature: in this sense nature was the supreme good, and artifice the ultimate evil.

Heroism was a key characteristic of man's essence, and was as such

---

[20] *Leviathan*, 89.   [21] Aron, *Paix et guerre*, 343.

[22] Hans Morgenthau, *Scientific Man Versus Power Politics* (Chicago: Chicago University Press, 1946), 202. See especially vol. ii of Niebuhr's *The Nature and Destiny of Man.*

[23] For the purposes behind Hobbes's use of rhetorical strategies see Q. Skinner, *Reason and Rhetoric in the Philosophy of Hobbes* (Cambridge: Cambridge University Press, 1996), esp. 376–437.

defined as a core value in the martialist tradition. For Machiavelli, man
at his best was a powerful and terrible creature, unbowed by fate
or circumstance. He was gifted with *virtù,* which symbolized the
conquering spirit. Freidrich Meinecke interpreted Machiavelli's use of
the word *virtù* in the following terms: 'this notion is exceedingly rich
in concept . . . but it was fundamentally intended to portray something
dynamic, which Nature had implanted in Man—heroism and
the strength for great political and warlike achievements'.[24] The celebration of this violent nature was a fundamental feature of martialist
writing. Isaiah Berlin evocatively summarizes this belief in the right-
eousness of man's savagery in his essay on de Maistre: 'History and
zoology are the most reliable guides to nature: they show her to be a
field of unceasing slaughter. Men are aggressive by nature . . . When the
destructive instinct is invoked men feel exalted and fulfilled.'[25]
Unlike Niebuhr's notion of the misguided egotistical search for glory,
martialists stressed the search for glory (a notion remarkably similar
to Machiavelli's *gloria*) was both a natural impulse and a noble
one.[26]

Secondly, rationality was not the essence of man. Indeed, 'reason' was
an artificial and dangerous construct which led man away from his true
path. Martialist man was instead a supremely irrational creature: he
did not reason, but simply existed. This existence was nonetheless
profoundly spiritual, emphasizing man's godlike nature. Drawing from
broader patterns of thought in anti-Enlightenment philosophy, this tradition defined spirituality (in either its Christian or pagan form) as an
essential element of human nature. Spirituality was divine, mystical,
transfiguring, the most powerful and absolute element in human nature.
It was a force which Meinecke described as the soaring spirit which
rose above the state, finding its expression in the supremacy of the
individual.[27]

[24] F. Meinecke, *Machiavellism: The Doctrine of Raison d'État and its Place in Modern History* (London: Westview, Routledge, 1984), 31–2. See also Skinner, *Machiavelli*, 35–6; Russell Price has shown the wide scope of understandings of Machiavelli's notion of *virtù*, with the majority of authors not assigning any ethical value to it, yet one or two concluding it was 'compatible with villainy': 'The Senses of *Virtù* in Machiavelli', *European Studies Review*, 3 (1973), 322–4.
[25] I. Berlin, 'Joseph de Maistre and the Origins of Fascism', *The Crooked Timber of Humanity* (London: John Murray, 1990), 21.
[26] Russell Price, 'The Theme of *Gloria* in Machiavelli', *Renaissance Quarterly*, 30 (1977), 625.
[27] F. Meinecke, *The Age of Liberation: Germany 1795–1815* (Berkeley and Los Angeles: University of California Press, 1977), 46.

Writers such as Clausewitz emphasized Machiavelli's portrayal of the pagan nature of this vital spiritual energy in contrast to its Christian formulation.[28] Christianity, Machiavelli wrote in the *Discourses*, was too timid to reflect adequately man's elemental and warlike nature. Holding up the example of the ancients who valued honour as *il sommo bene*, he praised the aspects of their religion which encouraged fierceness, highlighting sacrificial acts in which 'there was much shedding of blood and much ferocity; and in them great numbers of animals were killed', and praising their 'pomp' and 'magnificence'. These ceremonies 'because terrible, caused men to become like them'.[29] This view expressed an ethical dimension which was integral to the martialist approach. Although paganist, they would see Machiavelli arguing from a consummately moral position. Unlike the amorality of the realist's interpretation of Hobbes's and Machiavelli's natural man, the martialist tradition emphasized a coherent morality which was a true reflection of man's warlike nature. This point is underlined by those writers who have attempted to illustrate this aspect of Machiavelli's thought:

'Honour' and 'glory', far from placing [Machiavelli] within our moral universe, figure in his thought as expressions natural to a heroic and pagan moral code. Always missing [in the realist view] is an account of how disconcerting, how dangerous, how explosive Machiavelli's morality is ... It is Machiavelli's moral utterances that are disturbing, not his amoral calculations of the method of overthrowing any regime ... it is Machiavelli's very 'humanism', his morality derived from and imposed upon the classics that is so incompatible with our own humanism.[30]

Thus the martialists posited man as unafraid, unthreatened, and even unthinking. He was a Promethean being, delighting in his own strength and cruelty. There was a celebration of his godlike and god-given natural virtues, and he was engaged in a natural world which was as organic and glorious as he could become. The following account of the passing of the Prussian Marshall Von Moltke in a contemporary newpaper reflects some of these ideal martialist attributes: 'to the imagination of the Teutonic race Moltke seemed a type of the mythical gods, worshipped in the past by his pagan fathers; he had wielded the bolts of Thor and the axe of Odin.'[31]

---

[28] *Penser la guerre, Clausewitz,* 58, 86, 226.
[29] N. Machiavelli, *The Discourses* (London: Penguin, 1985), ii. 278.
[30] M. Hulliung, *Citizen Machiavelli* (Princeton: Princeton University Press, 1983), 227.
[31] W. O'Connor Morris, *Fieldmarshall H. Von Moltke* (London: n. p. , 1893), 12.

THE REALIST TRADITION AND
THE NATURE OF WAR

As shown, Hobbes's theory of human nature created the basis for his argument that war was a natural consequence of social intercourse. By fashioning an archetype for the state of war, Hobbes created one of the central themes of the realist perspective on war. His conviction was that although conflict was inescapable, it was also a predicament. As such it needed to be restrained and mitigated through rational attempts at control, which could be achieved by the creation of an all-powerful Leviathan. Accordingly, realist thinkers describing the nature of war rely heavily on the following explication:

Hereby it is manifest, that during the time men live without a common Power to keep them all in awe, they are in that condition which is called Warre; and such a warre, as is of every man, against every man. For WARRE, consisteth not in Battell onely, or the act of fighting; but in a tract of time.[32]

As explained in the first section, Hobbes's entire theory of human nature rested on his prescription of a rational solution to man's problematic nature. This premiss was the pivotal step which distinguished the traditional 'realist' approach from the martialist paradigm. Proponents of the realist tradition in international relations tend to cite a number of philosophers who describe war as inevitable and necessary. The two that tend to be most relied upon are Machiavelli and Clausewitz. However, the Machiavelli used by realists bears little resemblance to the Machiavelli portrayed in the martialist tradition. The realist Machiavelli is construed as a reasonable strategist, a calculating and passionless philosopher who attempted to come to terms with the grim business of conducting war by being pragmatic both about what he observed and could achieve. Thus E. H. Carr placed Machiavelli as the founder of this type of thinking—commonly known as 'machiavellian'.[33]

Similarly, a tempered view of Clausewitz which emphasizes only a portion of his writings has formed the basis of much of the realist perspective on war. Clausewitz's writings posit two completely different formulations of the phenomenon of war: 'absolute' war and 'real' war. 'Absolute' war was his normative account of how war should be fought, while 'real' war was his descriptive commentary on the military practice

---

[32] *Leviathan*, 88.
[33] E. H. Carr, *The Twenty Years Crisis 1919–1939* (London: Macmillan, 1946), 63. See also Kenneth Waltz, *Man, the State, and War* (New York: Columbia University Press, 1959), 212.

of his time and included limitations placed upon it. As Aron noted on the philosophical development of *On War*:

Whether we wish it or not, as we go from Books III, IV and V to Book VI, we breathe a different air. [In] Books III and IV . . . Clausewitz seems to exalt in battle, bloodbath, the grandeur of conflict and the cult of the supreme chief, mastering his emotions and still, at the height of the storm, clearsighted and cool. By contrast, Book IV lists the advantages that a military and political defensive can give.[34]

Martialists, typically, tended to find inspiration from his earlier Books, and indeed, it is ambiguous in Clausewitz's own writings on the subject whether or not he wanted to encourage this type of recognition for 'absolute war'. Realists, on the other hand tended not only to emphasize 'real' war as representing his central philosophy, but argued fiercely against the use of Clausewitz's other basic formulation of war, in spite of the fact that they were, in Raymond Aron's words, a 'conceptual pairing':[35]

The accepted view of Clausewitz's philosophy of war is that its core lies in his conception of war as the continuation of policy by the addition of other means, or, more simply, of war as a political instrument . . . It suggests that his real interest, even if it is focused in many of his chapters on specifically military questions, was of a wider kind: it was in politics, and more particularly, in the relations, tensions, and struggles between the different political units.[36]

According to Waltz, Clausewitz saw war as a political instrument of the state, which could therefore be mitigated and restrained: 'Clausewitz pointed out that he who uses force ruthlessly will gain an advantage if his opponent does not do likewise, but he noted that social institutions may moderate the extent and the savagery of the competition for power'.[37] Most realists defending Clausewitz against elements of his own theory in *On War* stress that it was unfinished.[38]

Like the martialist tradition, realist writers saw war as an inevitable

---

[34] See the English translation of his *Penser la guerre* entitled *Philosopher of War: Clausewitz* (London: Routledge & Kegan Paul, 1983), 237.

[35] See in particular part II, 'The Dialectic', ibid. 89–173. However, in the introduction, Aron's appeal to those reading Clausewitz is for them not to equate his notion of absolute war with 'total war' in spite of the text itself (and the very strong possibility that this is, indeed, his meaning), 5–7.

[36] W. Gallie, *Philosophers of Peace and War* (Cambridge: Cambridge University Press, 1979), 61.

[37] *Man, the State, and War*, 206.

[38] See Peter Paret's, 'The Genesis of *On War*' in M. Howard and P. Paret (eds.), *Carl von Clausewitz's On War* (Princeton: Princeton University Press, 1984), 3; and Aron's *Philosopher of War*, II, 236–7.

product of man's nature. But for the realists war was an unfortunate necessity, as opposed to a glorious opportunity. Because it was painful, destructive, and potentially unstable, realists regarded war as an instrument to be contained as far as possible, and wielded only in cases of extreme necessity. Realist war, in this sense, was not an end in itself but a means to a further set of (political) ends. Realism, in short, subordinated war to the higher political imperatives of the national interest. As will become clear in the following section, martialists saw no higher imperative than war.

MARTIALISM AND THE NATURE OF WAR

War occupied the highest position in the martialist scheme of values. Martialists saw their internal logic as being closer to the intrinsic values they ascribed to man's nature: war is a necessary feature of both human existence and, for one late nineteenth-century practitioner, the cosmos itself: 'war is not inherent only in man; it is the result of a more general law whose effects are not limited to the globe, but which extend across the entire universe'. Most importantly, war is derived from the inner self: 'man is an animal of struggle, driven strongly by his nature to fight, and for which he is supremely endowed'.[39]

Accordingly, the coherence of martialism was derived from advancing relentlessly towards the transformative goals which would make men achieve their heroic potential—to turn them, in the words of de Maistre, into heroic, irrational, and godlike creatures, 'half men, half beasts, monstrous centaurs'.[40] War was not merely, as Hobbes purported, a natural phenomenon; it was to be sought out, encouraged, idealized. These values naturally translated into conquest and expansion. As with the realists, the martialist tradition also invoked the philosophies of war of Machiavelli and Clausewitz. However, as we noted at the beginning of this chapter, the martialist interpretation of their writings differed dramatically from the realist version. Clausewitz admired Machiavelli enormously, especially his references to the greatness and violence of war. On Machiavelli's more radical anti-humanist views, Clausewitz wrote: 'no author is more necessary to read than Machiavelli, those that affect revulsion by his principles are nothing but *petits maîtres*

---

[39] Lieutenant Jean Montagne, *Les Avantages du militarisme au point de vue économique et social* (Paris: Berger-Levrault, 1908), 46, 53.

[40] J. de Maistre, *Œuvres complètes* (Paris: Vaton Frères, 1870), iv. 67.

donning the airs of humanists.'[41] So it was not the 'realist' Machiavelli that drew Clausewitz to the Florentine's writings, as a scholar of Clausewitz noted:

It is not difficult to recognise what impressed the young Clausewitz on his first reading of Machiavelli. Every passage he chose for discussion serves to confirm his growing sense, stimulated by the experience of his generation, that in war, psychological forces cannot be repressed by convention and system.[42]

Machiavelli, the foremost philosopher borrowed by the martial tradition, defined the object of war as the desire for conquest. Scattered throughout the *Prince*, the *Discourses*, and the *Art of War* are examples highlighting the glorious and transformative nature of war. A contemporary interpretation of Machiavelli's œuvre shows how he appealed to martialists' vision and could provide inspiration for less realist aims: 'By no means is imperialism an obscure or occasional topic in Machiavelli's writings. On the contrary, it is a central theme running throughout all his works, from beginning to end . . . Not even in his poetry can Machiavelli forget the question of empire.'[43] In contrast, the realist tradition looked to war as an inevitable result of the anarchic condition of the world and the legitimate need for security in that anarchic place. Conquest was only incidental to this search, and indeed was unnecessary if the state's borders were securely defended. However, for martialist writers, the desire for greatness had at its roots the search for expansion and mastery over others. War and conquest were therefore supreme imperatives.

The martialists also claimed war's absoluteness. There was a repudiation of military conflict in anything less than its unadulterated form. Any attempts to set limits (whether moral, prudential, or even political) to this natural phenomenon were to be rejected. As Clausewitz helpfully pointed out: ' "Laws of War" are self-imposed restrictions, almost imperceptible and hardly worth mentioning . . . To introduce into the philosophy of war itself a principle of moderation would be an absurdity . . . War is an act of violence which in its application knows no bounds.'[44] It was remarks like these that decided Liddell Hart on the

[41] The French term *petits maîtres* was used by Clausewitz in his original letter in German. This extract is from E. Carrias, *La Pensée militaire allemande* (Paris: Presses Universitaires de France, 1948), 184.

[42] Peter Paret, *Clausewitz and the State* (Oxford: Clarendon Press, 1976), 169.

[43] Hulliung, *Citizen Machiavelli*, 6. Also important to martialists in this context is his obvious fascination with danger. See John Dunn on this point in his 'The Identity of the Bourgeois Liberal Republic', in B. Fontana (ed.), *The Invention of the Modern Republic* (Cambridge: Cambridge University Press, 1994), 211.

[44] C. Clausewitz, *On War* (London: Routledge & Kegan Paul, 1962), i. 43.

point of whether or not Clausewitz was a martialist: 'if one weighs his influence and his emphasis, one might describe him historically as the Mahdi of the mass and mutual massacre. For he was the source of the doctrine "absolute war", and the fight to the finish theory.'[45] A generation after Clausewitz, this view was still paramount in the German army. General Julius Von Hartmann, of the German General Staff, also rejected the codification of war. His conception of the art of war was close to Clausewitz's; it glorified violence as natural, and was equally repelled by the introduction of legal notions into war. The series of essays written by Von Hartmann during 1877–8, entitled *Military Necessities and Humanity,* were the official reply of the Prussian Ministry of War to the proposal for a 'Codification of the Laws of War' suggested by the Institute of International Law, and proposed by Germany's lawyer Bluntschli. Von Hartmann believed that the notion of codifying war was 'obscene': 'When peace gives place to war, then passion and violence enter upon the great stage of history . . . the expression "civilised warfare", used by Bluntschli, seems hardly intelligible; for war destroys this very equilibrium.'[46]

Martialists shared an appreciation of war as divine, spiritual, and elemental; war was the manifestation of 'destiny' in the highest sense. Machiavelli warned that 'war must be considered fulfilment of a religious duty',[47] and Clausewitz wrote of 'the marvellously structured organic whole of all living nature'.[48] Other adherents to this tradition also extolled the religious and divine features of war. Considered the greatest German military thinker after Clausewitz, Von Moltke was greatly influenced by him.[49] He scathingly dismissed all Kantian projects for perpetual peace and law-based regulation of military conflict:

Perpetual peace is a dream, and it is not even a beautiful dream: war forms part of the universal order constituted by God. In war are displayed the most noble virtues which would otherwise slumber and become extinct: courage and abne-

---

[45] B. Liddell Hart, *The Ghost of Napoleon* (London: Faber & Faber, 1933), 124.
[46] J. Von Hartmann, *Militärische Notwendigkeit und Humanität—Military Necessities and Humanity* (Bonn: Deutsche Rundschau, 1877–8), xiii. 123; Andler, *Frightfulness in Theory and Practice*, 77.
[47] *The Discourses*, ii. 2, 278.   [48] Paret, *Clausewitz*, 149.
[49] Two works that point this out are H. Rothenberg, 'Moltke, Schlieffen, and the Doctrine of Strategic Envelopment', and H. Holborn's 'The Prusso-German School: Moltke and the Rise of the German General Staff', in P. Paret, G. Craig, and F. Gilbert (eds.), *The Makers of Modern Strategy* (Princeton: Princeton University Press, 1986).

gation, fidelity to duty, and the spirit of sacrifice which will hazard life itself; without war humanity would sink into materialism.[50]

Kant's 'Perpetual Peace' was also derided by Hegel, whose vision of war's imperious necessity was also incorporated by authors into the martialist tradition: 'War has the higher significance that by its agency . . . just as the blowing of the winds preserves the sea from the foulness which would be the result of a prolonged calm, so also the corruption in nations would be the product of prolonged, let alone "perpetual" peace.'[51] War was thus an act of redemption, a purifying 'bath of steel' which could bind a nation's soul. One writer who drew from this transfiguring notion of war an image which absolutely deified conflict was de Maistre. Here he extolled the glory of war as a god in itself:

War is thus divine in itself, since it is a law of the world. War is divine through its consequences of a supernatural nature which are as much general as particular . . . Who would doubt the benefits that death in war brings? . . . War is divine in the mysterious glory that surrounds it and in the no less inexplicable attraction that draws us to it . . . War is divine by the manner in which it breaks out . . . War is divine in its results which cannot be predicted . . . War is divine through the indefinable power that determines success in it.[52]

Whereas the realists saw war as a necessary evil, those in the martialist tradition regarded it as a necessary virtue. Some of these writers, especially at the second half of the nineteenth century, drew on contemporary social Darwinism in their understanding of war's healthy and transformative powers. In the words of General Von Bernhardi: 'War is not only a necessary element to the life of peoples, but also an indispensable element of culture, an expression of the highest vitality and force of civilised peoples . . . without war the races of lesser virtue or more degenerate could too easily snuff out healthy elements, and a general decadence will be inevitable.'[53]

This quasi-Darwinist approach, drawing analogies from the natural world, was extremely popular in mid to late nineteenth-century Europe.

[50] Von Moltke in a letter to M. Bluntschli, the lawyer representing Germany at the Brussels Conference of 1874. *Doctrines of War* in L. Freedman (ed.), *War* (Oxford: Oxford University Press, 1994), 217. I have used a section of the translation here from Andler, *Frightfulness*, 23.

[51] G. W. F. Hegel, *Philosophy of Right*, trans. T. M. Knox (Oxford: Oxford University Press, 1981), 211. Similarly, Embser declared in 1779 that universal peace would force men into 'stinking idleness'. Werner, *1914: les psychoses*, 17.

[52] *Œuvres complètes*, 255.

[53] Von Bernhardi, *L'Allemagne et la prochaine guerre*, in Carrias, *La Pensée militaire*, 70.

Dr Campeanu, for example believed that 'the instinct of battle exists in man's very nature', thus 'the influence of the sight of bloody spectacle' was important, as 'blood produces a kind of drunkenness in men engaged in battle as for animals, as one can see in the fury of fighting turkeys and bulls'. [54] War could not only be a healthy, restorative force—it could be art. War was continually glorified as a thing of infinite beauty. The artist Ruskin delivered the following speech at the Royal Military Academy at Woolwich in 1866: 'all the pure and noble arts of peace are founded on war; no great art ever yet rose on earth, but among a nation of soldiers. War, by eliminating the unfit, determined who were the best—those highest bred, most fearless, coolest of nerve, swiftest of eye and hand.'[55] War was even seen as a healthy exercise for nations who had it visited *upon* them. In a remark directed at Cobdenites, Treitschke represented conflict as a superior tool for inter-state communication: 'War does of course alienate nations, but it also teaches them to understand their neighbours; at times it is a better intermediary between nations than even international trade . . . war is a sacred, beneficial necessity.'[56] In one of de Maistre's most famous and quoted evocations of war, life itself is seen exclusively in terms of a preparation and consummation of its avatar, war: 'the entire earth, continually bathed in blood, is but an immense altar where all living things must be immolated without end, without restraint, without cease, until the consummation of all things, until the death of death'.[57] In sum, martialists drew from a wide range of extant doctrines to produce an image of war as the most essential affirmation of man's nature, a transcendental occurrence which was to be sought after and exalted. As it was a realization of humanity's essential greatness and god-liness, it was expansive and uncontrollable, and was in this sense a true reflection of man's deepest nature.

REALISM AND THE NATURE OF THE STATE

The central realist thesis concerning the nature of government was (and remains) the need for a strong and powerful state. The entire

[54] D. Campeanu, *Questions de sociologie militaire* (Paris: Giard et Brière, 1903), 5, 9.

[55] C. Eby, *The Road to Armageddon: The Martial Spirit in English Popular Literature 1870–1914* (London: Duke University Press, 1987), 1.

[56] A. Dorpalen, *Heinrich von Treitschke* (New York: Kennekat Press, 1973), 148.

[57] 'La terre entière, continuellement imbibée de sang, n'est qu'un autel immense où tout ce qui vit doit être immolé sans fin, sans mesure, sans relâche, jusqu'à la consom-mation des choses, jusqu'à la mort de la mort'. *Soirées de Saint-Petersbourg,* in M. Ferraz, *Histoire de la philosophie en France au XIXème siècle* (Paris: Perrin, 1880), 46–7; *Œuvres complètes,* 78.

logic of the realist paradigm rests on this requirement, which is derived from its interpretation of the nature of man and of war. Accordingly, Hobbes's notion of a Leviathan is reified: for realists, the adverse conditions of man's nature forced the creation of a strong and power-ful ruler who could maintain a strong and powerful state. The most important feature of this type of government was the artifice of its construct: it was a man-made response to nature and its dangers, and a means of mitigating the naturally destructive and unrestrained instincts of man. This realist view relies on Hobbes's description of the Leviathan's make-up:

But as men, for the atteyning of peace, and the conservation of themselves thereby, have made an Artificiall Man, which we call a Common-wealth; so also have they made Artificiall Chains, called *Civill Lawes*, which they them-selves, by mutuall covenants, have fastned at one end, to the lips of that Man, or Assembly, to whom they have given the Soveraigne Power; and at the other end to their own Ears. These Bonds in their own nature but weak, may nevertheless be made to hold, by the danger, though not by the difficulty in breaking them.[58]

In the realist approach, political power is limited functionally, as the state does not have the power to control all aspects of public and private life. It also derived its legitimacy from its fulfilment of the security needs of society; there were no other moral or philosophical justifications. Finally, power itself was a fragile and ephemeral construct, always threatened by failure and defeat. This led to another central argument of the realist tradition: the importance of the civilian character of the state. The creation of a Leviathan was intended to relieve men of the means of fighting each other. Although armies had to be used to wage war against other states, power and authority remained vested in civil-ian hands. Accordingly, the army had to occupy a subordinate position in the hierarchy of public institutions. Determining the priorities of battle was thus a matter for the state and its political leaders, not for the army.

Finally, realists highlighted the prudential aspect of states. As their sole responsibility was the pursuit of power for self-preservation, they could not be weighed down by absolutist moral considerations. As Hans Morgenthau stated: 'realism maintains that universal moral principles cannot be applied to the actions of states in their abstract universal formulation . . . There can be no political morality without prudence . . . Realism, then, considers prudence . . . to be the supreme virtue in politics.'[59]

---

[58] *Leviathan*, 147.   [59] *Politics among Nations*, 12.

THE MARTIALIST CONCEPTION OF THE STATE

Martialists did not formulate the idea of their state in the same way as the realists, nor did they place the same emphasis on state power. Other components ranked higher: the focus on individual greatness and heroism, the nature of war, and (as will be shown) cultural and 'natural' particularisms of the nation. Several values were central and indeed unique to this paradigm. First, the state had an individual identity; in the terms defined by Adam Müller, it was a living entity: 'the state is not merely a plaything or instrument in the hand of a person . . . *but it is itself a person*, a free whole, existing and growing in itself by means of endless interaction of contending and self-reconciling ideas. . . .'[60] The individual, the state, and society were not separate entities, but elements of an organic totality. In a passage rejecting both rationalist and natural law bases for the state Meinecke explained: 'the firm, organic bonds that connected society, state, and nation, and the individual to them, could not be overlooked—it was precisely the organic aspects of the state that were denied by natural law . . . beyond the world of conscious action stronger, more historical forces direct the paths of men.'[61] Advancing from this view was an emphasis on strong leaders and charismatic leadership (in contrast with the realist concern with the impersonal nature of the state structure). But leadership and human volition were not the final arbiter of state action in the martialist tradition; states themselves were driven by higher teleological purposes. Indeed, the martialist state was always presented as a natural and transhistorical institution, without the artificial aspects of Hobbes's Commonwealth, which was underpinned by the rational laws of men. The authority of the martialist state came not from written law, but from tradition itself. De Maistre was one of many writers who condemned written constitutions, declaring: 'the more that is written, the weaker is the institution', and went on to conclude that: 'the most essential, the most intrinsically constitutional, and the really fundamental is not written and even should not be if the state is not to be imperilled.'[62]

In further contrast with the realists, the purpose of the state was emphatically not the preservation of the individual's security. Indeed,

---

[60] *Briefwechsel zwischen Friedrich Gentz und Adam Heinrich Müller 1800–1829* (Stuttgart: Cottal, 1857), 23. Emphasis in text. Müller also believed strongly that the 'spirit' of ancient Rome was personified in its expansionist empire, and that the most alive and 'best' states grew naturally towards conquest. On Müller's thoughts on empire see K. Mannfield, 'Conservative Thought', *Essays on Sociology* (London: Routledge & Kegan Paul, 1953), 105.

[61] *The Age of Liberation*, 20.   [62] Joseph de Maistre, *Œuvres complètes*, 78, 151.

the state was entitled to expect the individual to sacrifice his safety for the higher purposes of the collectivity—a notion which we shall later see replicated (with some profound and essential differences) in the republican code. The individual's identification was not with a state which concerned itself with the security of its subjects, but only with their natural destiny, which was typically aggrandizing. In this respect too, the martialist tradition emphatically rejected the prudentalism and conservatism of the realists. Relevant to martialists was the militarized and hierarchical structure of government and society. This was an expression of a rejection of artificiality, and a belief in an innate sense of the natural order of the world. Whether tribal, feudal, religious, or monarchical, this order provided a preordained place for all members of society. These positions and roles were defined in a strict and unchanging hierarchy.

Unlike the civilian character of the types of society envisioned by realists, there was an honoured place near the pinnacle of this martialist hierarchy for the army. There were several dimensions to this relationship between army and state that were particular to the martialist approach. The first was that morality was an essential factor in cementing social relations. Alfred Vagts, a historian of militarism, noted that 'the principle of *honour* helped to unify the military state and protect it from civilian intervention', when examining this feature of essentially martial thought.[63] Furthermore, there was the attitude of the army towards a legitimate authority in the state. In nineteenth-century Prussia, for example: 'these officers did not regard themselves as soldiers of the nation, members of a single community, as once had been the case in the Wars of Liberation. They looked at themselves solely as paladins . . . loyal followers of the monarch to whom they had sworn personal fealty.'[64] Also distinctive was the manner in which the sovereign viewed his army. For example, Frederick the Great, the *roi connétable*, personally led his troops into the fray, and allowed no state agency to be interposed between himself and the army.[65] Even in civilian governments the army often had a specific place in the hierarchy of public institutions, which placed it above the government and just below the throne, as Stargardt observed: 'even at the Kaiser's table the Imperial Chancellor as a mere civilian gave his place to the military

---

[63] Vagts, *A History of Militarism*, 179.
[64] Heinrich von Treitschke in C. Paul and W. H. Dawson (eds.), *Treitschke's History of Germany in the Nineteenth Century* (London: Jarrold; Allen & Unwin, 1915), 39.
[65] Gerhard Ritter, *The Scepter and the Sword: The Problem of Militarism in Germany* (Florida: University of Miami Press, 1969), i. 7.

entourage, while the Minister of Finance felt he had really made it on his promotion from sergeant to lieutenant'.[66] Like many martialists, Macaulay believed this privileged status should be insulated from the machinations of elected assemblies as army officers were inextricably and morally bound to the fabric of the state.[67] And in contrast with the amoral character of its realist counterpart, the martialist state was endowed with moral qualities, lending the state moral calling. This distinction is captured by Hedley Bull, who here uses Hobbes to represent the realist position: 'Hobbes does not use the term reason of state, and the meaning it came to have for Hegel and his successors—of justification by reference to a state with an individual soul apart from the persons of which it is made up, and with a moral duty to assert itself—is entirely foreign to Hobbes.'[68]

In conclusion, the differences between the realist and martialist conceptions of the state were considerable. The martialist state was inherently conflictual, personalized, and charismatic, and acted on the basis of a broader teleological design; aggression and violence were its main virtues. The realist state was limited in its purposes, impersonal, and defensive: war was accepted as an instrument of policy, but only if circumstances absolutely dictated it.

THE NATURE OF LIBERTY: THE REALIST AND MARTIALIST TRADITIONS CONTRASTED

In the realist tradition, liberty was defined as an individual attribute; a quality belonging inherently to man in the state of nature, but which could be sacrificed to the state in order to gain security and civil peace. This evolved into the liberty (or right) of states to preserve their own security, and to do whatever was needed in this endeavour; realists again relying on Hobbes's formulation for this position: 'every sovereign hath the same right, in procuring the safety of his people, that any particular man can have in procuring the safety of his own body'.[69]

The concept of liberty as defined by realists thus occupied a subordinate position in their hierarchy of values. Security and order were seen as much more important goals. For martialism, however, liberty was

---

[66] V. Stargardt, *The German Idea of Militarism: Radical and Socialist Critics 1866–1914* (Cambridge: Cambridge University Press, 1994), 117.

[67] Vagts, *History of Militarism*, 169.

[68] H. Bull, 'Hobbes and the International Anarchy', *Social Research*, 48/4 (1981), 724.

[69] *Leviathan*, 162.

imagined in a framework full of contradictions and ambivalence. For example, the question of the objective value of natural rights was irrelevant; and, given its hierarchal and purposive ordering of society, martialism rejected the notion that individuals had any legal or moral claims over it. Indeed, individual liberty was merely a question of recognizing one's natural role in society. More importantly for the martialists, society needed to have the freedom to be true to itself. This 'natural' freedom was not so much in society, as of it. For the martialists, it represented the liberty to grow and to conquer; as Clausewitz admiringly agreed with Machiavelli, to strive for 'greatness'.[70] Accordingly, a 'free society' had a radically different connotation to that of the Enlightenment ideal. Unlike the realist scheme, where society took liberty away from the individual in exchange for security, this paradigm did not exclude the notion of personal liberty altogether, as long as the individual's purpose was to realize and fulfil his appointed role in the social and political hierarchy. Indeed, this exercise had to be approached in a 'semibarbaric swashbuckler's spirit'.[71] Looking at the history of his people in terms of expansion and conquest, Treitschke gave an example from the late Middle Ages which celebrated freedom as the quest for land and power. He applauded 'the northern and eastern rush of the German spirit and formidable activities of our people as conqueror, teacher, discipliner of our neigbours'.[72] These examples demonstrated a tendency to conflate the will of spirit and the desire for power with the true meaning of liberty. In the words of the German parliamentarian Dahlmann in 1849: 'The path of power is the only one that will satisfy and appease the fermenting impulse to freedom—for it is not solely freedom that the German is thinking of, it is rather power, which has hitherto been refused him, and after which he hankers.'[73]

Individual liberty was conflated with that of society. At the same time, its limits were also determined by the imperatives of the state and the nation. This understanding of liberty as a value which could be expressed only through the group, nation, or collectivity was a central component of the martialist perspective. The liberty of the nation to overpower others stimulated a glorification of expansionist ideas as will be noted later in the chapter. Few better examples of this conquering spirit could

---

[70] On Clausewitz's reading of Machiavelli see ch. 8, pp. 169–209 of Peter Paret's *Clausewitz and the State*.

[71] Ritter, *The Scepter and the Sword*, i. 117.

[72] F. Treitschke, *The Origins of Prussianism: The Teutonic Knights* (London: George Allen & Unwin, 1942), 18.

[73] Dahlmann speaking in the Frankfurt Parliament in 1849, in Meinecke, *Machiavellism*, 395.

be found than Viscount Wolseley. In this extract, he advanced a typical martialistic argument in favour of the liberty of empire:

If there were a Temple of Janus in England, its gates would seldom have been closed in her Majesty's reign. Until the British Empire be broken up by some mad minister, and his madness be so communicated to the English people . . . that . . . we force our loyal colonies to dissever their connection with us, and we lose all our foreign possessions, we cannot expect our swords ever to be sheathed for any number of years consecutively . . . without doubt we are the most warlike people on earth. No other armies have portions of it so constantly in the field as we have . . . The soldiers of Queen Victoria are to be found year after year in small numbers in remote corners of her empire, upholding the honour of England and fighting hard in its interests against hordes of barbarous foes.[74]

For the martialist tradition liberty was ultimately a collective phenomenon. As will be shown in the following section on nationalism and patriotism, the only manner in which an individual's true liberty could be expressed was through the burning crucible of the nation. Freedom, the nature of the individual, war, and nationalism were thus inextricably intertwined.

NATIONALISM AND PATRIOTISM IN THE MARTIALIST TRADITION

Twentieth-century realism, based as it is on the central theme of a powerful and prudential state, has little scope for patriotism and nationalism in its framework, and little place for these concepts in its writings; Hobbes's example of rational man understandably, if cravenly, escaping conscription is often quoted, as in the realist conception, the value of personal security is paramount. Although, for realists, it is the prerogative of the state to follow its own interests (often described as 'national'[75]), Morgenthau believed that nationalism as force in political life should and would wither away in the near future: 'in the atomic age, nationalism and the nation-state must make way for a political principle of larger dimensions, in tune with the world-wide configuration of interest and power of the age'.[76] As these two concepts are so much

---

[74] H. Bolitho, 'The Army', in T. Ward (ed.), *The Reign of Queen Victoria* (London: Collins, 1949) i. 185–6.

[75] H. Morgenthau, 'Nationalism', *American Political Science Review*, 16 (1952), 960.

[76] See in particular the use of the term 'national interest' in the writings of Morgenthau, for example. *In Defence of the National Interest: A Critical Examination of US Foreign Policy* (New York: Knopf, 1951).

more complex in the martial tradition, the following analysis will simply present the martialist formulation on these questions.

If the martialist paradigm were to be imagined as a cluster of concepts and values rather than a hierarchy, at its heart would be the dual notions of the nation and war. Driving them were the differing notions of nature, the individual, liberty, and society, where they were ignited in potent combustion. The nation and war were indissociable in the martialist tradition; they were envisioned as having a complementary and self-reconciling purpose. The nation and war were both the means and the ends to each other. The first strand of this totality concerned the notion of identity, and the means to achieve it. The individual was free to discover his identity through the nation, while the nation was free to discover its own character through war. Ultimately, the conceptions of nature, the individual, liberty, society, nation, and war formed a coherent and unique ontology, providing martialist doctrine with its underlying purpose and unity.[77]

NATION, WAR, AND PATRIOTISM

The nationalist of the martialist tradition believed that the fulfilment of the nation came with war. Stepping into the shoes of such a nationalist, Isaiah Berlin wrote:

if the satisfaction of the needs of this organism to which I belong turns out to be incompatible with the fulfillment of the goals of other groups, I, or the society to which I indissolubly belong, have no choice but to force them to yield, if need be by force. If my group—let us call it the nation—is freely to realise its true nature, this entails the need to remove obstacles in its path.[78]

War was credited with being a vehicle for the emergence of the nation, and an instrument for its further glory. One of the first writers who posited the dialectical relationship of the nation and war was Adolf Lasson, a German schoolteacher and polemicist. A contemporary of Fichte and Treitschke, Lasson wrote about the supremacy, and more importantly, the dynamic between military conflict and nationalism. His work had a tremendous influence on the thinking of Treitschke and Meinecke, and most importantly, military thinkers from the German

---

[77] See also a comparison with Roger Griffin's remarkable examination of both the ranking and the role of nationalism within the ideology of fascism in his *The Nature of Fascism* (London: Routledge, 1993).

[78] I. Berlin, 'Nationalism', in *Against the Current*, 343.

General Staff including Clausewitz and Von Moltke.[79] He also influenced later Pan-Germanist thinkers and propagandists such as Bottinger, Bley, Lange, Wirth, Tannenberg, and Frymann.[80] Lasson's writings undertook to show that war, while admittedly frightful, was equally glorious; they culminated in the claim that the ability to wage war to perfection was the highest manifestation of national culture: 'War is the only true judgement, for it is based on power—the powerful state is the better state, its people are the better people, its culture is the more valuable culture—such is the everlasting justice of history'; or, 'it is not only its own possessions which the state has to defend by war, but also those which it has not yet acquired and must conquer by means of war. It is absurd to profess indignation against the very idea of a war of conquest.'[81] Another illustration of how the individual's search for greatness could be completed only by means of the nation at war was given by the German journalist Konstantin Rössler. Writing in 1848, he propounded an expansionist, racialist, and culturally violent philosophy of national aggrandizement which typified the martialist view of the world:

Man begins with struggle and violence . . . Strength, power, constitute the earliest form of ideality, the first great impression man makes upon man . . . Every nation has the right, nay the duty, to extend its power as far as its strength reaches—reaches in earnest and for good. Sentimental considerations do not figure in this, such as the argument that people of different disposition have a right to live and must be spared—indeed possess all manner of estimable qualities that should be preserved for now and for all the future . . . That every kind of national vermin must be preserved is no more than a nonsensical tradition handed down to us by the sentimental eighteenth and doctrinaire nineteenth centuries. It is a duty and vocation of strong nations to divide the world among themselves.[82]

Two particular features should be noted here: first, as mentioned earlier, the nation was seen as an organic entity, which occupied a pre-eminent position over the state. Accordingly, the nation was not a political construction, but a natural association. So Meinecke used the term

---

[79] His main work was *Culture and War*, as yet untranslated into French or English, although selected paragraphs can be found in J. Dampierre's *German Imperialism and International Law* (New York: Charles Scribner, 1917), 50–7. See, for example, Dorpalen's *Treitschke*, 148; Ritter's, *The Scepter and the Sword*, 211; Meinecke's *Machiavellism*, 114–17.

[80] Smith, *Militarism and Statecraft*, 221.

[81] A. Lasson, *Culture and War*, in Ritter, *The Scepter and the Sword*, i. 211; in Dampierre, *German Imperialism*, 52.

[82] Ritter, *The Scepter and the Sword*, 212.

'nation' to signify something akin to its original sociological and pre-political sense. He quoted Wilhelm von Humbold's conception of the nation to explain this vision: 'like society, the nation was a spontaneous, natural union of like-minded individuals. The community was the means, but the end was the spiritual education of the individual towards energy and beauty.'[83] Another important attribute of the nation (as with other core values in the martial approach) was its interchangeability with the state. Not only was the nation superior to the state, but the latter's primary (and unique) purpose was to serve the moral, ethnic, and cultural ends of the nation. In the words of Treitschke:

> The state is the moral community, it is called to promote actively the education of mankind, and its ultimate purpose is to help a nation develop a distinct purpose in and through it; for this is the highest moral task for a nation as well as for an individual . . . Thus we may call the state a *Kulturstaat* and demand from it the positive actions in the promotion of the entire spiritual and material life of its people.[84]

This image of the nation as ethnically based, with a moral mission to colonize, was not restricted merely to thinkers and intellectuals. Military practitioners, such as Von Moltke, were also deeply imbued with this essentially chauvinistic ethos of nation.[85] In a pamphlet (rhetorically) entitled 'Is War Inevitable?' Ernest Jaeglé called upon his compatriots to 'engage all their strength . . . in order to accomplish the civilizing mission of the German race'.[86] The martialist notion of patriotism was a means of celebrating the individual's relationship to the nation; the locus where greatness was realized and transfigured through its warring spirit. Patriotism, therefore, was not so much an undesirable national duty as a spiritual consummation of man's ultimate being through self-immolation on a common altar:

> All known nations have been happy and powerful to the degree that they have faithfully obeyed the national mind . . . What is patriotism? It is this national mind of which I am speaking, it is *individual abnegation*. Faith and patriotism are the two great thaumaturges of the world. Both are divine. All their actions are miracles . . . They know only two words, *submission* and *belief*.[87]

The individual thus had to submit to an absolute patriotism so that

---

[83] *The Age of Liberation*, 20.
[84] Cited in Dorpalen, *Treitschke*, 234–5.
[85] See Ritter's chapter on Moltke's political thought in *The Scepter and the Sword*, and especially at 213.
[86] E. Jaeglé, *La Guerre est-elle inévitable?* (Paris: Heinrichsen, 1890), 97.
[87] Joseph de Maistre, *Œuvres complètes*, 108; emphasis in text.

the nation could be free to march towards its manifest destiny. It was the paladins and knights of the nation, its military, who were the sublime instruments of this greater purpose. This type of military, according to Herbert Spencer, saw 'success in war the highest glory' and that they are 'led to identify goodness with bravery and strength . . . they must have patriotism which regards the triumph of their society as the supreme end of action; they must possess the loyalty whence flows obedience to authority.'[88] Essential to this 'patriotic' feeling was lust for violence. Clausewitz wrote to Fichte the following: 'this true spirit of war seems to me to consist in mobilising the energies of every soldier to the greatest possible extent, and in infusing him with bellicose feelings, so that the fire of war spreads to every component of the army instead of leaving numerous dead coals in the mass'. Clausewitz explained this crucial aspect of what he called the 'spirit of war', emphasizing that it was neither technical nor mechanical: 'the modern art of war, far from using men like simple machines, should vitalise individual energies'.[89]

THE DEVELOPMENT OF
THE MARTIAL TRADITION FROM 1874

At Geneva, in 1949, the core values of martialism, and the norms of what will later be called its 'code of conquest' (i.e. the commitment to such practices as hostage-taking of occupied civilians and the concept of obedience by the occupied population owed to the occupying power) were fully represented. However, the traditionally perceived bearer of martial values in the Second World War, the Third Reich, had been defeated and no fascist state or Axis power was present. Instead, it was the British, who had fought against those very principles during the war, who proved to be the main agents of martialism at the conference. There was a simple explanation for this apparent paradox: the British War Office representative at Geneva was justifying the maintenance of martial practices in order to defend both the ideology of Empire, and, more importantly, the military policies of their colonial armies such as hostage-taking and the incineration of rebel villages.[90]

In the mainstream literature on the laws of war, and indeed in the broader writings of international theory, this ideological connection has

---

[88] H. Spencer, *The Principles of Sociology* (London: Williams and Norgate, 1876), 603–4.

[89] Clausewitz, *On War*, 169.

[90] B. Berman, *Control and Crisis in Colonial Kenya: the dialectic of domination* (London: Currey, 1990).

never been noticed, much less explored. Two reasons may be offered for this oversight: the conventional understanding of the roots of Nazism and early twentieth-century fascism generally, and equally the traditional view of British ideologies of empire and colonial practices.

A spirited debate exists on the intellectual origins of fascism in Europe.[91] The literature can be schematically divided into two tendencies. The first argues that fascism is the logical culmination of a range of ideas about man and society which were derived from earlier ideological tendencies in nineteenth- and early twentieth-century Europe. These ideas, which centred around a pessimistic and often irrationalist conception of human nature, a rejection of industrial capitalism and mass democracy, an affirmation of the vital and creative nature of force, and the celebration of authoritarian leadership, are seen to have deep roots in the political culture of continental Europe.[92] From such a perspective, twentieth-century fascist ideology has variously been presented as the natural extension of certain forms of conservative thought,[93] a derivation of specifically national forms of authoritarianism,[94] or even as a perversion of socialism or Marxism. The second tendency accepts the claim of ideological similarity between fascism and its conservative, nationalist, and authoritarian precursors, but stresses elements of discontinuity instead.[95] In this 'rupture' school, there appears a particular historical moment (which most date at or around the First World War) when traditional conservative authoritarianism changed into something new and qualitatively different. Most analysts here highlight the distinction between the 'revolutionary' aspect of fascism (particularly its egalitarian and racist notions, and its focus on modernization and industrialization) and the 'conservative' character of more traditional forms of authoritarian nationalist thinking.[96]

[91] For collections see W. Laqueur, *Fascism: A Reader's Guide* (Cambridge: Cambridge University Press, 1976), and P. Milza, *Les Fascismes* (Paris: Imprimerie Nationale, 1985). The most illuminating and comprehensive is Roger Griffin's. See his *Fascism* (Oxford: Oxford University Press, 1995) and his more recent *International Fascism: Theories, Causes and the New Consensus* (London: Arnold, 1998).

[92] Z. Sternhell, 'Fascist Ideology', in Griffin, *Fascism*, 315–76.

[93] I. Berlin, 'Joseph de Maistre', 91–174.

[94] Z. Sternhell, *Ni droite ni gauche* (Paris: Le Seuil, 1983), 15. See also his *La Droite révolutionnaire 1885–1914: les origines françaises du fascisme* (Paris: Seuil, 1978).

[95] F. Carsten, *The Rise of Fascism* (Berkeley and Los Angeles: University of California Press, 1969), 235–6.

[96] For example, see L. Dupeux's 'L'Hitlérisme et ses antécédents allemands', in P. Ory (ed.), *Nouvelle Histoire des idées politiques* (Paris: Hachette, 1987), 427. The work which makes the most helpful distinction between the authoritarian right and fascism is Juan Linz's 'An Authoritarian Regime: Spain', in Erik Allardt and Stein Rokkan (eds.), *Mass Politics: Studies in Political Sociology* (New York: Free Press, 1970).

Both approaches, however, share the common assumption that fascism is a continental European phenomenon. For this reason, Britain tends to be excluded from inquiries about its origins, and comparative patterns of thought remain unexplored. In the case of the first school, British political thought is ignored because there was no large-scale 'fascist' movement in Britain during the inter-war period; its political culture could therefore not have played a significant part of the intellectual genesis of 'fascism'. The second school, while recognizing the existence of authoritarian political traditions and values, neglects their 'martial' dimensions because these are seen as the exclusive property of 'fascist' ideologies. The focus of both schools has therefore obscured the existence of authoritarian and martial undercurrents in Britain which shared many core values with their continental counterparts.[97]

The avoidance of Britain is perhaps also due to two further factors: a belief that its political thought developed in isolation from the rest of Europe; and a general inclination to regard Britain as a 'practical' rather than 'theoretical' polity. The British, too, chose to view themselves this way. As Keir Hardie wrote to Engels: 'We are a solid people, very practical, and not given to chasing bubbles.'[98] Indeed, they often hoped this was the way they *were* seen: 'In European eyes the English had become in the nineteenth century a people given to deeds, to work in the world for its own sake . . . the Empire might have its energumens like Rhodes but its strength lay among the restless, practical, non-contemplative people.'[99] For these reasons, political developments and practical trends in the rest of the world are not seen to apply. For example, Michael Howard notes the emergence of a 'new militarism' in Europe in the early twentieth century, which emphasized 'demotic values'.[100] But the development of this spirit is located in continental Europe, the United States, and even Australia; its existence in Britain is not considered. Yet in another article, Howard argues that 'it was taken for granted—by all save a slightly larger minority—that the Empire,

---

[97] One of the few genuinely comparative exercises is in Hannah Arendt's *Imperialism*, but it focuses exclusively on race. *The Origins of Totalitarianism*, vol. ii: *Imperialism* (New York: Harcourt, Brace, & World, 1951).

[98] Cited in S. Macintyre, *A Proletarian Science: Marxism in Britain* (Cambridge: Cambridge University Press, 1980), 1.

[99] J. Grainger, *Patriotisms: Britain 1900–1939* (London: Routledge & Kegan Paul, 1986), 130–1.

[100] M. Howard, *The Causes of Wars*, 67; 'Empire, Race, and War', in V. Pearl, B. Worden, and H. Lloyd-Jones (eds.), *History and Imagination: Essays in Honour of H. R. Trevor-Roper* (London: Duckworth, 1981), 340.

having been built up might be legitimately extended by war, and would probably have one day to be defended by war. The military virtues were thus considered part of the essence of an Imperial Race'; thus for Britain, studies of Empire are far removed from the studies of British political thought and action in the nineteeth and twentieth centuries.[101]

A second reason for the lack of sources for this tradition is the conventional understanding of the historical origins of the ideologies of Empire. In the main, history has been written from the premiss that the British Empire had material rather than ideological roots. Historians have looked to the underlying purposes of empire, both economic and political, and rendered the underpinnings of empire in these 'realist' terms, reducing the element of ideology (in the construction, and especially the maintenance, of empire) to an instrumental position: 'imperialism was . . . a hybrid phenomenon, for which defencism provided the main motivation, crusading a common justification, and militarism no more than the occasional flash of rhetoric'.[102] However, upon closer examination of the historical and political origins of the imperial idea in Britain, it is clear that there were several radically different traditions of thought on empire at the end of the nineteenth century within mainstream political and social life.

One was developed out of the Liberal and Radical wings of British political life, which presented the (sometimes disputed) value of empire in purely rational, economic terms. These wings differed from the separatists—a loose coalition of Free Traders, Utilitarians, and 'Philosophical Radicals' who were not associated with the Colonial Reform Movement and were active at the beginning of the nineteenth century. The Colonial Reform Movement was succeeded by the 'Manchester School', which also attempted to reformulate the notion and structure of empire without altogether abandoning the benefits which accrued from it.[103] The second school, which was at its apogee during the period

[101] As one historian of empire noted, this martial sentiment seemed 'singularly removed from the much advertised English tradition of peaceful yeomanry and indigenous liberalism'. Raymond Betts, 'The Allusion to Rome in British Imperialist Thought of the Late Nineteenth and Early Twentieth Centuries', *Victorian Studies*, 15 (1971), 149.

[102] Ceadel, *Thinking about Peace and War*, 39.

[103] See C. Bodelson, *Studies in Mid-Victorian Imperialism* (Norway: Glydendalske Boghandel, 1924), 14–15. See also A. Thornton, *The Imperial Idea and Its Enemies: A Study in British Power* (London: Macmillan, 1959) for a discussion of the debate between ideologies of empire in the late nineteenth century. For an interesting approach to the critiques of empire in the nineteenth century see Miles Taylor's '*Imperium et Libertas?* Rethinking the Radical Critique of Imperialism in the Nineteenth Century', *Journal of Imperial and Commonwealth History* (1987), 1–18.

of 'jingoism' in Britain at the end of the nineteenth century, saw empire as a pure reflection of martial values. This tradition, which shared in the common European heritage of conservative and authoritarian thinkers, was the principal source for the martial spirit in Britain. The martialist *Zeitgeist* informed both the norms of the age, and the practices and policies of the architects, builders, and managers of empire—the army, as well as some of the ministers and civil servants within the Colonial and War Offices, right up to (and after) the Geneva Diplomatic Conference of 1949. Both these schools of thought on empire shared the common assumption that liberal political principles and practices were a central part of the British domestic infrastructure, but this system could not (and should not) be extended to the colonial possessions. This was a singularly British conception of the period commonly known as *imperium et libertas*.[104] Yet the two schools differed radically, and argued bitterly, about the nature of the ideological underpinnings of empire. For example, Seeley, an almost universally acknowledged martialist, described the political divisions thus: 'There are two schools of opinion among us with respect of our Empire . . . The one is lost in wonder and ecstasy at its immense dimensions, and at the energy and heroism which presumably have gone to the making of it; this school therefore advocates the maintenance of it as a point of honour or sentiment. The other is in the opposite extreme, regards it as founded in aggression and rapacity, as useless and burdensome, a kind of excrescence upon England.'[105] Additionally, the second school of martial imperialists gave form to the thesis that two distinct sets of ideologies could operate within a single paradigm and political culture; hence illustrating the ability of a liberal democracy to accommodate the ideology and values of martialism.

While noting the existence of such ideological dualism at the time, general histories of the period have tended to emphasize the more rational interpretation of imperialism advanced by the liberal school at the height of Empire—a school which was itself busy minimizing the value and importance of the contending martial school of thought, as one historian noted: 'historians perceived the problem of multiple

[104] Hugh Cunningham traces three distinct strands of political thinking within the 'Jingoists', of which the conservatives are only one. See his 'Jingoism in 1877–8', *Victorian Studies*, 14 (1971), 453. See B. Holland's comprehensive survey of the concept in *Imperium et Libertas: A Study in History and Politics* (London: Edward Arnold, 1901); also R. Faber's *The Vision and the Need: Late Victorian Imperialist Aims* (London: Faber & Faber, 1966), especially 117–20 on the ideological roots of reconciling *imperium* and *libertas*.

[105] Cited in Peter Burroughs, 'John Robert Seeley and British Imperial History', *Journal of Imperial and Commonwealth History*, 1 (1973), 208.

approaches that seemed to fragment the historiography of imperialism, but the upshot of their work remains a delineation of imperialism as a more or less practical, realistic, rational response to either strategic or political exigencies by men of (or co-opted to) the British ruling order.'[106] This has had the effect of minimizing a vibrant and authentic martial tradition with consistent patterns of thought on war from the nineteenth to mid-twentieth century. The remainder of this chapter will illustrate the commonalities between British martialism, which operated within a liberal democracy (although overseas), and the broader tradition of martialism outlined in the earlier parts of this chapter.

THE MARTIAL TRADITION AND ITS DEVELOPMENT WITHIN A LIBERAL DEMOCRACY

As it developed in Britain between 1874 and 1949, the martial tradition of war was a clear emanation of nineteenth-century European martialism. At the same time, it had a number of attributes which made it distinctive. In order to understand exactly how this tradition developed—internally, in both its core and peripheral values, and externally, in the way the tradition adapted itself to the prevailing norms and values of that era—this section will explore the interaction between two elements: how martialism functioned within a liberal democracy, and how its political thought developed in relation to empire. This will be undertaken by examining some of the features of the characteristics and work of the main agents and bearers of the tradition. Their personalities and style, language and rhetoric, and, above all, their political ideology will be traced in relation to the more general martialist doctrine extant in nineteenth-century Europe, showing the similarities between the martialist paradigm of empire and the broader martial tradition.

As noted above, traditional analysis of the purposes of empire focused on the pragmatic policies and the decision-making of the 'reluctant imperialists' of Whitehall. Yet the martial tradition was the ideology of an army, not of the bureaucracy in London. In his seminal article 'The Turbulent Frontier as a Factor in British Imperialism', John Galbraith pointed out that the most neglected factor behind the British

---

[106] H. Field, *Toward a Programme of Imperial Life: The British Empire at the Turn of the Century* (Westport, Conn: Greenwood Press, 1982), 15; see also P. Rich's fascinating account *Race and Empire in British Politics* (Cambridge: Cambridge University Press, 1990), especially at 54–5; and J. Kendle, *The Round Table Movement and the Imperial Union* (Toronto: Toronto University Press, 1975).

Empire was the fact that it tended to expand as a result of the policies on the ground, rather than in Whitehall. Even when ministers carried more liberal, and less interventionist political views, it was events just beyond the Empire's borders that continually drew the army outward, towards expansion and then annexation. 'In India, Malaya, and South Africa, governors, charged with the maintenance of order, could not ignore disorder beyond their borders, and turbulence, which pulled them toward expansion.' Galbraith points out that local administrators and armies on the ground were often responsible for the Empire's growth, making sense of the notion that it 'grew in spite of itself', or in Seeley's terms, that it was created in a 'fit of absence of mind'.[107]

Thus, as martialism in Britain was centred in the colonial army, it becomes evident how its representatives, who implemented the idea of empire, were highly inarticulate about their ethos and principles, never seeing themselves as thinkers or ideologues. The new 'imperial administrators', notably those assuming position and influence, rather saw themselves as 'men of action more than of contemplation'. Accordingly, their memoirs often consisted of picaresque and highly personalized anecdotes of skirmishes, long lists of battle sites in far-flung places, and amusing sketches of the peoples they conquered. Likewise, one of the core features of the martial spirit of the age was a reactionary loathing of thought and intellectualism, and the celebration of a certain animal-like dumbness. The colonial adventurer was thus someone who 'explored the world, not himself'. The 'epitome of the English', Carlyle had insisted, was not the spoken word or the written poem, but 'the done work'. He emphasized that 'what mattered in Empire, that escape from words and theory, from the cant of both religious and secular speculation, was a "cloudy-browed, Thick-soled, opaque Practicality", that which "transcends all logical utterances: a Congruity with the Unuttered" '.[108] Yet, as MacKenzie, a historian of colonialism, noted, the army had a clear ideology underpinning their policies:

the officer class saw itself as maintaining aristocratic traditions of war, power, and rule. They maintained romantic attachments to indigenous aristocracies and martial races, and often saw their role as the recreation of feudal relations in an imperial context . . . The imperial officer's conceptions of hierarchies, personal devotion, and relationship with servants and followers, together with his

---

[107] 'The Turbulent Frontier as a Factor in British Imperialism', *Comparative Studies in Society and History*, 2 (1960), 168. For the context of Seeley's remark see Deborah Wormell, *Sir John Seeley and the Uses of History* (Cambridge: Cambridge University Press, 1979), ch. 6.
[108] Betts, 'The Allusion to Rome', 152; Grainger, *Patriotisms*, 129.

loathing of dangerous professionals, educated elements among the indigenous population and visiting politicians were firmly rooted in this social conservatism.[109]

Even outside the world of the military, where in other European countries the educated classes were producing book after book on the subject, in Britain these same classes were largely defined by their silence, and this silence seemed to have been the result of a particular training: 'the public school was, as it has remained, one of the most powerful institutions in the kingdom. From it, and from the universities of Oxford and Cambridge that it nourished, were to emerge into public life a solid body of "pass-men", intrinsic Tories, uneasy with theory, unhappy with ideas, pillars of society.'[110] The select few who gave definition to the general spirit of British martialism, and a more substantive form to this 'unspoken code', were, in the main, individuals from the world of arts and letters. Literature in the form of Dilke's travelogues, Kipling's adventures and poems, the stirring accounts in the *Pall Mall Gazette*, *Blackwoods*, and the *Daily Mail* of the ardent imperialist Steevens, represented aspects of the more popular interpretations of martialism at home and abroad.[111] In particular, these journalists abroad saw their mission as articulating and translating the army's core ideology to the British public. At the same time, the history chairs at the universities of Oxford, Cambridge, and London were (somewhat more seriously) shaping the core values of the political ideology, constructing a suitable history for the tradition, and inviting the likes of Thomas Arnold and Charles Kingsley to give lectures to help 'forge' the thinking of the new generation (Thomas Arnold's inaugural lecture at Oxford in 1841 celebrated the vastly superior Germanic roots of the English nation, 'Our English race is the German race').[112]

By far the most renowned of these writers was Thomas Carlyle (1795–1881). Produced before the great swell of empire and martialism,

---

[109] *Popular Imperialism*, 12.

[110] Thornton, *The Habit of Authority* (London: Allen & Unwin, 1966), 241.

[111] On this subject, see J. MacKenzie's *Propaganda and Empire: The Manipulations of British Public Opinion 1880–1960* (Manchester: Manchester University Press, 1984). On literature, see Colin Graham's recent *Ideologies of Empire: Nation, Empire, and Victorian Epic Poetry* (Manchester: Manchester University Press, 1998); R. Jeffrey (ed.) *Imperialism and Juvenile Literature* (Manchester: Manchester University Press, 1989).

[112] A. Stanley, *The Life and Correspondence of Thomas Arnold* (London: Minerva, 1881), ii. 324. Charles Kingsley also took the same tack at Cambridge: 'The welfare of the Teutonic race is the welfare of the world'. *The Roman and the Teuton: A Series of Lectures Delivered before the University of Cambridge* (London: Macmillan, 1864), 305–6.

his work directly inspired the subsequent life and thought of two of the most prolific British martialists of the late nineteenth century, Froude and Kingsley—an inspiration which continued relentlessly down the generations to other figures who drew sustenance from his martial philosophy.[113] Carlyle himself was deeply influenced by German thought; his main influences were said to be Herder, Fichte, Goethe, Von Schlegel, and Novalis. The historian Harrold noted: 'he was imbued with a sense not only of the power of the individual hero, but also of the power of the individual race—the Teutonic. He saw in the vigour of that race a transforming power in the world.'[114] And his obsession with Goethe developed subsequently into an obsession for war. As one of his great admirers (and self-styled disciples), Professor Cramb explained:

The shaping thought of his work, tyrannous and all-pervading, is that of the might, the majesty, and the mystery of war. One flame picture after another sets this principle forth . . . To Carlyle, nineteen centuries after Christ, as to Thucydides, four centuries before Christ, war is the supreme expression of the energy of a State as such, the supreme, the tragic hour, in the life-history of the city, the nation, as such. To Carlyle war is therefore neither religious nor inhuman, but the evidence in the life of a State of a self-consecration to an ideal end; it is that manifestation of a world spirit of which I have spoken above—a race, a nation, an empire, conscious of its destiny . . . It was a profounder vision, a wider outlook, not a harder heart, which made Carlyle apparently blind to that side of war which alone rivets the attention of Tolstoi.[115]

Unlike Cramb's interpretation (and, indeed, Cramb's own views), Carlyle's brand of martialism, in particular his right-equals-might philosophy, did not directly relate to his concept of empire. This was due to various factors, not least his particular preferences for colonial expansion. According to one historian: 'the reason why the right-might theory and the abstract justification of conquest, in short the attempt to establish a special set of ethics for the use of Imperialism, plays a small part in Carlyle's theories of colonial policy is the fact that the obvious fields for the systematic colonisation recommended by Carlyle were Canada and Australia, empty countries in which there was practically no native population whose suppression had to be

---

[113] *Frederick* was Adolf Hitler's favourite book, and he had Goebbels read it to him in his last days in the bunker. J. Rosenberg, *Carlyle and the Burden of History* (Oxford: Clarendon Press, 1985), 117.

[114] C. Harrold, *Carlyle and German Thought: 1819–1834* (London: Yale University Press, 1934), 63.

[115] J. A. Cramb, *Origins and Destiny of Imperial Britain* (London: John Murray, 1915), 126–7.

justified.'[116] Carlyle's complex and dark work cannot be reduced to a martial mould.[117] However, his singular cast of mind, the prolific nature of his work and such phrases as: 'Might and Right do differ frightfully from hour to hour; but give them centuries to try it in, they are found to be identical', and 'man is created to fight; he is best of all definable as a born soldier, his life "a battle and a march"', made his writings a goldmine for subsequent generations of imperialists (and German fascists).[118]

Another important figure was the Scottish professor John Adam Cramb (1862–1913). His romantic ravings on war, blood, and the Roman Empire in particular gave his position as History Professor at London University a particular potency.[119] Furthermore, whilst occupying that post he also remained committed to his lectures on military history at the Staff College in Camberley, at York, at Chatham, and at other military and colonial centres. There, young officers were anxiously awaiting elucidation as to their moral purpose before being sent off to some far-flung corner of the Empire to represent England, empire, and the martial spirit. Cramb sought to carve out a history for the British martial tradition by stressing its similarity with the Roman Empire. In this he was aided by the Cambridge professor Sir John Seeley (1834–95), author of *Expansion of England*, whose work on Livy helped shape his thoughts, and by the emphasis on Roman studies at Oxford during the last quarter of the nineteenth century, which also influenced the likes of Cecil Rhodes. Rhodes, in fact, developed an obsession with his 'facial resemblance to certain Roman emperors'; his favourite expression was 'Remember always that you are a Roman' (*sic*).[120] Indeed, it appears that many of the dons and students at Oxford sought to create elites which would rule the world. The strongest cabal appeared to develop at Balliol, headed by George Parkin, a 'mature student'.[121]

The switch from the study of ancient Greece to the Roman Empire was heavily influenced by the core values of these academics who

[116] Bodelson, *Studies in Mid-Victorian Imperialism*, 32. Obviously the indigenous peoples of Canada and Australia would diverge from this view of their land as 'empty'. However, the point remains that Carlyle believed that they were so.

[117] See, for example, Arendt, *The Origins of Totalitarianism*, 105.

[118] T. Carlyle, *Chartism* (London: Everyman's Library, 1839), 210; id., *Past and Present* (London: Chapman & Hall, 1843), 163–4.

[119] For the cast of martialists who held positions of power and influence in Victorian England, see J. Bruce-Glasier, *Le Militarisme anglais* (Brussels: Norz, 1916).

[120] J. Lockhart, *Rhodes* (London: Hodder & Stoughton, 1963), 31.

[121] M. Girouard, *The Return to Camelot: Chivalry and the English Gentleman* (New Haven: Yale University Press, 1981), 223.

(mirroring Machiavelli), plundered the image of the ancient Roman Empire for its martialist underpinnings. Seeley put forward the reason for this substitution frankly: 'There was a time, no doubt, when the Roman Empire, because it was despotic and in some periods unhappy and half-barbarous, was thought uninteresting . . . but there are many other good things in politics besides liberty.'[122] Also important was the *Journal of Roman Studies*, launched by the Society for the Promotion of Roman Studies in London in 1911. Seeley saw the role of historians as 'formulators of public opinion'. Those claiming to be directly influenced by him, such as Sir Charles Lucas, Hugh Edward Egerton, and Arthur Newton went on to found the 'Imperial Studies Group' with other members of the Royal Colonial Institute in order to carry forward what they saw as the great task of educating the working class to a love and loyalty of empire. To Seeley's notion of expansion they added their own conceptions of 'organic evolution, inbred racial instinct, providential design and optimistic fatalism'.[123] This martialist view did not go entirely unchallenged in academia, however. An organized assault to this approach was made by the 'Round Table' in order to wrest the political ideology of empire away from martial thought. This was done by the introduction of ancient Greece as the political source for the British tradition of empire rather than Rome. This counter-attack was launched by Professor Alfred Zimmern, a classics scholar at Oxford, who encouraged an enthusiasm for Greek civilization which would 'represent a reaction away from the more authoritarian model of imperial Rome so favoured by late nineteenth century British imperial enthusiasts'.[124]

Other martialist academics included the professor of archaeology and classics at Cambridge, W. Ridgeway, and the first Chichele Professor of Military History at Oxford, Spenser Wilkinson (in his inaugural lecture, he declared his hero to be the architect of the Prussian invasion of France in 1870, Count Moltke, ranking him greater than Napoleon). As a more recent Chichele Professor remarked 'the occupants of the Chichele Chair of the History of War at Oxford were men of very diverse if equally distinguished qualities, but all shared a common perception of their duties of a kind unusual in academics. To a greater or

---

[122] J. Seeley, *The Expansion of England: Two Courses of Lectures* (London: Macmillan, 1883), 274–5.

[123] J. G. Greenlee, '"A Succession of Seeleys": The "Old School" Re-examined', *Journal of Imperial History*, 4/3 (1965), 280.

[124] Thornton, *The Imperial Idea*, 60–3. For Zimmern's distinction between Prussian and British cultures see his 'Germany', in R. W. Seton-Watson, *The War and Democracy* (London: Macmillan, 1915), in particular his introduction to the book, 10–12, and his section on Prussia, 75–120.

lesser degree they all saw the teaching of their subject as a means of serving the State. For Spenser Wilkinson, this was the purpose of the University as a whole.'[125]

The third example of a powerful promoter of martialist ideology was George Steevens, 'the Balliol Prodigy' (1888–92), whose career was symbolic of an emerging generation who crossed into the field of 'popular journalism' from more elitist backgrounds. He was one of 'a little army of Oxford men' who 'in the last 15 years invaded the realm of London journalism'. Along with his mentor William Henley (whom Chesterton described as a 'clever and unhappy man who lived in admiration of a vague violence'), he belonged to the 'Counter-Decadent' set.[126] They all, but in particular Steevens, took seriously the role of ideology in empire: 'What Mr. Kipling has done for fiction, Mr. Steevens did for fact. He was a priest of the Imperialist Idea, and the glory of the Empire was always uppermost in his writings.'[127] Steevens was highly influential with both the politicians of the day, and, more importantly, the public. As he was fond of boasting, the amount devoted to 'imperial topics' in his *Daily Mail* column was twice that of any other London daily. Kitchener called Steevens a 'genius, with a real insight into military affairs'.[128]

There was a crucial reason for his success and that of others like him. This group of men—none of them in himself an extraordinary talent—all flourished because they managed to ride the crest of what was an immensely powerful wave of popular sentiment which supported, indeed embraced, the martialist notion of empire. This existing culture was reflected in the work of the pamphleteers, in theatre performances, and the music halls of Victorian Britain. The historian Spiers described one of the most prominent popular organizations: 'The Tory based Prim-

[125] S. Wilkinson, *The University and the Study of War* (Oxford: Clarendon, 1909), 26; M. Howard, *War and the Nation State: An Inaugural Lecture Delivered before the University of Oxford on 18 November 1977* (Oxford: Clarendon, 1978).

[126] R. Stearn, 'G. W. Steevens and the Message of Empire', *Journal of Imperial and Commonwealth History,* 17 (1989), 212; Field, *Toward a Programme of Imperial Life*, 133. See Buckley's revealing (but sympathetic) biography of an extraordinary martialist: *William Ernest Henley: A Study of the 'Counter-Decadence' of the 'Nineties* (Princeton: Princeton University Press, 1945).

[127] V. Blackburn, 'The Last Chapter', in G. Steevens, *From Capetown to Ladysmith* (London: W. Blackwood & Sons, 1900), 176.

[128] Field, *Toward a Programme of Imperial Life*, 80; cited in Stearn, 'G. W. Steevens', 225. Stearn also noted that Kitchener privately admitted plagiarizing Steevens's work for his own dispatches, drawing from the popular, but rather rushed, martialist books: *With the Conquering Turk: Confessions of a Bashi-bazouk* (London: W. Blackwood & Sons, 1897); *Egypt in 1898* (Edinburgh: W. Blackwood & Sons, 1898), and the most famous *With Kitchener to Khartum* (Edinburgh: W. Blackwood & Sons, 1899).

rose League, claiming a membership of one million by 1890, was one of the more active bodies. By its lectures, pamphlets, exhibitions, magic lantern displays, and children's fiction, it generated an emotional enthusiasm for Empire.'[129] The effect that journalists such as Forbes, Villiers, and Steevens had on moulding the 'new imperial' spirit is important. Although one writer on Steevens said that 'Steevens and his writings were exceptionally eulogised by journalists, soldiers, defence publicists, navalists and imperialists, in private correspondence, reviews, obituaries, and memoirs', he noted that 'this praise all came from men who shared common political ground with Steevens'.[130] Yet it was not only political friends that believed in Steeven's influence—his critics, too, claimed the significance of his work on the political culture of Britain. Contemporary writers like Hobson, advancing a critique on the 'new imperialism' of the day, wrote: 'a biased, enslaved and poisonous press has been the chief engine for manufacturing Jingoism'.[131]They were certainly more influential than the academic imperialists. As Munro Smith noted, 'popularizers do more than "solid" writers to mould opinion'.[132] These journalists did not as much shape as capture the martialist ideology which already existed in Britain at the time, but, even more important for the martial tradition, they acted as the mouthpiece for the values of the Colonial Army. For the martial tradition also developed out of the practices of conquest and rule, as well as the ideological justification for it at home. Although their ideological 'code' remained largely unexpressed, the soldiers of empire relied upon the newly emerged 'war correspondents' to transmit martial values back to the British public; an obligation they took to heart, and discharged brilliantly. Correspondents became part of the army whilst 'covering' events. For example, 'they assumed officers' role in battle', were made honorary members of the officers' mess, enjoyed quasi-officer status, and were even asked to 'take command of some of the men by the senior officers on the spot'. More importantly, they 'shared officers implicit Social Darwinism and proudly ethno-centric imperial and racial beliefs, assuming "Anglo-Saxon" superiority and an ethnic hierarchy which was partly moral and martial'.[133] Their main creative

---

[129] J. Spiers, *The Late Victorian Army* (Manchester: Manchester University Press, 1992), 186.

[130] R. Stearn, 'G. W. Steevens', 212, 224.

[131] J. A. Hobson, *The Psychology of Jingoism* (London: MacMillan, 1901)

[132] *Militarism and Statecraft*, 221–2.

[133] R. Stearn, 'War Correspondents and Colonial War, c.1870–1900', in John M. MacKenzie (ed.), *Popular Imperialism and the Military: 1850–1950* (Manchester: Manchester University Press, 1992), 145, 147, 149.

contribution, perhaps, lay in founding the myth of the heroic soldier who symbolized the core values of a martial tradition already flourishing in Britain.[134]

THE DEVELOPMENT OF
THE MARTIAL TRADITION IN BRITAIN

As was noted earlier, the main characteristics of man's nature in the martial tradition were the celebration of the natural over the artificial, aggressiveness and restlessness, and a pagan, animal-like spiritual (rather than rational) energy as man's main driving agency. There are many examples of the celebration of the natural over the artificial, from Burke through to Carlyle and, as endlessly popularized by Steevens, natural man *was* the Englishman. 'Perhaps to Englishmen—half savage still on the pinnacle of their civilisation—the very charm of the land lies in its barbarism . . . there is life to defend, and death to face . . . You are unprejudiced, simple, free. You are a naked man, facing naked nature.' So for Steevens, the discovery of essential man was achieved through the revelatory experience of war: 'one day you start thinking and suddenly you see that sometime, somehow—you don't know when or how—you have really become a man . . . the sum of it was that everything artificial, conventional, social, had vanished, and you were left with base, natural man.'[135] As mentioned earlier, Steevens was part of the 'Counter-Decadence Movement', which H. G. Wells described as the return to the essential: 'a change is sweeping over the minds of thousands of educated men. It is a discovery of the insufficiency of the cultivated life and its necessary insincerities; it is a return to the essential, to honourable struggle as the epic factor of life.'[136] For some martialists with a Darwinist tinge, the Englishman's natural restlessness made him an obvious choice for the conquest of the world. Kidd identified this trait as responsible for the successful conquest and control of India by the English:

The love of action, the insatiable desire for strenuous energetic labour is everywhere characteristic of the peoples who have come to occupy the foremost

---

[134] J. MacKenzie, 'Heroic Myths of Empire', ibid. 126. The recognized patron of this type of symbolism and myth-making was Carlyle's *Hero Worship* (London: Chapman, 1842).

[135] *With Kitchener to Khartum*, 325–6; *With the Conquering Turk*, 310–11.

[136] B. Bergonzi, *The Early Life of H. G. Wells* (Manchester: Manchester University Press, 1961), 138.

places of the world . . . A certain restless energy, an always unsatisfied ambition to go forward, is one of the most pronounced aspects of the individual and racial characteristics of the winning sections of the human family.[137]

Other European Darwinists agree. There is an intriguing work by the French Darwinist, Edmond Demolins, whose book had a tremendous success (for reasons that will rapidly become obvious) when it was translated from the French and published in London in 1898. Rather poignantly titled *A quoi tient la supériorité des Anglo-Saxons?*, he faulted his compatriots for their over-indulgence in Cartesianism: 'We are inclined to dabble in general ideas, *they* are disposed to practical applications.'[138] Besides a similarity with Social Darwinist thought on the Continent, there were other direct parallels. As with earlier sources of martial thought used by nineteenth-century European thinkers, religious ritual in Britain had a strong paganist and folkloric element. Kingsley, a renowned advocate of empire, declared the official national religion as essentially martial in nature: 'I say that the Church of England is wonderfully and mysteriously fitted for the souls of a free Norse-Saxon race, for men whose ancestors fought at the side of Odin, over whom a descendant of Odin now rules.' Cramb continually referred to Saxon, Norse, and even Arthurian legends in his praise of warrior-cult religions, and Seeley too noted the public importance of religion for the construction and maintenance of a political ideology of martialism: 'the province of religion . . . is much more national and political, much less personal, than is commonly supposed'.[139]

In the martial view of government, it will be remembered, there was a strong emphasis on the hierarchical nature of society, the importance of leadership, the central role of the army in support of the emperor or monarch, and a highly personalized vision of the state. In addition, British martialists emphasized the hierarchical nature of races; making it the intellectual underpinning for both the distinction between the British and imperial types of governments, and for the treatment of any indigenous inhabitants foolish enough to reject British rule. In the novel

[137] *Social Evolution* (London: Macmillan, 1894), 57–8, 278–88. Semmel described him as a 'non-Spencerian Social Darwinist'. See Semmel's *Imperialism and Social Reform: English Social Imperial Thought 1895–1914* (London: G. B. Allen & Unwin, 1960); especially 'Social Darwinism: Benjamin Kidd and Karl Pearson', 18–42.
[138] E. Demolins, *A quoi tient la supériorité des Anglo-Saxons?* (Firmin-Didot, Paris, 1897); *Anglo Saxon Superiority: To What is it Due?* (London: Leadenhall Press, 1898), 153.
[139] *Charles Kingsley: His Letters and Memories of his Life*, ed. F. Kingsley (London: C. K. Paul, 1877), i. 253; Cramb, *Origins and Destiny of Imperial Britain*, *passim*; id., *National Religion* (London: Macmillan, 1882), 195.

Tancred, Disraeli declares: 'A Saxon Race, protected by an insular position, has stamped its diligent and methodic character on the century. And when a superior race, with a superior idea to work and order, advances, its state will be progressive . . . All is race; there is no other truth.'[140] And Froude, for example, argued that in the West Indies 'in many instances, perhaps in most, the slave trade was innocent and even beneficial', that the loss of slave status was bitterly regretted by the 'negroes', and declared that England must rule the West Indies despotically or 'accept negro supremacy' (which, he added, would be 'nothing less than a public disgrace').[141] As Rhodes rather famously said: 'we happen to be the best people in the world, with the highest ideals of decency and justice and liberty and peace, and the more of the world we inhabit, the better it is for humanity'. Cramb assumed this superiority had to be linked with political infrastructure: 'the imperialistic is the supreme form in the political development of the national as of the civic State, and that to the empires of the world belongs the government of the world in the future . . .'.[142]

However, although a liberal democracy was acceptable to many martialists at home, for most it was not their preferred system of government. At the height of empire many saw the Liberal government as the real enemy. Kipling believed that 'the only serious enemy to the Empire, within or without, is the very Democracy which depends upon Empire for its proper comforts', and he was vitriolic about the nature of Liberals: 'I don't suppose you could prevent a Liberal from lying any more than you could stop a little dog from lifting up his leg against a lamp post.'[143] For the influential Henley, if it had to be a democracy, it could only be one type of party that ran it: no other political doctrine went so well with imperialism as conservatism: 'Toryism, as I conceive it, is as much a matter of taste as a body of doctrine, and is as much a mental attitude as a set of principles . . . Toryism, to be plain, is in some sort a matter of aversions.'[144] But for many espousing martial values, the development of democracy was infecting the purity of empire. Steevens's

---

[140] B. Disraeli, *Tancred, Or the New Crusade* (London: Longmans Green, 1847), 34.

[141] J. A. Froude, *The English in the West Indies* (London: Longmans, 1888), 207, 196, 293.

[142] Eby, *The Road to Armageddon*, 150. Cramb, *Origins and Destiny of Imperial Britain*, 112.

[143] E. Birkenhead, *Rudyard Kipling* (London: Weidenfeld & Nicolson, 1978), 256. Birkenhead adds, concerning Kipling's reaction to the Liberals' gaining power: 'Kipling threw himself with almost despairing ardour into any cause likely to promote national virility or military preparedness', 256–7.

[144] *National Review*, 21 (1893), 268.

writings were thus not restricted to explaining and championing British rule: his philosophy of empire had implications for domestic politics as well. In 'The New Humanitarianism' the first of two seminal articles, he argued that the British people had become too soft, obsessed with the avoidance of suffering, believing that death and pain were the worst evils that could befall man. He cited the general concern with the well-being of cripples and incubator babies, and the opposition to hunting, as examples of this degenerate trend. He asserted that such faddish behaviour was 'throttling [the] patriotism and common-sense and virility of individual character . . . we became and are an Imperial race by dealing necessary pain to other men'. His article 'The New Gibbon', about the end of nineteenth-century Britain, was full of ominous descriptions of 'the latent causes of decay and corruption' in the country, and contained dire warnings about its future. Similarly, Froude argued for the regeneration of the English through vast expanses of green of the Empire, away from the 'fetid smell from the ill-made sewers'.[145] Yet other martialists were able to maintain a double standard of political enfranchisement for themselves, and complete servitude for the peoples in their dominions quite naturally and logically through racial ideology. Horsman argues that this belief in superiority began as 'long held beliefs in the superiority of early Anglo-Saxon political institutions which became a belief in the innate superiority of the Anglo-Saxon branch of the Caucasian race . . . [and] in a more general sense involved the whole surging Romantic interest in uniqueness, in language, and in national and racial origins. Both directly from Germany and by transmission through England.'[146]

In nineteenth-century European martial ideology, a core principle was the recognition of war's supreme value to man and society and this aspect was crucial to British imperialists as well. For Cramb, the purpose of war was all at the same time moral and historical, organic and sublime:

War, therefore, I would define as a phase in the life effort of the State toward completer self-realization, a phase in the eternal *nisus*, the perpetual omnipresent strife of all being towards self-fulfilment. Destruction is not its aim, but the intensification of the life, whether of the conquering or of the

[145] 'The New Humanitarianism' (1898) and 'The New Gibbon' (1899), in Field, *Toward a Programme of Imperial Life*, 187; J. A. Froude, *Oceana or England and her Colonies* (London: Longman, Green & Co. , 1886), 8. In Britain, during Steevens's era, the term patriotism held exclusively martialist connotations in socialist circles. H. Cunningham, 'The Language of Patriotism', *History Workshop Journal*, 12 (1981), 27.
[146] *Race and Manifest Destiny* (London: Harvard University Press, 1981), 9.

conquered State. War is thus a manifestation of the world-spirit in the form the most sublime and awful that can enthral the contemplation of man. It is an action radiating from the same sources as the heroisms, the essential agonies . . . conflicts, of all life . . . Thus the great part which war has played in human history, in art, in poetry, is not, as Rousseau maintains, an arraignment of the human heart, not necessarily the blazon of human depravity, but a testimony to man's limitless capacity for devotion to other ends than existence for existence' sake—his pursuit of an ideal, perpetually.

He was equally scathing about those who argued the practical ends of empire: 'The wide acceptance of the territorial theory of the origin of war as an explanation of war, and the enumeration by historians of causes and results in territory or taxation, can be ascribed only to that indolence of the human mind, the subtle inertia, which, as Tacitus affirms, lies in wait to mar all high endeavour.'[147] For Colonel Maude, a strong leader was needed to inspire individuals to die for glory:

Given a Leader who, conscious of the power latent in the Race and the means by which to develop it, applies all the means which science has now rendered available to the definite end of teaching men 'to know how to die'—not how to avoid dying—and we shall soon find men ready as ever were their ancestors to clamour for the right of rushing to what will appear to them to be certain death, when they know that thereby they will attain a great end.[148]

The glorification of violence was also expounded by the founder of the Anti-Decadent movement in Britain. In his *Sword Song* of 1892, dedicated to Carlyle, Henley wrote of the sword in mythical terms:

The War Thing, the Comrade, Father of Honour, And giver of kingship, The Fame-smith the songmaster . . . Ho! Then the sound, Of my voice, the implacable Angel of Destiny!—I am the Sword. Sifting the nations, The slag from the metal, The waste from the weak, From the fit and the strong, Fighting the Brute, the abysmal Fecundity, Clear singing, slicing, Making death beautiful, Archanarch, chief builder.[149]

Although he was both extremely anti-Prussian and anti-German, the unmistakable congruity of this work with the Prussian Körner's *Sword Song* is remarkable: 'I do indeed clank in the scabbard; I long for the strife, right wild and battle-joyous . . . Oh fair garden of love, full of little blood-red roses and blossomed death. Hurrah!'[150] War and conquest, for

[147] *Origins and Destiny of Imperial Britain*, 120–3, 116.
[148] Francis Maude, *War and the World's Life* (London: Kegan Paul, 1907), ii. 252.
[149] Buckley, *William Ernest Henley*, 138–9.
[150] Cited in R. Butler, *The Roots of National Socialism 1783–1933* (London: Faber & Faber, 1968), 53.

the British martialists, were principles that were inexorably wedded to each other. They were, for Carlyle, the natural inheritance of the English race, and indeed a holy 'task'.[151] For some, this 'task' of conquest was held to be by the race, for the race. For example, Steevens described the natives of imperial possessions as morally depraved. Of Omdurman he wrote: 'the whole city was a huge harem . . . a monstrosity of African lust . . . And foul. They dropped their dung where they listed.' Such conditions vindicated British rule: 'its abominations steamed up to heaven to justify us of our conquest'.[152] By others, it was seen to be the nation's task, in the interests of that nation, as Michael Howard noted, for Seeley, the British Empire was not made up, as past Empires had been, of the 'rule of a metropolis over alien peoples abroad'. Instead the current British Empire was the British nation itself, 'which had grown slowly and inexorably according to its own laws and was now spread all over the world; and which needed a new self-consciousness in order to realise the full potential of its greatness'.[153] Harold Fraser, the secretary of the Imperial Maritime League was fixated upon this noble task:

Has not a nation, like an individual, a certain appointed task which, beyond other nations, it is fitted to perform? Wilfully to neglect this ordained labour is, so to speak, an unforgivable sin, because it is to defeat the purpose of the Universe as shown in the aptitudes which have been produced by the previous course of things. To sustain worthily the burden of empire is the task manifestly appointed to Britain, and therefore to fulfil that task her duty, as it should also be her delight.[154]

The most famous of imperial Darwinists and avowed socialists Professor Pearson, endorsed 'racial and global violence as the outcome of cosmic laws'.[155] He also wedded the nation to war as a symbol of the most natural and inevitable of unions: 'a nation [is] kept up to a high pitch of external efficiency by contest, chiefly by way of war with inferior races'.[156] Finally, it was seen that in the martial tradition the definition of liberty was simply the freedom to find one's place within a hierarchical society. As Froude saw it, this extended to the freedom granted to oppress others—the conquered found their freedom here, too:

[151] *Chartism*, 214.   [152] Stearn, 'War Correspondents and Colonial War', 150.
[153] 'Empire, Race, and War', 341.
[154] H. Fraser, 'Ethics of Empire (1897)', in M. Goodwin (ed.), *Nineteenth Century Opinion* (London: Harmondsworth, 1951), 268.
[155] Paul Crook, *Darwinism, War and History: The Debate over the Biology of War from the Origin of the Species to the First World War* (Cambridge: Cambridge University Press, 1994), 29.
[156] K. Pearson, *National Life from the Standpoint of Science* (London: Walter Scott, 1892), 5.

A natural right to liberty irrespective of the ability to defend it, exists in nations as much as and no more than it exists in individuals . . . Among reasonable beings right is for ever tending to create might . . . The better sort of men submit willingly to be governed by those who are nobler and wiser than themselves . . . and the rights of man—if such rights there be—are not to liberty, but to wise direction and control . . . As a broad principle it may be said, that as nature has so constituted us that we must be ruled in some way, and as at any given time the rule inevitable will be in the hands of those who are then the strongest, so nature has allotted superiority of strength to superiority of intellect and character; and in deciding that the weaker shall obey the more powerful, she is in reality saving them from themselves, and then confers true liberty when she seems most to be taking it.[157]

This quotation from Froude suggests there was little to distinguish this form of thought from German and Italian fascists in the 1920s and 1930s. However, Michael Howard argues otherwise: 'One can by a selective quotation from a very narrow range of writers present an alarming picture of pre-1914 Britain as a proto-Fascist society, but in fact it was nothing of the kind. The ideas expressed by such writers as Maude existed generally in very mild solution,' and he believes that this 'pride in Empire, the belief in the superiority of Anglo-Saxon culture, the consciousness of military achievement in the past and the determination if necessary to parallel it in the future, all this was there, but without the rancour and fanaticism; still underpinned by a strong Christian ethic and leavened by values of Victorian liberalism'.[158] From the demonstration that an ideology such as martialism could flourish *within* a liberal democracy, it does not follow that Britain was a 'proto-Fascist society'. However, the purpose here has not been to demonstrate the existence of pre-fascist thinking in nineteenth-century Britain, but rather to illustrate the very wide range of writing and popular thinking which gave form to the ideology of the 'martial tradition', which may go some way towards explaining the British ideological position at the Geneva Conference in 1949.

CONCLUSION

This chapter had three objectives: to establish a clear contrast between the broad doctrine of realism and a distinct tradition on war, which has

---

[157] J. Froude, *The English in Ireland in the Eighteenth Century* (London: Longman, Green & Co. , 1872), i. 1–2, 5–6.
[158] Howard, 'Empire, Race and War', 353.

been called martialism; to define the main components of the martial tradition of war; and finally to argue that this tradition cannot be reduced to the deranged outpourings of a few Prussian cranks who provided bedtime reading for the intellectuals of the Third Reich, but instead was a broad and influential ideology with deep roots in the political culture of modern Europe. The evidence for this claim has come from the depiction of the British martial tradition, which has been seen to share most of the essential characteristics of the wider body of martial doctrines.[159] This tradition served as the political philosophy of armies of invasion and occupation, and informed military thinking in relation to the legal separation between lawful and unlawful combatants up to and including the 1949 Geneva Conference.

To summarize the findings as regards the first question, it has been seen that realism and martialism differed significantly in their views of the world. What the realist tradition accepted as facts to be wrestled with as effectively as possible, the martialist paradigm glorified as the supreme values of existence. Realists saw struggle as inherent in human relations, but needing to be subordinated to the higher purposes of civil peace and personal security. Martialists, however, glorified struggle as the highest activity of man, and romanticized war and violence. Realists had a pessimistic view of human nature as unchanging, fearful, and submissive; martialists were optimistic in their appreciation of man's qualities and potential, and indeed acknowledged the possibility of change through transformative action. Realists were conservative and prudent; martialists were expansive and willing to take risks to serve their ultimate ends. Realists saw power as a political instrument for the preservation of security, while martialists worshipped power as an end in itself. Realists rejected nationalism and other particularist ideologies, while martialists believed in the natural superiority of races and peoples. Realists, finally, had a static or cyclical view of history as essentially unchanging and purposeless, whereas martialists operated on the basis of a broader teleological design.

The second object of the chapter was to define the main components and *modus operandi* of a broad-ranging martial tradition, as it developed in Europe from the mid-nineteenth century. One of its most distinguishing features was its reactive quality. Martialist thinkers, from de Maistre and Von Bernhardi to their Victorian imperialists successors, all mounted a spirited counter-attack against the Enlightenment tradition

---

[159] For a striking example of the exclusion of Britain from a broad investigation of the intellectual origins of authoritarian and fascist thought, see J. Freund's *La Décadence* (Paris: Sirey, 1985).

of progress, and in particular against its 'degenerate' modern forms: English utilitarian liberalism; industrial society; socialist democracy; cosmopolitanism; and feelings of decadence and defeat. Martialist ideology came in a variety of shapes and forms: it could be the defining characteristic of a national culture, as in Prussia after 1866; a strongly defined and popular norm in a parliamentary democracy, which could mobilize millions of men and women in support of its principles; and it could even be restricted to a public institution within a democratic state, such as the British colonial army after 1919. At the same time, it is worth noting that martialism never relied on a single canonical text, such as a *Mein Kampf* or a *De Jure Belli ac Pacis*. Indeed, it was distinctive precisely in its refusal to cast itself as an explicit and fully articulated way of thinking; it saw itself more as a manner of being, a way of life in which fundamental principles were defined as a result of action. In this sense, the soldiers and military officers who implemented the imperial dreams of the European powers were more authentic to their tradition than the intellectuals who attempted to formulate it in logical and abstract categories.

As regards the third objective of this chapter, a number of claims have been advanced. First, it has been shown that martialism was neither a marginal nor a rhetorical device of Liberal politicians, but a fully-fledged ideology. Secondly, this ideology was not, as is too often suggested, an imitative response to Prussian imperialism and nationalism, but an indigenous *Weltanschauung*. For—and this is the third claim—British martialism arose and was given full expression in the practices and needs of empire. Although to some extent influenced by German political thought, British martialist thinkers were primarily inspired by the imperatives and experiences of their colonial army in far distant lands.

In this sense, it could be said—looking ahead at the traditions in existence in the twentieth century—that British martialists anticipated many of the values and sentiments of invading and conquering armies up to the present moment. Indeed, if conquering armies were to have a universal political theory, martialism would be it. This theory can be seen to express a particular conception of expansion, with a strong emphasis on notions of violence, racial and ethnic superiority, and subjugation of 'inferior peoples'. Sadly, this was a philosophy which had (and may still have) a bright future ahead of it.

5

The Enigma of the Middle Way: Grotius and the Grotian Tradition on War

The writings, unique methodology, and above all influence on successive generations of admirers identifies Hugo Grotius (1583–1645), a Dutch diplomat, lawyer, poet, mathematician, theologian, and historian as the primary source for a specific school of thought on war. The tradition set out in this chapter is the most powerful of the three to be presented for a number of reasons. In the first place the Grotian tradition defines the very project of the modern laws of war: to regulate, mitigate, and standardize practices of warfare. Most crucially, Grotian legal norms lie at the heart of the enterprise of distinguishing among types of war and classes of combatants. As the editors of the most recent compilation of work about Grotius pronounced: 'What is clear is that the issues Grotius addressed, the concepts and language he used, even the propositions he advanced, have become part of the common currency of international debate about war in general, and about particular wars.'[1] The tradition is also powerful because of its internal characteristics as a system of thought: flexibility, elasticity, and adaptability are its defining qualities. Although narrowly focused upon the problematic of war (in contrast with the broader Grotian traditions of war and peace and international society), the tradition outlined in this chapter draws from an extremely wide range of legal and political systems embedded in Grotius' writings. The potency of this tradition of war, finally, is manifested in its covert quality. Grotian language not only defined the terms of the debate on the laws of war, but succeeded in concealing its ideological purposes in doing so. The primary objective of this chapter will be to analyse this ideology, and show how its principles came to underpin the later Grotian rationale for the legal distinction between lawful and unlawful combatants.

The chapter begins by evoking the inherently enigmatic qualities of Grotius and the numerous (and often conflicting) traditions which he inspired. Next the distinct properties of the Grotian tradition of war are

[1] Hedley Bull, Ben Kingsbury, and Adam Roberts (eds.), *Hugo Grotius and International Relations* (Oxford: Clarendon, 1990), 26.

set out: they are seen to consist in a singular legal discourse, a pluralist method, and a strong attachment to order and power. The core components of this ideology are then examined with reference to Grotian conceptions of human nature, government, and liberty. These elements are shown to provide the necessary foundations of his conception of war, and in particular to inform the priority accorded to the rights of states and armies over those of civilian populations. The final section of the chapter examines how this ideology informed the practices and beliefs of the founders of the modern laws of war. These ideological changes highlight the adaptability of this tradition as it developed at the end of the nineteenth century, and defined the dominant paradigm of the laws of war.

THE GROTIAN ENIGMA

The challenge of setting out the work of such a complex figure is not to be shouldered lightly, since Grotius is legendary for his inexhaustible gift for mystification and obscurity. Indeed, the abiding image of Grotius the man remains that of an intellectual escape artist, famous for getting out of many a tight spot by relying on a great number of books.[2] The image of his scholarship was the use put to his main work, *De Jure Belli ac Pacis* by the great Gustavus Adolphus, who used it either as a pillow, or (even more charmingly) as a fetish in his saddlebags as he laid waste and conquered Europe.[3]

The greatest enigma in the study of Grotius is the man himself. Here is an author who clearly desired to establish that law was a public authority, yet first wrote in defence of private and mercenary wars (on the charge that the interests of Grotius' clients shaped his convictions; the example usually cited is the contradiction between his diplomatic position when representing the Netherlands at the Colonial Conference of 1613, and the position he took in *Mare Liberum*).[4] Grotius is famed

---

[2] This account, still taught to Dutch schoolchildren, is how Grotius escaped from prison by hiding in a trunk covered in books. Vicomte de Caix de Saint-Aymour, *Notice sur Hugues de Groot* (Paris: Charavay Frères, 1883), 18.

[3] J. de Burigny, *La Vie de Grotius: avec l'histoire de ses ouvrages* (Paris: Debure l'Aîné, 1752), i. 135–6.

[4] The most scholarly analysis which also offers an unusual defence of this charge is by Judge G. Ladriet de Lacharrière, 'The Controversy Surrounding the Consistency of the Position Adopted by Grotius', in Asser Instituut (ed.), *International Law and the Grotian Heritage* (The Hague: T. Asser Instituut, 1985), 207–13. See also Richard Tuck's defence (a contextualization of Grotius' life with that of lawyers in Holland in 1619) in his review: 'Peter Haggenmacher, Grotius et la doctrine de la guerre juste', *Grotiana*, 7 (1986), 89–92.

for his attempt to secularize natural law, but much of his work and interests were theological. As a polymath, his contribution to the fields of diplomacy, poetry, and law were all disputed, not least by Grotius himself on his deathbed: 'By undertaking many things I have accomplished little.'[5] Furthermore, the eclectic nature of his life seems to merge easily into the mystery of his works. One article even purports to offer guidance through the enigma of Grotius' work. However, the author, Willems, in keeping with his subject matter, declares: 'Underneath the Grotian myths, the Grotian legends is there a Grotian truth? Or only Grotian ambivalence? To be quite candid, I do no [*sic*] intend to answer these questions . . .'.[6] Haggenmacher remarks upon his 'intrinsic ambivalence'; Vaughan found his work riddled with 'perpetual confusion . . . a nest of sophistries and contradictions'; and Lauterpacht points out in his authoritative account that Grotius' 'evasions and contradictions' are not even the most 'conspicuous defects . . . which invite criticism'.[7]

Given the extent of this confusion over what his writings even contained, perhaps it is not suprising that so many other scholars, jurists, and rulers held so many contradictory opinions of their value. For example, while James I of England found him 'tedious and full of tittle-tattle . . . a pedant, full of words but of no great judgement', Henri IV of France hailed him as the 'Miracle of Holland'.[8] While Richelieu, Voltaire, Rousseau, and Wight were dismissive, others asserted he was 'a divine' whose contribution was as important as that of Copernicus, Galileo, and Descartes.[9] Although to some he justified and even pro-

---

[5] W. Knight, *The Life and Works of Hugo Grotius* (London: Grotius Society Publications, 1925), 289. An extremely charitable interpretation of his poetry can be found in 'The Minor Poetry of Hugo Grotius', *Transactions of the Grotius Society*, 13 (1928) 128.

[6] J. Willems, 'How to Handle Grotian Ambivalence? A Guidance towards some Recent Guides', *Grotiana*, 6 (1985) 106.

[7] P. Haggenmacher, *Grotius et la doctrine de la guerre juste* (Paris: Presses Universitaires de France, 1983), 623; C. Vaughan, *Studies in the History of Political Philosophy before and after Rousseau* (New York: Russell & Russell, 1960), i. 22; H. Lauterpacht, 'The Grotian Tradition in International Law', *British Yearbook of International Law*, 23 (1946), 12.

[8] R. Lee, 'Hugo Grotius', *Proceedings of the British Academy*, 16 (1930), 236. On 5 April 1598 in the gardens of Castle of Angiers, Grotius was presented to King Henry, who turned to his courtiers declaring: 'Behold the Miracle of Holland'. H. Vreeland, *Hugo Grotius, the Father of the Modern Science of International Law* (New York: OUP, 1917), 24.

[9] Wight famously called Grotius' work 'baroque thickets' full of 'giant rhododendrons': *System of States*, 127; Rousseau's objections to Grotius will be illustrated comprehensively in Chapter 6. In his *L'Examen important de Milord Bolingbroke*, Voltaire dismissed Grotius as a mere 'pedant': *The Complete Works of Voltaire* (Oxford, Taylor Institution, 1987), 62, 189. Bizarrely, Basdevant believed the difficulty Voltaire found with

moted barbarism and tyranny, he was proclaimed the 'jurist of humanity' by Vico, and 'un homme de la paix, de la paix entre Etats' by Van Eysinga, seemingly responsible for the Peace of Westphalia. As Hedley Bull declared: 'The idea of international society which Grotius propounded was given concrete expression in the Peace of Westphalia', affirming that 'Grotius must be considered the intellectual father of this first general peace settlement of modern times'.[10] Equally, Grotius was declared responsible (as a *revenant*) for either the entire arbitration process or for promoting the disarmament issue at the Hague Peace Conference in 1899. Indeed, a remarkable event in honour of Grotius took place there:

the ceremony of placing the wreath upon the tomb of Grotius took place on the 4th of July, in the Nieuwe Kerk, in the city of Delft. Representatives from the various delegations in the conference were present. Outside, the winds raged and the rain beat furiously, as if nature were trying to remind the assemblage of the storm and stress in which the life of the honoured dead was passed. Within, the great organ poured out its wondrous tones, and at eleven o'clock the ceremony began.[11]

Finally Grotius preached submission to all forms of alien rule, yet his writings were clandestinely republished in Holland during the Second World War as an 'act of faith in Justice'. So perhaps it is most bewildering of all to discover that, for Van Vollenhoven, Grotius' writings are 'frank and straightforward'.[12]

Although many have denied that he was the founder of any particular school or discipline, there is a long line of scholars who comfortably classify Grotius as the founder of the modern natural law tradition.

Grotius was a consequence of reading him too quickly, and could be resolved in the following manner: 'Il faut le lire attentivement et y revenir'; 'Hugo Grotius', in A. Pillet (ed.), *Les Fondateurs du droit international* (Paris: V. Giard & E. Brière, 1904), 266. Lord Acton, cited by H. Lauterpacht in 'The Grotian Tradition in International Law', 53, n. 1; E. Jímenez de Aréchaga, 'The Grotian Heritage and the Concept of a Just World Order', in Asser Instituut, *International Law and the Grotian Heritage*, 13; Abbé V. Hély, *Étude sur le droit de guerre de Grotius* (Paris: Le Clère, 1875), 193–4.

[10] 'The Importance of Grotius in the Study of International Relations', in *Hugo Grotius*, 75. On responsibility for the aspects of the Hague Conference see G. Sperduti, 'The Heritage of Grotius and the Modern Concept of Law and State', in Asser Instituut, *International Law and the Grotian Heritage*, 33. W. J. M. Van Eysinga, *Grotius Annuaire International* (1940–6), 29.

[11] Vreeland, *Hugo Grotius, the Father of the Modern Science of International Law*, 239–40.

[12] F. Rouge (ed.), *Hommage à Grotius* (Lausanne: University of Lausanne, 1946), 44; C. Van Vollenhoven, *The Three Stages in the Evolution of the Law of Nations* (The Hague: Martinus Nijhoff, 1919), 32.

Holding the former view, W. Knight, argues that *De Jure* was really 'no more than a restatement of principles which had already for generations been commonplaces of the schools, and particularly of the neo-scholastics of Spain'. The latter view is argued by Michael Donelan, who declares: 'His book is devoted to putting once again at unprecedented length the traditional case for saying that there is a law common to all men, the natural law . . . the deepest layer of Grotius' thought . . . is the natural law'. Of Lauterpacht's eleven contributions made by Grotius, the second in ranking is 'the Acceptance of the Law of Nature as an Independent Source of International Law'; and J. Figgis argues that natural law is 'at the very bottom of the whole system of Grotius in regard to international affairs'.[13] However, this view is juxtaposed against other (and apparently equally meritorious) claims that natural law was the last thing on Grotius' mind: his whole *engagement* was an attempt to jettison natural law in favour of, for example, positive law. The eminent jurist Stone decided that 'Grotius' use of the practice and other evidence of Consensus of States, as distinct from the vague consensus of mankind, belongs to modern positivism', and the jurist Di Vecchio added for good measure: 'Natural Law has in reality no function in the structure of his system.' Still others suggest he managed to introduce both.[14] More familiar is the contention that he is the 'father' of international law, without being too precise about which branches, if any. Indeed, there is a review of the debate concerning Grotius' responsibility in the 'fathering' of international law. At a gathering in Grotius' honour one international lawyer makes light of this commonplace conception: 'The Grotian Heritage *is* international law. It is not a coincidence that Grotius has been referred to as the "father of international law" . . . All too often today I had the feeling that I was in the presence of a group of theologians looking for authority in chapters and verses of a certain bible . . . Apparently, every development in international law in the last three and a half centuries is supposed by some

---

[13] W. Knight, *The Life and Works of Hugo Grotius* (London: Grotius Society Publications, 1925), 4, 202; M. Donelan, 'Grotius and the Image of War', *Millennium*, 12/3 (1983), 235, 239; Lauterpacht, 'The Grotian Tradition', 21. See also E. B. Midgley, *The Natural Law Tradition and the Theory of International Relations* (London: Elek, 1975), 154–67; V. Hraber, 'Le Rôle de Grotius dans le développement scientifique du droit international', *Revue de droit international et de législation comparée*, 6 (1925), 549; J. Figgis, *From Gerson to Grotius* (Cambridge: Cambridge University Press, 1907), 190.

[14] J. Stone, *Legal Controls of International Conflict: A Treatise on the Dynamics of Disputes and War-Law* (London: Stevens, 1959), 10; A. Di Vecchio, 'Grotius and the Foundation of International Law', *New York University Law Review*, 37 (1962), 263; C. Murphy, 'The Grotian Vision of World Order', *American Journal of International Law*, 76 (1982).

to have its source in holy scriptures by Grotius.'[15] Again, international relations theorists have claimed him as the source of the tradition of 'international society', 'solidarism', 'rationalism', 'progress', traditionalism, and even, according to more modern theorists, 'regime theory'.[16]

The second aspect of this particular enigma arises over the methods deployed to support or deny his paternity of these various traditions. There are two schools noted by Willems in Grotian literature: the historical, which offers a contextualization of 'the man in his time'; the second, commonly defined as the 'Grotian quest', is the introduction of Grotius' ideas into more current debates.[17] A minor offshoot of this second school endeavours to drag Grotius, like Banquo's ghost, into the very conference where they are speaking or to find him a place at the very desk where they are writing. One lawyer, Pinto, declared: 'If Grotius was present in spirit during the countless hours of the meetings of this Conference, he was silent, content to watch as a congress of nations such as he had foreseen, resolved conflicts . . . he was content to observe reason and the sociableness of man interact as he had conceived they would.' Another lawyer, Murphy, clearly found Grotius less silent with *him*, as he portentously reported to a gathering of experts: 'In closing this brief comment, may I express *my confidence* that Grotius would share the outlook of a modern Christian

[15] Basdevant, 'Hugo Grotius', 238. Y. Dinstein, in Asser Instituut, *International Law and the Grotian Heritage*, 229. See another discussion of this point with additional citations in Ben Kingsbury's: 'Grotius, Law, and Moral Scepticism: Theory and Practice in the Thought of Hedley Bull', in Clark and Neumann, *Classical Theories*, 44, n. 16.

[16] Bull is the most commonly cited author who classifies Grotius as the founder of both international society and solidarism. For the former, see his 'The Grotian Conception of International Society', in Butterfield and Wight, *Diplomatic Investigations*, 51–73; for the latter view, see his essay 'The Importance of Grotius in the Study of International Relations', in *Hugo Grotius*. For aspects of both views see Bull, *The Anarchical Society: A Study of Order in World Politics* (London: Macmillan, 1977), 24, 27, 152, and 153. See also C. Cutler, 'The "Grotian Tradition" in International Relations', *Review of International Studies*, 17 (1991), 54; Wight, *International Theory: The Three Traditions*, 13–15. For Lauterpacht the eleventh feature of Grotius is his 'Tradition of Idealism and Progress', 'The Grotian Tradition', 48; E. Balogh, 'The Traditional Element in Grotius' Conception of International Law', *New York University Law Quarterly Review*, 7/2 (1929), 270. In Krasner's introduction to *International Regimes*, he cites three contributors to the volume as being 'heavily influenced' by Grotius. *International Regimes* (London: Cornell University Press, 1983), ix.

[17] 'How to handle Grotian Ambivalence?', 106. A keener analysis of these trends is Roelofsen's 'Grotius and the "Grotian Heritage" in International Law and International Relations: The Quartercentenary and its Aftermath', *Grotiana*, 11 (1990), 6–29. The term 'Grotian Quest' was created by Richard Falk in his seminal introduction to Edwards's *Hugo Grotius, the Miracle of Holland: A Study in Political and Legal Thought* (Chicago: Chicago University Press, 1981), xiii–xxi.

humanist.'[18] Although most writers on Grotius can be divided between the first two approaches (with a few cautiously incorporating both strands), this division does not resolve the primary question of the motives behind Grotius—both the man and his work. So, amongst those who endeavour to place him 'in his time', several do not agree on the nature of his contribution, whether it be natural law or international society, nor on the interpretations of his character, nor indeed whether his aim was to defend order or justice, slavery or freedom, secularisms or God. This incoherence is equally manifest in the writings of the 'Grotian Quest' school.

This enigma is further complicated by those who see themselves as belonging to the Grotian tradition. Not only is there no consensus over the nature of the man, his work, and how it is to be used, these divisions have often obscured the fact that there is no agreement over what it actually means to be a 'Grotian'. Self-confessed members see themselves, and their tradition, in markedly distinct ways whilst claiming their often contradictory values to be quintessentially 'Grotian'. These contradictions were perhaps a consequence of the Grotian predilection for inconclusiveness. In the words of one devotee, the three principles of the Grotian method were 'aporetic (leaving philosophical questions open), antinomic (not seeking to solve apparent contradictions) and anti-apodictic (avoiding firm statements)'.[19] Two such examples are the disparity between Falk's and Murphy's interpretations of the role of a Grotian, as well as, for example, Hedley Bull's and Martin Wight's. A corollary of this problem is the apportioning and assigning of the 'duties' of membership of the tradition, over which, characteristically, there is immense controversy. For one, the method of placing Grotius within one of the two schools of thought has implications for the shouldering of Grotian responsibilities. When comparing Edwards's *Hugo Grotius: The Miracle of Holland* ('quest' approach), with Roelofson's *Grotius and International Law* ('mixed' approach), he warns: 'if Edwards' view is correct, then Grotius' view of human nature . . . may be, in light of the present, our main source of inspiration. Or, to form it more negatively, as for Grotian scholarship, any approach that mixes the scholarly—and therefore the critical—with the cynical seems to me

---

[18] M. C. W. Pinto, 'The New Law of the Sea and the Grotian Heritage' in Asser Instituut, *International Law and the Grotian Heritage*, 92; C. Murphy, 'The Grotian Vision', 27; emphasis added.

[19] J. C. Willems, 'Grotius and International Law', in F. Elchlepp et al. (eds.), *Hugo Grotius 1583–1983* (Assen: Maastricht Colloquium, 1983), 42–54.With such guiding principles, little wonder that Grotianism often comes across as an *auberge espagnole*.

a hazardous one.'[20] On this seemingly perennial problem of definition, one particularly anguished Grotian, seized with the terrible responsibility of choosing the correct interpretation in order to 'fulfil' the heritage, asks:

Does this lead to the conclusion that it is still too early for shadowland exploration, that for the moment the Grotian quest will not lead to any result? Or should we just base ourselves on the basic tenets of Grotius' work: the concept of a world community as a legal community; the doctrine of duties; the need for restraint and charity; and start the Grotian quest from there, in order to find paths that lead to new horizons? We can no longer appeal to the shared values emanating from the concept of natural law. Or can we?[21]

This leads to a further enigma, which bears on the question of taxonomy. There are several aspects to this problem. The first centres on the conditions that need to be met in order to classify a thinker (whether self-confessed or not) as Grotian. Classification by its very nature involves an element of elision, and leads to an emphasis on the 'essential' characteristics of a system of thought—an endearing image of this dilemma was conjured up by John Vincent, when he warned of the dangers of 'the whole enterprise of treating great thinkers like parcels at the post office'.[22] This essentialism is necessary but always brings with it the danger of reductionism. This can be particularly problematic for a writer who was both prolific and eclectic, and whose followers were faithful to him in this respect (if in no other). The second aspect, arising partly from this eclecticism, is the sheer diversity of 'the Grotian tradition'. How useful is it to include under the same theoretical roof two such contrasting figures as Cornelius Van Vollenhoven and Hedley Bull? The former believed in the radically transformative capacity of international institutions, while the latter never ceased to stress the limits of diplomatic voluntarism and solidarist agency in an 'anarchical' international society. This can be a problem for Grotians themselves. Bull, for example, lost no time in removing himself from any club which welcomed members such as Van Vollenhoven. However, if the club could

[20] J. C. Willems, 'How to Handle Grotian Ambivalence?', 114. The Roelofson piece cited by Willems is a chapter in K. Van Holk and C. G. Roelofsen (eds.), *Grotius Reader: A Reader for Students of International Law and Legal History* (The Hague: T. Asser Instituut, 1983), 3–21.

[21] P. Kooijmans, 'How to Handle the Grotian Heritage: Grotius and Van Vollenhoven', *Netherlands Journal of International Law*, 81 (1983), 91.

[22] J. Vincent, 'The Hobbesian Tradition in Twentieth Century International Thought', *Millennium*, 10 (1981), 96.

be limited to such pluralists as Oppenheim, Bull would have gladly renewed his subscription.[23]

The third aspect is the question of temporality. What is it that makes Emmerich de Vattel and Stanley Hoffmann members of the same 'Grotian' tradition? Is it merely their common acknowledgement of the importance of Grotius? Their engagement in an atemporal dialogue? Is this dialogue based on a common agenda and frame of reference, or simply on a common commitment to the understanding of certain atemporal ideals? Equally delicate is the relationship among the three-cornered 'Hobbesian-Grotian-Kantian' paradigms and competing schemes for the classification of political thought. For example, it is generally suggested that the Grotian category corresponds to the middle term in Wight's 'Realist-Rationalist-Revolutionist' trilogy. However, self-styled Grotians have often been included under the Realist and Rationalist denominations (and sometimes even under the Revolutionist). Hedley Bull demonstrated an equal ambivalence concerning his own position, deciding at times he was a Grotian and at others not. Stanley Hoffmann, in discussing Bull's contribution to international relations, is seized with the same taxonomical confusion: 'Bull's own kind of realism, however, was never left far behind. He always managed to correct his own Grotian inclinations by an infusion of what he called Oppenheim's pluralism.'[24] This ubiquity captures the enigma of Grotianism whose flexibility is such that it seems welcome under a plurality of theoretical roofs. For example, Cutler argues for a distinction between 'Grotians' and 'neo-Grotians' depending upon adherence to the foundations of natural law in constructing theories about international society. Lauterpacht's definition of a Grotian is similar, although he believes Grotians overlay practice on the underpinnings of natural law: 'We cannot even consider [Grotius] as what is usually described as a "Grotian" who has accomplished a workable synthesis of natural law and state practice.'[25] Finally, and perhaps most fundamentally, there is the relationship between domestic and international political theory. For some, its commitment to international improvement and progress, mitigation, consensus, and the rule of law marks Grotianism as a paradigmatic instance of liberalism.[26] But domestic liberal political theory is also concerned

---

[23] Bull's determining of the Grotian tradition as 'solidarist', based on natural law (hence his own exclusion from it) is ably dealt with in Cutler's 'The Grotian Tradition'; Bull, 'The Grotian Conception', 52.

[24] Wight, *International Theory*, 13–15; S. Hoffmann, 'Hedley Bull and his Contribution to International Relations', *International Affairs*, 62 (1986), 187.

[25] Cutler, 'The Grotian Tradition', 41–65; Lauterpacht, 'The Grotian Tradition', 5.

[26] Koskienniemi's study of international legal history argues that liberalism provides

with issues of democracy, distributive justice, equality, and human rights. The inclusion of these further values into international discourse is a source of serious controversy within the Grotian tradition. Francis Lieber, for example, held deeply conservative views on issues such as slavery in America, but nonetheless saw himself (and has been seen since) as part of the Grotian 'humanizing' tradition. A definition of his political stance was attempted by his friend and colleague, Bluntschli: 'He is a *Liberal* both as a man and as a scholar. But he was in no wise a follower of Rousseau, and by no means captivated with those airy systems of the philosophical school in which unwary and unpractical men had allowed themselves to be caught, like flies in cobwebs.'[27] Conversely, a domestic liberal such as Kenneth Waltz eschews the possibility of introducing liberal principles into the international system.[28]

The final enigma concerns the treatment of the more unpleasant aspects of his work which both methods of interpreting Grotius leave unresolved. For the advocates of the 'Grotian Quest', there is the obvious need to select aspects of his ideas which could be useful to their current problematic (in this respect, his views on slavery would not be considered valuable by most scholars in the second half of the twentieth century). Curiously, one desperate writer attempted to show that since Grotius did not actually *mean* what he was saying, the possibility had to be considered that he was trying to inspire horror (perhaps so, as a rhetorical device) for the *purpose* of moderation (although this argument is less satisfying).[29] However, this process inevitably results in a truncation and historicist censoring of his philosophy. Amazingly, in one case whole sections of *De Jure Belli ac Pacis* were censored from an edition edited by Van Vollenhoven. One defender of Van Vollenhoven's tactics in 'handling' Grotius believed the international lawyer (as opposed to the historian) does not have to depend 'as a minimum, on a correct

the doctrinal underpinning of international law. *From Apology to Utopia: The Structure of International Legal Argument* (Helsinki: Lakimiesliiton Kustannus, 1989), 53–130; Michael Freeden argues that an adherence to seven distinct core values identifies a (domestic) liberal: see 'The Family of Liberalisms: A Morphological Analysis', in J. Meadowcroft, *The Liberal Political Tradition* (Cheltenham: Edward Edgar, 1996), 14–39.

[27] Introduction, vol. ii of Lieber's *Miscellaneous Writings* (Philadelphia: Lippincott & Co., 1881), emphasis in text. However, a better analysis of Lieber's political thought can be found in B. Brown's *American Conservatives: The Political Thought of Francis Lieber and John W. Burgess* (New York: AMS Press, 1967).

[28] On the inherently conflictual properties of his 'third image' see his *Man, the State, and War: A Theoretical Analysis* (New York: Columbia University Press, 1960), 159–86.

[29] Hély's *Étude*, 180.

representation of the past'.[30] On the other hand, the advocates of the 'man of his time', by attempting to contextualize his life and work with what can be reconstructed about the prevailing philosophies of seventeeth-century Holland can simply relativize these unpleasant aspects away. One such scholar, when speaking of Hobbes and Grotius together noted: 'The common importance of the two seventeenth century thinkers lies less in their respective answers and solutions—plainly outdated though *meant to be valid for all times*—than in their exemplary formulation of the problem. This, it is submitted, forms the common, timeless core of their heritage.'[31] By relating his atavistic zeal for certain practices to the era of the Thirty Years War, there is a propensity to minimize the relevance of these principles. Indeed, this school often appears to be actually engaged in a prolonged *apologia* for the brutal principles and imagery littered thoughout *De Jure Belli ac Pacis*.

RECAPTURING THE SECOND PARADIGM OF WAR: GROTIUS' TRADITION ON WAR

As a Dutch Minister of Foreign Affairs once remarked: 'Grotius has survived because he was an enigma.'[32] This enigmatic figure has come to be seen as the source of at least two traditions: the broad tradition of international relations on the one hand, incorporating the concept of international society, solidarist and pluralist approaches, and that of international law on the other, based on either positive or natural law or a combination of the two. The tradition of war set out in this chapter is distinct from these Grotian conceptions of international relations and international law, although it draws discrete elements from both. Indeed, the approach outlined here differs from the traditional manner of defining the 'Grotian Heritage' in three key ways.

---

[30] See a masterly indictment of this method of transforming not only Grotius' reputation, but his texts as well, in J. Oudendijk, 'Van Vollenhoven's "The Three Stages in the Evolution of the Law of Nations": A Case of Wishful Thinking', *Legal History Review of the Netherlands*, 48 (1980), 3–27; Kooijmans, 'How to Handle the Grotian Heritage', 87.

[31] P. Haggenmacher, 'On Assessing the Grotian Heritage', in A. Dufour, P. Haggenmacher, and J. Toman (eds.), *Grotius et l'ordre juridique international: travaux du Colloque Hugo Grotius* (Lausanne: Payot, 1985), 160, emphasis added. Richard Tuck also argued that Grotius' entire project was to combat (rather than introduce) moral relativism. See his *Philosophy and Government 1572–1651* (Cambridge: Cambridge University Press, 1993), xv–xvii, 347.

[32] W. Van Eekelen, Opening Address, in Asser Instituut, *International Law and the Grotian Heritage*, xxii.

It will be argued that the nature of Grotius' character is central: his reality as an intellectual Houdini and servant of the powerful is not a detail to be mentioned in biographical sketches, or rejected as mere 'cynicism'.[33] Rather, this characteristic needs to be emphasized in order to present an authentic tradition which relies on moral, ideological, and intellectual ambivalence. Indeed, it is suggested that a separation between what Schwarzenberger called his *persona* and his *fama*—his personality and the body of his work—is not useful for setting out his central philosophy.[34]

Controversy over the methods used by both approaches to Grotius and his work have obscured the heritage bequeathed by the 'Miracle of Holland' to his tradition. An interesting example of the dangers of having to select single patterns of Grotius' thought can be found in the meticulously contextualized historical work by Haggenmacher, *Grotius et la doctrine de la guerre juste.* His thesis is that *De Jure Belli ac Pacis* cannot be seen as the precursor for the system of international law that developed subsequently; it is instead a much more scientifically rigid and limited work whose sole aim was to set out a general theory of the laws of war. He argues this persuasively (and I believe correctly) by situating *De Jure Belli ac Pacis* within what Tuck described as a 'medieval technical debate' continuing in Grotius' time. However, this historical approach still excludes the subsequent effect which the techniques and methods introduced (or believed to be introduced) by Grotius had on political ideologies of subsequent generations of international lawyers and theorists, and could be said to create a 'Grotian Tradition of War'. Haggenmacher's approach thus acknowledges the singular methodology of Grotius without assigning any 'heritage' value to it.[35] For the tradition which is introduced in this chapter, the 'truth' of whether he was a naturalist or a positivist is irrelevant. In explaining the distinction between the 'naturalist' school of international law and the 'positivist', Best rightly points out that there is more similarity between them than has been conventionally assumed: 'neither school in practice is as inattentive to the substance of the other as their philosophical champions . . . seem to expect . . . the fact is, they are not so far apart as some of them think'.[36] More

---

[33] Lauterpacht pays tribute to these textual acrobatics with a comment on one example: 'But here, once more, he retreats from his position by an ingenious piece of dialectics'.'The Grotian Tradition', 8; Willems, 'How to Handle Grotian Ambivalence?', 114.

[34] 'The Grotius Factor in International Law and International Relations: A Functional Approach', in Bull et al., *Hugo Grotius and International Relations*, 303.

[35] See Haggenmacher, *Grotius, passim*; R. Tuck, 'Peter Haggenmacher', 87.

[36] *Humanity in Warfare*, 39.

importantly, it is irrelevant since the debate over whether he was the founder of natural law or its negator conceals the fact that he founded a synthetic tradition which could encompass a variety of approaches within a single paradigm. This method is sometimes referred to by lawyers without addressing its political implications. For example, Kingsbury notes: 'For Grotius, law provides both a language and a mechanism for the systematic application of reasons to problems of social order and conflict.' Here there is an acknowledgement of an ideological purpose behind Grotius' use of particular methods (which Kingsbury notes is 'right reason'), but immediately thereafter there is a shift to a discussion of the general questions within Grotius' *De Jure Belli ac Pacis*, without an examination of the substantive issues raised by these very methods.[37]

The systems of thought within Grotianism all commonly acknowledge certain core 'Grotian values' such as the sociable nature of man, the subjection of international relations to law, the search for consensus and compromise, the principle of moderation, the recognition of state sovereignty, the endorsement of the principle of *pacta sunt servanda*, and the universality of international society. Nonetheless, they diverge in three ways. In the first place, the meaning and force attributed to some terms is contested, as with the notions of 'positive' or 'natural' law. Furthermore, there are differences over the precise ordering of the core values themselves—is consensus more important than universality? Does moderation inspire law, transcend it, or merely operate within its interstices? Finally, there are divergences over the content and ordering of such peripheral values as legal, political, and individual rights, and the notion of equality.

By approaching the subject in this fashion, this chapter transcends the taxonomical confusion over how Grotians are classified and classify themselves, and how the tradition sees itself. As to the latter, it will emerge that 'conservative' and 'progressive' clusters have always coexisted within the Grotian ensemble, expressing contrasting patterns of internal values. More generally, the ranking of the internal values of the Grotian tradition has not been addressed by most international relations theorists and international lawyers; those who have tried have often come up with singularly unhappy results. For example, this piece of *galimatias* by de Aréchaga:

when an act is permitted by natural law and forbidden by positive law or conversely permitted by positive law but forbidden by natural law, there is in fact no conflict which would determine a hierarchy between the two legal

---

[37] 'Grotius, Law, and Moral Scepticism', 45–6.

systems . . . but when there is real incompatibility and contradiction, when one system of law orders conduct forbidden by the other, then Grotius assigns primacy to international law.[38]

However, identifying the particular range of core and peripheral values within a tradition's ideology can provide new insights not only into its morphology, but also into the manner of its development over time. The values internal to an ideology are rarely static, but shift at different periods of time under the influence of internal and external pressures. This is clearly the case with the Grotian tradition. Furthermore, many of its values actually developed over time, acquiring a distinct shape in the process. The notion of consensus played a pivotal role here. Given that Grotians sought to define themselves as the *via media* between two extreme sets of values, it is those extremes that partly defined their identity as a tradition. But since those normative extremes necessarily changed over time (Erasmian values were not quite the same as Kantian ones, which in turn differed from Wilsonian), the content of the 'Grotian middle' shifted correspondingly. Another example of necessary change follows from the Grotian identification with order. For all Grotians, order remained one of the cardinal values in the international system; hence a tendency to situate themselves in relation to the dominant constellation of power in the states system. This method is not only noted but celebrated by Bull:

> one may also doubt whether it was a limitation of Grotius that like others in his time (and like many of us in Europe now) . . . as a professional lawyer his views were affected by the interests of his clients, that in his early life in Holland he taught and wrote as a representative of a powerful state or that kings and governments . . . thought highly of his views and were sometimes able to use them in support of his policies. It is *not a weakness but a strength of Grotius' contribution* to international law that he was no mere visionary but sought to found his views on the actual interests and policies of states.[39]

As the Grotian tradition was thus 'index-linked' to legitimate power, its values always exhibited strong affinities with the prevailing norms of any particular epoch. But dominant norms change: the notion of racial equality was not part of the international system's scheme of values in 1850 or even 1919, yet was becoming increasingly accepted by the end of the 1940s. A 'Grotian' answer to the question of the existence of slavery in international law would therefore differ significantly depending on whether it was given in the mid-nineteenth century or the

---

[38] 'The Grotian Heritage and the Concept of a Just World Order', 18.
[39] Asser Instituut, *International Law and the Grotian Heritage*, 137. Emphasis added.

mid-twentieth.[40] All these variations and differences notwithstanding, this chapter has the ambition of identifying a number of new and distinct elements of unity within the Grotian tradition. These elements are methodological as much as substantive, and will become clearer as the argument unfolds. One of their principal manifestations will be seen to lie in the very style, language, and rhetoric of Grotians—a style which is always controlled and tempered, seeking to extricate itself from the meaningless 'passions' of the ideological universe; a language which is formalistic and technical, often derived from the conceptual reservoir of lawyers, which artificially 'closes' arguments by imposing their particular terms of reference upon the debates; and above all a rhetoric which borrows heavily from the canons of reactionary thinking to forestall the introduction of substantive change. To borrow from Albert Hirschman's celebrated categories, it will be seen that the Grotian tradition of war subscribes to a considerable extent to the three principles of reactionary discourse: futility, perversity, and jeopardy.[41] Attempts to change the existing scheme of things, in other words, are either useless because impractical; or perverse because they may have the opposite effect to those intended; or hazardous because they endanger the fragile heritage of order and civilization which has patiently accrued through the ages. As will be seen, these arguments will be used both to justify the general Grotian conception of the laws of war, and in particular to resist all attempts to undermine its central notion of a distinction between lawful and unlawful combatants.

The unique methodology of the Grotian school of thought helped to create an entirely revolutionary manner of thinking about war, which set out a consensual paradigm on the laws of war. This approach initiated the most powerful ideology of the three traditions outlined in this book. It attempted to establish, through a complex system of highly sophisticated propositions, a paradigm which provided a means of justifying the priority accorded to states and their armies over civilian populations in occupied and conquered territories. In order to illustrate this unique doctrine, which later guided the founders of the laws of war in the nineteenth century, the next sections will set out the thoughts of Grotius on the following issues: human nature, government, liberty, and war. The first three themes will shed crucial light on the fourth; it will be seen that the Grotian notion of war makes sense

---

[40] On this theme see J. Vincent's 'Racial Equality', in H. Bull and A. Watson, (eds.), *The Expansion of International Society* (Oxford: Clarendon Press, 1984), 239–54.

[41] A. Hirschman, *The Rhetoric of Reaction: Perversity, Futility, Jeopardy* (Cambridge, Mass.: Harvard University Press, 1991).

only if viewed as operating within his broader framework of political values.

GROTIUS ON THE NATURE OF MAN

For Grotius, the laws of nature and the nature of man were indissociable. In the *Prolegomena* he established sociability as the primary characteristic of man's nature, and associated this feature with natural law:

> But among the traits characteristic of man is an impelling desire for society, that is, for social life—not of any and every sort, but peaceful, and organised according to the measure of his intelligence . . . This maintenance of the social order, which we have roughly sketched, and which is consonant with human intelligence, is the source of law properly so called. . . . From this signification of the word 'law' there has flowed another and more extended meaning . . . in such things it is meet for the nature of man, within the limits of human intelligence, to follow the direction of a well-tempered judgement, being neither led astray by fear or the allurement of immediate pleasure, nor carried away by rash impulse. Whatever is clearly at variance with such judgement is understood to be contrary also with the law of nature, that is, to the nature of man.[42]

Many have seen the purpose of these preliminary remarks as a means of introducing the concept of sociability. Both international law textbooks and many international relations theorists regard Grotius as having introduced sociability as the very basis of natural law.[43] In the traditional view, inherent natural sociability is seen as both apolitical and positive: 'there was no need for a political conception of international relations. The genius of Aristotle was acknowledged, an instinct for society or sociableness replaced the Aristotelian notion of a natural impetus towards political life.'[44] Equally, natural law, as the essential underpinning of sociability, is generally regarded as a moderating and progressive factor in Grotius' system. However, these traditional sources of the Grotian heritage can be challenged on several grounds. First, Grotius seemed to have as many definitions of natural law as he had varied opinions of himself:

[42] 'Prolegomena', *De Jure Belli ac Pacis*, trans. A. Campbell (London: Hyperion Press, 1990), vii, viii, ix; 8–11.
[43] T. Tadashi, 'Grotius's Method: With Special Reference to Prolegomena', in O. Yasuaki, (ed.), *A Normative Approach to War: Peace, War, and Justice in Hugo Grotius* (Oxford: Clarendon Press, 1993), 26; de Aréchaga, 'The Grotian Heritage', 11. D. Kennedy, 'Primitive Legal Scholarship', *Harvard International Law Journal*, 27 (1986), 79.
[44] Murphy, 'The Grotian Vision', 497.

Natural right is the dictate of right reason, shewing the moral turpitude, or moral necessity, of any act from its agreement or disagreement with a rational nature, and consequently that such an act is either forbidden or commanded by God, the author of nature. The actions, upon which such a dictate is given, are either binding or unlawful in themselves, and therefore necessarily understood to be commanded or forbidden by God. This mark distinguishes natural right, not only from human law, but from the law, which God himself has been pleased to reveal, called, by some, the voluntary divine right, which does not command or forbid things in themselves whether binding or unlawful, but makes them unlawful by their prohibition, and binding by its command. But, in order to understand natural right, we must understand that some things are said to belong to that right, not properly, but . . . by way of accommodation.[45]

Second, if one includes all of Grotius' definitions of natural law, it becomes immediately clear that it is not necessarily a moderating or progressive force. That it can be a conservative (rather than progressive) element is an important and overlooked feature of his system—except this one comment by Lauterpacht:

the fact is that we are often at a loss as to the true meaning which he attaches to the law of nature . . . it is by no means clear that the law of nature, as used by him, invariably fulfils a humanising function in the cause of the alleviation of suffering and of progress conceived as an assertion of the liberty of man . . . his conception of natural law approaches very much that of Hobbes' notion of the right of nature and of a law of nature as expressions of physical laws rather than as ethical and juridical norms. Most of the harshness of the law of war he deduces from the law of nature thus conceived.[46]

Another implication of Grotius' pluralist concept of natural law was that it did away with the necessity of maintaining an internal coherence, as contrasting and opposing precepts could be included within the same system. Grotius himself used mathematical equations as an analogy for illustrating the evident and 'not so evident' range of values within natural law. One writer, Remec, attempts to explain the structural ambiguity of Grotius' natural law: 'these fundamental principles [of natural law] are only the most indispensable safeguards of social life. They are therefore limited to certain prohibitions and commands', and notes that these principles 'leave free a broad area of what is permissible. Yet the strict law of nature does not consist merely of those general principles which are evident to a degree that admits no doubt. It consists also of inferences from those general principles.' Thus, Remec acknowledges that 'the problem is that these inferences sometimes gain recognition

[45] *De Jure Belli ac Pacis*, Book I, 21.   [46] 'The Grotian Tradition', 7, 9.

easily, while in some other cases they are not so easily accepted. The more extensive the deduction from the general principle is, the less self-evident is that particular rule of the law of nature.'[47]

Third, this pluralism introduced the potential for a further conceptual step, which formed the basis of the Grotian ideological tradition: moral relativism. Recognition was given to a plurality of possible moral outcomes, including even the freedom to detach from any moral framework whatsoever. But this relativism was constrained within specific limits. 'But among the traits characteristic of man', declared Grotius, 'is an impelling desire for society, that is, for the social life—not of any and every sort, but peaceful, and organized according to the measure of his intelligence, with those who are of his own kind.'[48] What is also important is his identification with a particular type of society: peaceful and organized, but also hierarchical. Society therefore, is not simply 'political' in the Aristotelian sense, but hierarchical in the tribal, or patriarchal sense. As a means of locating Grotius within the prevailing norms of his day, Haggenmacher highlights two types of law-based social 'links' in *De Jure Belli ac Pacis*, the second 'taking place between unequal persons such as the ruler and his subjects or the *paterfamilias* and the rest of the *domus*, including his wife and children', adding 'such a distinction remained quite useful to Grotius and his contemporaries in a civilisation where inequality was accepted and even slavery was not yet looked upon as utterly intolerable'.[49]

Accordingly, it can be seen that Grotius' conception of human nature, as defined in the 'Prolegomena', and derived from this concept of sociability, posited that man was perfectible, but not perfect. As Richard Tuck noted of Grotius' views on sociability: 'The natural society of men is one in which individuals pursue their own interests up to the point at which such a pursuit actually deprives another of something which they possess; it is not one of benevolence, as we would customarily understand the term.' Indeed, Tuck adds, crucially: 'It is this minimalist character of the principle of sociability which made it in Grotius' eyes a principle which a moral relativist could accept.'[50] Man's social condition thus had three distinct features. First, perfectibility was conditional; the achievement of progress depended on certain social and institu-

---

[47] P. Remec, *The Position of the Individual in International Law According to Grotius and Vattel* (The Hague: Martinus Nijhoff, 1960), 64.

[48] 'Prolegomena', 11.

[49] 'On Assessing the Grotian Heritage', 158. See also Tadashi's 'State and Governing Power', in Yasuaki, *A Normative Approach to War*, 128, and *De Jure Belli ac Pacis*, Book I, Chapter III.

[50] R. Tuck, 'Grotius, Carneades, and Hobbes', *Grotiana*, 4 (1983), 53.

tional prerequisites. Secondly, any improvement in man's situation was reversible. Perfectibility was hypothetical in the sense that it was not certain; Grotius rejected a teleological approach to man's nature. Finally, the idea of progress was hypothetical rather than categorical: all improvements were therefore reversible because there was no divine or earthly guarantee that any positive changes would be of an enduring character.

As will be shown next, both Grotius and his modern successors had a crucial purpose in their ideological construction of the world. There was a more formidable ambition behind this apparent ethical aimlessness: it was a direct attack on the ideologies prevalent at their particular times.

GROTIUS AND GOVERNMENT

The writings of Grotius indicate that he had contradictory views on the nature of government. He saw himself as a man of progressive moral and political views, whereas to others (notably Rousseau) he appeared to favour authoritarianism. In defence of the former view, Grotius set out a definition of the purpose of government which seemed to endorse justice:

Again, some governments may be formed for the advantage both of subjects and sovereign, as when a people, unable to defend themselves, put themselves under the protection and dominion of any powerful king. Yet it is not to be denied, but that in most governments the good of the subject is the chief object which is regarded: and that what Cicero said after Herodotus, and Herodotus after Hesiod, is true, that Kings were appointed in order that men might enjoy justice.[51]

However, in what can be seen as a typical 'Grotian' development, in the same breath (and next sentence) he retracted the substance of what he had just established:

Now this admission by no means goes to establish the inference that kings are amenable to the people. For though guardianships were invented for the benefit of wards, yet the guardian has a right to authority over the ward. Nor, though a guardian may for mismanagement be removed from his trust, does it follow that a king for the same reason be deposed. The cases are quite different, the guardian has a superior to judge him; but in governments as there must be some last resort, it must be vested either in an individual, or in some public body,

---

[51] *De Jure Belli ac Pacis*, 68.

whose misconduct, as there is no superior tribunal before which they can be called, God declares that he himself will judge. He either punishes their offences, should he deem it necessary; or permits them for the chastisement of his people.[52]

Both the vagueness and incoherence of his views on government were derived from Grotius' focus on the *basis* for instituting the state, rather than its internal composition. By the particular tools he employed to define this rationale, he was vulnerable to charges of supporting tyrants, both in actuality and by default. Yet this was not a flaw in Grotius' substantive political values, but rather a necessary consequence of his system of thought.

His main intention in thinking about the state was to undermine the various doctrinal foundations upon which it was established in his time, and to create different grounds from those provided hitherto. Although substantively different in their core values and institutional structures, in his view they shared one common feature: they were all based on ideologically absolutist doctrines of ends. Erasmus' conception of communitarianism was grounded in an axiomatic faith in the benign and pacific attributes of human nature. Dante's imperialism was founded on his unshakeable conviction in the temporal and spiritual supremacy of the Roman Church. The central premiss of Machiavelli's conception of *raison d'état* was an idea of the state unfettered by the bonds of law and society in its pursuit of power.[53]

In lieu of this ideological absolutism, Grotius offered an approach which could be termed ideological relativism. This relativism had several general features. The first was the rejection of the exclusivity of any one doctrine: neither realists, communitarians, nor religious imperialists could singly offer a comprehensive account of the world, or build a coherent normative foundation to state institutions. As shown in the previous section, Grotius demonstrated a willingness to choose from each of these paradigms in an eclectic fashion, using whichever aspects served his particular purposes. Furthermore, the range of doctrines from which he was prepared to draw was extremely broad, revealing a capacity to accommodate diversity and recognize the richness of different intellectual traditions. But recognition of this diversity was not an end in itself, but a means of systemic ranking. By setting opposing doctrines and values alongside each other, Grotius was able to carve out a middle

---

[52] Ibid.
[53] On the political doctrines prevailing in Grotius' time, see Hedley Bull's 'The Importance of Grotius', 71–2. See also, more generally, vol. ii of Q. Skinner's *The Foundations of Modern Political Thought*.

ground for himself. Finally, there was a relativization of ideology itself: in other words, a willingness to minimize it (and even discard it entirely) when practical imperatives so demanded.

Nonetheless, Grotius did not see himself as a complete relativist. His aim in attacking different ideological systems was to clear the rubble in order to make way for a society (both domestic and international) governed by certain key values and procedures. The supreme characteristic of civilized society was law; it was the bedrock upon which all notions of order were constructed. Accordingly, his goal in disputing various forms of political autonomy was to establish the concept of sovereignty as indissociable from the law, no matter what teleological purposes lay behind the achievement of sovereignty:

And here is the proper place for refuting the opinion of those, who maintain that, every where and without exception, the sovereign power is vested in the people, so that they have a right to restrain and punish kings for an abuse of their power . . . and upon the following grounds they may be refuted. From the Jewish, as well as the Roman Law, it appears that any one may engage himself in private servitude to whom he pleased. Now if an individual may do so, why may not a whole people, for the benefit of better government and more certain protection, completely transfer their sovereign rights to one or more persons, without reserving any portion to themselves? Neither can it be alleged that such a thing is not to be presumed, *for the question is not, what is to be presumed in a doubtful case, but what lawfully may be done.*[54]

Law not only occupied a key position in Grotius' scheme of values, it was the essential procedural means to establish a stable system of domestic and international politics. As Grotius defined it, law was both the ends and means of sovereign power:

to enquire into the matter of a right is not the same thing as to examine the nature of its tenure. A distinction which takes place not only in the corporeal but in the incorporeal possessions. For a right of passage of carriage through a ground is no less a right than that which entitles a man to the possession of the land itself.[55]

Grotius believed sovereign right was established through custom and practice, and his emphasis was on precedent rather than on principle: 'The opinion of those can never be assented to, who say that the power of the Dictator is not sovereign, because it was not permanent. For in the moral world the nature of things is known from their operations.'[56]

Legal relations, in the realist and martial tradition, are simply expres-

---

[54] *De Jure Belli ac Pacis*, 63. Emphasis added.   [55] Ibid. 71.   [56] Ibid. 72.

sions of power. Idealists such as Kant often derived legal norms from moral imperatives. In the republican tradition, as we shall see in the following chapter, legal authority drew its legitimacy from the principle of popular sovereignty. Distinct to these different traditions was a monistic conception of the sources of law. By introducing a pluralistic approach Grotius was able to establish new foundational principles for the sources of law. As Kingsbury explains: 'Grotius' account of sources is a theory of sources of law in general rather than a specific hierarchy of formal or material sources of the types found in modern international law.'[57] Focusing on the legitimacy of the state institutions themselves rather than the legal norms that underlay them, he was able to detach himself from ideological arguments about the foundation of state power. As Remec pointed out: 'it is possible that men consent to a wide range of possible systems of government, from the entirely democratic to the extreme absolutist one . . . There is no "best" form of government, according to Grotius.'[58] What mattered was not what the 'true' law or moral principle was, as we noted earlier, but simply that states were founded on laws, especially because these laws were expressions of agreement among dominant forces in society.

For in the first place the assertion that the constituent always retain a control over the sovereign power, which he has contributed to establish, is only true in those cases where the continuance and existence of that power depends upon the will and pleasure of the constituent: *but not in the cases where the power, though it may derive its origin from that constituent, becomes a necessary and fundamental part of established law.* Of this nature is that authority to which a woman submits when she gives herself to her husband. Valentinian the Emperor, when the soldiers who had raised him to the throne, made a demand which he did not approve, replied; 'Soldiers, your election of me for your emperor was your own voluntary choice; but since you have elected me, it depends upon my pleasure to grant your request. It becomes you to obey as subjects, and me to consider what is proper to be done.'[59]

This was an understanding of law which Grotius applied not only to the domestic sphere, but also (and especially) to inter-state relations. An important feature of this understanding was an image of a hierarchical state formulated on the model of the household, where a king occupied an analogous position to the head of a household.[60] The law of nations was not derived from abstract and absolute principles of justice, but

---

[57] 'Grotius, Law and Moral Scepticism', 47.
[58] *The Position of the Individual in International Law*, 75.
[59] *De Jure Belli ac Pacis*, 67. Emphasis added.   [60] Ibid. 23.

from the agreements reached by the world's most powerful nations, as heads of their respective households:

And in this sense we may readily admit also the truth of the saying that right is that which is acceptable to the stronger, so that we may understand that law fails of its outwards effect unless it has a sanction behind it. In this way Solon accomplished a very great results, as he himself used to declare: 'By joining force and law together, Under a like bond'.[61]

This linkage of power to law, similar to the Hobbesian interpretation, was one of the central features of Grotius' paradigm. Roelofsen cites Tuck as the foremost exponent of the similarity of Hobbes's and Grotius' philosophy: 'In many respects Tuck detects a close relationship between Grotius and the English philosopher, so much so, that the reader starts to wonder whether there was after all such a fundamental difference between them as is construed for instance by Bull.'[62] As will be seen in the next section, this linkage identified order, power, law, and sovereignty as the cluster of core values in Grotius' system. Kennedy noted that Grotius conflated sovereignty with natural justice and added: 'to Grotius, sovereignty is a type of power within the natural order'.[63]

GROTIUS AND THE NATURE OF LIBERTY

In Grotius' vision liberty was non-essentialist, subsidiary, conditional, reversible, and finally, profoundly ambiguous. In insisting on its non-essentialist nature, he took a position opposite to the realist and martial stances. Far from believing that the purpose of history and political institutions was to actualize this virtue (as with the martialists), he instead rejected the idea that liberty was an innate element in human nature at all. In his discourse, freedom was merely a subcategory of power which simply meant that one was not subject to another's rule. But even slavery was not inconsistent with the principle of human freedom. Grotius explained how this could work in *De Jure Belli ac Pacis*:

by the law of nature, in its primaeval state; apart from human institutions and customs, no men can be slaves: and it is in this sense that legal writers maintain

---

[61] 'Prolegomena', 15.

[62] 'Grotius and the "Grotian Heritage"', 20. See Tuck's 'Grotius, Carneades, and Hobbes' at 54. As will be seen in Chapter 6, an earlier exponent of this view (although with a substantially different analysis) was Jean Jacques Rousseau.

[63] 'Primitive Legal Scholarship', 85, 90.

the opinion that slavery is repugnant to nature. Yet in a former part of this treatise, it was shown that there is nothing repugnant to natural justice, in deriving the origin of servitude from human actions, whether founded upon compact or crime.[64]

More important, liberty was ranked very low as a political value. It was, at best, a subsidiary principle which was always conditional upon achievement of the dual imperatives of authority and order. Tadashi says of this: 'Grotius adopts an extremely negative stance towards the right of resistance. To recognise a right of resistance is contrary to the purpose for which a state is formed, i.e., the maintenance of public peace', and finds that, for Grotius, 'it is more prudent to have peace even with injustice or subjection than to cause domestic disturbance for the purpose of seeking justice or freedom.'[65] Although he defined the state as 'a complete association of free men', the freedom of a people could come only after the formation of the state. In the beginning of *De Jure Belli ac Pacis,* he defined liberty as a subsidiary right to sovereign authority:

Men call a faculty a Right, which every man has to own; but we shall hereafter, taking it in its strict and proper sense, call it a right. This right comprehends the power, that we have over ourselves, which is called liberty, and the power, which we have over others, as that of a father over his children, or a master over his slaves ... Right, strictly taken again, is again twofold, the one PRIVATE, established for the advantage of each individual, the other, SUPERIOR, as involving the claims, which the state has upon individuals ... Thus the Regal authority is above that of a father and a master, and a Sovereign has a greater right over the property of his subjects.[66]

Here, in an example where liberty must be sacrificed to peace, Grotius' definition of peace includes civil order, with slavery preferable to liberty:

An example of evils, that ought by all possible means to be avoided, is furnished by the consultations among the states of Gaul, who according to the account of Tacitus, deliberated, whether they should make the choice of liberty or peace. By liberty here is meant civil liberty, that is, the right of governing themselves, and remaining independent states; and by peace is meant such a peace as would prevent the whole people from being exterminated, a calamity like that which befell the Jews, when their city was besieged by Titus. In such cases reason itself dictates the choice of peace, as the only means of preserving life, which is the immediate gift of God, and the foundation of every blessing. So that the almighty, as we read in his sacred volume, deems it a kindness, when instead of

[64] *De Jure Belli ac Pacis*, 19–20. [65] 'State and Governing Power', 143.
[66] *De Jure Belli ac Pacis*, 19–20.

destroying a people, he permits them to be reduced to slavery. Therefore he admonishes the Hebrew, by the mouth of his prophet, to surrender to the Babylonians, rather than to die by pestilence and famine.[67]

His philosophy emphasized an association of law with order and authority (rather than giving expression to moral and political rights). This is again a function of the ambiguous position of liberty in Grotius' writings. In a telling paragraph, he both accepts and rejects the notion of man's liberty as part of the laws of nature:

> For where liberty is said to be a natural right belonging to all men and states, by that expression is understood a right of nature, antecedent to every human obligation or contract. But in that case, liberty is spoken of in a negative sense, and not by way of contrast to independence, the meaning of which is, that no one is by the law of nature doomed to servitude, though he is not forbidden by that law to enter into such a condition: as Albutius pertinently remarks, 'the terms, freedom and servitude, *are not founded in principles of nature, but are names subsequently applied to men according to the dispositions of fortune'*.[68]

Grotius' approach to the question of obedience to sovereign power relied heavily on the principle that rebellion or resistance to tyrannical rule was illegal. As Onuma notes:

> Grotius stresses the virtue of obedience and thereby reveals his penchant for maintenance of the *status quo* between ruler and ruled . . . Must one obey this law of non resistance even in cases of extreme danger? Despite hesitating at times, Grotius basically advises submission in this world, i.e. martyrdom, so that eternal salvation might be attained. In this way, while prohibiting the execution of an order contrary to natural or divine law, Grotius seeks to resolve the question of resistance against tyrants *quoad exercitium*, not through disobedience but through submission and eternal salvation.[69]

As noted in an earlier section, his focus was on states' rights rather than those of individuals; accordingly, many of his limits on individual freedom were proposed to argue for the liberty of action of states. His rights of slavery within the state thus provided the foundation for the right of conquerors to enslave others. As summarized by Naoya: 'Grotius starts from the premise that, in the primary state of nature, no human beings are slaves. But if the institution of slavery came into being as a result of wrongful conduct, it could not be regarded as a violation of justice under natural law. In the law of nations, slavery is permitted to a large extent.' Therefore, according to Grotius, 'since there was no

---

[67] *De Jure Belli ac Pacis*, 283.　　[68] Ibid. 270. Emphasis added.
[69] 'War', in Yasuaki, *A Normative Approach*, 102.

element of agreement between captor and captive, the captor never promised not to kill his captive, but was completely free to do whatever he wished, including killing, or enslaving him.'[70] Grotius wrote a great deal on the rights of slavery, a fact which many of his modern admirers are understandably reluctant to dwell upon. In a paragraph of Book II of *De Jure Belli ac Pacis* entitled 'The Right over Slaves', he presented voluntary subjection for basic necessities as one of the legitimate foundations of slavery:

That is complete slavery which owes lifelong service in return for nourishment and other necessities of life; and if the condition is thus accepted within natural limits it contains no element of undue severity. For the lasting obligation to labour is repaid with a lasting certainty of support, which often those do not have who work of hire by the day . . . To his own manger many a slave returns, Who once had run away and lived as free . . . 'if I were free I'd live at my own risk, But now I live at yours'.[71]

According to the Grotian law of nations, there is not even a requirement of consent on the part of a people in times of war in order to justify enslaving them arguing that 'as to persons, not only those, who surrender those rights, or engage themselves to servitude, are considered in the light of slaves, but all, who are taken prisoners in public and solemn war, come under the same description from the time that they are carried into places, of which the enemy is master'. He adds the conclusive: 'nor is the commission of crime requisite to reduce them to this condition, but the fate of all alike, who are unfortunately taken within the territories of an enemy, upon the breaking out of war'.[72]

GROTIUS AND THE NATURE OF WAR

Much like Hobbes's *Leviathan*, the ambition of Grotius' *De Jure Belli ac Pacis* can be found in its title. Grotius' goal was not to establish whether there could be rules that governed war and peace, but what those rules were. He proceeded by first defining war as broadly as possible, in order to include a comprehensive range of permissible activity within the scope of its laws:

In treating of the rights of war, the first point, that which we have to consider, is, what is war, which is the subject of our enquiry, and what is the right, which we seek to establish . . . war is the state of contending parties, considered as

[70] 'The Laws of War', in Yasuaki, *A Normative Approach to War*, 267–8.
[71] *De Jure Belli ac Pacis*, Book II, 719–20.   [72] Ibid. 345.

such. This definition, by its general extent, comprises those wars of every description, that will form the subject of the present treatise.[73]

He also created a system of law which could offer bilateral rights to both belligerents in war, an additional principle to traditional *jus ad bellum*. Writers on the laws of war before Grotius had argued that either there could be bilateral rights in war (that is, each belligerent could have an equal right to make war on the other), or that there was only one just party. Grotius, unsurprisingly, took a position in between these two, and suggested an entirely new legal approach. He argued that although sovereigns could *not* have bilateral rights, their subordinates *could*, so that belligerents in the field of battle could both be lawful and just. This was put forward as a custom of war, sourced in a type of contractual *jus gentium*. It allowed Grotius to put forward a theory which claimed that states had tacitly agreed that, irrespective of the objective justice of their claims, their representatives in battle (commanders and soldiers) could be recognized as having mutual and legitimate rights against each other in war.[74]

Grotius' method of analysis was driven by both principal and subsidiary purposes. The principal goal was to counter what he believed were the two established theories of war and peace, thus advancing his own system in their place. He claimed the alternative philosophies of war and peace were both too excessive and too absolute in the extent and limits they sought to place upon war. In his famous statement in the introduction to his book on the laws of war and peace, the 'Prolegomena', Grotius defined his philosophy as a response to the problems encountered in each extreme view:

Confronted with such utter ruthlessness, many men who are the very furthest from being bad men, have come to a point of forbidding all use of arms to the Christian, whose rule of conduct above everything else comprises the duty of loving all men. To this opinion sometimes John Ferus and my fellow countryman Erasmus seem to incline, men who have the utmost devotion to peace in both Church and State; both their purpose, as I take it, is, when things have gone in one direction, to force them in the opposite direction, as we are accustomed to do, that they may come back to a true middle ground. But the very effort at pressing too hard in the opposite direction is often so far from being helpful that it does harm, because in such arguments the detection of what is extreme is easy, and results in weakening the other statements which are well within the bounds of truth. *For both extremes therefore a remedy*

---

[73] *De Jure Belli ac Pacis*, Book I, 17–18.
[74] See Haggenmacher, *Grotius et la doctrine de la guerre juste*, 397–9.

must be found, that men may not believe either that nothing is allowable, or that everything is.[75]

His secondary purpose was to introduce a concept of 'moderation' into the practice of warfare. His appeal for the application of this virtue formed several chapter headings of Book III of *De Jure Belli ac Pacis*, which was concerned chiefly with the customs and practices of war. The manner in which Grotius introduced the notion of *temperamenta* was typical. After listing a particularly brutal range of customs which he described as acceptable under various types of law, he began 'I must retrace my steps, and must deprive those who wage war of nearly all the privileges which I seem to grant them'.[76] Indeed, his system of introducing improvement was to illustrate the possibility and limits of change. His method of seeking moderation, *temperamenta*, was crucial, and laid a foundational stone for the Grotian tradition. Although it was the last phrase in his quotation about finding the middle way which is most remembered, it was his method of introducing change stated earlier which was much more consequential: the search for a *via media* between 'both extremes' which he believed so disastrous.

Here Grotius develops a concept, which was aptly captured in Hirschman's theories of perversity and jeopardy, which posits the idea that any substantive change was hazardous, because it either has the reverse effect to that intended, or imperils the positive values already achieved, endangering some 'previous, precious accomplishment'. (This concept in practice will also be illustrated in more depth later in this chapter by an illustration of the development of the Grotian tradition of war.)[77] Further, Grotius maintained this method of seeking change by 'pressing too hard in the opposite direction', actually undermining various customs which ought to be maintained; this amounted to a belief on his part that the more utilitarian and harsh practices of war had a recognized place *within* the law.

Accordingly, Grotius' system defined all customs and practices as legitimate in wartime, but advanced a more normative claim to moderate these customs. Both the normative claim and the customary practices could, according to Grotius, be sourced from divine law, natural law, the law of nations or volitional law. His method in establishing a theory using this eclectic procedure represented his unique contribution to the foundations of a new school of thought on war. There are five

[75] 'Prolegomena', 21. Emphasis added.
[76] *De Jure Belli ac Pacis*, 716. Unfortunately, this remark introduces the chapter which gives legal grounds for extensive rights over slaves.
[77] Hirschman, *The Rhetoric of Reaction*, 7.

features of the Grotian system that are particularly worthy of mention. The first of these concerns his way of defining what were customary practices of war, searching for illustrations of these customs in ancient history and examples from his own century. He explained the reasons for choosing this procedure:

History in relation to our subject is useful in two ways; it supplies both illustrations and judgements. The illustrations have greater weight in proportion as they are taken from better times and better peoples. Thus we have preferred ancient examples, Greek and Roman, to the rest. And judgements are not to be slighted, especially when they are in agreement with one another; for by such statements the existence of the laws of nature, as we have said, is in a measure proved, *and by no other means, in fact, is it possible to establish the law of nations.*[78]

His selection at first may appear simply arbitrary; on a complete reading of his work, however, it is apparent that the examples used are purposely and selectively chosen. Among the Romans he had a particular devotion to Livy, Machiavelli's favoured promoter of savage war.

The second theoretical feature concerned the artificial contrivance Grotius deemed necessary to achieve his desired *via media*. As he compiled an enormous collection of brutal practices of war, a structural imbalance developed within his system. As the architectural pillar supporting barbaric practices at one end of his scale was so heavily loaded, its weight destabilized the more normative pillar which he had constructed to embody the other end, thus abandoning a true middle ground. The hypothetical *via media* was not merely conjectural, it was not even in the middle. Accordingly, Grotius' work drew more heavily from the conservative view of history than the progressive in constructing this ersatz 'middle'.

A third feature was the moral relativism in Grotius' vision of war which, along with the ideological relativism set out earlier, remained unresolved both in his work and tradition. This was a conflict between procedural and substantive conceptions of pluralism. The normative pillar, which held up one end of Grotius' theoretical edifice, claimed to need the more 'realist' positivist pillar in order to constitute a balanced structure. This was perceived as the only means of finding the just route: the gate at the centre of Grotius' edifice through which one had to pass in order to navigate a true middle path between the absolutist claims of any single ideology. Yet the normative pillar, by its nature, consisted of moral claims which established the absolute virtue of specific values and

---

[78] 'Prolegomena', 30. Emphasis added.

principles, such as the justness of choosing such a middle path. Likewise the positivist pillar claimed that the theoretical structure must encompass both extremes of the discourse on war. Yet the pluralistic procedures took precedence over the pluralistic substance. These discourses embodied a mechanism which allowed different moral visions to coexist, making adherence to any one ethical claim near impossible.[79]

The fourth feature lay in his declared attempt to make a moral claim for moderation in warfare, using the techniques of inclusivity. The contradiction between making a moral claim, based on Christian law, the law of nature, or any other law, whilst simultaneously maintaining the ability to detach from any ethical scheme whatsoever, created irreconcilable tensions. Yet the uniqueness of this approach had to do with Grotius' ability to cite ethical claims within the same system (and alongside others) which denied other moral claims; these precepts could equally be claimed by the humanitarian, 'normative' Grotian tradition, of the more 'realist' Grotian lawyers.

And finally, a notable feature in Grotius' theory of moderation in war was his audience. The appeal for moderation was made specifically to rulers and princes in authority. His entire argument rested on the fact that only by writing for, and about, power and powerful leaders, could incremental change be brought about. By sustaining, and indeed constructing, legitimizing arguments which endorsed rulers' actions, the entire body of the work assumed an asymmetrical character, seeming to offer an endless range of rights for rulers, and mere obligations for subjects and slaves.

Indeed this was the essence of the Grotian legacy to the founding of the laws of war. At the heart of the Grotian system was an essential dichotomy between the rights of states and armies on the one hand, and the position of ordinary members of society on the other. Although he devoted some effort to justifying private wars, the thrust of Grotius' writings was to concentrate the legitimate recourse to war in public hands. Within these limits, however, states and armies were given an open field to visit destruction and mayhem upon each other; these actions were justified by the hallowed principles of practice and custom. On the other side of the equation lay the hapless subjects of their respective states, condemned to wallow in the private sphere, enjoying no political or civic rights either in war or peace, and with the peculiar formulation of Grotian charity as their only hope for salvation. Between

---

[79] Adapting a model from Hans Kuhn, Koskenniemi has set out a similar analysis of international law in general, positing 'descending and ascending patterns of arguing about international order'. *From Apology to Utopia*, 84.

the public sphere of the state and the private realm of the subject, there was no question in Grotius' mind as to which enjoyed the primary position. Sown by Grotius, the seeds of the distinction between the rights of states and armies and the subordinate position of civilians—expressed in the legal dichotomy between lawful and unlawful combatant—germinated in the later nineteenth century. The remainder of this chapter will be devoted to examining how this development occurred, who were its principal agents, and what it revealed about Grotian ideology itself.

THE GROTIAN TRADITION OF WAR

The Grotian tradition of war developed in a particular manner from 1874 to 1949 in the context of the framing of the laws of war. Central to the Grotian position was the ambition to limit the rights of belligerency to a particular class of participant (the soldier), and to exclude all others from the right to become actively involved in it. In order to understand exactly how the tradition developed internally, in both its core and peripheral values, and externally, in the way the tradition adapted itself to the prevailing norms during that era, this section will explore some of the characteristics and works of the main agents and bearers of the Grotian tradition of war. Their general personalities and demeanour, the language and method of the discipline (which they themselves largely constructed), and, above all, their political ideology will be traced in relation to Grotius' main contributions.

Although many personalities among the publicists of the era could be classified (or classified themselves) as 'Grotian', there were three pivotal members. The term 'publicist' as a nineteenth-century occupation was suitably described by one historian as 'meaning not journalists, as the term implies today, but those learned men, philosophers with a practical bent, who specialized in what we now call public international law and international relations.' But neither, explains Geoffrey Best, were they 'international lawyers—they were too close to moral and political philosophy for that, and much of what they wrote was meant for a readership stretching well beyond courts, cabinets, colleges and military academies'.[80] Fedor Fedorovich de Martens, Johann Caspar Bluntschli, and Francis Lieber were collectively responsible for structuring both the discourse and the actual texts on the laws of war in the second half of the nineteenth century. Another powerful agent was the very conserv-

---

[80] *Humanity in Warfare*, 34.

ative Belgian publicist and first head of the Institute of International Law, Rolin-Jacquemyns. However, his role was more that of a supporter and consolidator of the views of the three above-mentioned agents. These men had many features similar to Grotius himself, indeed Best described Grotius as 'the prime proto-publicist'.[81] Often overlooked are the more personal aspects of their careers, and how these influenced their views of the world.

As noted earlier, the broad nineteenth-century doctrine of international law, both in its structure and practitioners, was liberal in its political assumptions and underpinnings. Many liberal political concepts can be described as conservative in nature, notably the attachment to law, order, political stability, hierarchy, continuity, and tempered progress.[82] Yet within the Grotian tradition of war in the late nineteenth century there appears evidence of strong reactionary principles as well, similar in their formulation and core values to Grotius' own. Hirschman's characteristic features of reactionary thought over the last three centuries—perversity, futility, and jeopardy—were echoed in the personal and political ideologies of these three men, and were generally reflected in much of the consensual thinking about the laws of war during this period.

Of the three, Francis Lieber was the most influential. A Prussian by birth, his legal contribution, *Instructions for the Government Armies in the Field, issued as General Orders No. 100 of 24 April 1863* commonly known as the 'Lieber Code' (or to his intimates and himself, 'The Old One Hundred') was written while in America, and was designed for their civil war. However, he never lost his association and love for all the glory of Prussia, and celebrated Germany's invasion of France seven years after his code was published. As one biographer wrote: 'he was delighted, in his old age, with the German conquest of France', and another biographer, on reading his letters, noted that 'his spirits soared' on hearing of the Prussian invasion of France.[83] He held an anti-abolitionist stance on slavery while holding a professorship in the American South: 'Lieber felt he could not speak out publicly on the issue of slavery', and in any case 'he believed that immediate emancipation would solve nothing; it would only lead to social equality and consequent intermarriage and amalgamation', an idea which was 'repugnant

[81] Ibid. 53.
[82] For further discussion see Michael Freeden, *The New Liberalism: An Ideology of Social Reform* (Oxford: Clarendon Press, 1986), and Pierre Manent, *An Intellectual History of Liberalism* (Princeton: Princeton University Press, 1994).
[83] Brown, *American Conservatives*, 17; Frank Freidel, *Francis Lieber: Nineteenth Century Liberal* (Baton Rouge: Louisiana University Press, 1947), 408–9.

to Lieber's Anglo-Saxon mind'. Accordingly, he believed the only
ethical approach, was to 'reduce the number of Negroes in the population by having the state legislatures carry out a program of colonisation
... In 1835, when he came to South Carolina, he had to demonstrate
that he was not an abolitionist, for he believed that only states could
deal with slavery.'[84] He also held a deep love of war which was based
on his belief that, among many other virtues it possessed, it was a means
of development of civilization. As he declared to General Halleck:
'Blood is occasionally the rich dew of History.'[85] Equally, his desire
for fame and recognition all offered strong echoes of Grotius' persona.
He wrote to his patient friend Charles Sumner: 'I will not rest until
I *force* the political and legal world to quote me,' and to another
friend: 'I know that my work belongs to the list which begins with Aristotle, and in which we find the names of Thomas More, Hobbes, Hugo
Grotius, and Pufendorf.' Unlike Grotius, however, who questioned his
contribution on his deathbed, Lieber 'died firmly convinced of his own
greatness'.[86]

Fedor Martens was an ardent servant of the Russian Emperor. Best,
in describing Martens as 'a jurist in the service of the Tsar' quite rightly
wonders 'the extent to which de Martens was his own man or the Tsar's';
however, it will be shown here that, according to his ideology, being the
Tsar's man was identical to being 'his own' man.[87] He was instrumental
in convening (and more importantly, devising the political and legal
rules at) the first international diplomatic conference on the laws of war
in 1874 in Brussels, and carried a reputation for being as much a self-
publicist as a publicist. Martens's book on the conference at Brussels,
La Paix et la guerre, begins his account with the declaration: 'In Europe
an entire myth has formed on the subject of the origin of the Brussels
Conference, and of the causes which produced it.' In setting out his own
authoritative version of the Brussels and Hague Conference, where he
played a pivotal role, the legend he constructed about the purposes of
the conference clearly reveal his own political inclinations.[88] He was

[84] Brown, *American Conservatives*, 20–1; Freidel, *Francis Lieber*, 235.

[85] A comprehensive account of this Darwinian explanation of war by Lieber, and its
other virtues, can be found in J. Childress, 'Francis Lieber's Interpretation of the Laws
of War: General Orders No. 100 in the Context of his Life and Thought', *American
Journal of Jurisprudence*, 21 (1976), 44.

[86] T. Perry, *The Life and Letters of Francis Lieber* (Boston: Osgood, 1882), 17, 18;
emphasis in text; Freidel, *Francis Lieber*, 417.

[87] Best, *Humanity in Warfare*, 163. For details of the conservative liberalism of the
Russian legal school from which his political philosophy was based, see A. Walicki, *Legal
Philosophies of Russian Liberalism* (Oxford: Clarendon Press, 1987), 214–27.

[88] Martens, *La Paix et la guerre*, 99.

deeply disliked by diplomats of all political persuasions (the Belgian and German delegates, separated by a yawning political gulf, drew together only in their mutual dislike of Martens), but was tireless in promoting his essential vision of the laws of war based extensively on Lieber's Code.[89] His bullying behaviour towards delegates of lesser powers at Brussels in 1874 and especially The Hague in 1899 (the diplomatic archives in Brussels and Nantes abound with examples of his arrogance and petulance towards what they considered their own vital concerns of self-defence) includes a particularly unpleasant episode of legal plagiarism on a grand scale at The Hague.

In the archives of the Belgian Ministry of Foreign Affairs, the depressing tale of the real origins of the so-called 'Martens' Clause' (the famous preamble to the Hague Regulations) appears. As one internal report on the matter baldly stated, when matters came to an impasse at The Hague in 1899, the two Russian delegates (de Staal and Giers) appealed for help from the Belgian diplomat Baron Lambermont (who had represented his country at the first conference on the laws of war at Brussels in 1874). He sent them, through the Belgian representative at The Hague, a M. de Beernaert, a draft text of a preamble which he thought might solve the current problems in the text (which the smaller countries had found unacceptable). The next day at the Commission, Beernaert made a shocking discovery: 'M. de Martens simply presented the declaration as if it was his and made no mention of its real origin.' However, this was the least of it. Martens then truncated the Lambermont draft dramatically, vitiating its original substance ('Peu après, M. de Martens s'occupa de transformer les textes adoptés par la Commission'). When challenged on this issue, in writing (and after Lambermont sent another, fresh draft of the complete version, highlighting the fact that the original also had the word 'draft' written all over it), Martens then speciously claimed, in a response made ten days later, that he had not received this second draft in time, and that the text was now impossible to change anyway.[90]

Johann Bluntschli, although by birth and legal training a Swiss national, made his way across the border to his natural political home in Prussia. Besides his legal and scholarly activities at the University of Heidelberg, he was an active member of the First Chamber in Germany, a representative of a party which sought 'l'unité allemande et

---

[89] On the German delegate's impression at The Hague, see Best, *Humanity in Warfare*, 164, and below for the Belgian Lambermont's in 1874.

[90] Brussels, Ministry of Foreign Affairs, Direction P, No. 6120, Annexe 3, 24 July 1899.

l'hégémonie prussienne' from 1862.[91] It was Bluntschli who established the highly political parameters of the Institute for International Law, involving his friend, Rolin-Jacquemyns. Bluntschli wrote to Jacquemyns in 1872: 'The idea of a gathering of jurists of international law has often preoccupied me . . . the crucial point appears to be that one must create a permanent and durable institute which can become an authority for the entire world.'[92] It was Bluntschli who plagued delegates at Brussels with his pedantic manner. As Baron Lambermont commented in his daily journal of the Brussels Conference: 'Anyway, the arrival of Bluntschli has got on the nerves of all the other delegates . . . we can foresee long harangues and tirades without end . . . it seems understood in Berlin that this Russian project harmonizes extremely well with Prussian military practices.'[93] And it was Bluntschli who took the failed Brussels project under his wing at the Institute, and pushed through, practically single-handedly, the creation of a Manual on the Laws of War in 1880 (commmonly known as the 'Oxford Code'), which subsequently provoked such a violent response from his political masters. As noted in Chapter 1, his correspondence over the Manual became something of a legal scandal, with both Field Marshal Moltke and the head of the German General Staff Hartmann repudiating his Manual in a famous exhange of letters and articles.[94]

Bluntschli saw himself as part of a 'scientific clover leaf' (so-called by Lieber) which included Lieber, but excluded Martens. The third member of his greenery was the French jurist Edouard Laboulaye, who broke off with them after 1870 and the Franco-Prussian War, unable to keep up with their pro-occupier views. Fedor Martens has been offered as the more authentic third man, as his core values were more similar to Bluntschli's and Lieber's than Laboulaye's (even before their rupture).[95] These three Grotians, instruments and promoters of a particular view of the laws of war, shared a distinct political ideology, which, while similar in many instances to conservative liberalism, also contained the three principles of Hirschman's theory. Indeed, Hirschman noted that his arguments are not the exclusive property of 'reactionar-

[91] G. Rolin-Jacquemyns, 'Bluntschli—Necrologie', *Revue de droit international et législation comparée*, 13 (1881), 626. Bluntschli is better known to political scientists as the author of *The Theory of the Modern State* (Oxford: Clarendon, 1885).
[92] *Annuaire de l'Institut*, 1 (1873), 11–28.
[93] Brussels, Archives of Ministry of Foreign Affairs, 29 July 1874, Dossier B 748.4.
[94] See H. Von Moltke, *Moltke's Military Correspondence*, ed. S. Wilkinson (Oxford: Clarendon Press, 1923).
[95] Bluntschli, Introduction to Lieber, *Miscellaneous Writings*, ii. 13.

ies': 'they can be invoked by any group that opposes or criticizes new policy proposals or newly enacted policies'.[96]

The first core element of the political ideology of these three men was the cardinal position assigned to the notion of order. As noted above, Grotius was seen to be a 'man of peace' exactly in the same way as Hobbes desired the preservation of order. Lieber's notion of order was so absolute that it appeared to be reified, especially when one looks at the main (but not only) justification he uses for the maintenance of slavery: 'Lieber at that time also believed that the preservation of the Union was more important than the extinction of slavery.' This ranks order as a supreme value, coming as it does for Lieber before a very limited concept of freedom.[97] Equally, any attempt to challenge this notion of order was met with the principles of jeopardy and perversity. Likewise, as both de Martens and Bluntschli argued in their works on the laws of war, regularizing armies was the best means of preserving order. Bluntschli, in citing the purpose of the distinction between lawful and unlawful combatant, recognizes that keeping war the preserve of professional soldiers serves the interests of conquerors:

The victor, on his part, enjoys the fruits of the peaceful labours of the inhabitants. It is easier for him to feed himself and to satisfy his needs in enemy territory when the inhabitants are not troubled, when the fields are cultivated, when factories continue to produce goods, and when commerce continues to distribute them.[98]

This argument could be seen to be advanced to appeal to the interests of the military in an attempt to stop them slaughtering civilians. Yet there is also a direct lineage from this argument back to a medieval concept of the rights which accrued to those privileged to bear arms—the rights of conquest. This notion of order was as much a central belief of Grotius as it was a highly Vattelian one; it viewed states as the primary locus of legitimacy and law. Interestingly, however, Lieber dismissed Vattel because of his 'moderate' views, complaining 'it makes me impatient to find old Vattel so often quoted'. He later described Vattel as 'Father namby-pamby' for restricting some methods of warfare, e.g. the use of poison, and the retention of all means of destruction in order to wage war (both of which Lieber clearly desired to maintain). Martens preferred him, and indeed, in the preface to the 1916 edition of

---

[96] Hirschman adds that nonetheless these arguments are used 'most typically' by conservatives, *The Rhetoric of Reaction*, 7, 8.
[97] Brown, *American Conservatives*, 21
[98] J. Bluntschli, *Le Droit international codifié* (Paris: Guillaumin et Cie., 1870), 300.

Martens's *La Paix et la guerre*, La Pradelle notes that Martens reminds him of Vattel as he is 'clear-minded but slightly superficial'. This is confirmed by the Vattelian comments Martens makes in it, such as: 'The relations between States rest upon the principle of complete independence. States do not recognize any superior power, neither sovereign, nor legislative, nor juridical. They are omnipotent, and submit to no outside authority.'[99]

Another strain that runs through each of the publicists is a similar understanding of the harmony of interests of the Great Powers in the second half of the nineteenth century, which reflected the hegemonic nature of the two Empires of Bluntschli and Martens, and Lieber's Prussian views. Martens believed that others, too, would come eventually to see that this hegemony (which buttressed his conception of 'international law') was the only means of preserving international peace. As he opined:

However the history of the attempts by Russia to improve the lot of all nations confirms us in the view that, on the one hand, it is one of the goals of Russian national policy to promote the principles of international law, and on the other, that at the end of the day the principles proclaimed by Russia are eventually generally accepted, even by the powers which opposed them most energetically.[100]

A third shared core value was their elitism, which informed their view of the world around them and their place within it. Martens, like Grotius before him, believed that the peoples outside Europe were too uncivilized to meet the standards of his 'universalist' conception of international law. 'This agreement can evidently exist only among nations which have achieved more or less the same level of civilization and which do not significantly differ in their conceptions of law and morality'. This is why 'it would be impossible to expect Turks or Chinese to observe the laws and customs of war'.[101] Lieber's own views on the matter have already been illustrated with reference to the question of slavery. On the universality of international law his views were predictable: 'The fundamental idea of all international law is the idea that all civilized nations of our race form a family of nations.' His views on race mirrored those of the Prussian martialist, littered as his works were with Teutonic superiority, as to the inferiority of the 'Latin Culture' of

[99] Childress, 'Francis Lieber's Interpretation of the Laws of War', 59, and n. 82; La Pradelle cited in Best, *Humanity in Warfare*, 164; Martens in *La Paix et la guerre*, 47.
[100] Martens, *La Paix et la guerre*, 83.
[101] Ibid. 47. That Russia was involved in a war with Turkey should be noted.

the French, and to the danger of 'Mexican degenerates' (this latter when arguing for the annexation of Mexican territory).[102] Elitism also shaped the way they perceived their own function and role in society. Bluntschli, in a letter to Lieber describing the task before him in writing his book about the laws of nations, declared that one of the purposes of his *Droit international codifié* was to conform to the 'needs of the age'.[103] Additionally, as the founder of the Institute of International Law, he believed that the correct method of influencing state policy was to create an exclusive body of men like himself:

What would be necessary to-day and what we are about to propose would be the intimate meeting of a *select* group of men already known in the sciences of international law through their writings or their deeds ... This meeting would attempt to fix the first landmarks of collective scientific action, first, by studying out in principle a system of usefulness, examining its effectiveness and devising the best form to be given it; secondly, by adopting the constitution of an academy or international institute of the law of nations.[104]

He wrote the same to Lieber, who concurred. Indeed, as one biographer noted, on this subject 'Lieber's mind spouted forth a ceaseless and variegated deluge of international ideas'. Lieber thought that international laws should gain acceptance through the 'sheer authority of the distinguished jurists who drafted them', and was 'unqualifiably adverse' to the introduction of international codes into the domestic legislature of individual states, and voted through their Parliaments democratically, because 'the strength, authority, and grandeur of the Law of Nations rests on, and consists in, the very fact that Reason, Justice, Equity speak through men "greater than he who takes the city"'.[105]

Disguised under the notion of 'public opinion', all three developed a concept which in effect empowered a select group of unaccountable servants of state like themselves. Bluntschli, in particular, developed the theoretical notion of 'public conscience' in international law. This theory, however, did not imply grounding law in popular norms; rather, its purpose was to lay the ideological foundation for a central role for publicists in the formation of law.[106] Lieber declared that his personal ambition was to emulate Grotius: 'Hugo Grotius was quoted as

---

[102] 'Twenty-Seven Definitions and Elementary Positions Concerning the Laws and Usages of War', *Miscellaneous Writings*, ii. 223; 125.

[103] Rolin-Jacquemyns. 'Necrologie', 625.

[104] James Scott (ed.), *Resolutions of the Institute of International Law*, xvii. Emphasis in text.

[105] Freidel, *Francis Lieber*, 400; Perry, *Life and Letters*, ii. 255.

[106] Sperduti, 'The Heritage of Grotius', 33.

authority at the Congress of the European nations at Vienna; but he was thus quoted above monarchs, ministers, and nations, *because* he was an unofficial man, absent from the strife.' Another more poignant example was when he declared that he wanted his work to be taken seriously: 'I mean [to] *settle* as Grotius *settled.*' Lieber's dream was to come true at Brussels in 1874, when the Russian delegate Baron Jomini made several references to his code in the opening address, acknowledging it as the basis of the draft text. But of course, in order to take this challenging role in creating rules it helped to have Lieber's personality (of whom the publisher Putnam declared after meeting him: 'Lieber is the most conceited man in the country').[107] Grotius' thesis that the only means of moderating states' behaviour was to appeal to rulers found enthusiastic disciples over 200 years later.

Such ideological values were underpinned by an essential part of their political *animae*: a deep fixation with power. It was the strongest chain that united them with a central aspect of Grotius' own neglected persona and hidden heritage which was highlighted earlier in this chapter. As one of Grotius' biographers wrote of him: 'He himself was not, and never had been, merely a philosopher of the armchair in disposition and fact. By nature he loved, and was most comfortable in, association with people of rank and importance, negotiating either their business or that of a ruling class.'[108] An examination of the private worlds of these three men and the link with Grotius invites two important conclusions. The symbiosis between more private politics and public personas illustrates the fact that their personal political ideologies and convictions were deeply embedded in their written works. It also highlights the importance of linking the notions of the good life inside the state with the good life outside it. For Grotius as with Lieber, Bluntschli, and de Martens, these two facets of political philosophy were indissociable.

Therefore, these men, pivotal in influencing the legal construction of the modern laws of war, can be said to reflect a harsher side of the Grotian tradition of war. In the next section, it will be shown that some of Hirschman's premises remained central to the tradition until 1949, whilst others were abandoned as the ideological priorities of the Grotians shifted.

---

[107] Lieber in a letter to Halleck, 1863, emphasis in text; Childress, 'Francis Lieber's Interpretation of the Laws of War', 39, emphasis in text; 'Actes de la conférence réunie à Bruxelles, du 27 juillet au 27 août 1874, pour régler les lois et coutumes de la guerre', *Nouveau Recueil général de traités*, 4 (1879–80); Freidel, *Francis Lieber*, 413.

[108] Knight, *The Life and Works of Hugo Grotius*, 191–2.

THE DEVELOPMENT OF THE
GROTIAN TRADITION OF WAR

Although there is a plethora of works about the laws of war and the law of nations in Europe in the nineteenth century, it has been argued that its modern founders were Bluntschli, Martens, and Lieber. This is claimed for two reasons. First, and most obviously, because these individuals were both best placed, and used their positions, to advance their own formulations on the legal agenda of war with their rulers at international conferences and with their Institute colleagues. Second, although there were many other works about the laws of war before and during their time, much like Grotius they demonstrated a supreme talent for synthesizing these legal rules into a particular framework. This intellectual construction involved several elements, each of which represented a central tenet in the modern Grotian tradition of war: the elaboration of a distinct language and methodology of law; the standardization of ideological relativism; the institutionalization of moral relativism; the manner of introducing moderation in war; and the affirmation of the centrality of order. All these elements came together to justify the Grotian emphasis on denying all rights of belligerency to civilians, even in situations of self-defence.

The language of law is perhaps one of the most difficult of all disciplines to penetrate. The founding agents of the Grotian tradition were part of a wider discipline of international law which used a particular language not only to map out their distinct concerns, but also as a political tool. In an illuminating work on the subject, which tackles some of the mechanisms and morphology of legal traditions in general, Martin Krygier noted two key features in the formulation of legal language:

Legal traditions provide substance, models, exemplars and a *language* in which to speak within and about the law. Participation in such a tradition involves sharing a way of speaking about the world which, like language though more precisely and restrictively than natural language, shapes, forms and in part envelops the thought of those who speak it and think through it. For better or for worse (almost certainly for better *and* for worse) it is difficult for insiders to step outside it or for outsiders to enter and participate in it untutored. It moulds the thinking of insiders even where, perhaps especially where, they least realise, and evades the grasp of outsiders determined to pin it down.[109]

[109] Martin Krygier, 'Law as Tradition', *Law and Philosophy*, 5 (1986), 244. On this issue see also the interesting article by F. Boyle, 'Ideals and Things: International Legal Scholarship and the Prison-house of Language', *Harvard International Law Journal*, 26/2 (1985), 327–59.

For the language of the laws of war, there were several Grotian inno-
vations in methodology, which introduced restrictions in the discourse
itself. The first was the introduction of specific customs which were
imbued with particular (in this case conservative) political ideologies.
A central criticism of Grotius' method mentioned by both Voltaire and
Rousseau was the inclusion (indeed selection) of barbaric Roman
customs as examples of precedent ('history as fact'). This method was
also used by Martens, Lieber, and Bluntschli when describing existing
customs, thus defining the 'correct' manner of selecting history in the
structuring of laws of war. In a section of his work which referred to the
question of civilian uprisings at the Brussels Conference, Martens chose
to quote Napier, who (as was shown in the first two chapters) gave an
extremely unbalanced and prejudiced account of the guerrilla war
against Napoleon's occupying army:

Thus the war of the Spanish against Napoleon has up to now been celebrated;
it is held up as evidence that a levée en masse can achieve great results . . . But
in reality, the war in the Iberian peninsula suggests rather different considerations to us. The famous British historian Napier . . . was brought to the following conclusions: 'It is perhaps easy', he noted, 'to raise a people against an
enemy which is attempting to occupy its country; but it is a very perilous task
to control this energy once it has been awakened. The slightest mistake in the
choice of methods could bring more harm than good'. These judicious
observations from this military historian can serve to refute the objections
raised by the British government in 1875 against the inclinations of the
Brussels Conference.

He also cites an 'impartial' book by Brialmont, an anonymous tome
entitled '*L'Angleterre et les Petits États* about the Brussels Conference,
where the author 'General T' rather untruthfully stated that there had
never actually been such a thing as a *levée en masse* in Europe during
the 'Christian era'.[110] Lieber also used Napier to the same effect. He was
also partial, like Grotius, to citing Roman practices as inscribed by
Cicero, and Machiavelli's favourite Roman historian Livy, especially in
his 'Guerrilla Parties Considered with Reference to the Law and Usages
of War'.[111] Another aspect was how this language became restricted by
the establishment of value-laden concepts in accepted 'neutral' legal ter-
minology. For example, 'innocent' civilians, a term used invariably by the
three synthesizers to classify the category of passive civilians under
occupation, had a moral rather than merely descriptive connotation.

[110] *La Paix et la guerre*, 377–8; 376.
[111] *The Miscellaneous Writings of Francis Lieber*, ii. 282.

'Innocent' if passive implied, of course, 'guilty' if politically or militarily active.[112]

It should be noted that although the purpose of structuring the modern laws of war through the selective use of history was strongly conservative, the method of using history as a political tool remained, as did the employment of 'neutral' and 'apolitical' terms. Most modern Grotians working in the laws of war continue to use, and indeed celebrate, this technique. In an attack on Richard Falk, Hedley Bull rejects overtly political terms, apparently in preference for a political ideology which is embedded within a neutral language: 'The task of an academic inquirer is not to jump on bandwagons but to stand back and assess, *in a disinterested way*, the direction in which they are going' and continues, dismissively, 'any writer can join a political movement and devote his intellectual talents to supplying the rhetoric, the exaggeration, the denunciation and the slurring of issues that will help speed it on its way,' and concludes that 'it does not seem the best uses for the talents of the Albert C. Milbank Professor of International Law'.[113] What Hedley Bull had in mind as legitimate legal theory is argued as follows:

> In order to come to grips with himself as an organizer of the present and the future—his first and foremost calling—the lawyer above all has to find his bearing within time and *vis-à-vis* the extraneous forces constantly in operation. As a means to that end, his own view of the past is essential—and saying so, I wish to emphasize that a lawyer's view of past events and circumstances should not necessarily coincide with a historian's conception of the same. Out of the continuous stream of factual elements, the lawyer as an organizer will make his own choice, selecting what is important from an organized perspective. And in order to structure his findings, he may apply a particular technique of recording periodization according to events that in his estimation heralded a new phase . . . It is my profound belief that lawyers as organizers are entitled to their own view of, and compartments in, history, including the concept of growth.[114]

The International Committee of the Red Cross began a reconstruction of the language of the modern laws of war to reform what they

[112] See the following theoretical arguments, where nonetheless all three accept without question the Grotian definition of 'innocence'. G. Mavrodes, 'Conventions and the Morality of War', *Philosophy and Public Affairs*, 4/2 (1975), and two replies to his article: R. Fullinwider, 'War and Innocence', *Philosophy and Public Affairs*, 5/1 (1975), and L. Alexander, 'Self-Defence and the Killing of Non-combatants: A Reply to Fullinwider', *Philosophy and Public Affairs*, 5/4 (1976). For further discussion see M. Walzer's, *Obligations: Essays on Disobedience, War, and Citizenship* (Cambridge: Harvard University Press, 1970).

[113] H. Bull, 'International Law and International Order', *International Organization*, 26 (1972), 588; emphasis added.

[114] M. Bos, *Netherlands International Law Review*, 39 (1992), 1.

believed was its regressive substance, yet, in this progressive project they nonetheless remained guided by the same methodological principles as Martens, Lieber, and even Grotius. For example, the expression 'International Humanitarian Law', a term promoted by the ICRC to replace 'The Laws of War', advanced the notion of a set of laws established to protect the lives of humans rather than a set of rules and customs providing guidelines for fighting war. David Forsythe explains that 'it has been privately argued by some governmental officials that the ICRC has such an extensive view of humanitarian law in armed conflict that the ICRC and "its law" are getting in the way of the process of war,' and explains that what follows from this is apparently 'the ICRC is making a surreptitious contribution to peace by so restricting the parties in the conduct of war as to make war impossible as a viable means of state policy'.[115] The way in which this is done is by a distinctive use of language:

ICRC members expressed themselves in a neutral, impartial language, making skillful uses of litotes, euphemisms, omissions, allusions, extrapolations, and abstractions. The result was a wooden dialect that tried to blend ideals with neutrality. With rare exceptions, it expressed no clear political intentions, emotions, or personal feelings.[116]

Also standardized was the notion of ideological relativism. Indeed eclecticism was heralded as the cornerstone of the Grotian system: in the words of Schwarzenberger the Grotian approach 'offers splendid opportunities *for arguments either way*'.[117] This struck to the heart of the Grotian heritage—the notion of different legal arguments being advanced from a single methodological blueprint. Eclecticism laid the cornerstone of the concept of pluralism in the construction of the laws of war. Lauterpacht noted:

The fact seems to be that on most subjects which he discusses in his treatise it is impossible to say what is Grotius' view of the legal position. He will tell us, often with regard to the same question, what is the law of nature, the law of nations, divine law, Mosaic law, the law of the Gospel, Roman law, the law of charity, the obligations of charity, the obligations of honour, or considerations of charity. But we often look in vain for a statement as to what is *the* law governing the matter.

[115] D. Forsythe, *Humanitarian Politics: The ICRC* (Baltimore: Johns Hopkins University Press, 1977), 122.

[116] Junod, *The Imperilled Red Cross and the Palestine-Eretz Israel Conflict: 1945–1992*, 49.

[117] 'The Grotius Factor in International Law', in Bull et al., *Hugo Grotius and International Relations*, 306, n.14.

He went on to remark with the admirable sang-froid of a lawyer: 'There is almost a touch of levity in this indiscriminating and confusing eclecticism in the use of sources.'[118] As was illustrated above, early Grotians used this method to entrench the hegemonic position of the Concert of Europe. Later Grotians, of the more progressive school, were able to draw on the methodology to argue for progressive ethical and juridical norms. In a well-known example, Falk uses Grotius' methodology to fashion a much more liberal and progressive 'Grotian quest' than that of nineteenth-century jurists such as Martens and Bluntschli: 'the Grotian question, because it is normatively grounded and future oriented, synthesizes the old and the new while it cherishes continuities and legitimizes discontinuities'. Accordingly, the 'Grotian quest should probably concentrate more on mobilizing the consciences of the people than on activating the consciences of their rulers'.[119] Accordingly, the method clearly instituted a system which was based on a flexible ranking of values.

The third feature of the Grotian tradition of war was the relativism of its ethical and legal reasoning. This was not a complete form of relativism. It was established by Grotius that in order to define his philosophy as the *via media* between two extremes, certain ideologies which threatened the position of his philosophy as the true middle ground had to be challenged.[120] This was done by classifying them as perverse, or replete with Hirschman's concept of jeopardy, or indeed simply by dismissing them as 'ideologies'. Once the paradigmatic theory was adequately established as the middle way, however, it was then possible to include certain features which could encompass both progressive and conservative strands of Grotian thought. As the Professor of Law at Yale remarked dryly: 'Rules, as Grotius presented them, ordinarily travelled in pairs of opposites.'[121] This pluralism confirmed the practice of moral relativism and gave a semblance of coherence to the rhetorical language of neutrality.

Equally noteworthy was the means of controlling the parameters of the legal discourse on moderation in war. The notion of *temperamenta* was extremely limited in the Grotian tradition of war in the late nineteenth century. Accordingly, the element of futility was introduced to highlight the limited nature of moderation. Grotius was the first to make use of the notion of the inevitability of war (which was 'in perfect accord

---

[118] 'The Grotian Tradition', 5.
[119] 'The Grotian Quest' in Edwards, *Hugo Grotius*, xxi.
[120] Grotius used this argument almost exclusively against Erasmian pacifism.
[121] M. McDougal, in Asser Instituut, *International Law and the Grotian Heritage*,166.

with the first principles of nature') as a means of justifying the futility of banning it (hence his main criticism of the Erasmian approach). Basdevant noted, 'Grotius only took international society as it then was . . . he didn't believe that an organisation could eradicate war . . . he also didn't believe in abolishing war, but in regulating it'.[122] Lieber not only thought war was inevitable, but was half in love with it, denouncing as sacrilegious those who sought to outlaw it: 'indiscriminate railing against war' involves a 'degree of impiety', he declared to General Halleck in 1864.[123] In his *La Paix et la guerre*, de Martens also deployed the concept of the futility of banning war on the grounds of its inevitability. 'War thus appears as a positive historical fact, which cannot be denied. This fact proves that the causes of war are profound and that they stem, on one hand, from man's nature, and on the other, from the external world.' Although citing this as an example of 'Prussian thinking' he goes on to see it as common currency, and only to be changed by the gradual development of civilization.[124] Equally, he adopted the Grotian method of arguing for the middle way in the introduction of limited moderation. Many twentieth-century Grotians of the more conservative school adopted both these methods, highlighting the inevitability of war and the middle-way approach. An absolutely characteristic example of this approach was Hedley Bull's, whose argument synthesizes futility, jeopardy and even perversity (on the part of small states rejecting his analysis): 'Grotius saw that international society is threatened not only by an absence of restraint on the right to resort to war, but also a refusal to countenance any resort to force at all', then goes on to cite the Grotian liturgy: 'the needs that are served by the doctrine of "the middle way" are not ultimately those simply of strong states but of weak states also; it is the doctrine that no distinction can be made between just and unjust causes of war'.[125] However, the more progressive Grotians focused on the 'middle-way' approach almost exclusively.

The final element in the Grotian tradition of war which united both conservative and progressive strands was the central notion of order. The threats of disorder to the Grotian system of rules in general (and rules on war in particular) were countered by two arguments: perversity and jeopardy. In the first case, Grotian lawyers repeatedly argued that any concession to the rights of civilian belligerency would merely

---

[122] *De Jure Belli ac Pacis*, 52; see also *Prolegomena*, vii; Basdevant, 'Hugo Grotius', 256, 257.
[123] Childress, 'Francis Lieber's Interpretation of the Laws of War', 44.
[124] Martens, *La Paix et la guerre*, 27.
[125] Asser Instituut, *International Law and the Grotian Heritage*, 136–7.

serve to exacerbate the condition of occupied populations; the remedy was in this sense nothing but an aggravation of the disease. The Grotian founders also sought to safeguard the sanctity of the existing system of legal rules by reference to the notion of jeopardy: the threat to all existing benefits and virtues. As a loyal imperialist, Martens strongly opposed the republican notions of popular sovereignty and mass participation in civic life. From this perspective, he was also strongly opposed to any effort to involve citizens in the defence of their country. Such efforts were seen as having the potential effect of endangering all forms of civilization. He offered the example of the Paris Commune in 1870:

Given the advancing sophistication of modern armies, one can easily appreciate how little use for the motherland were popular masses who were not well organized. Furthermore, the history of the Paris Commune is an example destined forever to remind all nations of this fundamental truth: it is easier to hand out weapons than it is to retrieve them.[126]

Ideologically dangerous terms such as patriotism and notions of just war also threatened the existing order of states. De Leer, the Russian military delegate at Brussels in 1874 used this method when trying to promote a strict limitation on who could qualify as legitimate belligerents. He declared: 'There are two kinds of patriotism, that which is regulated and that which is not. Which one is preferable for the defence? It is of course the one which is regulated', and a typical jeopardy argument by a French military jurist claimed that the patriotic acts of civilians:

creates an inevitable and dangerous confusion, becomes the cause of daring and heroic acts which cause their authors—in all good faith—to disregard the laws of war, and through an exalted sense of patriotism to carry out acts which irritate the enemy and often provoke terrible reprisals. Finally, the levée en masse is, in a certain sense, in contradiction with the principle that war is a relationship between States.[127]

In the words of a Grotian lawyer, popular expressions of patriotism only served to make wars harsher and more intractable: 'we must be especially wary of individual initiatives which could develop under the impulsion of this most beautiful and noble of sentiments: patriotism. When this occurs, the inevitable result is to render war more brutal and

---

[126] Martens, *La Paix et la guerre*, 381.
[127] 'Actes de la conférence', 99; A. Mérignhac, *Les Lois de la guerre sur terre* (Paris: Perrin, 1903), 76.

harsh'.[128] The substance and the method of these traditionalists was replicated in the works of certain later Grotian theorists on war. Modern Grotian theorists such as Hedley Bull argued for order as the supreme principle of international society, overriding in most cases concerns for alternative claims such as justice. When in doubt, they fell back on the Grotian methodological blueprint, which released them from specific moral commitments in order to continue to uphold order as the supreme value. Hedley Bull's views on this matter are worth setting out, as he deemed international order the cornerstone of any society, or, indeed, system. For Bull, order preceded concerns of justice—the goal of order was a core value, whereas justice was a secondary one. In any conflict between the two, he took the 'conservative or orthodox view' which prioritized order, arguing that it would be too difficult to find a 'consensus' on the demands of justice if it entailed change: 'the prospect is opened up that the consensus which does exist about order or minimum coexistence *will be undone*'. This is another example of Bull's use of the notions of perversity and jeopardy to defend threats to order .[129]

CONCLUSION

This chapter has outlined the contours of a new tradition of the laws of war derived from the writings of Grotius. It is a tradition that drew on his writings on international relations and international law, yet was distinct from both of them. This Grotian tradition of war was based on a hierarchical reading of the notion of sociability; the dualist potential of natural law both as progressive and regressive guides for human action; the overriding concern with state sovereignty and law; the subordination of the demands of liberty to those of order; the occupation of a middle path between two contending political ideologies; and a claim to neutrality which concealed an ideological *parti pris*. From the perspective of the laws of war, whose terms of reference it defined, this Grotian tradition was strongly attached to the notion of maintaining a clear distinction between lawful and unlawful combatants.

As an ideological construct, this tradition of war had a number of strengths and weaknesses. On the positive side, one of its greatest assets was its sheer discursive power; its capacity to articulate the proper fron-

---

[128] A. Rolin, *Le Droit moderne de la guerre* (Brussels: Seycourt, 1920), 267.
[129] *The Anarchical Society*, 94–7; emphasis added.

tiers of legitimate discourse in the field, and, in so doing, to represent the political interests of hegemonic powers. Grotian ideology performed this function with notable skill and consummate elegance. This sensitivity was also apparent in the tradition's flexibility and adaptibility, ensuring that its principles were always attuned to the needs of the times (as defined at least by the dominant powers). Finally, of the three traditions presented here, this is the one which most accurately captured the ambivalent nature of military occupation itself; this has been illustrated in greater depth in Chapter 2. But if this ambivalence was a source of the tradition's strength, paradoxically it was its certainties which exposed many of its weaknesses. The power of Grotian language (rhetorically but not substantively universalist) actually excluded ideologies and groups which did not conform to its conception of the status quo, thus giving the lie to its claims of inclusivity. Likewise, the Grotian certainty of the necessity of moral relativism blinded its devotees to an essential feature of the human condition, namely its propensity to subscribe to ethically absolutist doctrines.

The formulation of this tradition also has a number of broader implications for the understanding of Grotius and influence of his work; the taxonomy of the Grotian traditions of international relations and international law; the internal structure of Grotian ideology; and, finally, the impact of this ideology on the construction of the laws of war. It has been shown that excluding the *persona* and *fama* of Grotius has vitiated a proper understanding of the substance of his philosophy on war. These two factors are also essential for appreciating the *Weltanschauung* of subsequent generations of Grotians, and the practical and intellectual methodology they acquired from him. This point has a wider bearing on the manner in which Grotian traditions of thought have usually been systematized. Contrary to convention, it has been argued here that personal political values and preferences exercised a significant influence on the construction of the Grotian paradigm; in other words, individual political convictions and published output were inexorably intertwined. Further, recapturing their political world view highlights the importance of linking the notions of the good life inside the state with the good life outside it. How Grotians situated themselves in domestic politics had a crucial bearing on how they theorized about and practised international law and international relations.

This tradition served as the basis for the elaboration of a Grotian 'normative code' which informed the practices and approaches of Grotian agents at the negotiations on the laws of war at Brussels in 1874, The Hague in 1899 and 1907, and Geneva in 1949. Central to this normative code was an essential attachment to the distinction between lawful and unlawful combatants. In the Grotian scheme of things, states were the exclusive subjects of international law. This system of rules was therefore designed to protect and maintain their interests. This conception was even more deeply embedded in the laws of war, which was a project defined by Grotians during the second half of the nineteenth century. Essential to the Grotian position was the contention that these laws could be made to work only if states and civilians were recognized to operate in different spheres. Wars were waged by soldiers, on the orders of their political and military commanders, while civilian populations remained entirely outside its framework. Indeed, the crux of the Grotian argument was that this removal was in the civilians' best interests; for the consequences of a war fought between armies were likely to be less destructive if local inhabitants were excluded from it. Hence the 'neutral' and 'impartial' posture of the Grotian system, which presented itself as completely separated from ethical considerations of justice and right.

But the neutrality which lay at the heart of the Grotian approach was deeply slanted. In wars of conquest and occupation, it effectively conceded all rights of belligerency to one party (the invaders and occupiers) and none to the other (the populations fighting invading armies). What this chapter has established, furthermore, is that this ideological imbalance was not an accident. All rights of belligerency were denied to civilians because the arming of the citizenry was part of a system of values which was entirely alien to the Grotian understanding of the world. In a political and philosophical system which prioritized order over liberty—and indeed slavery over freedom—there was only room for dependent and subservient subjects, operating within a restricted framework of sociability. Citizens struggling to defend their communities, properties, and ways of living did not belong to that world, and perhaps even threatened its very essence. Hence the rather frantic Grotian invocations of the notions of perversity and jeopardy whenever attempts were made to broaden the range of permitted belligerents, for such attempts represented an ideological challenge to a broader notion of consensual order which was quintessentially 'Grotian'. Hence, equally, the strength (but also the limits) of the system of legal rules which they devised to circumscribe the practices of belligerents.

6

Hope and Heroic Action:
Rousseau, Paoli, Kosciuszko,
and the Republican Tradition of War

I open my books about rights and morals, I listen to scholars and legal experts, and inspired by their suggestive discourses, I deplore the miseries of nature, admire the peace and justice established by the civil order, bless the wisdom of public institutions, and console myself for being a man by seeing myself a citizen. Well instructed as to my duties and my happiness, I close the books, leave the lecture room, and look around me. There I see a miserable people groaning under an iron yoke, the human race crushed in a grip of oppressors, and an enraged mob overwhelmed by pain and hunger whose blood and tears rich men drink in peace. And everywhere the strong are armed against the weak with the formidable power of the law.

All of this happens peacefully and without resistance. With a tranquility like that of Odysseus' imprisoned companions as they wait to be devoured by the Cyclops, we groan and are quiet. But I must draw a veil over these horrors. I lift my eyes and look towards the horizon. There I see fire and flames, deserted countrysides, pillaged villages. Monstrous men, where are you dragging these poor creatures? I hear a terrible noise, an uproar, screams! I draw near. Before me is a panorama of murder—ten thousand, the dead piled up in heaps, the dying trampled under the feet of horses—and everywhere the sight of death and agony. Yet all of this is the fruit of peaceful institutions. Pity and indignation rise up from the depth of my heart. Barbarian philosopher, come read to us your book on the battlefields![1]

---

[1] Jean Jacques Rousseau, *Principles of the Rights of War*, trans. Grace Roosevelt, *Reading Rousseau in the Nuclear Age* (Philadelphia: Temple University Press, 1990), 233. See also her article on this work, 'Rousseau's Fragments on War', *History of Political Thought* (1987), 8; and 'The Role of Rousseau's Writings on War and Peace in the Evolution of the Social Contract', in G. Lafrance (ed.), *Studies on the Social Contract* (Presses de l'Université d'Ottawa: Ottawa, 1989). For original French text see the authoritative *Œuvres complètes* (hereafter *OC*), ed. B. Gagnebin and M. Raymond (Paris: Pléiades, 1964–95), iii.

THE REPUBLICAN TRADITION OF WAR

The above quotation captures the essential features of both J. J. Rousseau's philosophy of war and his particular formulation of the laws of war. These principles were markedly different from the two traditions delineated in Chapters 4 and 5, the martial and the Grotian. One of the aims here is to demonstrate that Rousseau's thought formed part of a pattern of political ideas about war which were themselves embedded in a distinctive tradition of war in Europe. These principles were not isolated, nor were they drawn from abstract theory. Instead, they were part of a larger understanding of republican war which was both articulated and practised across Europe in the mid-eighteenth and nineteenth centuries. The doctrinal positions were present in force at all the relevant conferences: Brussels in 1874, The Hague in 1899 and 1907, and Geneva in 1949. These principles, together with the practices of republican war in continental Europe, beginning with Corsica and Poland in the eighteenth century, helped forge the republican tradition of war which this chapter will illustrate.

As the quotation from *Fragments on War* (originally entitled *Principles of the Rights of War*) shows, Rousseau was driven by the desire to refute what he claimed were the flaws in the writings of other thinkers on war, in particular Thomas Hobbes and Hugo Grotius. Yet his purpose here was more ambitious. It was, equally, to articulate a new paradigm of republican action. Although Rousseau's thoughts on republican war were complex and highly distinctive, they were not isolated from the broader patterns of thought about republican war in his time. And although he is usually juxtaposed with other *philosophes'* thinking—such as Montesquieu, de Mably, and the Abbé de St Pierre[2]— and contextualized within the intellectual debate on republics in mid-eighteenth-century political thought, this chapter will demonstrate that Rousseau's thinking on republican war was reflected in another arena entirely: the realm of practical politics and the international crises of his

---

[2] For example, see the recent and sympathetic interpretation of de Mably's republican thought by Johnson Kent Wright in *A Classical Republican in Eighteenth Century France: The Political Thought of Mably* (Stanford: Stanford University Press, 1997), especially at 121–4 and 164–76. Montesquieu's morally ambivalent version of republicanism is aptly captured in Nannerl Keohane's *Philosophy and the State in France: The Renaissance to the Enlightenment* (Princeton: Princeton University Press, 1980). See especially the 'small republic debate' at 408–19; and Montesquieu's *Œuvres complètes* (Paris: Seuil, 1964), in particular, his previously unpublished, early views on republicanism in *Dialogue de Xantippe et Xenocrate*, 153–4; on the Abbé see Fernand Maury's classic *Étude sur la vie et les œuvres de Bernardin de St.-Pierre* (Paris: Hachette, 1892).

day. The cases of eighteenth-century Corsica and Poland were the two most obvious examples from which he drew inspiration for his thought.[3] Accordingly, as this tradition was not theoretical, but grounded firmly in the practices of republican war on the Continent, the two great republican military leaders of the eighteenth century, Pasquale Paoli of Corsica (1725–1807), and Tadeusz Kosciuszko of Poland (1746–1817), will also be presented here as pivotal founders of this tradition. Their actions, their legislation, their political philosophy and, above all, their military struggles made them exemplars of the notion of republican war as the good life.

REPUBLICANISM

Republicanism as an ideology (and even a single concept) is currently under intense scrutiny in both its historical and theoretical forms. However, the way in which it is understood in this chapter will differ greatly in certain key respects from other current approaches. First, there is no attempt to attach the same chronological lineage to the tradition, as has already been so successfully accomplished by scholars in the recent literature. The broader ideas being forged in eighteenth-century continental Europe created a multitude of strands of republican thought, some drawing on more classical associations than others. These patterns helped to articulate the principles which lay behind the attempt to fashion modern republics through force of arms in the nineteenth century. The political battles against empire gave rise to an array of republican forms: from the nineteenth-century liberation theology of Lamennais, who inspired many active republicans from Denmark to Greece and Poland, to the radical anti-clericalism of Buonarroti; from La Fayette's *Charbonnerie* to Pasquale Paoli's Machiavellian republican policies and fraternal masonic republican associations;[4] from the exiled 'Portsmouth' group of egalitarian socialist

---

[3] His two 'advisory pieces' on republican practices *Considérations sur le gouvernement de Pologne*, and *Projet de constitution pour la Corse*, in *OC* iii. 953–1041, 901–50. Most instructive on Rousseau and Poland remains B. Lesnodorski's seminal article: 'Rousseau vu de Pologne', *Annales historiques de la Revolution Francaise*, 34 (1962).

[4] On Lamennais see René Rémond, *Lamennais et la démocratie* (Paris: Presses Universitaires de France, 1948), François Tuloup, *Lamennais et son époque: sa vie, son œuvre, son influence, son prophétisme* (Dinan: Impr. Commerciale 1961), Georges Hourdin, *Lamennais: prophète et combattant de la liberté* (Paris: Perrin, 1982), and for the development of the republican tradition of war see Gaston Bordet's useful *La Pologne, Lamennais et ses amis 1830–1834* (Paris: Éditions du Dialogue, 1985). A biography of Buonarroti in English is Elisabeth Eisenstein, *Filippo Michele Buonarroti, The First*

peasant-soldiers of Poland who had fought in the 1831 November insurrection to the ambitious pan-Slavic republican secret societies of Joachim Lelewel and Alexander Herzen of the 1860s.[5] Fascinating though these separate narratives may be, it is not the purpose here to attempt to trace all of these diverse branches and movements of republican martialism. Instead, the ambition will be to offer two basic claims. First, that within the wider republican ideologies of war in nineteenth-century Europe there were two highly distinct branches: the defensive and the expansive. Republicans of the defensive branch sought to fight within their national borders to establish states of a republican political character and for the establishment of sovereign nations. Summarized very crudely, republicans of the expansive branch, on the other hand, sought to export and impose republican values upon other nations through military force in the creation of a republican way of life. Second, that the defensive tradition of war was both a philosophical articulation and a concrete political practice, and that its founders established a paradigm for republican struggle in modern Europe. Accordingly, it is the defensive branch that will be explained and developed here, as it was exclusively this doctrine that was advanced so extensively and consistently at Brussels in 1874, The Hague in 1899, and Geneva in 1949.

THE THREE FOUNDERS

The reasons why the republican leaders of Corsica and Poland can be identified as founders of the republican tradition of war stem directly

Professional Revolutionist, 1761–1837 (Cambridge, Mass.: Harvard University Press, 1959). A powerful summary of his intellectual and political career is given by Jean Crozier in his edition of Buonarroti's *La Conjuration de Corse* (Bastia: Editions Centofanti, 1997), 9–48, which also contains the most recent bibliography on various aspects of Buonarroti's life and work, 165–85. On La Fayette's work in the *Charbonnerie* and with the Poles see Adam Lewak's fascinating, *General M. R. La Fayette o Polsce: listy—mowy—dokumenty* (Warsaw: Gebethner i Wolff, 1934). On Paoli's influences and associations see F. Ettori's 'La Formation intellectuelle de Pascal Paoli (1725–1755)', *Annales historiques de la Révolution Française*, 46 (1974), especially at 491, 501–4.

[5] For the group of illiterate peasants who had fought in the 1830 insurrection and ended up in Portsmouth see Peter Brock's 'The Political Programme of the Polish Democratic Society', in his *Nationalism and Populism in Partitioned Poland* (London: Orbis, 1973), especially at 78; for Herzen and Lelewel, see Joan Skurnowicz, *Romantic Nationalism and Liberalism: Joachim Lelewel and the Polish National Idea* (New York: Columbia University Press, 1981); on Herzen see *My Past and Thoughts: The Memoirs of Alexander Herzen* (Knopf: New York, 1968) and especially E. H. Carr's, *The Romantic Exiles: A Nineteenth-century Portrait* (Harmondsworth: Penguin, 1949).

from the predicament of their countries, yet go beyond them in several ways. Most importantly, Pasquale Paoli and Tadeusz Kosciuszko have been selected as 'founders' of nineteenth-century continental republican war through the remarkable representation of their lives—the example which they set (and which they sought to set) in the minds of their peers and of future generations waging war with republican aims in nineteenth-century Europe. Also of primary significance was the fact that both were men of action rather than 'mere philosophers'. It will be demonstrated below that the republican principles which they espoused led them to engage in war in the first instance. Accordingly, their principles (republican in faith) and the practice of these principles (republican in form) are both central aspects of the political philosophy of the republican tradition of war. Finally, the model they set for the practice of republican virtue—in their political and military work, in the values they professed, in the policies, declarations, letters, and manifestos they wrote—all demonstrated a coherent set of defensive and creative practices to be followed when waging republican war. There was a level of consistency between the republican aims of these two leaders and the means they deployed to achieve these ends.

Jean Jacques Rousseau (1712–78) has been selected from a different set of criteria. Crucially, his writings provided the most comprehensive articulation of defensive republican war in the mid-eighteenth century. Indeed, he claimed to be inspired by the actions of the Corsican people and Pasquale Paoli's own role in the creation of a free republic in Corsica, and also by the predicament of the Polish people facing her hungry and powerful neighbours.[6] Although he did not adhere entirely to the life of Plutarchian virtue as the others appeared to have done, two aspects of his life as a model are relevant. Not only did he make it clear that he was attempting to live such a life, but he claimed that this public attempt was an integral part of his active political position and republicanism.[7]

---

[6] On Corsica, see Rousseau's correspondence with M. Buttafuoco in *Correspondance complète*, ed. R. A. Leigh (Geneva, Voltaire Foundation, 1967–95), xxi. 3475; Sven Stelling-Michaud's introduction to *Projet de constitution pour la Corse*, *OC* iii. cc–ccxiv; Rousseau's *Confessions*, *OC* i. 612–19. On Poland see Jean Fabre's excellent introduction to *Considérations*, in *OC* iii. ccxvi–ccxlv, and also Maurice Cranston's biography *The Solitary Self: Jean Jacques Rousseau in Exile and Adversity* (London: Allen Lane Penguin Press, 1997), 94, 177–9.

[7] An illustration of exactly how Rousseau set himself up as 'public example' is given in R. A. Leigh's touching 'Jean-Jacques Rousseau and the Myth of Antiquity in the Eighteenth Century', in R. Bolgar (ed.), *Classical Influences on Western Thought A.D. 1650–1870* (Cambridge: Cambridge University Press, 1979). For a completely different view of the effect on his life and his work see Denise Leduc-Lafayette, *Jean-Jacques Rousseau et le mythe d'antiquité* (Paris: Librairie Philosophique, 1974), especially 33–69.

Although some recent literature has amply demonstrated his authentic and active republicanism as a Genevois, in no substantive manner did his life follow the same trajectory as the other two.[8] It is primarily in his political writings, rather than his personal example, that one finds the clear expression of the defensive republican paradigm.

ROUSSEAU'S REPUBLICAN WAR

The quantity of literature devoted to Jean Jacques Rousseau is immense, and continues to grow apace. Yet within this vast scholarship, there are a few compelling contributions to the understanding of Rousseau's political philosophy which give a varied, and generally sympathetic treatment of his work, avoiding the anachronisms of earlier periods.[9] In spite of this, and excluding the lonely example of Grace Roosevelt's work, there is a discouraging dearth of such scholarship on his vision of international affairs, and absolutely none on his writings on the laws of war.[10] Such studies as do exist have tended to support—and sometimes magnify—either the 'multipolar' or the traditional 'bipolar' view of his work.[11] For example, scholars on international relations in the first half of the twen-

His fascination with the Laconian model is extensively covered in Elizabeth Rawson's *The Spartan Tradition in European Thought* (Oxford: Clarendon, 1991), 231–41, 243–6, 277–9.

[8] Most recent is Helen Rosenblatt's compelling *Rousseau and Geneva: From the First Discourse to the Social Contract 1749–1762* (Cambridge: Cambridge University Press, 1997).

[9] A good place to begin is with Robert Wokler's elegant *Rousseau* in the Past Master series (Oxford: Oxford University Press, 1995), or see N. Dent's *Rousseau: An Introduction to His Psychological, Social, and Political Theory* (Oxford: Basil Blackwell, 1988). See also Arthur Melzer, *The Natural Goodness of Man*, which, as its title would suggest, focuses on Rousseau's belief that all his ideas were developed from the central postulate of man's natural goodness: *The Natural Goodness of Man: On the System of Rousseau's Thought* (Chicago: University of Chicago Press, 1990). Christopher Kelly's *Rousseau's Exemplary Life: The 'Confessions' as Political Philosophy* (Ithaca, NY: Cornell University Press, 1987) is in a similar vein.

[10] There were three writers on Rousseau and the laws of war in the first part of this century: Cuno Hofer, *L'Influence de J.-J. Rousseau sur le droit de la guerre* (Geneva: Georg. et Cie., 1916); George Lassudrie-Duchène, *Jean-Jacques Rousseau et le droit des gens* (Paris: Imp. Henri Jouve, 1906); and G. Beaulavon 'Les Idées de J.-J. Rousseau sur la guerre', *Revue de Paris* (1917), 11. However, they were all convinced Grotians, with the inevitable result.

[11] Jean Wahl, 'La Bipolarité de Rousseau', *Annales de la Société Jean-Jacques Rousseau*, 33 (1953–5), 49–55. See also, for example, Judith Shklar, borrowing Wahl's term, and in her own work on Rousseau emphasizes the duality in his writings: *Men and Citizens: A Study of Rousseau's Social Theory* (Cambridge: Cambridge University Press, 1969).

tieth century often seemed to confuse Rousseau with the Abbé de St Pierre.[12] Hinsley argued that Rousseau was 'confused', his work fraught with 'inconclusiveness', and described its overall sensibility as one of 'defeatism'.[13] In Stanley Hoffmann and David Fidler's *Rousseau on International Relations*, Rousseau is presented as an over-idealistic pessimist.[14] In Hoffmann's earlier article, however, Rousseau appears as merely charmingly fatalistic, thus not really worth taking seriously ('his work is hardly relevant to the world we live in').[15] A book based almost entirely on Hoffmann's interpretation, Carter's *Rousseau and the Problem of War*, describes him as a man stuck between a rock and a hard place; the former his 'moralism' and the latter his 'pessimism'.[16]

One reason for the scarcity of work on Rousseau's thinking about war is the spotlight put upon Thomas Hobbes, considered by many to be Rousseau's main opponent. At first this appears to be a natural predilection of political philosophers familiar with Hobbes's work, where there is an emphasis on the civil foundations of the state. Indeed, much has been written contrasting the two writers.[17] Without wishing to underestimate Hobbes's influence as a stimulus, what is conspicuous in domestic political philosophers' interpretations of Rousseau is the absence of his equally infuriating antagonist Hugo Grotius. In the vast majority of works on Rousseau, Grotius tends to be marginalized, lumped together with Pufendorf, or reduced to the status of 'natural law' writer in a footnote explanation.[18] As this chapter will show, Rousseau's key principles

[12] For example, J. Windenberger, *Essai sur le système de politique étrangère de J.-J. Rousseau: la République Confédérative des Petits États* (Paris: A. Picard et Fils, 1899).

[13] F. H. Hinsley, *Power and the Pursuit of Peace: Theory and Practice in the History of Relations among States* (Cambridge: Cambridge University Press, 1963), 46–62.

[14] S. Hoffmann and D. Fidler (eds.), *Rousseau on International Relations* (Oxford: Clarendon Press, 1991). The collection of his works in this volume are extracted from other, earlier, translations of Rousseau's work and are sadly incomplete at crucial points (especially *Corsica* and *Fragments on War*); no mention is made of Roosevelt's recovery of the essential and original texts (unlike Victor Gourevitz's recent translation for Cambridge, which makes good use of her scholarship and acknowledges it).

[15] S. Hoffmann, 'Rousseau on War and Peace', in *American Political Science Review*, 57 (1963), 317–33.

[16] C. Carter, *Rousseau and the Problem of War* (New York: Garland Press, 1987), 209–10.

[17] For example M. Cranston and R. Peters (eds.), *Hobbes and Rousseau* (New York: Anchor Books, 1972), or H. Cell and J. MacAdam's *Rousseau's Response to Hobbes* (New York: Peter Lang, 1988).

[18] See Robert Wokler's helpful: 'Rousseau's Pufendorf: Natural Law and the Foundations of Commercial Society', *History of Political Thought*, 15/3 (1994), 384–7. In an invaluable analysis, Wokler focuses on Pufendorf as Rousseau's main adversary on the principles of natural law. In his article, Wokler notes that there are 'only five specific references to Pufendorf . . . There are, by contrast, abundant references to Grotius throughout Rousseau's major political writings and most especially in the *Contrat Social*', 380.

on the laws of war were asserted through launching a deliberate attack on the first two traditions of war identified in this book, the martial and the Grotian. Rather than directly challenge the Martialist paradigm, he demonstrated instead how similar it was to both Grotius' and Hobbes's ideas on war. For Rousseau, Hobbes's and Grotius' philosophy was identical on these issues: his views of what happened inside the state was intimately linked to what was happening outside its borders.

In the literature of the laws of war, Jean Jacques Rousseau is mistakenly perceived as the founder of the fundamental principle that underlies the entire project of the modern laws of war: the distinction between combatant and non-combatant. Nearly all international lawyers and writers on the philosophy of war confer upon him the accolade of establishing this principle, citing this famous passage from the *Social Contract*:

War is then not a relationship between one man and another, but a relationship between one State and another, in which individuals are only enemies accidentally, not as men, nor even as citizens, but as soldiers.[19]

As Pillet wrote in his classic work on the laws of war: 'The ideas were significantly modified on this issue in the course of the [eighteenth] century.' The 'progress of the laws of war' was in recognizing this 'idea, set out for the first time by Rousseau, that war is between states and not between individuals'. In a similar vein, the nineteenth-century lawyer and scholar Lieut. Brenet explains, it is 'J.-J. Rousseau who, in the "Social Contract", formulated the primordial principle of the laws of war distinguishing between combatants and non-combatants'. Even the Rousseauian scholar Robert Derathé accepts this interpretation: 'Rousseau is the first, in the history of international law, to say that war is a relation between States, and that the citizen is, in principle, completely excluded of war.' He goes on to assert the commonplace view on its merit: 'it is the principle that we currently uphold: the population should be controlled. Unfortunately, the evolution of modern war goes against this conception.'[20] Another typically 'Grotian' interpretation of this concept is Windenberger's *Essai sur le système de politique étrangère de J.-J. Rousseau*: 'this axiom, which is ex-

---

[19] *OC* iii. 356.

[20] A. Pillet, *Le Droit de la guerre* (Paris: A. Rousseau, 1892), 113–14; Lieut. Amédée Brenet, *La France et L'Allemagne devant le droit international, pendant les opérations militaires de la guerre 1870–71* (Paris: A. Rousseau, 1902), 1; R. Derathé, 'Jean-Jacques Rousseau et le progrès des idées humanitaires du XVIe au XVIIIe siècle', *Revue internationale de la Croix Rouge*, 40 (1958), 523.

plained by the role of self defence, is a role reserved uniquely for the state'.[21] In Cuno Hofer's lengthy treatise we find he understands the 'humanitarian idea of Rousseau, which distinguishes between citizen and soldier'. He explains that 'this legal principle of his argues that war must remain localised; that is, between regular military forces, since war constitutes a relation between states'.[22] Yet this prevailing interpretation of Rousseau as the founder of the legal notion of the distinction is fundamentally misguided. Its received wisdom on Rousseau's political position in the literature on the laws of war—and especially as the founder of the notion of distinction—has permeated interpretations of other aspects of his writings in both international relations and political philosophy, theory, and history. Yet Rousseau was arguing the exact opposite of the usual understandings of his words. Indeed, the manner in which he has been construed would probably have him spinning in his *sarcophage* at the Pantheon.

ROUSSEAU, PAOLI, AND KOSCIUSZKO

This chapter will begin by setting out Jean Jacques Rousseau's articulation of the nature of man, war, liberty, government, patriotism, and nationalism, and will finish with the views (and the policies and practices that reflected the views) of the other two founders of the tradition, Pasquale Paoli and Tadeusz Kosciuszko. Rousseau's political thought was centrally engaged with these moral and institutional questions, and his specific conclusions had a direct bearing on two core themes of republican war. First, he concerned himself with the birth, development, and maintenance of young republics.[23] Franco Venturi has argued that Rousseau's work on Poland was driven by an 'aversion to civilisation brought by conquest'.[24] Yet as will become clear, it is exactly a 'civilised' civic society which Rousseau sought to construct, through the process of resistance to tyranny itself. Accordingly his advice was directed at securing and forging republican values and institutions in the face of

---

[21] Windenberger, *Essai*, 133. Emphasis added.

[22] Hofer, *L'Influence de J.-J. Rousseau sur le droit de la guerre*, 24.

[23] See two detailed studies on his work on Corsica, both originally theses: Ernestine Dedeck-Héry's *Jean Jacques Rousseau et la constitution pour la Corse* (Philadelphia: University of Pennsylvania, 1932); Ange Moretti, *La Constitution corse de Jean Jacques Rousseau* (Paris: Librairie Recueil Sirey, 1910).

[24] F. Venturi, *Utopia and Reform in the Enlightenment* (Cambridge: Cambridge University Press, 1971), 194.

adversity. He also developed a complex and sophisticated set of practical codes to guide republican and proto-republican nations, as well as their citizens, when at war.

Rousseau's views are the first to be set out below, yet the claim here is not that he is a more influential founder than the other two, nor that he chronologically predates them, nor even that they are influenced by, or helping to construct, a 'Rousseauian paradigm'. Indeed, it will be shown that Rousseau's writings were directly affected and inspired by the actions of Paoli as well as the predicament of Kosciuszko's Poland. Rather, he appears as the first founder because his writings on war possessed the greatest degree of theoretical and philosophical elaboration. This was partly because his targets were not Genoa or Russia as much as they were two other philosophers of war: Thomas Hobbes and Hugo Grotius. His ambition was to show how their formulations could be used to serve the policies of such imperial powers. Hence Rousseau used the method of appearing to 'construct' a theory in response to the limits and flaws of the two main rival paradigms of war. Although this technique has been conventionally understood largely as a device employed to illuminate his own rather elaborate system, his critique was an integral element in establishing the foundations of his political vision. So the complex republicanism he proposed to create, and the means which he claimed were needed to create it, arose directly from the context against which he was reacting. As Peter Winch remarked with some accuracy, for Rousseau 'conceptions of justice are only developed through discussions of injustice'.[25]

Moreover, it was *within* the context of the tyranny and the oppressive actions of the Genoese Republic that Pasquale Paoli was motivated to create his virtuous Corsican Republic; as, for Kosciuszko, it was his service in the American Revolution, as well as the repressive policies of Catherine the Second's Russia which helped to formulate his republican sentiments. Rousseau set out his principles on the rights of war with the aim, first, of revealing the inadequacies of the methods Hobbes and Grotius used to establish their theories of war, and, second, of uncovering what he considered the highly political motives that underlay these methods. By drawing on his advice to Poland, to Corsica, and his unfinished work *Principles of the Rights of War*, we shall be reading a

---

[25] P. Winch, 'Man and Society in Hobbes and Rousseau', in M. Cranston and R. S. Peters (eds.), *Hobbes and Rousseau: A Collection of Critical Essays* (New York: Doubleday, 1972), 253. See also an interesting recent study by Pierre Hassner: 'Rousseau and the Theory and Practice of International Relations', C. Orwin and N. Tascov (eds.), *The Legacy of Rousseau* (Chicago: University of Chicago Press, 1997).

far different Rousseau, whose moderation is matched only by an almost prescient awareness of the nature of international and national politics.

THE NATURE OF MAN AND THE STATE OF NATURE: ROUSSEAU *CONTRA* HOBBES AND GROTIUS

Before setting out his own vision of the nature of man, Rousseau was able first to illuminate the contours of Hobbes's vision of the world as a place of false assumptions and failed imagination:

Who can imagine without shuddering the insane system of a natural war of every man against every man? What a strange animal this man must be who believes that his own well-being depends upon the destruction of his species! And how could anyone think that this species, so monstrous and detestable, could last even two generations? But it is to extremes such as these that the desire, or rather the fury, to establish despotism and passive obedience has led one of the greatest geniuses that ever lived.[26]

He went on to criticize Grotius' methods for suggesting that man's sociability was a basic tenet of natural law, declaring that both he and Hobbes used flawed reasoning to construct man's natural state, and that both equally forced a vision of a world which was tainted by a dishonest political agenda. Here, he paints the absurd but vivid picture of what he believed would be the consequences of Hobbes's view:

If a destructive and mutual enmity were essential to our constitution, it would make itself felt even more and would burst forth, in spite of ourselves, from within every social bond. The fierce hatred of humanity would eat away at the heart of man. He would mourn at the birth of his children, rejoice at the death of his brothers, and kill every sleeping man he happened to come across.[27]

Rousseau did not set out to authenticate an irrefutable historical and anthropological basis for man's nature. His intention in advancing such an account had, as its central aim, to uncover the nature of man's ethical worth, through countering the claims of other philosophers.

I have said before and I cannot repeat too often that the error of Hobbes and the *philosophes* is to confuse natural man with the man that they have before their eyes, and to transport into one system a being that could only exist in another ... A superficial philosopher observes souls that are endlessly kneaded

---

[26] *Principes du droit de la guerre*, 187 (*OC* iii. 611).   [27] Ibid. 235.

and allowed to ferment in the yeast of society and believes he has observed man. But in order to know man well, he must know how to separate out the natural growth of the sentiments.[28]

It was of primary importance for Rousseau that this state be both correctly explained and understood; he saw it as the crucial intellectual first step in the journey towards self-mastery. The individual had to imagine himself in the original state of nature as a means of discovering, and beginning to recapture, what he really is, was, and could be. Therefore the purpose of his portrait of natural man was not to illustrate his historical or anthropological origins (although he does portray them in his writings), but for man to retrieve his moral core which modern society has corrupted. Rousseau's 'looking back' was driven by a specific ambition: to lay the basis for a just society. This could be achieved only through the affirmation of the cardinal principle that man was, in essence, good. So Rousseau offered a gentle creature in the state of nature, who wished harm to no person or object. This also demonstrated that war had no place in the state of nature:

Man is naturally peaceful and shy; at the slightest danger his first movement is to flee. He only becomes emboldened by the force of habit and experience. Honour, self-interest, prejudice, vengeance—all the passions which can make him brave the perils of death—are far from him in the state of nature. It is only after having socialised with man that he determines to kill another.[29]

By establishing the correct basis of man's condition and character, Rousseau could then set out his true needs, and construct an authentic political project for man in society. As demonstrated in *Emile*, but also in *Considerations on the Government in Poland*, Rousseau's natural man could become (after first assuming his true self) a citizen through a radical programme of education. Education was the means to replicate man's essential nature on a different plane; the creation of the new world of the virtuous republic. Finally, in illustrating the first step that man had to take in his ethical development, Rousseau sets out his system: his project was to reflect the internal world on an external plane and (as the sections on liberty, war, and government will show), demonstrate how the act of uncovering man's essential qualities could recreate this condition artificially in the republic. It would be these very republican qualities which would be needed when situations of war and foreign occupation had to be confronted. Indeed, Rousseau claimed that these moral and

---

[28] *Principes du droit de la guerre*, 187–8 (*OC* iii. 611–12).
[29] Ibid. 236 (*OC* iii. 602).

civic qualities may be nurtured through the dialectical act of forging republics through war. In his guidance for emerging republics, he stressed that the political and civic virtues he believed were necessary could be brought about through the struggle against the old world of slavery and empire. The other point Rousseau stressed was that, rather than Hobbes's hate-filled creature, man was naturally filled with both love and pity. Man was not motivated to act by reason alone; sentiments played a central role in determining man's actions.

If natural law were inscribed only on human reason, it would hardly be capable of directing most of our actions. But it is also indelibly engraved in the human heart. It is from the heart that natural law speaks to man more powerfully than all the precepts of philosophers. It is from there that it cries out to him that he may not sacrifice the life of his fellow man except to save his own, and that even when he sees himself obliged to do so, he cannot but feel a sense of horror at the idea of killing in cold blood.[30]

As we shall see, man's capacity for love in Rousseau's state of nature—not for himself alone, but for his fellow man—is significant for the eventual creation and maintenance of the republic, through the development of civic love. This sentiment, beginning as it does with the individual love of a common humanity also develops, in the republic, into a firm principle of fraternity—both between peoples and between nations, and of course, also within nations.

THE NATURE OF WAR

In his opening paragraphs of *Principes du droit de la guerre,* Rousseau descends upon Hobbes's and Grotius' philosophy of war with an utterly martial literary force. After attacking their methods, he goes on to address their motives in equally scathing terms:

What human soul would not be sickened by such sad scenes? But one is no longer considered a man if one pleads the cause of humanity. Justice and truth must be bent in the interests of the strongest. That is now the rule. Since the poor cannot provide pensions or employment, since they do not grant tenure or endow university chairs, why should we protect them?[31]

Finally he assaults the principles upon which their version of the nature of war is based. His aim is not only to destroy their logic,

---

[30] Ibid. 189 (*OC* iii. 602).   [31] Ibid. 233 (*OC* iii. 604).

demonstrate the poverty of their principles, or illustrate the viciousness of the ethics of the old world, but also to reveal his own system with as much lucidity as possible. Only by dramatically crushing the opposition could he clear the way for an entirely new formulation. Within his system was a way to guide relations between states with radically different political structures. Accordingly, he needed to juxtapose the new world of his virtuous republic with the old world of power politics, brute force, and conquest, and in so doing demonstrate that there was no fatality about the latter phenomena. Wars of occupation did not have to be endured with stoic resignation, but could (and in fact needed to) be met with a firm collective response by the citizenry.

Rousseau illustrates the nature of war by defining it in a wholly original way. As he repeatedly professed in *Principes*, and went on to argue in the *Social Contract* as well, there is a political nature to both just and unjust war. In his *Principes du droit de la guerre*, he argues that in fact war arises directly from Hobbes's unjust 'peaceful' institutions:

For a moment let us put these ideas in opposition to the horrible system of Hobbes. We will find, contrary to his absurd doctrine, that far from the state of war being natural to man, war is born out of peace, or at least out of the precautions men have taken to assure themselves of peace.[32]

He next focuses his attack on Grotius' claims in *De Jure Belli ac Pacis*. Grotius' world of unjust war endorses three principles which Rousseau rejects: private war, conquest, and the rights that naturally accrue to conquest—in short, slavery and the principle of might is right. Chapter 3 of the *Social Contract* is actually entitled 'The Right of the Strongest'. As he explains 'the "right of the strongest", a right that apparently seems to be ironic, is in reality an established principle', and asks, rhetorically, 'but will no one ever explain to us this phrase?' Rousseau argues that force is only a 'physical power, and I cannot see what morality can result by its effects. To yield to force is a necessity and not an act of will; at most it is prudence.' He concludes: 'in what sense can it become a duty? . . . this so-called right can only produce a bewildering nonsense.'[33] In his next chapter on slavery he points the finger more directly:

Grotius and the others claim to find another justification in war for the alleged right of slavery. According to them, the victor's having the right to kill the vanquished implies that the vanquished has the right to purchase his life at the

---

[32] *Principes du droit de la guerre*, 186–7 (*OC* iii. 610).   [33] *OC* iii. 354.

expense of his liberty; a convention thought to be the more legitimate because it proves profitable to both parties. But it is clear that the so-called right to kill the vanquished cannot be derived from the state of war . . . the right of conquest has no other foundation than the law of the stronger. And if war gives the conqueror no right to massacre a conquered people, no such right can be invoked to justify their enslavement . . . Hence far from the victor having acquired some further authority besides that of force over the vanquished, the state of war between them continues; their mutual relations is the effect of war, and the continuation of the rights of war implies the absence of a treaty of peace. A convention has been made, but that convention, far from ending the state of war presupposed its continuation.[34]

Hence unjust war, in his definition, emanated from the 'first world' of empire and inequality—the worlds inhabited by Hobbes and Grotius and all those who subscribed to their 'desolate philosophies'. Just war, as derived from the true principles of the nature of man, was a war fought not by the professional soldiers in the pay of kings, but by citizens of the republic, who rallied to its aid in times of crisis. Rousseau explained the difference between the two in no uncertain terms in his advice to Poland: 'Regular troops, the plague and depopulators of Europe, are good for only two purposes, to attack and conquer neighbours, or to shackle and enslave Citizens.' He then added, 'I know that the state should not remain without defenders; but its true defenders are its members. Each citizen ought to be a soldier by duty, none by profession.'[35]

An essential feature of his paradigm, however, is the fact that this republic was not utopian. Unlike the Abbé St Pierre's *Projet*, Rousseau did not believe that total peace was always possible, because within his system these two worlds could coexist simultaneously. A natural consequence of this multi-dimensional vision was that once these two worlds were juxtaposed, wars coming from the old world were unjust wars of conquest, while wars from the new world were just wars of self-defence. Here, in a recommendation to the Polish people on how to preserve their sovereignty, he juxtaposed the old world with their potential new one to illustrate this point:

To look for a means of guaranteeing yourselves against the will of a neighbour stronger than you is to seek a chimera. It would be of an even greater one to try and make conquests and to acquire offensive force; it is incompatible with the form of your government. Whoever wants to be free ought not to want to be a conqueror.[36]

[34] Ibid. 356, 357.   [35] *Considérations, OC* iii. 1014.   [36] *OC* iii. 1013.

In summary, Rousseau's perception of the nature of war was under-pinned by his belief in its political nature. War, he believed, was the result of a particular type of government. He expressly rejected any justification for wars of conquest, but did not imagine they might be banned from existence; rather they would cease only when corrupt empires transformed themselves into virtuous republics (and he had no illusions about the time this might take). Even so, his belief that republics were less aggressive towards their neighbours was heavily qualified as he noted the ability of unprincipled leaders to pervert or confuse the general will.

Even more ingeniously, as his system allowed for the past and the future to coexist, he could suggest policies for the republic, and rules which could guide relations between states during different stages of their development, thus allowing for prescriptions to proto-republics such as Poland. Central to this view was that citizens could not be detached from the defence of the state. A just war of self-defence was by its nature a war in which the state was defended by the sovereign citizens, who acted in the very name of public authority under such circumstances.

LIBERTY

Rousseau's challenge to Hobbesian and Grotian conceptions of man and war highlighted two core values within his system: man was born free and good, and war resulted from unjust and tyrannical political structures. His conception of the natural liberty of man was ranked as the ultimate value and, in contrast to Grotius and Hobbes, the republic and social contract were the means to preserve (or replicate as closely as possible in civil society) man's 'noblest faculty': freedom. For, as he rhetorically inquired in the *Social Contract*, how could the purpose of government possibly be slavery? Thus, although Rousseau aspired to peace, it was not peace at any price. As he remarked rather pointedly, there were many more desirable values than that of 'tranquillity'. He enquired, 'what do men gain, if this very tranquillity is one of their miseries? There is tranquillity in the dungeons, but is that enough to make them pleasant?'[37] One of these values greater than peace is liberty. In his advice to the Poles, he explains that one has to rank these values accordingly:

37 OC iii. 356, 357.

You love liberty, you are worthy of it; you have defended it against a powerful and cunning aggressor who, under pretence of offering you the bonds of friendship, shackled you with the chains of servitude. Now, weary of your fatherland's troubles, you sigh for tranquillity. I believe it is very easy to attain; but to preserve it together with liberty, that seems to me to be difficult. The patriotic souls that protected you against the yoke were formed in the midst of the anarchy you find so hateful. They fell into a lethargic sleep; the storm awoke them. Having broken the chains intended for them, they are weighed down with weariness. They would like to combine the peace of despotism with the sweetness of freedom. I am afraid that they want things that are contradictory. Repose and liberty seem to me incompatible; one has to choose.[38]

Even more absurd, in Rousseau's eyes, was Grotius' limited notion of sociability and the patriarchal view of man which established grounds for the principle of slavery, a notion as distant from Rousseau's natural freedom as was possible. Grotius' hierarchical conception of sociability, which put severe limitations on man's natural liberty, was directly challenged by Rousseau's understanding of the essential quality of natural man's liberty: for him, man's primary condition was one of independence and autonomy from others. In his *Principes,* he derides the Grotian laws of modern society which favour despotic authority:

Thus the whole face of the earth is changed. Everywhere nature has disappeared and human art has taken its place, independence and natural liberty have given way to laws and to slavery, and there no longer exists a free being. The philosopher searches for man and does not find him.[39]

Thus the journey to recapture man's essential and natural goodness was necessary in order to uncover man's freedom. Indeed this was the primary purpose of the journey back to the hypothetical state of nature. Rousseau resolved the Hobbesian dilemma of purchasing security at the cost of natural liberty in two ways. First, by including the concept of equality as a core value within that society, and second, by recreating on the external plane what was essential to man's internal plane. Rousseau did this by suggesting that in fact two types of liberty existed; both replacing the individual's liberty in the state of nature and enhancing man's condition of freedom by giving it moral qualities. These freedoms would prove invaluable when circumstances arose which necessitated the involvement of citizens in the defence of the state. But the cornerstone of Rousseau's approach was that the denial of freedom in the 'public sphere' in circumstances of occupation and alien rule

---

[38] Ibid. 954–5.   [39] *Principes du droit de la guerre*, 190 (*OC* iii. 603).

should not be allowed to annihilate the spirit of freedom in the hearts and thoughts of the citizenry. Indeed, such circumstances could act as a spur for the awakening of individual notions of moral and political liberty. In his advice to Wielhorski on Poland, he explains:

In the present state of things I see only one way of giving it the stability it lacks: to infuse, so to speak, the soul of its confederates into the entire nation, to establish the Republic in the hearts of the Poles so thoroughly that it endures there in spite of all its oppressors' efforts. That, it seems to me, is the only refuge where force can neither reach nor destroy it. We have just witnessed a uniquely memorable proof of this. Poland was in Russia's chains, but the Poles remained free. A great example which shows you how you can defy your neighbours' power and ambition. You may not be able to keep them from swallowing you; at least make sure that they cannot digest you. No matter what is done, Poland will have been overwhelmed by its enemies a hundred times before it can be given everything it needs in order to be in a position to resist them. The virtue of its Citizens, their patriotic zeal, the particular form which its national institutions may give their soul, this is the only rampart that will ever stand ready to defend it, and which no army could subdue by force. If you see to it that a Pole can never become a Russian, I assure you that Russia will never subjugate Poland.[40]

Yet he was extremely modest in his understanding of what was possible, and in his section on maintaining the constitution of Poland he warns its leaders:

To emancipate the peoples of Poland is a grand and fine undertaking, but bold, dangerous, and not to be attempted thoughtlessly. Among the precautions to be taken, there is one that is indispensable and that requires time. It is, before everything else, to make the serfs who are to be emancipated worthy of freedom and capable of tolerating it. . . . Recognize that your serfs are men like yourselves, that they have in them all the stuff to become all that you are: work, first of all, at activating it, and emancipate their bodies only once you have emancipated their souls.[41]

Accordingly, his view of liberty had two purposes; he believed that a martial republican spirit was needed to serve both the construction of the *polis*, and to maintain it in its republican liberty: 'In the plan I imagine and shall soon finish outlining, the whole of Poland will become warlike as much for the defence of its freedom against undertakings by the Prince, as against those by its neighbours . . .'[42]

Finally, as Rousseau was concerned with identifying exactly how to restore and maintain people's political liberty, he argued that this repub-

[40] *OC* iii. 959–60.   [41] Ibid. 974.   [42] Ibid. 1017.

lican liberty was often recognized, and then fought for, only in situations where this selfsame liberty had already been lost—in a war of conquest. As he remarks, 'I see all the other States of Europe rushing to their ruin. Monarchies, Republics, all these ever so wisely balanced governments, have grown decrepit and threaten soon to die.' All the while 'Poland, this depopulated, devastated, and oppressed region, wide open to its aggressors, at the height of its misfortunes and its anarchy, still displays all the fires of youth.' Even more, it 'dares to call for a government and laws, as if it had only just been born'. Poland 'is in chains, and debates the ways to keep its liberty! It feels within itself the kind of power which the force of tyranny cannot subjugate.'[43]

GOVERNMENT, SOCIETY, AND THE REPUBLIC

In all his works Rousseau asserted that his views on nature, man, and society were driven by his desire to define the basis for legitimate political structures. His examination proceeded through a critique of two central premises of Hobbes and Grotius. Of Hobbes's theory of state his main refutation is the relationship between force and law; with Grotius it is the theory of slavery as a right, in particular the right to enslave oneself. The substance of his disagreement concerned two aspects of the same idea. To return to nature is to return to freedom. Rousseau points the finger for the condition of slavery at both Grotius and Hobbes. He developed his attack to include his other main adversary, Hobbes, who like Grotius rested his theory of government on force:

If an individual, says Grotius, can alienate his freedom, and enslave himself to a master, why could not a whole people alienate its freedom and subject itself to a king? . . . To speak of a man giving himself in return for nothing is to speak of something absurd and unthinkable; such an action is illegitimate and null, if only because no one who did it could be in their right mind. To say the same of a whole people is to conjure up a nation of lunatics; and right cannot rest on madness.[44]

Rousseau demonstrated the unjust and unequal nature of despotism, and by so doing challenged the moral premiss of Hobbes's *Leviathan*:

It will be said that a despot gives his subjects the assurance of civil tranquillity. Very well, but what does it profit them, if those wars against other powers which

---

[43] Ibid. 954.   [44] Ibid. 355, 356.

result from a despot's ambition, if his insatiable greed, and the oppressive demands of his administration, cause more desolation than civil strife would cause? What do the people gain if their very condition of civil tranquillity is one of their hardships?[45]

Rousseau, in his refutation of Hobbes's and Grotius' philosophy, was setting out his own conceptions of the just republic. But while engaging in this critique he set forth one of his most controversial concepts in the elaboration of this tradition: the Lawgiver.

REPUBLIC

There are many formal components in the paradigm of the virtuous republic: sovereignty, democracy, law, the general will, rights, and citizenship, amongst others. For the purposes of setting out the republican tradition of war, it is important to avoid assigning any internal hierarchy to them. First, because each element of the republic was equally significant, and second, because varying emphases placed on the importance of these features are the basis for the still raging controversies amongst Rousseauian scholars concerning the philosopher's intentions and their political implications.

In contrast to his two antagonists, Rousseau's theory of the good life centres around the man's preservation of his dual core values of freedom and equality through entering the social contract and constructing the republic. Rousseau's articulation of popular sovereignty was defined via his image of democracy, which he described as the general will in action. The general will was the sole source of the law. It was citizens who made the laws, and Rousseau's definition of the virtuous citizen was the image of the individual's true, interior self made manifest on the external plane. Individual attributes were transformed into the mechanisms of the republic in order to uphold the core values of equality and freedom. This aim is clearly laid out in the *Social Contract*, equally it is to be found in his *Principes*:

It is from the social pact that the body politic receives its unity and its *moi commun*. The government and the laws determine the robustness of its constitution, the hearts of its citizens give it its life, their courage and their customs determine its durability, and the only actions that it undertakes freely and that it can be accountable for are those dictated by the general will.[46]

[45] *OC* iii. 355.   [46] *Principes du droit de la guerre*, 192 (*OC* iii. 1899).

This section will focus upon the highly contested means Rousseau suggested were crucial to create and preserve a young or emerging republic which could reflect the two central values of liberty and equality: the Lawgiver. Rousseau's Lawgiver has been defined as a totalitarian ruler, a judge, a (temporary or permanent) dictator, a Supreme Being, and sometimes merely (although rarely) a political leader. So why did Rousseau need the Lawgiver when the aim was to create a democratic and free people living in a free republic? As has been indicated above, Rousseau's ambition was to go beyond (and indeed to counter) those who merely attempted to establish what was the right thing to do. Instead, his aim was to try and understand (and make understood) how exactly to 'move men to do it'. Just before introducing the notion of the Lawgiver in his advice to Poland, he sets out his general quest: 'How, then, can one move hearts, and get the *patrie* and its laws loved?' And he answers himself: 'Dare I say it? With children's games; with institutions which appear trivial in the eyes of superficial men, but which form cherished habits and invincible attachments.'[47] Accordingly the Lawgiver's task was both delicate and difficult: he must persuade his people to give up selfish interests and work for the *moi commun* before one has been created. And reason cannot be used. As Rousseau explains in the *Social Contract*: 'For a nascent people to be capable of appreciating sound maxims of politics and of following the fundamental rules of reason of State, the effect would have to become the cause, the social spirit which is to be the work of the institution would have to preside over the institution itself, and men would have to be prior to laws what they ought to become by means of them.' Therefore, since the Lawgiver 'can use neither force nor reasoning, he must of necessity have recourse to an authority of a different order, which might be able to rally without violence and to persuade without convincing'.[48] For Rousseau the Lawgiver is the forger and protector of the republic, and his qualities are listed in his various *Discourses* and the *Social Contract*; the application of these qualities are quite explicitly highlighted in his work on Poland, Corsica, and his unfinished early work on war. The skills, wisdom, talents, and tools that a Lawgiver needs are set out in his advice to Poland, where, in a chapter entitled 'Spirit of the Ancient Institutions', he writes of the moral and spiritual qualities of three ancient Lawgivers: Moses, Lycurgus, and Numa:

The same spirit guided all ancient Lawgivers and their institutions. All of them sought bonds that might attach the Citizens to the *patrie*, and to each another,

---

[47] *OC* iii. 955.   [48] Ibid. 383.

and they found in them distinctive practices, in religious ceremonies which by their very nature were always exclusive and national (see the end of the *Social Contract*),[49] in games which kept the Citizens frequently assembled, in exercises which increased their pride and self-esteem together with their vigour and their strength, in spectacles which by reminding them of their history of their ancestors, their misfortunes, their virtues, their victories, stirred their hearts, fired them with a lively spirit of emulation, and strongly attached them to the *patrie* with which they were being kept constantly engaged.[50]

From each of the three Lawgivers he writes about, he selects those virtues which made them, in his eyes, a leader and architect of the republic. 'Moses dared to make out of this wandering and servile troop a body politic, a free people' by creating 'all the bonds of fraternity he introduced among the members of the republic'. Whereas Lycurgus undertook to 'institute a people already degraded by slavery and the vices which are its effects' by imposing on it 'an iron yoke the like of which no other people has ever borne'. Yet he 'attached it to this yoke: he, so to speak, identified with it, by always keeping it occupied with it.' Lycurgus constantly 'showed it the *patrie*, in its laws, in its games, in its home, in its loves, in its feasts. He did not leave it a moment's respite to be by itself.' Rousseau concludes that from 'this constant constraint, ennobled by its object, arose in it that ardent love of *patrie* which was always the Spartans strongest or rather their sole passion, and made of them beings above humanity'. Finally, he restores what he sees as Numa's tarnished reputation: 'Numa was the true founder of Rome.' It was Numa 'who made it solid and lasting by uniting these brigands into a dissoluble body, by transforming them into Citizens, not so much by means of laws … as by means of gentle [*doux*] institutions which attached to them one to another and all of them to their soil'.[51] Rousseau believed that these Lawgivers all had certain virtues in common, which were critical in the task of fashioning first the nation, the *patrie,* and finally the republic— and sometimes all three responsibilities at the same time.

The Lawgiver must first have achieved virtue for himself in order to be able to capture and make manifest, in the public sphere, the will of the people. It was for Lawgivers to help construct the law that would guide the republic, for, as Rousseau notes in the introduction to this chapter, 'No constitution will ever be good and solid unless the law rules the citizens' hearts.' This is because so long as 'the legislative force does

[49] This refers to chapter 8 in Book IV, which argues for the construction of a civil religion as the backbone to a virtuous republic. *OC* iii. 460–9.
[50] *OC* iii. 956.   [51] Ibid. 956, 957, 958.

not reach that deep, the laws will invariably be evaded'. He asks, rhetorically, 'but how can men's hearts be reached?' His answer, of course, is through and by means of the Lawgiver. Thus the sovereignty of popularly enacted law is not meant as an institutional solution that can work anywhere and automatically; it will work only if men have been made into virtuous and patriotic citizens. It is, then, the Lawmaker's role to both create and, if needs be, represent the structures that have not yet come into being until such time as an active and virtuous citizenry had emerged.

Accordingly, Rousseau does not argue for immediate freedom for peoples under the yoke when it is a domestic one. Although he urges them to fight for it against a foreign occupier as a means of understanding freedom and acquiring virtue, in his advice to the Poles he does not suggest that the serfs rise up against their Polish overlords. This gradualism and moderation is repeated in the advice he gives to the nobles of Poland as he urges rather than demands them to give up their own powers:

And where does Poland propose to get the power and forces which it wantonly stifles in its own bosom? Nobles of Poland, be something more: be men. Only then will you be happy and free, but never flatter yourselves that you are so, as long as you keep your brothers in chains.[52]

It can therefore be seen that, unlike Hobbes's form of government, which was premissed on a government based on fear, Rousseau's republic relied upon a positive commitment to the community. He resolved the dilemma of participatory political structures based on the *volonté* of the individual by devising an educational philosophy which was as least as important as the more formal mechanisms of the republic. This was the theory of a complementary political culture which could give birth to the virtuous qualities of the republican citizen: patriotism and nationalism. Only then could people, according to Rousseau, bear the weight of public freedom:

Freedom is hearty fare, but hard to digest; it takes very healthy stomachs to tolerate it. I laugh at those degraded peoples who, letting plotters rouse them to riot, dare to speak of freedom without so much as an idea of it, and, their hearts full of all the vices of slaves, imagine that all it takes to be free is to be unruly. Proud and holy freedom! If these poor people only knew you, if they only realized at what price you are won and preserved, if they were only sensible to how much your laws are more austere than the tyrant's yoke is hard; their weak

---

[52] Ibid. 974.

souls, the slaves of passions that should be stifled, would fear you a hundred times more than servitude; they would flee you in terror as a burden about to crush them.[53]

PATRIOTISM AND NATIONALISM

Patriotism (and to a lesser extent nationalism) was the key which unlocked the entire Rousseauian paradigm, and particularly lay at the heart of its conception of civic participation in just wars of self-defence. In both *Discourse on Political Economy*, and in the *Social Contract*, he argued for the development of patriotic virtue as the primary safeguard of republican liberty. He set it out as an almost mathematical formula in the *Discourse on Political Economy*: 'The *patrie* cannot endure without patriotism, nor patriotism without liberty, nor liberty without virtue, nor virtue without citizens.' He finishes this point by warning: 'you will have everything if you form citizens; if you do not, you will have nothing but nasty slaves, beginning with the heads of state.'[54] But it is in his advice to Corsica and to Poland that he illustrates what a valuable defensive tool patriotism can be in the construction and preservation of republican nations.[55]

Patriotism was thus a significant notion in two distinct ways. It is the primary educational tool by which Rousseau's man could develop from the individual plane to the public sphere. It also encapsulated a political culture necessary to sustain the formal instruments and institutions of the republic, and defend it in times of war. Besides being the tool to create the republic, the other important function of patriotism was that it was the means to maintain its existence. The means by which the individual could become amenable to surrendering individual will for the general good was by becoming imbued with the virtue of patriotic education and fraternal sentiment, both essential in the making of citizens. Man needed to acquire three basic qualities in order to achieve the moral status of the sovereign citizen. A central quality was the education of the individual to self-mastery. Through the guidance of patriotic education, individual liberty was transformed into virtuous moral freedom. The enlightened Rousseauian citizen also participated in the public sphere on the basis of will, not compulsion. Finally, there was an emphasis on the unity of man's passion and reason. Natural sentiment

---

[53] *OC* iii. 974.   [54] Ibid.   [55] Ibid. iii. 901–50; 951–1041.

and reason were united through the catalyst of patriotism to produce civic virtue:

But make the people love the commonwealth, seek virtue, and do not concern yourself with great talents; they would do more harm than good. The best motive force for a government is love of country, and this love is cultivated together with the land. Common sense suffices to govern a well-constituted state; and common sense develops quite as much in the heart as in the head, since men who are not blinded by their passion always behave well.[56]

Rousseau did not encourage the sublimation of the senses and the exclusive promotion of reason as Kantians, and some mid-nineteenth-century republicans proposed, because in his mind a citizen without passion could not form the living organism which was the republic. In *Considerations on the Government in Poland*, he suggests the creation of a body of citizens can be advanced through encouraging a people's love of particular national institutions. He adds:

It is upon souls such as these that legislation will take hold. They will obey the laws and not elude them because they will suit them and will have the inward assent of their wills. Loving their *patrie*, they will serve it out of zeal and with all their heart. With this sentiment alone, legislation, even if it were bad would make good Citizens; and only good Citizens will ever make for the strength and prosperity of the State.[57]

Individual compassion, precisely actualized on a higher plane, was transmuted into civic love. Rousseau believed the creation of the republic was the creation of a living organism, kept alive by the participation of its citizens: 'A thousand writers have dared to say that the State is without passion and that there is no *raison d'état* other than reason itself. And yet anyone can see on the contrary that the essence of society consists of the activity of its members and that a State without motion would be dead.'[58]

Accordingly, natural sentiments could be transformed into patriotism through the agency of patriotic education. The maintenance of the republic through this patriotic culture is the second feature of Rousseau's system of citizenship. The most critical stabilizing function of patriotism is its power to bring about both the awareness and the ability to defend the republic—what Rousseau refers to in his advice on Poland as an 'enlightened patriotism'.[59]

---

[56] *Constitution pour la Corse* (fragments séparés), *OC* iii. 940–1.
[57] *OC* iii. 960, 183–4.
[58] *Principes du droit de la guerre*, 192, *OC* iii. 605.   [59] *OC* iii. 995.

The first level of this twofold obligation, understanding the need for the defence of the republic, is again brought about through the sentimental education of the citizen. Rousseau insists both that duty must be given freely, and that all citizens protect themselves when they defend the republic. Early on in his advice to Poland, he has an all-important section entitled 'Education':

This is the important subject. (*C'est ici l'article important*). It is education that must give souls the national form (*force nationale*), and so direct their tastes and opinions that they will be patriotic by inclination, passion, necessity. Upon opening its eyes, a child should see the *patrie,* and see only it until his dying day. Every true republican drank love of the *patrie,* that is to say love of the laws and of liberty with his mother's milk. This love makes up his whole existence; he sees only the *patrie*, he lives for it alone; when he is alone, he is nothing: when he no longer has his *patrie*, he is no longer, and if he is not dead, he is worse than dead.[60]

Accordingly, in advising a large but vulnerable country like Poland, Rousseau suggests that defence can come only through the acquisition of patriotic virtue:

A single thing is enough to make Poland impossible to subjugate; the love of the *patrie* and of freedom animated by the virtues inseparable from that love. You have just given a forever memorable example of it. This love, so long as it burns in your hearts, may not secure you against a temporary yoke; but sooner or later it will burst forth, shake off the yoke, and make you free. Work then, without relief, without respite, to carry patriotism to its highest pitch in all Polish hearts.[61]

The defence of the republic goes to the heart of the conception of Rousseau's system of just political institutions: the ability to volunteer one's life in its defence. In order to encourage this devotion in citizens, a different public perception of the army is thus necessary: 'in order to succeed in this operation, one would have to begin by changing public opinion'. This would be done by seeing to it that in Poland 'a soldier is no longer looked upon as a bandit who sells himself for a few pennies a day in order to live, but as a Citizen who serves the *patrie* and does his duty'.[62]

This sentiment, emerging from a more general love for humanity established in his all-important reformulation of the nature of man, and inspired by it, has now developed into a public bond achieved through love of the active citizen and their common commitment to the common

[60] *OC* iii. 966.   [61] Ibid. 1019.   [62] Ibid. 1016.

good. Accordingly, Rousseau established the concept of patriotism as a virtue which combined reason and sentiment in a moral apogee; the raw fuel upon which his conceptions of the individual, nature, war, liberty, and the republic were conveyed. For the future survival of Poland, a sentimental education was crucial to the defence of the individual's (and accordingly the republic's) two core values of liberty and equality, using, primarily, the instrument of fraternity (and the virtues associated with it).

REPUBLICAN NATIONALISM

In Rousseau's system, patriotism was the most reliable instrument for creating the citizen, and equally the method for sustaining the republic. However, he believed aspects of nationalism could also perform an important function, and he formed a complex view of its role and relationship to both patriotism and the state. Nationalism, a powerful ideology in itself, is the most easily misunderstood aspect of Rousseau's system. Most negative interpretations derive directly from the unhealthy emphasis scholars place on his attachment to nationalism, without recognizing its position within the overall structure of his system. For Rousseau, it is only within (and as a result of) a system that upholds liberty and equality, that a true fraternity and common love for the *patrie* can indeed emerge. He makes the distinction clear in the dedication to the Republic of Geneva in *The Discourse on Political Inequality* 'if I could have chosen the place of my birth, I should have chosen' a society '... where this gentle habit of seeing and knowing one another would have made love of the *Patrie* a love of the Citizens rather than of its soil'.[63]

However, Rousseau believed that a nascent republic could develop before having time to create the type of patriotic citizen able and willing to risk his life for it: for this were needed citizens motivated by a purely civic love for the particular principles, values, and institutions of their republic. In his advice to young republics he argues that a permissible, but temporary, substitute to the sentiments of patriotism could be the passions of nationalism, a powerful weapon in rallying a people in the defence of the republic. In his advice to the Poles (in the paragraph immediately following a description of how to promote love of country as a means of defence against

---

[63] Ibid. 111–12.

aggressive invaders) he explicitly portrays nationalism as a defensive tool:

It is national institutions which form the genius, the character, the tastes, and the morals of a people, which make it be itself and not another, which inspire in it that ardent love of *patrie* founded on habits impossible to uproot, which cause it to die of boredom among other peoples in the midst of delights of which it is deprived in its own. . . . Give a different bent to the Poles' passions, and you will give their souls a national physionomy which will set them apart from all other peoples, which will keep them from merging . . . you will give them a vigour which will take the place of deceptive appeals to empty precepts, which will make them do by preference and passion the things one never does well enough when one does them only by duty or interest.[64]

Although he does not ignore the risks involved, Rousseau saw the promotion of nationalism as an important defensive tool of young republics. However, he was at pains to distinguish it from patriotism, and to demonstrate its lower ranking within his system. Moreover, it is important to remember that even patriotism was the means to an end— the creation of a virtuous republic—and that nationalism was even more a temporary expedient on the road to making men free. Nationalism was never an end in itself but simply a way of guaranteeing freedom in order to develop collective ethical capacities—virtues necessary to maintain and protect a society—with a modicum of public safety. In circumstances of wars of self-defence and the imposition of alien rule, furthermore, it offered a powerful instrument for defending the integrity and identity of the civic community (which could be national or even regional or local). In short, just as the republic was inseparable from its citizens, just wars of self-defence could not be imagined—let alone successfully waged—without the active participation of the population. Nationalism cannot be abstracted from his system—none of these instruments or tools can—and it coexists within a framework of republican liberty, equality, and, last but not least, a very republican love of humanity.

REPUBLICAN FOUNDERS OF THE TRADITION OF WAR: PAOLI AND KOSCIUSZKO

Pasquale Paoli

In his day Pasquale Paoli was celebrated as the 'hero of the enlightenment' and during the 1750s and 1760s his Corsican Republic became

[64] *OC* iii. 960.

the focal point for European *pèlerins de la liberté*.[65] This interest developed in the midst of the island's revolt against Genoa, *La Dominante*; the visitors hailed as heroic and virtuous both Corsica's resistance to Genoese rule and Paoli's creation of a democratic republic in the island.[66] The historical context from which Paoli emerged, gaining such a reputation for himself and his people, and both representing and constructing the republican tradition of war in the mid-eighteenth century, will be briefly set out in order to explain his pivotal position in the founding of defensive republican war for those practising it in the nineteenth century. Next, his thought and the specific practices of republican war will be detailed.[67]

The Corsican insurrection against the Genoese occupation lasted nearly fifty years.[68] It began in late 1729 when a village near Corte refused to pay taxes to the Genoese Governor after two successive failed harvests. The Corsican rebellion ended in 1769 when Paoli embarked at Porto-Vecchio for exile in London, after being defeated by the forces of the Genoese, fortified with French arms and, eventually, over 30,000 French troops at the battle of Ponte Nuovo.[69]

Pasquale Paoli was not yet 30 years old when he was elected, by the national *Consulte* held at Caccia, to lead the Corsicans in their fight against the Genoese Republic.[70] He had accompanied his father

---

[65] 'Pilgrims of Liberty'. The seminal work on this is Frances Beretti's profoundly elegant work: *Pascal Paoli et l'image de la Corse*, in *Studies on Voltaire and the Eighteenth Century*, 253 (Oxford: Voltaire Foundation, 1988); also the earlier work by Thadd E. Hall, *France and the Eighteenth-Century Corsican Question* (New York: New York University Press, 1971).

[66] A short essay on this subject, also by Thadd E. Hall is: 'The Development of Enlightenment Interest in Eighteenth Century Corsica', again in *Studies on Voltaire and the Eighteenth Century*, 64 (Oxford: Voltaire Foundation, 1968), 165–85.

[67] The best work on Paoli and the period arguably remains Franco Venturi's 'Patria e libertà la rivoluzione di Corsica', in vol. v of id., *Settecento Riformatore: L'Italia dei Lumi* (Torino: Einaudi, 1969–87). See also his chapter 'Pasquale Paoli', in S. Woolf (ed.), *Italy and the Enlightenment: Studies in a Cosmopolitan Century* (New York: New York University Press, 1972), 134–53, and the other two articles, as yet untranslated, 'Il dibattito francese e britannico sulla rivoluzione di Corsica', *Rivista storica italiana*, 86 (1974), 643–719, and 'Il dibattito in Italia sulla rivoluzione di Corsica', *Rivista storica italiana*, 88 (1976), 40–89.

[68] A useful general history of this period is by Fernand Ettori, former director of the Centre d'Études Corses, and scholar of the Paolist and French Revolutionary period. See his 'La Révolution de Corse', in Paul Arrighi and Antoine Olivesi's *Histoire de la Corse* (Toulouse: Privat, 1986), 306–68.

[69] A full account of the extraordinary military struggle of the Paolist forces against the Genoese Republic and France can be found in the *maîtrise* of Didier Rey: 'L'Armée corse 1755–1769', University of Provence, unpublished Master's thesis, 1978.

[70] On Paoli's election, see D. P. Marini, 'La Consulte de Caccia et l'élection de Pascal Paoli 1752–1755', *Bulletin de la Société des Sciences Historiques et Naturelles de la Corse* (1913), 352–4.

Hyacinth into exile in Italy (after Hyacinth, a patriotic leader himself, had taken part in directing the failed national uprising against the Genoese rulers as a member of a nationally elected *junte*); and whilst there had trained as a soldier specializing in engineering.[71] Upon his election as General-in-Chief of the Corsican nation in 1754, Pasquale Paoli immediately continued with the development of a democratic regime, while enhancing its republican elements with a written constitution.[72] He established ports for trade that avoided the Genoese blockade, developed a thriving local agriculture, founded a university in Corte, an armoury, and a printing press.[73]

The French consul at that time confirmed what appeared to be the irreversible character of the insurrection, and noted that once Paoli arrived from Naples in 1754, the struggle began to acquire a twofold aim: 'both the independence of the land, and the *installation of a republican form of government*'.[74] It was this latter goal which constitutes a decisive break from the leadership of Gaffori, who was assassinated by the Genoese in 1753, and singles Paoli out as a founder of the republican tradition of war. Indeed Paoli's republican vision was inextricably interwoven with the desire for freedom from foreign occupation. Although Corsica already practised a rudimentary form of indigenous popular rule, it was the Paolist republic, and especially the Constitution written in 1755 which contained (a full seven years before Rousseau's *Du contrat social*) principles not yet introduced into European political life in the eighteenth century. The Corsican Constitution begins with the remarkable phrase 'the General Diet of the People of Corsica, *legitimately Master of itself*, convoked according to the form established by the General Paoli in the city of of Corte . . . November, 1755'. It goes on to set out the republican aims of the Corsicans in their fight against the Genoese, and the instruments and mechanisms of democratic self-

[71] A general biography which includes this early period is Peter Adam Thrasher's *Pasquale Paoli: An Enlightened Hero, 1725–1807* (London: Constable, 1970).

[72] There is a very recent edition of the 1755 constitution which has been translated (into French), edited, and includes a helpful commentary by Dorothy Carrington, as well as a preface by Jean-Marie Arrighi. *La Constitution de Pascal Paoli, 1755* (Ajaccio: La Marge, 1996). See also Carrington's two (largely similar) articles on the subject: 'The Corsican Constitution of Pasquale Paoli (1755–1769)', *English Historical Review*, 88 (1973), 481–503; 'Pascal Paoli et sa "Constitution" (1755–1769)', *Annales historiques de la Révolution Française*, 46 (1974), 508–41.

[73] Ettori, 'La Révolution de Corse', 332–51.

[74] Emphasis added. ('L'indépendance du territoire insulaire et l'instauration d'un gouvernement à forme républicaine'.) René Boudard, *La 'Nation corse' et sa lutte pour la liberté entre 1744 et 1769: d'après la correspondance des agents français à Gênes et en Corse avec la cour de Versailles* (Marseille: Jeanne Lafitte, 1979). Letter of 9 Sept. 1754 Correspondance consulaire B. I. 590. Tome 80 (Archives nationales).

government enacted by the Corsican people.[75] The Corsican republican tradition could draw upon such works as the early 1730s debate by theologians at Oretta concerning the legitimate justifications, and rights, to go to war against the Genoese,[76] and the two classic Corsican works *Il Disinganno* by Natali, published in 1736, which was concerned with justifying the revolt against Genoa, and the later *Giustificazione* of the Abbé Salvini, published in 1758 at Paoli's press in Corsica itself. Equally important were the customs and practices of earlier national *consultes*.[77]

Although the constitution itself is clearly of some historical significance, it is through his actions as a Lawgiver, through the practical policies he pursued, and, most particularly, through the effect of his example that Paoli was to provide such rich material for generations of republicans after him. He was seen not only as the living proof of the *virtù* of a republican leader, but he also embodied throughout this period the notion that republican actions must be fully consistent with republican thought. This was demonstrated by the way he represented his relationship to his *fortuna* (Paoli read Machiavelli rather differently from the martialist thinkers of the nineteenth century outlined in Chapter 4).[78] Accordingly, he allowed himself to be used by the young Boswell ('I have bagged a leader, and I'm off to bag another', Boswell had said after meeting Rousseau, and on route to Corsica to meet Paoli), in order to use him in turn to gain popularity for the cause of an independent Corsica.[79] Indeed Boswell was to become an ardent lifelong

[75] Carrington, 'The Corsican Constitution', 482. An extensive study of most aspects of Paoli's constitution can be found in Mathieu Fontana's *La Constitution corse du Généralat de Pascal Paoli en Corse 1755–1769* (Paris: Imprimerie Bonlauvot-Jouve, 1907).

[76] See Ettori's fascinating study of this debate in 'Le Congrès des Théologiens d'Orezza, 4 Mars 1731: mythe et réalité', in *Études corses* 1 (1973), 77–96. Cf., however, Philippe Castellin and Jean Marie Arrighi's comments in their edited and annotated *Projets de Constitution pour la Corse* (Ajaccio: La Marge, 1979), 55, 56, 57.

[77] *Disinganno intorno alla Guerra di Corsica Scoperto da Curzio Tulliano ad un suo Amico Dimorante nell'Isola.* This has been recently republished in French (Ajaccio: La Marge, 1982). *Giustificazione della Rivoluzione di Corsica et della Ferma Risoluzione presa dai Corsica di Mai piu Sottomettersi al Dominio di Genova* (Corte, 1758). For earlier *consultes* see Fontana's *La Constitution corse*, 19. For the political and historical context of these two works see R. Emmanuelli's ' "Disinganno", "Giustificazione", et philosophie des lumières', *Études corses* (1974), 2, 83–113.

[78] An account of the paramount influence of Machiavellian thought on the young Paoli (over that of other writers, such as Montesquieu or even Genovese) is advanced by Fernand Ettori: 'La Formation intellectuelle de Pascal Paoli (1725–1755)', especially at 498–501, and 507.

[79] A work that touches directly on this aspect of Boswell's career, and on his peculiar relationship with Paoli is Joseph Foladare's *Boswell's Paoli* (Hamden, Conn.: Archon Books, 1979), 48. See also Jean Viviès, 'Boswell, La Corse, et *l'Encyclopédie*', in *Studies on Voltaire and the Eighteenth Century* (Oxford: Voltaire Foundation, 1986), 245, 407–9.

campaigner for the Corsican cause after meeting Paoli. The book he eventually wrote about General Paoli, *Journal of a Tour to Corsica, with the Memoirs of Pascal Paoli* made him a best-selling author, and he became known in Britain as 'Corsica Boswell'.[80] Paoli's life as republican 'example' in the *Memoirs* made him a hero of the American colonists, who named their conspiratorial meeting places after him, toasted him as one of the 'Sons of Liberty', and held up the military aspects of his republican struggle as an example to emulate.[81] Paoli himself claimed he was inspired throughout his life by particular heroes of ancient Greece and Rome as described in Plutarch's *Lives*, and that he modelled his own behaviour on them (much like Rousseau was to claim before him, and Kosciuszko after); many contemporary figures had observed that Paoli was himself a man of Plutarchian proportions, 'the likes which haven't been seen for 2000 years'.[82]

The Republican Thought and Practices of Paoli

After his election as leader of the nation in 1755, Paoli set out, in printed circulars and public meetings, the nature of the problems facing the Corsican people. He constantly likened their fight to a struggle against slavery, as well as a battle against the tyranny of the Genoese. One of the Corsican Republic's first national publications, an insurrectionary text aimed at encouraging Corsicans in exile (many of them serving in foreign armies) to join the national insurrection, argues against a false peace in a similar manner to Rousseau. It suggests, despite claims to the contrary by Genoa, that the state of war had continued: 'Are these the advantages of peace? All writers, sacred and profane, set peace out as the first of goods (*premier des biens*).' and adds, 'we would never contradict this, but we also mustn't forget that this is not the true question. Of course, if one could be enjoying the gentlenesses of such a sincere and durable peace, yet claim to prefer the hazards and misfortunes of

[80] See M. McLaren's *Corsica Boswell: Paoli, Johnson, and Freedom* (London: Secker & Warburg, 1966) on this. This work also offers an interesting comparison of Scottish notions of liberty and those of Corsica during the same period.

[81] George Anderson, 'Pascal Paoli: An Inspiration to the Sons of Liberty', *Publications of the Colonial Society of Massachussetts*, 6 (1925), especially 188–205.

[82] Rousseau, Genovese, John Wesley, Voltaire, Horace Walpole, Napoleon, the poet Thomas Grey, and the 'pilgrims of liberty' to Corsica in the 1760s (such as James Boswell, Andrew Burnaby, and Christopher Hervey), all compared Paoli to the ancients, claiming he reflected the genius (as described in Plutarch's *Lives)* of Epaminondas, Solon, Lycurgus, Themistocles, but above all, of Timoleon. See Beretti, *Pascal Paoli et l'image de la Corse*, 4–5, and section b. of ch. 7: 'Pascal Paoli: un héros de Plutarque', 190–210.

war, surely we are utter fools deserving of the saddest fate that Genoa could hold in store for us.' If, on the contrary, 'the assurances of peace and of moderation by our enemies were never more than a blood-soaked irony, how does one define those partisans of peace? That they must choose either between the title of coward or that of traitor.' The 'peace' offered by the Genoese was thus an illusion. As it explains, 'Genoa will not offer peace until she can no longer see a way of continuing the war.' Therefore, 'to desire it [peace] will be only weakness; to accept it, deception; to solicit it, the height of calumny. Our interest, as our honour, rests in the perseverance of a brave insurrection.'[83] For Paoli, clearly, this was a time for virtuous republican action rather than abstract thought. 'I much prefer Themistocles to Demosthenes, because one spoke without acting, and the other acted without speaking.'[84] Yet for Paoli this was not a recommendation of action for its own sake. Paoli deemed man gentle and good by nature, and he believed that the 'greater happiness was not in glory but in goodness'. He explicitly preferred the example of William Penn in America, who had 'established a people in quiet and contentment' over 'Alexander the great after destroying the multitudes at the conquest of Thebes'.[85] He went on to conclude: 'Penn the legislator of Pennsylvania seems to me infinitely superior to Alexander the Great; one founded a republic of free and happy men, the other ravaged a half of the entire world by his conquests.' He ended, rather rhetorically, 'which of these two glories is the more pure?'[86] Also crucial was the role of sentiment in the Republic, vital for the development of virtues such as patriotism. As he explains in the *Memoirs*:

If a man would preserve the generous glow of patriotism, he must not reason too much. Mareschal Saxe reasoned; and carried the arms of France into the heart of his own country. I act from sentiment not from reasonings. Virtuous sentiments and habits are beyond philosophical reasonings, which are not so strong, and are continually varying.[87]

As was clear by his every action as Corsican leader during the insurrectionary years, liberty was a cardinal concept in Paoli's political

---

[83] 'La Corsica ai suoi Figli Sleali', published in Orette in 1760, and cited in A. Arrighi, *Histoire de Pascal Paoli, ou La Dernière Guerre de l'Indépendance (1755–1807)* (Paris: Librairie de Charles Gosselin, 1843), ii. 43.
[84] Arrighi, *Histoire de Pascal Paoli*, ii. 354.
[85] James Boswell, *Journal of a Tour to Corsica, with the Memoirs of Pascal Paoli* (London: In Print, 1996, facsimile of the 3rd edition of 1769), 51.
[86] Ibid. 89.   [87] Ibid. 60.

thought. He believed that the Corsican *patrie* enjoyed a natural liberty; its presence was absolute, even in the midst of the Genoese tyranny. In the pamphlet addressed to Corsicans in France and Italy, he wrote that it was 'evident that the breaking of promises and violation of conventions have delivered the Corsicans into the fullness of their rights. Ours was a conditional submission, which ought therefore to have those conditions rigorously observed.' Paoli believed that the violation of this contract ended the duty of the Corsicans to honour it, and therefore 'the country returns to its *primitive* liberty'.[88]

One of Paoli's main tasks was to draft republican laws and to create the conditions for the emergence of a self-sufficient and autonomous political community. This was done through the codification of a Corsican constitution of 1755, and the legislation enacted in the annual *consultes* which followed. Upon being elected leader, he demanded of his own national assembly to circumscribe his powers to a greater extent than they had for his predecessors. No matter the national emergency, he argued that he should not be granted the supreme powers of a wartime *junte*. In a circular published in 1757 he wrote, 'My authority, that of the Council of State, of the parliament, of all officials from the lowest to the highest function in the hierarchy', are only a 'delegation of sovereignty, a temporary mandate, and through which we owe a severe and rigorous account to our electors'. He maintained this was 'how we have a moral force; it is in the name of the electoral college that we fulfil our duties. On the day that 'this confidence is withdrawn', we will 'cede to those who inspire it. This is justice.'[89] Thus Paoli understood his own role as the 'Lawgiver' and founder of the *patrie* as a temporary one, and as both expressing and forming the general will at the same time. He told Boswell that his 'great object was to form the Corsicans in such a manner that they might have a firm constitution, and might be able to subsist without him'. He explained:

our state is young, and still requires the leading strings. I am desirous that the Corsicans should be taught to walk of themselves. Therefore when they come to me and ask who they should choose for their Padre del Commune, or other Magistrate, I tell them, You know better than I do, the able and best men among your neighbours. Consider the consequence of your choice, not only to yourselves in particular, but to the island in general. In this manner I accustom them to feel their own importance as members of the state.[90]

[88] 'La Corsica ai suoi Figli Sleali', 44.   [89] Arrighi, *Histoire de Pascal Paoli*, i. 67.
[90] *Memoirs of Pascal Paoli*, 47–8.

A stream of the important legislation emerged from the elected Assembly. Much was concerned with fostering agriculture, but also it took all responsibilities for setting the levels of taxation. By government decree a mint was set up in Murato in 1761, and coinage began to be issued, perceived in Europe as a vital symbol of sovereignty.[91] But Paoli saw two other institutions of his nascent republic as being of more importance for the recognition of Corsica's sovereign power. The first was the role of disseminating the written word through a national printing press: 'the press will be one day the greatest power in society. The inventor of the printing press will be seen to have killed despotism. The establishment of a press at Corte was the best possible response to the heavy calumnies inflicted by my enemies. It proved to the world that my leadership was by the rule of the general will.'[92] Yet it was with the establishment of the University, at Corte, that he saw himself creating the most important institution of the free republic. Paoli was devoted to its construction, and spent a great deal of time elaborating the role of education in making citizens and maintaining the *patrie*.[93]

He often wrote of liberty, especially from his exile in London after 1769. Using the exact analogy (and even a similar phrasing) as Rousseau did in his *Considerations on the Government of Poland,* he explained in a letter to a British naval commander: 'I have sucked with my milk the love of my country; I came into the world at a time that its tyrants openly concerted its destruction.' He continued: 'after the example of my father, the first rays of reason made me pant after its liberty'. Emphasizing the value of republican fortitude, Paoli stressed that 'neither the most disastrous vicissitudes, exile, danger, distance, nor even the conveniences and honours of life have ever been able to make me lose sight of an object so dear', and towards which 'all my actions have been directed'.[94]

Another key republican concept for Paoli was equality, and a central

---

[91] Jean-Baptiste Marchini, *Pasquale Paoli: Correspondance, 1755–1769: la Corse, état, nation, histoire* (Nice: Serre, 1985), ix.

[92] See F. Flori's, 'L'Imprimerie Nationale', *Études corses*, 18 (1982), 19. Letter from Paoli to M. Grimaldi of Caccia, Arrighi, *Histoire de Pascal Paoli*, ii. 398.

[93] The university established by Paoli in Corte was ransacked then closed down by French soldiers in 1769. It was not reopened until 1982. The current site of the Centre de Recherches Corses is in Paoli's old National Palace.

[94] D. Carrington, *Sources de l'histoire de la Corse au Public Record Office de Londres avec 38 lettres inédites de Pasquale Paoli* (Ajaccio: Société des Études Robespierristes, Librairie la Marge, 1983), 61. Letter to Sir Gilbert Elliot written in Corte, 8 Oct. 1794. Foreign Office General Corsica 20, 61. Rousseau wrote: 'Every true republican drank love of the *patrie*, that is to say love of the laws and of liberty with his mother's milk', *OC* iii. 966.

reason for the military struggle against Genoa: 'my political system is extremely simple: make predominate the general interest over the private one. Equality in all its forms has always been the principle and the foundation.' He suggested that Genoa's failure lay in this very 'separation of their interest with that of the peoples'. In the following sentence he made clear the connection of this republican equality to republican liberty. Having posed the question 'what is the definition of a good social regime?', he offered this answer: 'that in which all citizens enjoy, in peace, the greatest liberty possible.'[95] His notion of justice arose from this notion of liberty and equality. 'Of all the moral virtues, that which I respect most is justice.'[96] Paoli's views on nationalism and patriotism were also similar to Rousseau's. National pride and passion were to be utilized mainly as a force to confront the Genoese with, but in true republican fashion this did not override the continuing necessity of fraternity. Paoli wrote that the 'hatred against foreign oppressors' was the 'true virtue of free peoples', but, as Boswell said: 'when I . . . talked with violence against the Genoese, Paoli said, with a moderation and candour which ought to do him honour even with the republick: "It is true the Genoese are our enemies; but let us not forget, that they are the descendants of those who carried their arms beyond the Hellespont."'[97]

In the *Memoirs*, Paoli spoke constantly of the need to preserve the independence of Corsica from foreign powers: 'We may, said he, have foreign powers for our friends; but they must be *Amici fuori di casa*, Friends at arm's length . . . we may make an alliance, but we will not submit ourselves to the dominion of even the greatest nation in Europe', so the 'less assistance we have from allies, the greater our glory'.[98] It followed, therefore, that he believed in the imperative of military self-reliance. Citizen armies were required both for reasons of republican virtue and, more practically, for the successful defence of the island. He declared that the 'best of all armies is a people who are proud of their independence, jealous of their rights', and 'always ready to defend them', going on to note that in antiquity the most 'warlike' of nations had never sent for 'mercenary soldiers from afar to replace a national army'. He added 'neither Agesilas nor Cimon commanded regular troops'.[99] He further developed the implications of this argument,

---

[95] Letter to P. J. Arrighi, *Bulletin de la Société des Sciences Historiques et Naturelles de la Corse*, 95 (1888), 673.
[96] Marchini, *Pasquale Paoli: Correspondance, 1755–1769*, 45.
[97] Boswell, *Memoirs of Pascal Paoli*, 71.   [98] Ibid. 65, 66.
[99] Ibid. 174.

writing that 'to confide the depository of our welfare, our constitutions, in the hands of foreign mercenaries, is to implicitly admit we are not equal to keep them'. And, even worse, it shows that one has 'ceased to attach the same value to them', which is 'an equally injurious supposition to a people who have sworn to place no good higher than that of their independence'.[100] For Paoli, one should 'leave to wealthier nations the puerile vanity of showing off plumes and epaulettes, or to salute the passage of marching armies with the drumroll or with fanfares'.[101] Not only did he subscribe to the classical republican view that a 'civil militia' was preferable, but he could not 'think of a better guarantee for the continued liberty of the country' as a whole.[102] Although he set out the case for limiting defence to a civil militia at great length in a number of letters, circulars, and open meetings, he was overruled on this issue by the National *Consulte*, who unsurprisingly were concerned to engage as many soldiers as possible in their struggle against the professional soldiers of the Genoese Republic.[103]

Tadeusz Kosciuszko and the Polish Insurrection of 1794

The last figure whose practices and writings provided a direct inspiration for future generations of republicans fighting for independence and against military conquest was the Polish leader Tadeusz Kosciuszko (1746–1817). Kosciuszko was born to an impoverished noble family in 1746. He went to a military school in his youth, and later studied at the Académie Royale de Peinture et de Sculpture in Paris.[104] He volunteered and then distinguished himself as a soldier fighting for republican ideals in revolutionary America; an engineer like Paoli, he founded West Point, and spent seven long years in the struggle for American independence.[105] In spite of his noted modesty and reticence, and his

---

[100] Ibid. 175.   [101] Arrighi, *Histoire de Pascal Paoli*, ii. 370.

[102] Marchini, *Pasquale Paoli: Correspondance, 1755–1769*, 175.

[103] See J. Pulicani's illuminating 'Le Palais National', *Études corses*, 11 (1978), which gives an account of the workings between the different departments of government.

[104] The most detailed general biography of Kosciuszko in English is by Monica Gardner, *Kosciuszko: A Biography* (London: G. Allen & Unwin, 1920), which is (apparently) almost entirely an unacknowledged translation and synthesis of Tadeuz Korzon's renowned two-volume work in Polish: *Kosciuszko: Biografia z Dokumentow Wysnuta* (Cracow, n.p., 1894).

[105] See M. Haiman's *Kosciuszko in the American Revolution* (New York: The Kosciuszko Foundation and the Polish Institute, 1943); and the article by M. Dziewanowski, 'Thaddeus Kosciuszko, Kazimierz Pulaski, and the American War of Independence', in J. Pelenski (ed.), *The American and European Revolutions, 1776–1848* (Iowa City: University of Iowa Press, 1980).

passionate views against slavery, he was eventually rewarded with
a variety of honours from the founding fathers Washington and
his great friend Jefferson, who described him as: 'the noblest son of
freedom'.[106]

When Kosciuszko returned to Poland from America after the second
partition, he found a country already divided by Catherine the Great of
Russia, Frederick the Great of Prussia, and Marie Theresa of Austria
(the first, secret partition having taken place while Rousseau was writing
his *Considerations on the Government of Poland*).[107] Kosciuszko was
delegated to Paris in the summer of 1793 by the group of Poles who had
consolidated themselves in order to organize a national resistance
against the dismemberment of Poland.[108] Arriving there on the day the
king was executed and the Jacobin ascendancy began, his mission was
to gain support for military action from the French government.
Although he had achieved a considerable agreement with the
Girondist-led government in the preceding months (and in spite of
having been made a *citoyen français* by the Legislative Assembly in
August 1792 along with Pasquale Paoli and several other 'leaders of
liberty' of America), he spent a miserable summer there, desperately
seeking support from an increasingly hostile French republic which
itself was becoming subject to a siege mentality and eventually suc-
cumbed to an incoherent foreign policy with regard to Poland.[109] He was
to return empty handed, and went on to lead the so-called 'Kosciuszko
Insurrection' against the Russian and German empires in 1794 with only
Polish forces and Polish arms and money. After a heroic summer of

[106] On his friendship with Jefferson and the Kosciuszko–Jefferson correspondence see
A. W. W. Evans, *Memoir of Tadeusz Kosciuszko: Poland's Hero and Patriot, an Officer in
the American Army of the Revolution, and Member of the Society of the Cincinnati* (New
York: William Abbatt, 1915).

[107] See Jean Fabre's introduction to *Considérations*, in *OC*; also see Lydia Scher-
Zembitska, 'Considérations sur le gouvernement de Pologne', *Conférence sur Rousseau
et la Pologne* (Paris: Bibliothèque Polonaise, 1996).

[108] The best intellectual history of Poland during the period is B. Lesnodorski's *Les
Jacobins polonais* (Paris: Presses Universitaires de France, 1975). On the organization
of the exiled leadership, see Jerzy Lukowski, *Liberty's Folly: The Polish Lithuanian
Commonwealth in the Eighteenth Century 1697–1795* (London: Routledge, 1991), 256;
and Daniel Stone's chapter 'Democratic Thought in Eighteenth Century Poland', in M.
Biskupski and J. Pula (eds.), *Polish Democratic Thought from the Renaissance to the Great
Emigration: Essays and Documents* (London: East European Monographs, 1990), 55–72.

[109] Julien Grossart, 'La Politique polonaise de la Révolution Française jusqu'aux
traités de Bâle', *Annales historiques de la Révolution Française* (1929, 1930). See also M.
Kukiel, 'Kosciuszko and the Third Partition of Poland', in W. Reddaway, J. Penson, O.
Halecki, and R. Dyborski (eds.), *The Cambridge History of Poland* (Cambridge: Cambridge University Press, 1951), 155–6.

battles, the Poles, vastly outnumbered, were defeated by the combined forces of the Russian and German imperial armies, with Austria joining in at the end. Marx and Engels were later to note that it was the Kosciuszko Insurrection, over the summer of 1794, which saved the French from the concentrated military might of the empires themselves, and provided crucial strategic breathing space in which to consolidate their republic.[110] As for the Republic, it had only elected to send help after the public uproar: the decree of the National Assembly was signed on the day that the Polish resistance finally collapsed and Kosciuszko, gravely wounded, was captured.[111] He spent the next two years in one of Catherine the Great's prisons in St Petersberg, and was only released after her death by her son, the new emperor Paul. Still bearing open wounds on his head and thigh and paralysed in one leg, he travelled back to America via London where, to his dismay, he was celebrated as a Plutarchian hero.[112] He submitted to this attention in the hopes of helping his Polish compatriots still in prison and in order to draw attention to the Polish cause.[113]

In America, he re-established his friendship with Thomas Jefferson which lasted the remainder of his life, and on his behalf he returned secretly to France in order to improve relations between the American and French governments. He was to remain in Europe, always in exile, for the rest of his life. Together with his secretary, Josef Pawlikowski (who had been a pivotal figure in the planning of the 1794 insurrection), he published (anonymously) the seminal handbook on insurrectionary and partisan warfare *Can the Poles Fight their Way to Freedom?* in 1800.[114] The pamphlet could be seen as a direct attack on Napoleon's Polish policies; indeed, one Polish notable loyal to Napoleon complained to Talleyrand that the book was hostile to French interests (it

---

[110] 'In 1794, when the French Revolution was only with difficulty resisting the forces of the coalition, its deliverance came from the famed Polish insurrection'. 'Address to the Meeting in Geneva Called to mark the 50th anniversary of the Polish revolution of 1830', *Marks i Engels o Polsce*, ed. H. Michnik and C. Bobinska (Warsaw: Wyd. 1, 1960), ii. 112.

[111] Grossart, 'La Politique polonaise de la Révolution Française', 151.

[112] Poems were written about him by S. T. Coleridge ('Kosciuszko', 1794), and later by Leigh Hunt ('To Kosciuszko, Who Never Fought for Bonaparte or the Allies'); and Keats ('To Kosciuszko', 1816).

[113] The poet Julien Niemciewicz (1758–1841) who accompanied him to America, published a book about their imprisonment in the Russian fortress, *Notes sur ma captivité à Saint-Pétersbourg: en 1794, 1795 et 1796* (Paris: La Bibliothèque Polonaise, 1843), and on their travels in America, see W. Kozlowski, 'Niemciewicz en Amérique et sa correspondance inédite avec Jefferson, 1797–1810', *Revue de Littérature Comparée*, 8 (1928), 29–45.

[114] ('Czy Polacy moga wybic sie na niepodleglosc'), *Pisma Tadeusza Kosciuszki*, ed. Henryk Moscicki (Warsaw: Pnastowe Zaklady Wydawnictw Szkolnych, 1947).

emphasized the fact that no one would come to the Poles' help and they must become self-reliant). He also reported that Kosciuszko's secretary had smuggled 300 copies of the pamphlet into Poland via Frankfurt, resulting in Pawlikowski being placed under police supervision and Kosciuszko being sent an official warning from the government.[115] Kosciuszko moved increasingly further away from Napoleon's political position, in spite of Bonaparte's attempts to entice the Polish leader with offers of senatorial posts, money, military positions, and veiled threats: he needed the Poles to fight and die for him, which, indeed, they did in their thousands.[116]

Tadeusz Kosciuszko became a model to generations after him in America and in Europe for a number of reasons: his remarkable (and almost singular) bravery in standing up to the First Consul Napoleon; his own military valour in the summer of 1794; his passion for justice, his radical egalitarianism illustrated through his anti-abolitionist position whilst fighting in the American Revolution; but especially for his renowned modesty, kindness, and decency, in which he saw in his own role as leader merely an opportunity to serve the needs of the people, in the hope of achieving republican virtue. The republican historian Jules Michelet, in his *Légendes démocratiques du Nord*, wrote a life of Kosciuszko as a way of inspiring French republican commitment and as a model for the civic education of French citizens in the 1860s; as Michel Cadot noted, with his life of Kosciuszko, Michelet was attempting an 'international manual of civic instruction'.[117] Kosciuszko influenced not only republican thinkers like Michelet, but also (as we shall see later) subsequent generations of republican insurrectionary fighters in Europe. Indeed, his classic pamphlet was to become the starting point for all theoretical debates on insurrectionary warfare by republicans in the nineteenth century; it had gone into seven editions by 1843.[118] Those

[115] M. Kukiel, 'Les Origines de la stratégie et de la tactique des insurrections polonaises au XVIIIe et au XIXe siècle', *Revue internationale d'histoire militaire*, 3 (1952), 529.

[116] When Bonaparte asked him to be a member of the French Senate, Kosciuszko responded: 'Et que voudriez vous que je fisse là?' C. Falkensten, *Thadée Kosciuszko dans la vie politique et intime* (Paris: Brockhaus et Avenarius, 1839), 199. See the two-volume work by Leonard Chodzko, *Histoire des légions polonaises* (Paris: Barbezat et Roret, 1829–30), and W. Kozlowski's 'Kosciuszko et les légions polonaises en France', *Revue historique*, 119 and 120 (1915–1916), 86–116, 56–84.

[117] M. Cadot, 'Introduction', in J. Michelet, *Légendes démocratiques du nord* (Paris: Presses Universitaires de France, 1968), v.

[118] A. Walicki, *The Enlightenment and the Birth of Modern Nationhood: Polish Political Thought from Noble Republicanism to Tadeusz Kosciuszko* (Notre Dame: University of Notre Dame Press, 1989), 105.

whose writings on republicanism and war he had directly influenced, notably Mazzini, are generally seen as the progenitors of the ideas he first established. Nonetheless, two Polish military theorists have translated large parts of his writings into English and French, and others have traced both his own debt to Rousseau, his broader political philosophy, and his subsequent influence on the nineteenth-century republican tradition of war.[119] Kosciuszko himself claimed to be strongly influenced by both Rousseau's *Émile,* and by the *Social Contract* in his youth. One friend said in his memoirs: 'Kosciuszko told me that he had an uncle who ignited his zeal for sacrifice by telling him stories about great heroes', adding that his 'study of Rousseau is confirmed by a close friend of his, Jozef Pawlikowski, who states clearly that "in social teaching" Kosciuszko "valued Rousseau's views over others"'.[120] Lesnodorski has also traced the relationship between the two, noting: 'one sees traces of the influence of Jean Jacques Rousseau's thought on Kosciuszko himself, and this well before the Insurrection'.[121]

Another important influence on his thought and actions was the writings of Plutarch on models of ancient republican lives, especially on his childhood hero Timoleon. Kosciuszko later recalled that already in his 'very early years' out of all ancient heroes the one who touched his heart was 'Tymoleon' who 'burned with hatred towards all tyranny'. Kosciuszko liked 'especially the disinterestedness with which Tymoleon overthrew tyrants, set up republics and never demanded power for himself'.[122] Much like the other two founders, he looked to classical republican exemplars in order to create an entirely modern polity.[123]

[119] This has been examined by Emanuel Halicz in *Partisan Warfare in 19th Century Poland: The Development of a Concept* (Odense: Odense University Press, 1975), and especially in his 'Kosciuszko and the Historical Vicissitudes of the Kosciuszko Tradition', *Polish National Liberation Struggles and the Genesis of the Modern Nation* (Odense: Odense University Press, 1982); also M. Kukiel, 'Les Origines de la stratégie et de la tactique des insurrections polonaises au XVIIIe et au XIXe siècle', and 'Military Aspects of the Polish Insurrection of 1863–4', *Antemurale 1863–1963*, 7–8 (1963).
[120] Waclaw Sobieski, 'Kosciuszko's Early Years (Kosciuszko à Rousseau)', *Rok Polski* (1917), 516.
[121] B. Lesnodorski, 'Jean-Jacques Rousseau vu de Pologne', *Voltaire et Rousseau en France et en Pologne,* Actes du Colloque (Warsaw: Éditions de l'Université de Varsovie, 1982), 31.
[122] Sobieski, 'Kosciuszko's Early Years (Kosciuszko à Rousseau)', 13–14.
[123] Pocock's *The Machiavellian Moment* (p. viii) traces just such an ideological shift in America by those seeking new theoretical structures which could underpin the intellectual transition from subject to citizen.

The Republican Thought and Practices of Tadeusz Kosciuszko

> The first step towards casting off slavery is to have the courage to
> be free. The first step towards victory is to appreciate one's own
> strength.[124]

As with Rousseau and Paoli, the other founder of the republican tradition of war cast the conditions of his country's predicament in terms of
foreign oppression and slavery. Kosciuszko began his pamphlet *Can the
Poles Fight Their Way to Freedom?* describing Poland as a great nation
and added:

Shouldn't a nation like that endure, and count, and be highly respected among
the great powers? But, alas! Amongst nations justice is only an illusion! It is
the bandits' iron that determines everything with an eager rage; that embraces,
loots and nominates, and with millions of innocent people going under the yoke
of riotous scoundrels.[125]

Kosciuszko's declaration at the start of the insurrection in 1794 begins
with a description of the Polish plight. Referring to Catherine II and
Frederick, he wrote, 'They have compelled the subjects to take an oath,
and to a state of slavery, by imposing upon them a most grievous
burden.' Having subdued the country, these 'plunderers' had divided
among them the 'spoil', and in 'usurping the name of a National Government, tho' the slaves of a foreign tyranny, they have done whatever
their wills dictated'.[126] So immediately it can be seen that, for
Kosciuszko, the enemy is cast in precisely the same terms Rousseau and
Paoli had used before him. He had brought to this understanding of
slavery a sense of its grim reality: when his commanding officer in the
American Revolution, General Gates, had given him a slave named
Agrippa Hull in gratitude for services, Kosciuszko immediately freed
him, taking the opportunity to point out that all slavery was immoral
and repugnant.[127]

He also concurred with Rousseau's more practical analysis on how
to face the enemy confronting Poland. Referring to *Considerations*,
Kosciuszko explained: 'our country is open, flat, easy to enter; but as
Jean-Jacques Rousseau rightly says: Polish enemies should not be con-

[124] 'Kosciuszko's Act of Insurrection, Cracow, March 24, 1794, in an Assembly of Citizens', cited in Appendix A, M. Haiman, *Kosciuszko: Leader and Exile* (New York: The
Kosciuszko Foundation and the Polish Institute, 1977), 131.
[125] *Can the Poles Fight Their Way to Freedom?*, 169.
[126] 'Kosciuszko's Act of Insurrection', 131.
[127] Dziewanowski, 'Tadeusz Kosciuszko, Kazimierz Pulaski, and the American War of
Independence', 27.

cerned with entering the country, but rather with trying to remain in it'.[128]

Equally, Kosciuszko's republican vision of the nature of man shared certain aspects of Rousseau's central principles. According to Kosciuszko, man was by nature (and could be again) both happy and free, and was driven largely by a common love of humanity. In his call to arms with the famous *Polaniec Manifesto* at the start of his national insurrection of 1794, he declared that in face of tyranny, man would fight for happiness, as it was part of his nature, adding that, 'the enemy exerts his entire energy to prevent our using this occasion. He's using weapons, but these are the least dangerous force at his disposal.' Kosciuszko presents the image of his citizens facing Russian soldiers thus: 'against the mass of frightened and already enslaved [whom] we oppose, the united force of free citizens, who, fighting for their own happiness, cannot fail of victory'.[129] In the extraordinary 'memorial' written to Czartoryski (Tsar Alexander's Foreign Minister, himself a Pole), he set out his view that both man and the state should only practise a 'natural religion', and that the central motivation for man's actions was emotional—what he called the 'sphere of the heart'.[130] He wrote to a friend from his earlier days as an officer in the American Revolution: 'Oh! How happy when we think our Self when Conscious of our deeds, that were started from [the] principle of rectitude, from [a] conviction of the goodness of the thing itself, from [a] motive of the good that will come to Human Kind.'[131]

Kosciuszko repeatedly emphasized his people's natural courage which he understood as an intrinsic virtue similar to natural goodness. He also believed that if man could retrieve his true self, this would inevitably lead to just action. In *Can the Poles*... he explained: 'The human mind adheres to truth, the heart finds pleasure in justice, and if its zeal rises in the soul, it adds particular firmness in actions and causes exceptional events.'[132] Yet it is something that he argued should be sought out and secured as well, thus he set out the need for courage over other virtues. 'We must admit that the Poles hate their yoke, that they have an ardour for freedom and virtue.' But desire for 'order and

---

[128] *Pisma*, 180.

[129] *The Polaniec Manifesto*, in M. B. Biskupski and J. Pula (eds.), *Polish Democratic Thought from the Renaissance to the Great Emigration: Essays and Documents* (London: East European Monographs, 1990), Document 6, 190.

[130] This 'memorial', written in 1814, was not published until the 1960s. Cited in Josef Zuraw's 'Tadeusz Kosciuzcko: The Polish Enlightenment Thinker', *Dialectics and Humanism*, 6 (1971), 155.

[131] Haiman, *Kosciuszko in the American Revolution*, 133.   [132] *Pisma*, 174.

justice is not sufficient': one 'also needs courage to maintain them'.[133] For Kosciuszko, this courage could come through an understanding of the experience of liberty. He thus defined liberty as a physical force as well: 'liberty is the strongest spring to awaken the courage of those who fight. Spartans made miracles with it . . . If we pour its enthusiasm into the souls of our people, not only can it be unbeaten, but it necessarily must be victorious.'[134]

One of the ways in which to achieve this freedom was through education, but, unlike Rousseau in his advice to Poland, he did not believe that freedom for the Polish peasant should wait until they were educated. Liberty always had priority over everything else: 'Some people are of the opinion that it is necessary to educate the people first, before giving them freedom. I argue just the opposite, that if we want to educate the people, we must set them free.'[135] His views on education were derived from egalitarian principles since he believed that 'only riches and education differentiate people'.[136] During the Insurrection itself, the newly created 'Instruction Department of the Supreme National Council' issued several proclamations on patriotic education: 'All meetings and God's temples should occupy themselves with enlightenment, with the stimulation of love of the country, and the commitment to devote all for the country's good.' His insurrectionary pamphlet of 1800 contained the following motto:

Let us read and learn;
let us only will and we shall be free,
as a nation of sixteen million has not and ought not to be born to serfdom.[137]

To the end, Kosciuszko remained convinced of the importance of education as the way of keeping the republican spirit alive in Poland, spending much of his final two years in Switzerland devising a new educational system for his country with J. H. Pestolozzi.[138] This belief in education was connected, as with Rousseau before him, to the creation of citizens. An example can be found in the will he wrote for the use of the money

---

[133] *Pisma*, 173.   [134] Ibid. 189.

[135] Halicz, 'Kosciuszko and the Historical Vicissitudes of the Kosciuszko Tradition', 22.

[136] T. Kosciuszko, *Listy, Odezwy, Wspomnienia*, ed. H. Moscicki (Warsaw: Gebethner i Wolff, 1917), 35.

[137] *Pisma*, 169.

[138] Ibid. 171. In almost every letter written to Jefferson over the years, Kosciuszko mentioned the vital role that education should play in the development and construction of republics. See Tadeusz Kosciuszko, *Autograph Letters of Tadeusz Kosciuszko in the American Revolution: As well as those by and about him*, ed. M. Budka (Chicago: Polish Museum of America, 1977).

which had accrued from his unpaid arrears from the several years' fighting for the American cause. In it he authorized his 'friend Thomas Jefferson', to buy out 'his own or anyone else's slaves, give them land, and, more importantly, give them an education,' so that: 'each should know before, the duty of a Cytyzen in the free government, that they must defend their country against foreign as well as internal enemies'.[139]

Kosciuszko thus argued that education only served a purpose in the context of a republican process of citizenship which included both civic rights and responsibilities: 'Light is only acquired if everyone sees the need and the use of it.' He gives the example of the French, who 'did not involve themselves in a public cause before the revolution'. Only once an individual actually 'receives the right to participate in the legislative process, he is taught and considers interests of the nation. J.-J. Rousseau manifested people's rights.' Once that had occurred, 'eloquent Mirabeau encouraged the French to regain them'.[140]

Like Paoli, he referred to William Penn, but he did not hold him up as an example to follow. In a letter to Jefferson, he wrote: the 'Quakers are a moral people—but they are certainly not citizens'.[141] For Kosciuszko, to be a citizen meant one must defend the *patrie*. He was convinced of the importance of military struggle, remarking that 'the Swiss and the Dutch with rocks and bayonets, with populations ten times smaller, maintained their independence against equally powerful enemies'. Should we, with our more 'numerous resources and national treasures, be abandoned to disgraceful slavery? Prejudice and crime are far more harmful than military battles.'[142] Yet his views of the rights of insurrectionary republics to fight for their freedom were directed at defensive, not expansive, war. He held out the image of a Polish nation 'which desired only to preserve itself and not to invade others, which sought no insidious profits from others, but wanted only to improve the life of its compatriots'.[143] His experience looking for aid from the French republic in 1793 helped crystallize the defensive republican view also held by Rousseau and Paoli. He categorically rejected association with

---

[139] Jefferson never executed the will. In 1836 after three Presidential Commissions, the first school for blacks was founded in the United States (in the North) using Kosciuszko's bequest. See Haiman, *Kosciuszko: Leader and Exile*, 119–30. For other versions of the will, see B. Grzelonski (ed.), *Jefferson–Kosciuszko Correspondence* (Warsaw: Interpress, 1978), 9–10; Evans, *Memoir of Tadeusz Kosciuszko*, 247–8.

[140] *Pisma*, 208.

[141] Original in French. Appendix, correspondence, Haiman, *Kosciuszko: Leader and Exile*, 151.

[142] *Pisma*, 143.   [143] Ibid. 168.

other powers, believing it one of the most dangerous mistakes a nation could make:

It is necessary for a nation which desires independence to trust its own abilities. If this sentiment cannot be found, if to maintain its existence a nation does not make an effort, but instead looks for support and generosity from others, then it can be boldly stated that it will achieve neither happiness nor virtue nor fame.[144]

The struggle was not only to free oneself from tyranny, but also for the goal of equality: 'if the Poles want it now, and with unbroken zeal, to win their freedom', they can 'rise in revolution, and (if it interests all citizens equally) fight the enemy. Only cold souls and narrow minds calculate that we have little chance'.[145] Accordingly, just war was one which was fought for defensive as well as for republican principles. As Kosciuszko declared: 'Who would think to start a revolution, without the principles of freedom and equality, would want to shed the blood of his countrymen in vain, and would gain nothing.' And besides, he added, 'why would one begin fighting without having the happiness of all as its objective?'[146] For Kosciuszko, as for Rousseau, citizen defence was also the way to create citizens: 'Our war has its own specific character which only now can be fully understood.' Its success is based 'largely on the widespread arousal of enthusiasm and on the general arming of the inhabitants of all of our lands'. For that purpose, but also for the sake of the 'future of the republic itself' it is necessary to 'arouse love for the country among those, who, up to now, did not even know that they had a fatherland'.[147]

Kosciuszko came very close to Rousseau's definition of a lawgiver when he took an oath swearing: 'the Safety of the Nation is the Supreme Law' at the start of the national insurrection. His powers as leader were immense.[148] Yet while in his role as lawgiver of the nation Kosciuszko held up the principles of equality, liberty, and fraternity, and he constantly stressed that these powers should never be abused, substantiating this position through the various statements and actions he took during the insurrection. Through a more symbolic representation he also underlined that the virtues of kindness, modesty, and humility must accompany such a (temporary) supreme power. Thus he always dressed like a peasant, and during the insurrection, at the thanksgiving mass for

---

[144] *Pisma*, 169, 173.   [145] Ibid. 180.   [146] Ibid. 189.   [147] Ibid. 134.
[148] Articles 1–3, 'Kosciuszko's Act of Insurrection of Cracow, March 24, 1794, in an Assembly of Citizens', written by its organizers (Kosciuszko, Potocki, and Kollataj), Haiman, *Kosciuszko: Leader and Exile*, 131; and also Lukowski, *Liberty's Folly*, 256–9.

the liberation of Warsaw, he did not come into the church with the other generals, nor did he take his place next to the king, but entered alone and through the back door.[149] Michelet noted that Kosciuszko's gentle spirit was not merely a 'noble error of the human heart'. Rather, it was the most significant element of his character: 'I am convinced that it was precisely his extraordinary goodness' (*bonté extraordinaire*), 'kindness of a high order', which brought such 'countless, endlessly beneficial results for the future of his fatherland'.[150]

Kosciuszko believed strongly in the possibility of a multi-national, multi-religious, and multi-ethnic Polish republic.[151] Progressive and deeply humanistic ideas of fraternity of nations also found considerable resonance in his philosophy. The slogan 'for our freedom and yours', which was to become famous in the nineteenth century, originated in his work: 'he was father of the motto which caused whole generations of Poles to die in the fight of freedom under different latitudes'.[152] He wrote to the Russian enemy in their own language: 'Join your hearts with Poles, who fight for their freedom and yours. The Poles join hands with you and assure you that they will not throw down their arms until you and they are happy.'[153] So for Kosciuszko, the theory of republican war was indissociable from the practice of republican sentiment and action. In the first 'Act of Insurrection', the republican theory and practice of Kosciuszko came together to represent the general will of the *patrie* in one of the most remarkable documents of the age:

Borne down by an immense pressure of evils, vanquished by treachery, rather than by force of foreign enemies . . . having lost our country, and with her the most sacred rights of liberty, having been deceived, and becoming the derision of some nations, while we are abandoned by others; we citizens, inhabitants of the Palatinate of Cracow, by sacrificing to our country our lives, the only good which tyranny has not condescended to wrest from us, will avail ourselves of all the extreme and violent measures that civic despair suggests to us. Having formed a determined resolution to perish and entomb ourselves in the ruins of our country, or to deliver the land of our fathers from a ferocious oppression, and the galling yoke of ignominious bondage, we declare in the face of Heaven

[149] *Pisma*, 56.   [150] *Légendes*, 10–11.

[151] See ch. 3: 'Autour des idées de liberté et d'égalité' of Lesnodorski's *Les Jacobins polonais*, 115–67.

[152] Walicki, *The Enlightenment*, 113. H. Moscicki's article on this is illuminating: 'Relations de Kosciuszko avec le peuple russe', in Adam Mickiewicz, *La Tribune des peuples* (Warsaw: Institut National Ossolinski, 1963), 6.

[153] *Tadeusz Kosciuszko, jego dezwy I raporta–T.K. His Proclamations and Reports* (Cracow: Nabielak, 1918), 181.

and before all the human race, and especially before all the nations, that know how to value liberty above all the blessings of the universe, that to make use of the uncontestable right of defending ourselves against tyranny and armed oppression, we do unite, in the spirit of Patriotism, of civicism and of fraternity, all our forces.[154]

THE REPUBLICAN TRADITION IN THE NINETEENTH CENTURY

In its broad and general formulation as it developed in the eighteenth century, the republican tradition in Europe stood for a specific but loosely defined cluster of values: the ideals of public virtue or public spirit, civic involvement, dedication to the common good, active participation in the affairs of the commonwealth, deliberation with one's peers, political equality, liberty understood as independence.[155] By the middle of the nineteenth century this dynamic tradition was deeply entrenched in European political culture; republican ideas had also played a defining role in the American struggle for independence.[156]

The French Revolution of 1789 had given the republican idea a powerful impetus, and its notions of individualism, constitutionalism, patriotism, citizenship, and the nation-in-arms exercised a powerful appeal for the European imagination during much of the nineteenth century.[157]

---

[154] 'Kosciuszko's Act of Insurrection, in Cracow, March 24, 1794', 132.

[155] On the development of republican thought and themes before the eighteenth century, see, for example Gisela Bock and Q. Skinner (eds.), *Machiavelli and Republicanism* (Cambridge: Cambridge University Press, 1990); M. Peltonen, *Classical Humanism in English Political Thought from 1570 to 1640 with Special Reference to Classical Republicanism* (Helsinki: University of Helsinki, 1992); and Q. Skinner, *Liberty before Liberalism* (Cambridge: Cambridge University Press, 1997).

[156] For an overview see Franco Venturi's marvellous volumes on Europe (and republicanism) during the Enlightenment: *Utopia and Reform in the Enlightenment*; *Settecento riformatore (The End of the Old Regime in Europe), 1768–1776* (Princeton: Princeton University Press, 1989), and *Caduta dell'Antico Regime (The End of the Old Regime in Europe), 1776–1789* (Princeton: Princeton University Press, 1991), i, ii. On America see John Pocock's *The Machiavellian Moment*; P. Higonnet's *Sister Republics: The Origins of French and American Republicanism* (Cambridge, Mass.: Harvard University Press, 1988); D. Lacorne, *L'Invention de la république: le modèle américain* (Paris: Hachette, 1991); and J. Appleby, *Liberalism and Republicanism in the Historical Imagination* (Cambridge, Mass.: Harvard University Press, 1992).

[157] J. Godechot, *La Grande Nation: l'expansion révolutionnaire de la France dans le monde de 1789 à 1799* (Paris: Aubier, 1983); Colloque de Belfort, *L'Idée de nation et l'idée de citoyenneté en France et dans les pays de langue allemande sous la Révolution* (Belfort: Université de Belfort, 1989); Société des Études Robespierristes, *Colloque révolution et*

Yet for republicans in continental Europe fighting against the Holy Empire in the early nineteenth century, the cases of Corsica, Poland, and America (as well as some of the more classical republican images), provided appealing and more practical examples from which to draw inspiration.[158] In France, where the republican tradition was given a complex theoretical articulation, republicans were a polymorphous community, held together by an attachment to powerful principles and common historical experiences.[159] Although French republicans celebrated the Revolution, the principles of popular sovereignty and patriotism, the necessity of political freedoms and mass education, and the centrality of law, there were frequent and often acrimonious divisions over the definition and ordering of their core values.[160] This disunity was reflected in the French republican approach to questions of war and peace. During the nineteenth century, French republicans were at various moments tempted by aggressive and expansionist nationalism, pacifism, and even radical cosmopolitanism.[161] But none of these doctrines represented the true defensive manifestation of the republican philosophy of war, as outlined earlier in this chapter. As will be seen, this defensive tradition was instead mainly articulated by Polish and Italian republi-

république, l'exception française (Paris: IHRF, 1994); G. Best, *The Permanent Revolution: The French Revolution and its Legacy* (London: Fontana, 1988).

[158] For a general history of the broad insurrectionary movement in nineteenth-century Europe (including both the republican and more radical strands), see Geoffrey Best's chapters 'The Insurgent Underground', and 'People's Wars of National Liberation', in *War and Society in Revolutionary Europe 1770–1870* (Leicester: Leicester University Press, 1982), 252–64, 265–72, and R. F. Leslie's *The Age of Transformation* (London: Blandford Press, 1964).

[159] Notable studies include Claude Nicolet's *L'Idée républicaine en France* (Paris: Gallimard, 1982); François Furet, *La Gauche et la révolution au milieu du XIXeme siècle* (Paris: Fayard, 1986), and especially Tchernoff's exceptional two volumes: *Le Parti Républicain sous la monarchie de juillet: formation et évolution de la doctrine républicaine* (Paris: Pedone, 1901) and *Le Parti Républicain au coup d'état et sous le Second Empire* (Paris: Pedone, 1906), and also G. Weill's *Histoire du Parti Républicain en France* (Paris: Alcan, 1900).

[160] For a sense of the continuing importance of these themes in nineteenth-century French republicanism, see F. Furet and M. Ozouf (eds.), *Le Siècle de l'avènement républicain* (Paris: Gallimard, 1993); S. K. Hazareesingh *From Subject to Citizen: The Second Empire and the Emergence of Modern French Democracy* (Princeton: Princeton University Press, 1998); R. Alexander, 'Restoration Republicanism Reconsidered', *French History* (Dec. 1994), 442–69; P. Pilbeam, *Republicanism in 19th Century France* (London: Macmillan, 1995); Philip Nord, *The Republican Moment: Struggles for Democracy in 19th Century France* (Cambridge: Harvard University Press, 1995).

[161] Godechot's *La Grande Nation*, 211–32, is invaluable on expansive republicanism. For examples of republican 'anti-patriotism' see G. Hervé's *Leur patrie* (Paris: Librairie de Propagande Socialiste, 1906) and Larulot, *L'Idole Patrie et ses conséquences* (Brochure Datée de la Prison de Valenciennes, 15 May 1907).

cans from the early decades of nineteenth century.[162] Their French counterparts only fully embraced this doctrine after the impact of the Franco-Prussian War; it had become the mainstream republican view of war in France by 1914.[163] But if France did not provide the intellectual cradle for this doctrine, it certainly provided a more practical refuge for European republican insurrection: Polish and Italian exiles escaping persecution from their Empire's police and military forces met on French soil, and there began the process of organizing republican insurrection.

The determining moment for the construction of republics is traditionally seen as 1848, the 'Springtime of Nations'.[164] However, it will emerge that a particular event in the early 1830s which collected a small group of (largely) anonymous young men together was decisive in the founding of defensive republican war. They embarked on a project which was to have strong social and political ramifications for the development of the tradition of war in the nineteenth century, and indeed for modern republicanism in general. This project was a *Carbonari*-organized military expedition to liberate the Savoie, and included republican Germans as well as Poles, Italians, and a Scandinavian.[165] Although the attempt ended in failure, the people who had participated in the campaign had succeeded in creating something manifestly original, but that nonetheless drew on late eighteenth-century republican war in several ways. They forged a new set of principles which were to underpin the way in which republican war was waged in Europe for the rest of the century, both mirroring and enhancing the paradigm of three founders outlined earlier in this chapter.

[162] Italian republicans were articulating this philosophy from the 1820s. See L. Migliorini, 'L'Héroïsme militaire dans l'Italie après Napoléon', in Viallaneix and Ehrard, *La Bataille, l'armée, la gloire 1745–1871*, especially 497–8.

[163] Jules Michelet, *France et Français: Textes patriotiques* (Paris: Armand Colin, 1893), 160. The ideological evolution of socialists such as Jaurès was particularly critical; see for example his article on 'patriotism' in *Revue de Paris*, 1 Dec. 1898. More generally, G. Goyau's *L'Idée de patrie et l'humanitarisme: essai d'histoire française 1866–1901* (Paris: Perrin, 1902).

[164] Peter Stearns, *The Revolutions of 1848* (London: Weidenfeld & Nicolson, 1974), and the more recent Jonathan Sperber, *The European Revolutions, 1848–1851* (Cambridge: Cambridge University Press, 1994).

[165] A general account of the expedition is given in E. E. Y. Hale, *Mazzini and the Secret Societies: The Making of a Myth* (London: Eyre & Spottiswoode, 1956), ch. 6 (which is almost exclusively based on Harro Harring's account); Paul Harro Harring, *Mémoires sur la Jeune Italie et sur les derniers évènements de Savoie par un témoin oculaire ou mémoires d'un rebelle*, part I (Paris: Librairie M. Dérivaux, 1834), part II (Dijon: Imprimerie de Mme. Veuve Brugnot, 1834); see also Mazzini's version in his *Life and Writings of Mazzini*, 340–68.

As it developed in the nineteenth century, the republican tradition of war grew into two separate but on occasion overlapping branches; one defensive, one expansive. The defensive tradition was committed to preserving and building democratic republican institutions based on distinct nation states. The expansive tradition, however, focused almost exclusively on the projection of republican power through force. Each of these schools understood the concept of equality and fraternity in a different manner, leading to contrasting formulations in their structure, shape, and ideological development. The expansive branch drew on a different interpretation and image of Jean Jacques Rousseau from the version presented here. This difference was caused by its reliance on different works and also its emphasis on particular notions (as typically found in the representation of Rousseau by individuals such as Filipe Buonarroti).[166] The expansive tradition neither drew upon the other two founders of the defensive tradition, Pasquale Paoli and Tadeusz Kosciuszko for inspiration, nor on the predicaments of their nations for examples to learn from or emulate. It also did not associate views on republican war with Rousseau's work on war. Rather it drew almost exclusively from the principles and events of the French Revolution, and their interpretation of it. These differences, although often minor, emphasized quite distinct notions—and purposes—of patriotism for the republican tradition of war, as well as more generally for wars of national liberation. The unity and diversity of this broader tradition of war will be outlined at the end of this chapter, but it will be the nineteenth-century defensive tradition that will be traced in the following section, beginning with an introduction to key individuals, all of whom took part in the intellectual birth of Young Europe in Berne in 1834.

THE NINETEENTH-CENTURY REPUBLICAN TRADITION OF WAR

There were a number of central personalities in the development of the republican tradition of war in Europe but, as mentioned above, the main figures of the tradition to be examined in the first half of the nineteenth century were Polish and Italian. The nature of Polish exile had provoked involvement in other republican causes in Europe, and, under Napoleon, the Poles fought for France and for an expansive republican dream which could evoke (if not actually bring back) their lost

---

[166] See Eisenstein, *Filippo Michele Buonarroti, The First Professional Revolutionist.*

homeland. But there were Poles that did not look to France for salvation. One such was a young captain who led one of the exile columns out of Poland after the suppression of the long insurrection of 1830–1, Karol Bogul Stolzman. He had been part of the famous defence of the capital, and had clearly assumed a pivotal role since his name was on the short list of wanted 'criminals' who were tried *in absentia*.[167] The work of Polish military theorists who had participated in the Polish insurrection of 1830–1 were much studied in Europe throughout the nineteenth century,[168] and none more so than the military manual of this young republican officer, first published in 1844.[169] His own participation in the expedition to liberate the Savoie as a *Carbonaro*, and to forge the principles of Young Europe and Young Poland represented a decisive break from the expansive republican revolutionary movements many Poles preferred, in favour of the defensive republican paradigm. 'Young Poland' was the inspiration for other republican Polish groups planning yet more insurrections in exile, such as the 'Association of Polish People' in Paris and London, and the 'Confederation of the Polish Nation', which united with Young Poland in 1836. Along with other members of the Polish Democratic Society in Paris, Stolzman was clearly influenced by Rousseauian republican ideals.[170] Lesnodorski writes of the 'interest carried for the thought of J. J. Rousseau' by the Poles who had emigrated to France after the failure of the 1830–1 uprising, 'above all by the members of the Polish Democratic Society,

---

[167] A short biography of Stolzman is Boleslaw Limanoski, 'Karol Bogumil Stolzman: Steadfast Patriot and Partisan from 1831–1848', in *Szermierze Wolnosci* (Warsaw, 1911).

[168] The works of L. Bystrzonowski, *Notice sur le réseau stratégique de la Pologne, pour servir à une guerre des partisans* (Paris: Bourgogne et Martinet, 1842), W. Chrzanowski, *Sur la guerre des partisans* (Paris: Imp. de Pinard, 1835), and Pradzynski, *Mémoire historique et militaire sur la guerre en Pologne en 1831* (Paris: Nien, 1840) were known in the West and in Russia. These were all translated into foreign languages and used by military writers and theorists in France and Italy.

[169] K. Stolzman, *Partisan Warfare: The Warfare Most Appropriate to Insurgent Nations, Partyzantka czyli wojna dla ludów powstajacych najwalasciwsza*, ed. A. Anusiewicz (Warsaw: Wydawn Ministerstwa Obrony Narodowej, 1959), 2nd edition. Stolzman's 'remarkable' treatise is acknowledged as having an impact well into the twentieth century. W. Laqueur, *Guerrilla: A Historical and Critical Study* (London: Weidenfeld & Nicolson, 1977), 115. Halicz states that Stolzman's manual was among the most widely read books in Poland during the years 1840–60, and that future generations were 'brought up on it'. *Partisan Warfare in 19th Century Poland*, 100.

[170] On Rousseau's powerful influence on Polish insurrectionary thought see J. Fabre, *Stanislas-Auguste Poniatowski et l'Europe des lumières* (Paris: Éditions Orphrys, 1951); both B. Lesnodorski's 'Les Jacobins polonais', and his 'Jean-Jacques Rousseau vu de Pologne'; M. Tomaszewski, 'Rousseau, éducation des Polonais', *Rousseau, l'Émile et la Révolution*, Actes du Colloque International de Montmorency 1989 (Paris: Robert Thiéry, 1992).

founded in Paris in 1832 who relied upon Rousseau's theories'. One such member, Joseph Wiende, translated a new edition of *Social Contract* in 1839, which was re-edited and reissued in both 1860 and 1862 in Polish, on the 'eve of the Insurrection of 1863'.[171]

The other founder of 'Young Europe' was Giusseppe Mazzini (1805–72), who adapted Koscuiszko's theories to embrace the central platform of the republican tradition of war.[172] As with most republicans of the era, Mazzini was driven by the ambition of overturning the 1815 Vienna settlement, which had divided Italy, Hungary, and Poland among the Austrian, German, and Russian empires. Mazzini's acknowledged mentor in these early years was Carlo Bianco, Conte Di Saint-Jorioz (1795–1843), a former law student and Piedmontese officer who, after 1821, took part in the Italian, Spanish, and Greek insurrections. Bianco was the military chief of staff of the *Carbonari*. His two-volume masterpiece, published in 1830 on the subject of uprisings, entitled *Della Guerra Nazionale d'Insurrezione per Bande applicata all'Italia*, was drawn directly from Kosciuszko's work, *Can the Poles Fight Their Way to Freedom?*[173] Through joining Bianco's smaller society, the *Apofasimeni*, of which Buonarrotti was a member, Mazzini became initiated into one of the most secret of all revolutionary movements of Europe. After 1831 he published a short paper based entirely on Saint-Jorioz's book entitled: *La Giovine Italia* (Young Italy).[174] Mazzini was to become the central exponent of the ideology of insurrectionary and partisan war as the most useful method of constructing democratic republics, providing intellectual, moral, military, and material support for Polish, Hungarian, and French republicans.[175] Besides Carlo Bianco, Mazzini had close links with Stolzman and the Danish republican Harro Harring: all had been members of the *Carbonari*, the secret society opposed to the Vienna settlement; all had also rebelled against its secrecy and institu-

---

[171] Lesnodorski, 'Jean-Jacques Rousseau vu de Pologne', 34.

[172] For an account of the post-expedition Mazzini see Dennis Mack Smith's engaging *Mazzini* (London: Yale University Press, 1994); for a different, younger Mazzini see Hale's *Mazzini and the Secret Societies*.

[173] C. Bianco, *Della Guerra Nazionale d'Insurrezione per Bande applicata all'Italia: Trattato Dedicato ai Buoni Italiani da un Amico del Paese*, Marseilles, 2 vols. See Piero Pieri's 'Carlo Bianco Conte di Saint Jorioz e il suo trattato sulla guerra partigiana', chapter 4 of his *Storia militare del Risorgimento; guerre e insurrezioni*, Biblioteca di cultura storica, 71 (Torino: Einaudi, 1962), 104–29.

[174] *Life and Writings*, i. 58–65. A contemporary portrait of Bianco can be found in Harro Harring's work, especially at 28–9.

[175] See Stefan Kieniewicz's 'La Pensée de Mazzini et le mouvement national slave', *Atti del Convegno sul tema Mazzini e l'Europa* (Roma: Accademia Nazionale dei Lincei, 1974), especially 115–19.

tional hierarchy.[176] Harro Harring had joined in the Philhellene Brigade to fight for Greek liberation before joining the Poles in their struggle against the Russians in 1830. He had founded several underground republican newpapers in Germany and elsewhere, written several books, and was a crucial member of the exiles' group. All took part in a plan to liberate the Savoie from tyranny through military insurrection in 1833.[177]

THE DEVELOPMENT OF THE REPUBLICAN TRADITION OF WAR

Paoli and Kosciuszko, when facing the Genoese Republic and the combined forces of the Russian, German, and Austrian empires, described their predicament as a struggle against foreign tyranny and slavery. As seen earlier in the chapter, this was also how J. J. Rousseau depicted the enemy. However, the men who had embarked on the construction of republics in the 1830s saw themselves facing not only foreign forces but also fighting against what they perceived as less ethical attempts to overthrow empire. Thus the members of the Young Italy expedition broke away from their backers, the *Carbonari*, whilst at the same time attempting to complete their mission of insurrection in the Savoie. Mazzini complained of Carbonarism's 'fatal tendency to seek its chiefs in the highest spheres of society rather as the business of the superior classes than as the duty of the people, sole creators of great revolutions'. Although he and his friends were fighting for a republican vision, 'Carbonarism had no such principle. Its only weapon was mere negation. It called upon men to overthrow: it did not teach them how to build up a new edifice upon the ruins of the old.'[178] Harro Harring's memoirs are full of accounts of the high farce and the low treachery of these secret organizations, which he believed helped rather than hindered the cause of empire.[179] However, it was their cosmopolitanism which he believed was

---

[176] See Alessandro Luzio, *Giuseppe Mazzini, carbonaro: nuovi documenti degli archivi di Milano e Turino* (Torino: Fratelli Bocca, 1920), and more generally, Giuseppe Leti's *Carboneria e massoneria nel Risorgimento italiano* (Bologna: A. Forni, 1966).

[177] A short account of the extraordinary life of Harro Harring can be found in the preface of a collection of his watercolours of South American slaves done in the 1840s, and reprinted by the Brazilian government: P. Harro Harring, *Tropical Sketches* (Rio de Janeiro: Instituto Historico e Geográfico Brasileiro, 1965), drawn largely from the *Allgemeine Deutsche Biographie*.

[178] *Life and Writings*, i. 68–9.

[179] For a fascinating account of only a fraction of Buonarroti's activities see Julien Kuypers, *Les Égalitaires en Belgique: Buonarroti et les sociétés secrétes d'après des docu-*

the most dangerous feature of their ideology. He also did not hesitate to denounce all 'despots and their filthy satellites who encircle them'.[180]

Thus, although this later generation saw itself as carrying out the struggle on two fronts, there were striking continuities between the ideology of the nineteenth-century republican tradition of war and that of the founders of the tradition in the late eighteenth century. The historical context they used to explore answers to their predicament was similar. Writing on the failure of the 1830 insurrection, Stolzman evoked Kosciuszko's writings on the failure of 1794, in using examples from other nations facing stronger enemies than Poland herself: 'was the servitude of the Spaniards more dreadful, the yoke which oppressed them more cruel than that which crushed us before the Insurrection of November 29th?', and added, 'was the love of freedom and the desire for it more widespead, more diffused' among all 'classes of the inhabitants than here?'[181] A little later he quoted Kosciuszko's *Can the Poles Fight Their Way to Freedom?*: 'whoever thinks to start a revolution without the rights of freedom and equality, wishes to spill the blood of his fellow brothers in vain. And, moreover, why begin the struggle not having as the goal the happiness of all?'[182] 'He who has fought more than once for the cause of humanity', wrote Harro Harring after the failure of the expedition, 'will not weaken in his personal conviction'. Just because the 'enemies of the human race have managed to impede the open struggle for liberty and the rights of nations, having understood the goal of existence and the laws of progress', such a person could only 'take more strength and courage after these obstructions; it proves that a deeper hatred of his enemies' cause can strengthen his love for humanity and make it both more powerful and more profound'.[183] Stolzman, in a Swiss prison with other Polish exiles after the failure of the insurrection, published an appeal on their behalf addressed to the people of the canton of Vaud, and to the members of its *conseil d'état*. In it, he described their collective nature in an image that recalled

---

ment inédits 1824–1836 (Brussels: Librairie Encyclopédique, 1960); and (for the period from the French Revolution up until the year before the expedition) the seminal article by A. Lehning 'Buonarroti and His International Secret Societies', *International Review*, 1 (1956), 112–40. For the first expedition to liberate the Savoie, partially organized by Buonarroti, see F. Rude's 'La Première Expédition de Savoie', *Revue historique*, 189 (1940), 413–43.

[180] 'I pointed out the comic and ridiculous nature of such a committee, and declared that I should be ashamed to submit to such a crass dictatorship . . . who are so infiltrated that they are better known to our enemies than they are to themselves'. *Mémoires sur la Jeune Italie*, ii. 10, 4.

[181] *Partisan warfare*, xvii.

[182] Ibid. xxiv.   [183] *Mémoires sur la Jeune Italie*, ii. 4.

Rousseau, Paoli, and Kosciuszko: 'We declare, before the Being who has created men equal and free on all the earth, that we . . . children of misfortune, errant and fugitives of the earth, rebuffed by all governments, attach no more of a price on our life than that it could serve towards the emancipation of oppressed peoples'.[184]

Thus, as can be seen, the centrality of the core values of liberty, equality, and fraternity remained. Unlike other political groups who sought to advance national struggles in nineteenth-century Europe, the republican tradition viewed these principles as indissociable. The 'Young Italy' organization went further. Its members also developed a sophisticated view of republicanism as a complex combination of thought, action, principle, and sentiment. So the 'General Instructions for the Members of Young Italy' started with listing the following principles (before going on to develop them in depth): 'Liberty, Equality, Humanity, Independence, Unity'.[185] As Young Italy's epigram, the way in which these principles could be achieved, Mazzini declared, was if one recognized 'the duty and necessity of harmonizing thought and action'.[186] These principles must be affiliated because, as Mazzini declared: 'Merely to shout liberty, without reflecting what is intended the word should imply, is the instinct of the oppressed slave—no more.'[187] Indeed, republicanism, for Harro Harring, was everything: 'I am *Republican* in the most sacred intent of the word. . . . I am a rebel, an insurrectionary.' Just as Paoli had celebrated being cast as a 'rebel' by the Genoese, both as proof of his legitimate representation of his people and as a fighter against tyranny; so, too, Harro Harring defined rebellion as a metaphor for this republican philosophy. In his account of the expedition, *Jeune Italie*, subtitled *Memoirs of a Rebel* he asks:

What is a rebel? A Man whose heart revolts against injustice and lies, the prerogatives of birth, and against favour by the grace of God. A Man whose heart burns for justice and truth, for virtue and for liberty, who is ready to sacrifice, for humanity, his goods, his blood, and his life. A man who takes up arms to defend the honour of his *patrie*, and who prefers death to slavery: There! That is what a rebel is![188]

Marion Kubalski, another Polish member of the expedition both paraphrased and cited Rousseau in the frontispiece of his *Mémoires* by con-

---

[184] *Europe centrale*, 18 Feb. 1834.
[185] *Life and Writings*, i. 96. 'Unity' carried an instrumental rather than philosophical significance, and was in the main countering Sismondi's then popular theory of federalism for Italy; ibid. 43.
[186] *Life and Writings*, i. 65.   [187] *Life and Writings*, i. 157.
[188] *Mémoires sur la Jeune Italie*, iii. 2.

trasting the combined notions of liberty and democracy with those of slavery and peace: 'An eloquent and profound voice' who seems to be 'speaking to his own *patrie* tells us: it is, above all, for a democratic and popular government that the citizen needs to arm himself; with strength and constancy', and in 'such a manner that he may write every day of his life "I much prefer a perilous liberty to a tranquil slavery" J. J. Rousseau, Contrat Social, III, IV.'[189] Young Italy's commitment was to action, its epigraph: '*Ora e sempre, Fais ce que dois, advienne que pourra*'. This action was entirely republican. Mazzini's declared method to achieve republicanism was through education, but this was to be done by affiliating education to the notion of liberty; insurrection and education were thus fused in a unified approach: 'my idea of an association', was 'one calculated to serve an educational as well as insurrectional purpose'. Thus the 'means by which Young Italy proposes to reach its aim are: education and insurrection, to be adopted simultaneously, and made to harmonize with each other'. Education must 'ever be directed to teach by example, word, and pen, the necessity of insurrection'. Insurrection, on the other hand, 'whenever it can be realised, must be so conducted as to render it a means of national education'.[190]

Ultimately drawing on the earlier paradigm, the main formulators of the nineteenth-century tradition argued that self-reliance and self-respect were key aspects of a successful insurrection for national freedom.[191] As noted above, Kosciuszko was the first to argue this, although it made him extremely unpopular in Polish circles devoted to Napoleon, with royalist clans playing power politics between the diplomats of the empires of Austria and Russia, and with the more radical European groups like the *Carbonari* who believed the purpose of social revolution was to create a cosmopolitan, supra-national Europe.[192] Harro Harring complained about the Carbonari's attempt to 'involve itself arrogantly in the affairs of a foreign nation', and that, 'on the contrary, patriots being on the interior of an oppressed country always know better which were the means and the opportunities towards

[189] *Mémoires sur l'expédition des réfugiés polonais en Suisse et en Savoie dans les années 1833–4* (Paris: Merrlein Imp. P. Baudoin, 1836), i.

[190] *Life and Writings*, i. 155. 'Now and Forever, do what you must, come what may'; ibid. 65, 106.

[191] B. Negroni, 'Introduction', *Considérations sur le gouvernement de Pologne* (Paris: Flammarion, 1990), 33–50.

[192] For a detailed account of the diplomatic role the remnants of the Polish court played in Paris, see M. Dziewanowski, '1848 and the Hotel Lambert', *Slavonic and East European Review*, 26 (1948).

234 The Republican Tradition of War

emancipation'.[193] Stolzman also made this principle the credo of a successful partisan war: 'in order to complete this sacred mission, one must have faith in one's own strength, not depend on others and not count on external factors'. He appealed 'to our fellow countrymen: do not look to the French because they have no need as urgent and as sacred as ours to rise in arms'.[194] Young Italy was based on the idea that 'Italy is strong enough to free herself without external help'.[195]

Yet this self-reliance did not imply a lack of concern for others struggling for the same goals: as illustrated above, it was a core feature of republican internationalism to volunteer to help any other nation facing a similar predicament. The fraternal principles of Young Europe were explained as an association of 'all the peoples, and of all free men in one mission of progress embracing the whole of HUMANITY'.[196] Stolzman's *Partisan Warfare* was dedicated to his companions of the 1830 insurrection, 'my countrymen who first gave the call to national insurrection' and had on the frontispiece a combination of Adam Mickiewicz's motto of 'together young friends', and Kilinski's words: 'we took God as our aid and began immediately the search for friends to embark on our enterprise.'[197] The fraternity was even extended, as in Paoli's and Kosciuszko's political thought, to the enemy. The slogan under which Stolzman fought in Warsaw was a reversal of two words of Kosciuszko's slogan to the Russians 'for both our freedom and yours'; it had become, a generation later: 'for your freedom and ours'.[198] Mazzini also attempted to distinguish the political nature of the conflicts between peoples and states: 'the oppressed is not, whatever one says, the natural ally of the enemies of his master . . . one ought not to confuse the love of liberty with sentiments of hatred and vengeance.'[199]

---

[193] Harring, *Mémoires sur la Jeune Italie*, ii. 9.   [194] *Partisan Warfare*, ix.
[195] Mazzini, *Life and Writings*, iii. 107.
[196] Ibid. i. 165.
[197] *Partisan Warfare*. On this fraternalism (both within and across national movements) in the 1830s, see Kenneth F. Lewalski's 'Fraternal Politics: Polish and European Radicalism during the Great Emigration', in *Polish Democratic Thought, from the Renaissance to the Great Emigration: Essays and Documents* (London: East European Monographs, 1990), 93–108.
[198] This was adopted as the slogan of the resistance when facing the Russians, as advanced by the historian Joachim Lelewel, one of the leaders of the insurrection (whose younger brother was later to go on the expedition under Stolzman's command). See Skurnowicz, *Romantic Nationalism and Liberalism: Joachim Lelewel and the Polish National Idea*, 74. See also K. Olszer, *For Your Freedom and Ours: Polish Progressive Spirit from the 14th Century to the Present* (New York: New York University Press, 1981).
[199] G. Mazzini, *Lettre à M. Léon Plée sur la question européenne* ('*L'Europe entière sera libre ou cosaque*') (Geneva: A. Brasset et Cie., 1857), 2.

All republicans within this tradition of war also shared a common understanding of just and unjust war, and the methods to wage it. In 'Young Italy', Mazzini himself declares: 'Insurrection—by means of guerrilla bands—is the true method of warfare for all nations desirous of emancipating themselves from a foreign yoke.' Guerrilla warfare was 'invincible, indestructible'. Their programme argued that popular uprisings and partisan warfare were legitimate methods for achieving republican goals. Thus, in Mazzini's *Rules for the Conduct of Guerrilla Bands*, modelled on Bianco's earlier work, the role of insurrectionary war had to be distinguished from its goal: the 'political mission of [guerrilla] bands is to constitute the armed apostate of the insurrection . . . Guerrilla bands are the precursors of the nation, and endeavour to rouse the nation to insurrection. They have 'no right' to 'substitute themselves for the nation.'[200] Carlo Bianco argued that insurrectionary war was a war of people against 'one or more professional armies. At such a time every Italian who loves his country and is brave of heart will pursue the barbarian oppressors.'[201] Bianco's own work was shown to rely on Kosciuszko's in many parts, referring often to the 1794 uprising and *Can the Poles Fight their Way to Freedom?*, although believing that Kosciuszko's last battle was strategically mistaken and that he should have transformed the nature of the struggle into partisan warfare.[202] Stolzman believed that a partisan war was the means to republican goals: 'Guerrilla warfare causes minds to adapt themselves to independence and to an active and heroic life; it makes nations great.'[203] Like Rousseau, Harro Harring thought professional soldiers the worst type of criminal: 'the word soldier is an infamous one, by its very etymology "sold" which indicates payment and a bought creature'. This word ought to be 'erased forever from our Dictionary, or at least used with more circumspection'. He thus described himself a 'trooper-citizen', as an exile in the fifth company of the 'Polish republic'.[204]

As noted in Rousseau's paradigm of the republic at war, the main generator of self-defence was the culture of patriotism, which, through education, encouraged a sense of duty towards the republic. As in Rousseau's formulation, this education was primarily sentimental. The

---

[200] *Life and Writings*, i. Appendix; iii. 109. An assessment of the extent of Mazzini's debt to Bianco can be found in Pieri, *Storia militare del Risorgimento*, 129–30.

[201] Carlo Bianco di Saint-Jorioz, *Ai Militari Italiani (1833)* (Torino: Comitato di Torino dell' Instituto per la storia del Risorgimento Italiano, 1975), 25.

[202] In M. Kukiel's review of Piero Pieri's 'Carlo Bianco Conte di Saint Jorioz e il suo trattato' in *Teki Historyczne*, 59 (1958), he compares the two works in some detail.

[203] *Partisan Warfare*, 20.   [204] *Mémoires sur la Jeune Italie*, i. 7–8.

central concern of defensive republicans was the need to involve the entire populace in resistance through their political identification with *la patrie*. Mazzini explained Young Italy's organization as contrasted with that of the Carbonari and Buonarrotti's secret societies of the day: 'Ours was not a sect, but a religion of patriotism. Sects may be extinguished by violence—religions never.'[205] Stolzman argued that the qualities that were needed to lead a people in an insurrection were not based on wealth or property, but on a 'genuine love of the Motherland together with a sense of justice'.[206] In contrasting the life of a mercenary with the life of a guerrilla volunteer, Carlo Bianco saw the volunteer as the 'Italian citizen who, animated by a sacred enthusiasm, freely dedicates his life and possessions to his country', who 'takes up arms to serve Italy', to play his part in the 'sublime purpose of her regeneration', who is 'imbued with the pure joy that gladdens the heart of one devoted to a good cause', who 'feels a love of humanity, and for what is just and true'.[207]

The nation had an almost interchangeable role with the *patrie* for these republicans, especially for Mazzini. As with Rousseau, both these entities needed to be created but also already had to exist: 'In order to found a nationality, it is necessary that the feeling and consciousness of a nationality should exist.'[208] For Stolzman, both the nation and the *patrie* were born through military struggle: 'this war will give birth to strength, trust, and free education for the people', because 'struggle tempers nations, and rebellion wipes out the stigma of bondage from the rebels' brows'.[209]

At the end of the expedition named 'notre république ambulante' by Harro Harring, the four republicans went off on different trajectories, but all had determined a single course for the shape of sovereign republics and provided its military blueprint for much of the rest of the century.[210] Stolzman eventually found haven in England, was active in exile community politics organizing the next insurrection, and writing *Partisan War*. Mazzini went on to fulfil his brilliant future as symbol of the Italian nation, although Carlo Bianco had a less successful transition to the career of professional exile.[211] Harro Harring continued to

---

[205] *Life and Writings*, iii. 6.   [206] *Partisan Warfare*, 5, 6, 8.
[207] *Della Guerra Nazionale d'Insurrezione*, Discorso Preliminare, LXXXIX.
[208] Mazzini, *Life and Writings*, i. 108.   [209] *Partisan Warfare*, 20–1.
[210] 'Our movable republic', or more precisely, 'walking republic'. *Mémoires sur la Jeune Italie*, i. 38.
[211] Bianco, reduced to penury but refusing to accept commission in a professional army, eventually killed himself in Belgium in 1843. See Pieri's *Storia militare del Risorgimento*, 105.

wreak havoc on empire wherever and whenever he could for the next twenty-five years, in prison and out, founding newspapers and planning republican insurrections from Oslo to Latin America. What had brought them together was a desire for a modern, secular, vision of Europe constructed on democratic sovereign states that were above all republican; but most important was that they all displayed the willingness to fight for them.

The strength of this paradigm lay in the extent to which it developed its own trajectory, but, also in the sense in which it influenced other strands of republicanism, even some elements of pacifism. It is true that some pacifists were absolutely and unconditionally opposed to war. One of the arguments used by pacifist liberals was that nothing of permanent political value could come from military solutions;[212] in the late nineteenth and early twentieth centuries this disposition was perhaps best symbolized by Jean Jaurès.[213] However, closer examination shows that many republicans who were active anti-militarists remained strongly committed to defensive war throughout this period. This commitment is normally traced in France as a direct consequence of the experience of the Franco-Prussian war of 1870–1, but there is evidence of widespread support for defensive war among republicans during the 1850s and 1860s.[214] The French republican intellectual, Jules Barni, for example, is comfortably classed as one of the pre-eminent engineers of the large peace conferences of the 1860s, but a more detailed look at his views on war and peace reveals that he was in favour of intervention and defensive republican war. In his book *La Morale dans la démocratie* in 1868 Barni argued for a type of patriotism where 'each citizen has two outfits, one for his profession and the other for military life'; he also added that 'it is the intrinsic right of all human beings to resist by force those who wish to oppress them'.[215] The republican

---

[212] See for example F. Passy, *Conférence sur la paix et la guerre* (Paris: Guillaumin, 1867), 36.

[213] Jean Jaurès argued a particular kind of socialist case against partisan and insurrectionary war—'ces armées d'improvisation et de catastrophe'. He argued that tactics had irrevocably changed, and presented the case for a total demilitarization of all political action, especially class politics: 'la tactique des peuples opprimés change aujourd'hui par la nature des choses, comme la tactique du prolétariat lui-même. Le prolétariat a renoncé à la guerre des rues.' He believed in focusing on international peace and was radically anti-colonial. *L'Armée nouvelle* (Paris: J. Rouff, 1911).

[214] As is comprehensively shown in Alice Conklin's *A Mission to Civilize: The Republican Idea of Empire in France and West Africa, 1895–1930* (Stanford, Calif.: Stanford University Press, 1997), France's republican tradition becomes purely defensive in Europe after 1870, but remains excessively expansive abroad.

[215] J. Barni, *La Morale dans la démocratie; suivi du manuel républicain* (Paris: Ed. Kimé, 1992), 165, 116.

philosopher Eugène Pelletan argued that the only war a republic could wage was a defensive one, as compared to the aggressive war of monarchies.[216] Garibaldi was even invited to attend the Geneva peace conference in 1867 where he announced (to loud acclaim): 'the slave alone has the right to wage war against tyrants'. This argument was embedded within a cluster of republican values: 'All nations are sisters. Wars between them are impossible. Democracy and the propagation of democracy by instruction, education and virtue. Only democracy can remedy the evil of war and reverse the lies of despotism.'[217]

CONCLUSION

This chapter has advanced a number of claims concerning what has been termed the republican tradition of war. Both the expansive and defensive strands of the republican tradition shared a number of features. They came to life and were embedded in situations of wars of conquest, military occupation, and foreign rule. It was exclusively in such conditions that republicans such as Mazzini and Stolzman, Bianco and Harro Harring constructed their theories of popular sovereignty, the good life, and practices of insurrectionary war.

Much of the current study of republicanism tends to ignore the centrality of martial values in the construction of modern republics. By examining the historical practices of republicans in the late eighteenth and nineteenth centuries, it is hoped that a broader account of the intellectual foundations of republicanism has emerged. Modern republicanism was not constructed merely within national boundaries (and by liberal nationalists). It expressed a vision of the human subject through the agency of republican patriotism rather than nationalism. And finally, war is often seen as destructive of social and civic identities, whereas it is possible to see its constructive—and even creative—character for the republicans who waged it. War was not, in other words, a means to achieving the good life of the peaceful republic, but the good life in itself.

Next, republican war can be seen to be intricately implicated in core republican principles. Accordingly, if freedom is to be understood as independence, and dependence as any kind of slavery, then one needs to find the means to avoid becoming dependent not only on tyrants who

---

[216] Eugène Pelletan, *La Tragédie italienne* (Paris: Pagnerre, 1862), 29.
[217] A. Campanella, 'Garibaldi and the First Peace Congress in Geneva in 1867', *International Review of Social History*, 5 (1960), 468–9.

arise (by means of faction) from within but also from without (by way of conquest). But if conquest ends liberty, and liberty is the basic value, then one needs to stand ready as a community to repel enslaving conquerors no less than tyrants. Just as this makes participation in civil government an aspect of the *virtù* needed to stop tyranny, so participation in a civic militia becomes part of the *virtù* required to stop conquest. This is also why the trajectory of republican war is essentially one about defensive wars, as can be seen by the arguments advanced at the various diplomatic conferences on the laws of war between 1874 and 1949.[218]

This chapter has also shown that the republican tradition of war is truly something of a 'lost tribe', given that one of its principal founders, Rousseau, has been customarily aligned with the 'Romantic' tradition. This interpretation has typically placed Rousseau alongside Vico as part of an intellectual movement which developed in Germany in the writings of Herder, Fichte, and, ultimately, Hegel. This is a substantial misalignment, for which there are at least two reasons. The first is the usual emphasis on the rationality of the Enlightenment, with the 'Romantics' forming its heterodoxy. Hence the tendency either to interpret a violence-based morality as a dangerous type of radicalism (which could find its feet only in absolutist, totalitarian, and revolutionary models of thought), or to conflate heroic and epic narratives and practices with mysticism, nationalism, and quasi-religious or proto-Marxist doctrines. Both interpretations deny the genuineness of a moderate republicanism which was radical only in its activism, and was constructed in response to particular political predicaments in the modern European system of states (the experience of oppression, subjugation, and political domination). Second, some have argued that the kind of moral action upon which the republican tradition of war rested had fragmented by the end of the eighteenth century. As can be seen by a small sample of the rich literature of some of the members of Young Europe, Young Poland, and Italy, this is manifestly untrue.

Through affiliation with Pasquale Paoli and Tadeusz Kosciuszko, Rousseau can be seen and understood as (contrary to received wisdom among many theorists) one of the founders of a tradition of hope, rather than a tradition of despair. This hope is manifested in several dimensions. Their relentless unmasking of corrupt political structures provided the impetus for many republican blueprints for change; a positive appreciation of the essential goodness of man underlined the capacity for self-

---

[218] I am very grateful to Quentin Skinner for highlighting this aspect of my argument and for offering this extremely elegant formulation of it.

mastery and heroic action; and their calls for active citizen resistance to occupation and tyranny clearly represented a belief that such action was among the worthiest of human endeavours. At the same time this hope is not analogous to the Erasmian irenic tradition, especially as there is no teleological purpose which informs the actions of mankind—even those who are members of virtuous republics.

The final claim bears on Rousseau's contribution to the theories of *jus ad bellum* and *jus in bello*. It has been shown that his famous axiom on rights in war has been signally misinterpreted by virtually all subsequent writers and publicists. It was never his intention to limit the rights of belligerency to soldiers; rather, his two main purposes were to deny the very legitimacy of soldiers of conquest, and to protect citizens participating in the defence of their country from reprisals. It was true, as he said, that war was not between individuals, but it was most often between occupying armies and peoples. So Rousseau's practical advice on resisting foreign rule and occupation, coupled with Pasquale Paoli and Tadeusz Kosciuszko's epic acts, inspired and legitimized a vibrant, creative, and authentic body of writing on partisan and insurrectionary warfare across Europe in the nineteenth and twentieth centuries. This literature and the numerous organized uprisings it codified were systematically buried by mainstream writers and publicists on the laws of war. This burial was perhaps explained by the eminently Grotian claim that any civilian involvement in belligerent acts jeopardized the entire project of introducing 'humanity in warfare'. This all-or-nothing argument denied the republican paradigm, which blended just war and justice in war, because its formulation would demand a radical change in Grotian thinking. At a deeper level, the argument over the distinction between combatant and non-combatant was rooted in conflicting notions of human nature and the good life. For the Grotians, the Hobbesian imperative of purchasing peace at any price—be it collaboration or even slavery—was natural to the condition of man. Occupation was therefore something to be endured, or at best observed from the (hopefully) distant spheres of private life. In the republican vision, occupation was an affront to both individual and collective freedom; it was a pervasive and invasive phenomenon from which no retrenchment was possible.

Conclusion

By the end of the Geneva negotiations in 1949, significant progress had been made in the codification of the laws of war. Many ancient customary instruments of repression against occupied civilians were prohibited by treaty law. However, the question of the distinction between lawful and unlawful combatants remained essentially unresolved. This book has outlined both the conceptual and the practical historical contexts within which this problem was confronted, and in so doing has offered a particular explanation of its intractability. The argument has been that at the heart of this problem lay three fundamentally divergent philosophies of war, whose differing conceptions of lawful belligerency could not be reconciled.

The martial tradition celebrated the virtues of war, which was defined as inherent in man's nature, and indeed the expression of his most noble ends. While recognizing the inescapable quality of conflict, the Grotian paradigm sought to regulate its conduct and effects. For its part, the republican tradition defined war as an inherently political phenomenon, and sought to identify a normative framework for citizen participation in it. Beyond their ideological articulations, it has emerged that these paradigms were advancing the claims of distinct constituencies. Martialist ideology was in effect a philosophical justification of the practices of conquering and expanding armies; republicanism championed the rights of citizens in captured and occupied territories; and Grotian philosophy articulated the rights of states—a characteristic middle position dictated here by the need to serve the interests of both invading and invaded parties.

A number of central themes have run through this work, and their importance may now be drawn out. In terms of the study of international relations, this book has underlined that in situations of wars of conquest and military occupation, many of the traditional dichotomies in both international relations theory and political theory are lost: distinctions between state and society, individual and collective identities, and notions of public and private become completely and hopelessly enmeshed. For example, the concept of state sovereignty is central to the way in which most realist and rationalist international theorists conceive the world. The state is portrayed as the exclusive object of individual and group loyalty, and irrespective of its ideological configuration, enjoys a monopoly of the legitimate use of force. At the same time, this state is not absolutist: it recognizes the importance of the distinction between the public and private spheres. These neat and rigid categories lose much of their substance under conditions of invasion, occupation, and foreign rule. Individual and group loyalties become fragmented, the locus of sovereignty is fractured and often alienated, and no single group can maintain control over how force is to be used.

From the perspective of international law one central feature is highlighted in this book. In contrast with the conventional depiction of the legal arena as an exclusive instrument for advancing and reconciling state interests, this analysis has illustrated that legal systems are also (and perhaps primarily) the expressions of ideological norms and values. Although lack of space has prevented their full delineation, there were explicit and coherent normative legal codes on occupation, belligerency, and resistance in the martial, Grotian, and republican traditions. In this sense the inability to resolve the distinction between lawful and unlawful combatants was not a failure of diplomacy or negotiating technique, or for that matter a question of 'getting the law right'. The ideological framework within which the laws of war were embedded compounded their problematic nature, most particularly the recurrent tension between *jus ad bellum* and *jus in bello*. In the Grotian scheme, the introduction of any notion of just war was seen to jeopardize the entire project of laws of war. Indeed, they often accused republicans of moral duplicity in demanding protection from laws which they themselves were not prepared to apply to their enemies. However, this Grotian claim rested on a spurious formulation of the republican position. Although the republican paradigm of war was founded on the principle of just war, this did not obviate the necessity of laws of war. Indeed the central republican contention was that it was artificial to separate *jus ad bellum* from *jus in bello*, because considerations of morality applied with equal force to both the origins and the conduct of war. So, for defensive republicans, the ends never justified the means, contrary to the Grotian contention.

A central theme of this book has also been the importance of ideological traditions. As patterns of thought which held together, engaged with each other, and extended across time, the three traditions identified here constitute neglected strands in the history of international thought. The martialist contribution to the concept of war has been ignored, misunderstood, or at best underestimated. The only political theory of conquest whose roots have been exhaustively investigated is fascism. As shown in Chapter 1, however, martialism is in many (crucial) respects distinct from fascist ideology. Indeed, part of the object of illustrating the development of the martial tradition in Britain was precisely to demonstrate how martialist ideas and values could flourish in a 'liberal' society and within specific state structures such as the army. As for the Grotian tradition of war, its presence has been concealed within the broader Grotian approach to international relations and international law. Once presented as a tradition in its own right, Grotian claims to represent neutrality, common sense, and enlightened consensus are revealed as elements of an ideology with an overriding interest in preserving the existing status quo. The republican tradition of war, finally, has been retrieved from the wider republican framework within which liberal patriots were made to cohabit with radical pacifists, revolutionary anarchists, and internationalist eccentrics.

In its treatment of the themes of war and military occupation, finally, this work has highlighted a number of points. The opaque nature of occupation has been illustrated in relation to nineteenth-century Europe. Under these circumstances, all the traditional structures of political and civic life were dissolved. However, what appeared in their place was highly complex and not easy to define. Neither occupying soldiers nor civilian populations could operate according to clear-cut standards, and the final result was often a situation of permanent ambiguity. Nonetheless, Chapter 2 pointed to one incontrovertible fact (minimized and even dismissed by the makers of the laws of war): the existence of a powerful custom of civilian resistance to occupation and foreign rule. These practices of resistance took numerous forms, and were driven by many variants of patriotism, over which the republicans by no means held a monopoly. Of course, not all classes of civilians engaged in these acts of political or military resistance, but these manifestations helped to underline a broader feature of this type of war: the impossibility of maintaining a distinction between the private and public spheres. The Grotian notion of war relied upon this very separation for its advocacy of distinction between combatants and non-combatants. The republicans' formulation—which captured an essential reality—was that war touched the lives of each and every citizen, and in this sense private and public realms were inseparable. In any event, the incoherence of the

Grotian formulation was fundamentally exposed by the army practices of meting out reprisals on 'innocent' civilians—a martialist policy which brutally tore down the barrier between public and private life.

Yet that very act of destruction, by an irony of history, proved to be a catalyst for an act of creation: the structuring of notions of modern political identity. Foreign military occupation brought home that much of what was taken for granted as 'private'—property, language, customs, and social rules—were elements of a greater normative entity. When this way of life was threatened, personal identity and notions of the good life had to be reformulated to include the public sphere. Hence the explicit articulations of doctrines and sentiments of patriotism and nationalism in the face of wars of conquest and military occupation. Little wonder, then, that the attempt to introduce a distinction between lawful and unlawful combatant in the face of such developments proved such a Sisyphean task. The essential truth of wars of military occupation and conquest was captured in the opposition between the martial and republican paradigms. To the first, war was a moral imperative whose defining essence was force. To the second, war was also moral; it was through war that man became a citizen, and citizens acquired a true sense of their collective identity and moral legitimacy. It is only from this perspective that the republican quest for combatant status can be properly understood. This story will conclude on someone else's words, which capture both the mood and poignant melody of wars of occupation, and which evoke all those who participated in them. Writing in 1862 about the Italian struggle for independence, the French republican thinker and politician Eugène Pelletan gave this haunting account of the martialist and republican worlds of war:

National war is by its nature a spontaneous and capricious war, dependent on the contingencies of the unexpected and the inspirational. Wherever a man stands, there is a soldier; wherever there is a place to position the barrel of a gun, a shot is fired. If the enemy appears somewhere, church bells immediately give him away; and from every country crossroad, and from every bush, and from every heath, and from every house, and every wood, the shots ring out from right, from left, from the front, from behind, dying out here, only to resume there: a moving cordon of fire which constantly opens before the enemy as he advances, and closes upon him as he retreats.

Every locality is nothing but a fortress open to the sky. Not a single blade of grass that is not a stronghold; not a hollow that is not a retrenchment. The ground is mined everywhere, charged everywhere; the enemy cannot take a single step forward without it going off under his foot or at his ear. He thus wanders at random, in the midst of a terrible enchantment, where nature itself seems armed against him in order to repel him from the land. The trunk of a tree, the peak of a rock is an isolated sentinel, a mysterious sniper, always firing from close range. He walks in this mist of perpetual ambush, finding death at every minute, but without ever finding the enemy. If a soldier strays to forage, he's killed; if another stops to rest for a moment, he's dead.

The hostile army thus disappears, slowly devoured man by man, victims of a perpetual and ceaseless battle, without truce or armistice. Battle of watch, of guard, of detail, of copse, of each day, of each minute. Sinister battle for the conqueror, who drags behind him, melancholically, his instruments of artillery, without ever managing to line them all up. Battle omitted in all the treatises on strategy, battle of inspiration against science, but where science is always confounded and genius routed, even the genius of Turenne. There is no human means of subjugating by brute force a people who intend to preserve its *patrie*. Let us remember Spain.[1]

---

[1] Eugène Pelletan, *La Tragédie italienne* (Paris: Pagnerre, 1862), 13–14.

BIBLIOGRAPHY

Conference Records, State Archives, and Private Papers

Actes de la Conférence réunie à Bruxelles, du 27 juillet au 27 août 1874 pour régler les lois et coutumes de la guerre, in *Nouveau Recueil général de traités*, 2nd series, vol. iv (1879–80).

The Final Record of the Diplomatic Conference of Geneva of 1949, 3 vols., Federal Political Department, Berne (n.d.).

The Proceedings of the Hague Peace Conferences: Translations of the Official Texts, ed. J. Scott, 4 vols. (New York: Oxford University Press, 1920–1).

Private Documents of Georges Cahen-Salvador, Conseil d'État, Paris.

Archives of the Ministry of Foreign Affairs, Nantes, France.

Archives of the Ministry of Foreign Affairs, Brussels, Belgium.

Archives of the State Department, Washington, DC, USA.

Archives of the War and Foreign Offices, Public Record Office, Kew, United Kingdom.

Books, Manuals, and Articles

ALEXANDER, D., *Rod of Iron: French Counter Insurgency Policy in Aragon during the Peninsular War* (Wilmington, Del.: Scholarly Resources, 1985).

ALEXANDER, L., 'Self-Defence and the Killing of Non-combatants: A Reply to Fullinwider', *Philosophy and Public Affairs*, 5/4 (1976).

ALEXANDER, R., 'Restoration Republicanism Reconsidered', *French History* (Dec. 1994).

ANDERSON, G., 'Pascal Paoli: An Inspiration to the Sons of Liberty', *Publications of the Colonial Society of Massachusetts*, 6 (1925).

ANDLER, C., *Frightfulness in Theory and Practice* (London: T. Fisher Unwin, 1913).

ANGELL, N., *Prussianism and its Destruction* (London: Heinemann, 1914).

APPLEBY, J., *Liberalism and Republicanism in the Historical Imagination* (Cambridge, Mass.: Harvard University Press, 1992).

ARENDT, H., *The Origins of Totalitarianism*, vol. ii: *Imperialism* (New York: Harcourt, Brace, and World, 1951).

ARON, R., *Machiavelle et les tyrannies modernes* (Paris: Gallimard, 1993).

——*Paix et guerre entre les nations* (Paris: Calmann-Lévy, 1962).

——*Penser la guerre, Clausewitz: l'âge européen* (Paris: Gallimard, 1976).

——*Philosopher of War: Clausewitz* (London: Routledge & Kegan Paul, 1983).

ARRIGHI, A., *Histoire de Pascal Paoli, ou La Dernière Guerre de l'Indépendance (1755–1807)* (Paris: Librairie de Charles Gosselin, 1843).

AUDOIN-ROUZEAU, S., *1870: la France dans la guerre* (Paris: Armand Colin, 1989).

BALOGH, E., 'The Traditional Element in Grotius' Conception of International Law', *New York University Law Quarterly Review*, 7/2 (1929).

BARNI, J., *La Morale dans la démocratie; suivi du manuel républicain* (Paris: Ed. Kimé, 1992).

BASDEVANT, J., 'Hugo Grotius', in A. Pillet, *Les Fondateurs du droit international* (Paris: V. Giard & E. Brière, 1904).

BATHURST, M. E., 'The United Nations War Crimes Commission', *American Journal of International Law*, 39 (1945).

BAXTER, R., 'Le Premier Effort moderne de codification du droit de la guerre: Francis Lieber et l'Ordonnance no. 100', *Revue internationale de la Croix Rouge* (April–May 1963).

—— 'So Called "Unprivileged Belligerency": Spies, Guerrillas, and Saboteurs', *British Yearbook of International Law*, 28 (1951).

BEAULAVON, G., 'Les Idées de J.-J. Rousseau sur la guerre', *Revue de Paris* (1917).

BERETTI, F., *Pascal Paoli et l'image de la Corse*, in *Studies on Voltaire and the Eighteenth Century*, 253 (Oxford: Voltaire Foundation, 1988).

BERGHAHN, V., *Militarism: The History of an International Debate* (London: Berg Publishers, 1981).

BERGONZI, B., *The Early Life of H. G. Wells* (Manchester: Manchester University Press, 1961).

BERLIN, I., *Against the Current* (Oxford: Clarendon Press, 1991).

—— *The Crooked Timber of Humanity* (London: John Murray, 1990).

BEST, G., *Humanity in Warfare* (London: Methuen, 1983).

—— *The Permanent Revolution: The French Revolution and its Legacy* (London: Fontana, 1988).

—— *War and Law since 1945* (Oxford: Clarendon Press, 1994).

—— *War and Society in Revolutionary Europe 1770–1870* (Leicester: Leicester University Press, 1982).

BETTS, R., 'The Allusion to Rome in British Imperialist Thought of the Late Nineteenth and Early Twentieth Centuries', *Victorian Studies*, 15 (1971).

BIANCO C., di Saint-Jorioz, *Ai Militari Italiani (1833)* (Torino: Comitato di Torino dell' Instituto per la storia del Risorgimento Italiano, 1975).

—— *Della Guerra Nazionale d'Insurrezione per Bande applicata all'Italia: Trattato Dedicato ai Buoni Italiani da un Amico del Paese* (Marseilles, 1830).

BIRKENHEAD, E., *Rudyard Kipling* (London: Weidenfeld & Nicolson, 1978).

BIRKHIMER, W., *Military Government and Martial Law* (Washington, DC, 1892).

BISKUPSKI, M. B., and PULA, J., *Polish Democratic Thought from the Renaissance to the Great Emigration: Essays and Documents* (Boulder, Colo.: East European Monographs, 1990).

BISMARCK, *Les Mémoires de Bismarck*, ed. Busch (Paris: Fasquelle, 1898).

BLACKBURN, V., 'The Last Chapter', in G. Steevens, *From Capetown to Lady-smith* (London: W. Blackwood & Sons, 1900).

BLANCPAIN, M., *La Vie quotidienne dans la France du Nord sous les Occupations: 1814–1944* (Paris: Hachette, 1983).

BLANNING, T. C. W., 'The Death and Transformation of Prussia', *History Journal*, 29/2 (1986).

——*The French Revolution in Germany: Occupation and Resistance in the Rhineland 1792–1802* (Oxford: Clarendon Press, 1983).

BLAZE, S., *La Vie militaire sous le Premier Empire: mœurs de garnison, du bivouac ou de la caserne* (Paris: Librairie Illustrée, 1888).

BLUNTSCHLI, J., *Le Droit international codifié* (Paris: Guillaumin et Cie., 1870).

——*The Theory of the Modern State* (Oxford: Clarendon, 1885).

BOCK, G., and SKINNER, Q. (eds.), *Machiavelli and Republicanism* (Cambridge: Cambridge University Press, 1990).

BODELSON, C., *Studies in Mid-Victorian Imperialism* (Norway: Glydendalske Boghandel, 1924).

BOLITHO, H., 'The Army', in T. Ward (ed.), *The Reign of Queen Victoria* (London: Collins, 1949).

BONAPARTE, NAPOLÉON, *Correspondance de L'Empéreur Napoléon Ier* (Paris: Panckoucke, 1857–69).

BORDET, G., *La Pologne, Lamennais et ses amis 1830–1834* (Paris: Éditions du Dialogue, 1985).

BORDWELL, P., *The Law of War between Belligerents: A History and Commentary* (London: Stevens & Sons, 1908).

BOSWELL, J., *Journal of a Tour to Corsica, with the Memoirs of Pascal Paoli* (London: In Print, 1996, facsimile of the 3rd edition of 1769).

BOUDARD, R., *La 'Nation corse' et sa lutte pour la liberté entre 1744 et 1769: d'après la correspondance des agents français à Gênes et en Corse avec la cour de Versailles* (Marseille: Jeanne Lafitte, 1979).

BOULART, J. F., *Mémoires militaires sur les guerres de la République et de l'Empire* (Paris: Librairie Illustrée, 1892).

BOWER, G., 'The Nation in Arms: Combatants and Non-Combatants', *Transactions of the Grotius Society*, iv (London: Grotius Society, 1919).

BOYLE, F., 'Ideals and Things: International Legal Scholarship and the Prison-house of Language', *Harvard International Law Journal*, 26/2 (1985).

BRAY, J., *L'Occupation militaire en temps de guerre* (Paris: A. Rousseau, 1900), 154.

BRENET, A., *La France et l'Allemagne devant le droit international, pendant les opérations militaires de la guerre 1870–71* (Paris: A. Rousseau, 1902).

BREUCKER, J. DE, 'La Déclaration de Bruxelles de 1874 concernant les lois et coutumes de la guerre', *Chroniques de politique étrangère*, 27/1 (1974).

BRIALMONT, Gen. T., *Angleterre et les Petits États* (Brussels: C. Muquardt, Librairie Militaire, 1875).

BROCK, P., 'The Political Programme of the Polish Democratic Society', in id., *Nationalism and Populism in Partitioned Poland* (London: Orbis, 1973).

BROWN, B., *American Conservatives: The Political Thought of Francis Lieber and John W. Burgess* (New York: AMS Press, 1967).

BRUCE-GLASIER, J., *Le Militarisme anglais* (Brussels: Norz, 1916).

BRULLÉ, A., *Les Murailles dijonnaises pendant la guerre 1870–1871* (Dijon: Imp. Darantiere, 1875).

BUCKLEY, J. H., *William Ernest Henley: A Study of the 'Counter-Decadence' of the 'Nineties* (Princeton: Princeton University Press, 1945).

BULL, H., *The Anarchical Society: A Study of Order in World Politics* (London: Macmillan, 1977).

——'International Law and International Order', *International Organization*, 26 (1972).

——'Recapturing the Just War for Political Theory', *World Politics*, 31/4 (1979).

——KINGSBURY, B., and ROBERTS, A. (eds.), *Hugo Grotius and International Relations* (Oxford: Clarendon, 1990).

BUONARROTI, F., *La Conjuration de Corse*, ed. J. Crozier (Bastia: Editions Centofanti, 1997).

BURIGNY, J. DE, *La Vie de Grotius: avec l'histoire de ses ouvrages* (Paris: Debure l'Aîné, 1752).

BURROUGHS, P., 'John Robert Seeley and British Imperial History', *Journal of Imperial and Commonwealth History*, 1 (1973).

BURROW, J., *Evolution and Society: A Study in Victorian Social Theory* (Cambridge: Cambridge University Press, 1968).

BUTLER, R., *The Roots of National Socialism 1783–1933* (London: Faber & Faber, 1968).

BUTTERFIELD, H., *The Statecraft of Machiavelli* (London: G. Bell, 1944).

——and WIGHT, M. (eds.), *Diplomatic Investigations: Essays on the Theories of International Politics* (London: Allen & Unwin, 1966).

BYSTRZONOWSKI, L., *Notice sur le réseau stratégique de la Pologne, pour servir à une guerre des partisans* (Paris: Bourgogne et Martinet, 1842).

CAHEN-SALVADOR, G., 'Protéger les civils', *Hommes et mondes*, 67 (Feb. 1952).

CAIX DE SAINT-AYMOUR, Vicomte de, *Notice sur Hugues de Groot* (Paris: Charavay Frères, 1883).

CALVOCORESSI, P., and WINT, G., *Total War: The Causes and Courses of the Second World War* (London: Penguin Press, 1972).

CAMPANELLA, A., 'Garibaldi and the First Peace Congress in Geneva in 1867', *International Review of Social History*, 5 (1960).

CAMPEANU, D., *Questions de sociologie militaire* (Paris: Giard et Brière, 1903).

CARLYLE, T., *Chartism* (London: Everyman's Library, 1839).

——*Hero Worship* (London: Chapman, 1842).

——*Past and Present* (London: Chapman & Hall, 1843).

CARR, E. H., *The Romantic Exiles: A Nineteenth-century Portrait* (Harmondsworth: Penguin, 1949).

——*The Twenty Years Crisis 1919–1939* (London: Macmillan, 1946).

CARRIAS, E., *La Pensée militaire allemande* (Paris: Presses Universitaires de France, 1948).

CARRINGTON, D., 'The Corsican Constitution of Pasquale Paoli (1755–1769)', *English Historical Review*, 88 (1973).

——(ed.), *La Constitution de Pascal Paoli, 1755* (Ajaccio: La Marge, 1996).

——'Pascal Paoli et sa 'Constitution' (1755–1769)', *Annales historiques de la Révolution Française*, 46 (1974).

——*Sources de l'histoire de la Corse au Public Record Office de Londres avec 38 lettres inédites de Pasquale Paoli* (Ajaccio: Société des Études Robespierristes, Librairie la Marge, 1983).

CARSTEN, F., *The Rise of Fascism* (Berkeley and Los Angeles: University of California Press, 1969).

CARTER, C., *Rousseau and the Problem of War* (New York: Garland Press, 1987).

CASTELLIN, P., and ARRIGHI, J.-M. (eds.), *Projets de Constitution pour la Corse* (Ajaccio: La Marge, 1979).

CEADEL, M., *Thinking about Peace and War* (Oxford: Oxford University Press, 1989).

CELL, H., and MACADAM, J. (eds.), *Rousseau's Response to Hobbes* (New York: Peter Lang, 1988).

CHARRAS, E., *Histoire de la guerre de 1813 en Allemagne* (Paris: Armand le Chevalier, 1870).

CHILDRESS, J., 'Francis Lieber's Interpretation of the Laws of War: General Orders No. 100 in the Context of his Life and Thought', *American Journal of Jurisprudence*, 21 (1976).

CHODZKO, L., *Histoire des légions polonaises* (Paris: Barbezat et Roret, 1829–30).

CHRZANOWSKI, W., *Sur la Guerre des Partisans* (Paris: Imp. de Pinard, 1835).

CHUQUET, A., *L'Alsace en 1814* (Paris: Plon-Nourrit, 1900).

CLARK, I., *The Hierarchy of States: Reform and Resistance in the International Order* (Cambridge: Cambridge University Press, 1980).

——*Waging War: A Philosophical Introduction* (Oxford: Clarendon Press, 1988).

——and NEUMANN, I. (eds.), *Classical Theories of International Relations* (London: Macmillan, 1996).

CLARKE, M., GLYNN, T., and ROGERS, A., 'Combatants and Prisoner of War Status', in M. Meyer (ed.), *Armed Conflict and the New Law: Aspects of the 1977 Geneva Protocols and the 1981 Weapons Convention* (London: British Institute of International and Comparative Law, 1989).

CLAUSEWITZ, C., *On War* (London: Routledge & Kegan Paul, 1962).

CLERC, C., *Guerre d'Espagne, Capitulation de Baylen* (Paris: A. Fontemoing, 1903).

COIGNET, A., *Les Cahiers du Capitaine Coignet, 1799–1815* (Paris: Hachette, 1883).

COLIN, M., 'Mythes et figures de l'héroïsme militaire dans l'éducation patriotique des jeunes Italiens (1860–1900)', *Mythes et figures de l'héroïsme militaire dans l'Italie du Risorgimento* (Caen: Université de Caen, 1982).

COLLEY, L., *Britons: Forging the Nation 1707–1837* (New Haven: Princeton University Press, 1992).

Colloque de Belfort, *L'Idée de nation et l'idée de citoyenneté en France et dans les pays de langue allemande sous la Révolution* (Belfort: Université de Belfort, 1989).

CONKLIN, A., *A Mission to Civilize: The Republican Idea of Empire in France and West Africa, 1895–1930* (Stanford, Calif.: Stanford University Press, 1997).

COOPER, S., *Patriotic Pacifism: Waging War on War in Europe 1815–1914* (Oxford: Oxford University Press, 1991).

CRAMB, J. A., *National Religion* (London: Macmillan, 1882).

—— *Origins and Destiny of Imperial Britain* (London: John Murray, 1915).

CRANSTON, M., *The Solitary Self: Jean Jacques Rousseau in Exile and Adversity* (London: Allen Lane Penguin Press, 1997).

—— and PETERS, R. (eds.), *Hobbes and Rousseau* (New York: Anchor Books, 1972).

CROOK, P., *Darwinism, War and History: The Debate over the Biology of War from the Origin of the Species to the First World War* (Cambridge: Cambridge University Press, 1994).

CUNNINGHAM, H., 'The Language of Patriotism', *History Workshop Journal*, 12 (1981).

CUTLER, C., 'The "Grotian Tradition" in International Relations', *Review of International Studies*, 17 (1991).

DAMPIERRE, J., *German Imperialism and International Law* (New York: Charles Scribner, 1917).

DAVIES, N., *God's Playground: A History of Poland* (Oxford: Clarendon Press, 1981).

—— *A Short History of Poland* (Oxford: Clarendon Press, 1981).

DAVYDOV, D., *Essai sur la Guerre des Partisans*, trans. R. Polignac (Paris: J. Corréord, 1841).

—— 'Partisans against Napoleon', *Behind the Lines: Twenty-eight Stories of Irregular Warfare* (London: Cassel & Co., 1956).

DEDECK-HÉRY, E., *Jean Jacques Rousseau et la constitution pour la Corse* (Philadelphia: University of Pennsylvania, 1932).

DEDEM DE GELDER, A., *Un Général hollandais sous le Premier Empire: mémoires* (Paris: Plon-Nourrit, 1900).

DELAGRAVE, A., *Mémoires du Col. Delagrave, campagne du Portugal 1810–11* (Paris: C. Delagrave, 1902).

DE LA PRADELLE, P., *La Conférence diplomatique et les nouvelles Conventions de Genève du 12 août 1949* (Paris: Éditions Internationales, 1951).

DEMOLINS, E., *Anglo Saxon Superiority: To What is it Due?* (London: Leaden-hall Press, 1898).

——*A quoi tient la supériorité des Anglo-Saxons?* (Firmin-Didot, Paris, 1897).

DERATHÉ, R., 'Jean-Jacques Rousseau et le progrès des idées humanitaires du XVIe au XVIIIe siècle', *Revue internationale de la Croix Rouge* (1958).

D'ESPINCHAL, H., *Souvenirs militaires 1792–1814* (Paris: Masson et Boyer, 1904).

DETTER DE LUPIS, I., *The Law of War* (Cambridge: Cambridge University Press, 1987).

DIGEON, C., *La Crise allemande de la pensée française 1870–1914* (Paris: Presses Universitaires de France, 1959).

DISRAELI, B., *Tancred, Or the New Crusade* (London: Longmans Green, 1847).

DI VECCHIO, A., 'Grotius and the Foundation of International Law', *New York University Law Review*, 37 (1962).

DONELAN, M., 'Grotius and the Image of War', *Millennium*, 12/3 (1983).

DORPALEN, A., *Heinrich von Treitschke* (New York: Kennekat Press, 1973).

DOSTIAN, I., 'L'Attitude de la société russe face au mouvement de libération national grec', *Les Relations gréco-russes pendant la domination turque et la Guerre d'Indépendance grecque* (Thessalonica: Institute for Balkan Studies, 1981).

DOYLE, M., *Ways of War and Peace* (London: W. W. Norton & Co., 1997).

DRAPER, G., 'The Ethical and Juridical Status of Constraints in War', *Military Law and Law of War Review*, 55 (1972).

——*The Red Cross Conventions* (London: Stevens, 1958).

DROOP, H., 'On the Relations between an Invading Army and the Inhabitants, and the Conditions under which Irregular Troops are Entitled to the Same Treatment as Regular Soldiers', *Transactions of the Grotius Society (Papers Read before the Juridical Society)* (London: Wildy, 1871).

DUNANT, H., *Un souvenir de Solférino* (Geneva: Éditions l'Âge d'Homme, 1969).

DUNNE, T., 'Mythology or Methodology? Traditions in International Relations', *Review of International Studies*, 19 (1993).

DUPEUX, L., 'L'Hitlérisme et ses antécédents allemands', in P. Ory (ed.), *Nouvelle Histoire des idées politiques* (Paris: Hachette, 1987).

DZIEWANOWSKI, M., '1848 and the Hotel Lambert', *Slavonic and East European Review*, 26 (1948).

——'Thaddeus Kosciuszko, Kazimierz Pulaski, and the American War of Independence', in J. Pelenski (ed.), *The American and European Revolutions, 1776–1848* (Iowa City: University of Iowa Press, 1980).

EBY, C., *The Road to Armageddon: The Martial Spirit in English Popular Literature 1870–1914* (London: Duke University Press, 1987).

EDWARDS, C., *Hugo Grotius, the Miracle of Holland: A Study in Political and Legal Thought* (Chicago: Chicago University Press, 1981).

EDWARDS, H., *The Germans in France: Notes on the Method and Conduct of the Invasion, the Relations between Invaders and Invaded, and the Modern Usages of War* (London: E. Stanford, n.d.).

——*The Private History of a Polish Insurrection: From Official and Unofficial Sources* (London: Saunders, Otley, & Co., 1865). ·

EISENSTEIN, E., *Filippo Michele Buonarroti, The First Professional Revolutionist, 1761–1837* (Cambridge, Mass.: Harvard University Press, 1959).

EMMANUELLI, R., ' "Disinganno", "giustificazione", et philosophie des lumières', *Études corses*, 2 (1974).

ETTORI, F., 'Le Congrès des Théologiens d'Orezza, 4 Mars 1731: mythe et réalité', in *Études corses*, 1 (1973).

——'La Formation intellectuelle de Pascal Paoli (1725–1755)', *Annales historiques de la Révolution Française*, 46 (1974).

——'La Révolution de Corse', in P. Arrighi and A. Olivesi (eds.), *Histoire de la Corse* (Toulouse: Privat, 1986).

EVANS, A. W. W., *Memoir of Tadeusz Kosciuszko: Poland's Hero and Patriot, an Officer in the American Army of the Revolution, and Member of the Society of the Cincinnati* (New York: William Abbatt, 1915).

FABER, R., *The Vision and the Need: Late Victorian Imperialist Aims* (London: Faber & Faber, 1966).

FABRE, J., *Stanislas-Auguste Poniatowski et l'Europe des lumières* (Paris: Éditions Orphrys, 1951).

FALKENSTEN, C., *Thadée Kosciuszko dans la vie politique et intime* (Paris: Brockhaus et Avenarius, 1839).

FERRAZ, M., *Histoire de la philosophie en France au XIXème siècle* (Paris: Perrin, 1880).

FIELD, H., *Toward a Programme of Imperial Life: The British Empire at the Turn of the Century* (Westport, Conn.: Greenwood Press, 1982).

FIGGIS, J., *From Gerson to Grotius* (Cambridge: Cambridge University Press, 1907).

FLORI, F., 'L'Imprimerie Nationale', *Études corses*, 18 (1982).

FOLADARE, J., *Boswell's Paoli* (Hamden, Conn.: Archon Books, 1979).

FONTANA, B. (ed.), *The Invention of the Modern Republic* (Cambridge: Cambridge University Press, 1994).

FONTANA, M., *La Constitution corse du Généralat de Pascal Paoli en Corse 1755–1769* (Paris: Imprimerie Bonlauvot-Jouve, 1907).

FORD, W., 'Resistance Movements and International Law', being extracts from the *International Review of the Red Cross*, Geneva (Oct., Nov., Dec. 1967, Jan. 1968).

FORDE, S., 'Varieties of Realism: Thucydides and Machiavelli', *Journal of Politics*, 54/2 (1992).

FORSYTHE, D., *Humanitarian Politics: The ICRC* (Baltimore: Johns Hopkins University Press, 1977).

FRASER, H., 'Ethics of Empire (1897)', in M. Goodwin (ed.), *Nineteenth Century Opinion* (London: Harmondsworth, 1951).

FREEDEN, M., 'The Family of Liberalisms: A Morphological Analysis', in J. Meadowcroft, *The Liberal Political Tradition* (Cheltenham: Edward Edgar, 1996).

——*Ideologies and Political theory* (Oxford: Oxford University Press, 1996).

FREEDMAN, L. (ed.), *War* (Oxford: Oxford University Press, 1994).

FREIDEL, F., *Francis Lieber: Nineteenth Century Liberal* (Baton Rouge: Louisiana University Press, 1947).

FREUND, J., *La Décadence* (Paris: Sirey, 1985).

FROUDE, J. A., *The English in Ireland in the Eighteenth Century* (London: Longman, Green & Co., 1872).

——*The English in the West Indies* (London: Longman, 1888).

——*Oceana or England and her Colonies* (London: Longman, Green & Co., 1886).

FULLINWIDER, R., 'War and Innocence', *Philosophy and Public Affairs*, 5/1 (1975).

FURET, F., *La Gauche et la révolution au milieu du XIXeme siècle* (Paris: Fayard, 1986).

——and OZOUF, M. (eds.), *Le Siècle de l'avènement républicain* (Paris: Gallimard, 1993).

GALBRAITH, J., 'The Turbulent Frontier as a Factor in British Imperialism', *Comparative Studies in Society and History*, 2 (1960).

GALLIE, W., *Philosophers of Peace and War* (Cambridge: Cambridge University Press, 1979).

GARDNER, M., *Kosciuszko: A Biography* (London: G. Allen & Unwin, 1920).

GEAMANU, G., *La Résistance à l'oppression et le droit de l'insurrection* (Paris: Domat-Monchrestien, 1933).

GELLMAN, P., 'Hans J. Morgenthau and the Legacy of Political Realism', *Review of International Studies*, 14/4 (1988).

GILDEA, R., *Barricades and Borders: Europe 1800–1914* (Oxford: Oxford University Press, 1987).

GIROUARD, M., *The Return to Camelot: Chivalry and the English Gentleman* (New Haven: Yale University Press, 1981).

GLAHN, O. VON, *The Occupation of Enemy Territory* (Minneapolis: University of Minnesota Press, 1965).

GOBINEAU, A. DE, *Ce qui est arrivé à la France en 1870* (Paris: Klincksieck, 1970).

GODECHOT, J., *La Grande Nation: l'expansion révolutionnaire de la France dans le monde de 1789 à 1799* (Paris: Aubier, 1983).

GOYAU, G., *L'Idée de patrie et l'humanitarisme: essai d'histoire française 1866–1901* (Paris: Perrin, 1902).

GRABER, D. A., *The Development of the Law of Belligerent Occupation 1863–1914: A Historical Survey* (New York: Columbia University Press, 1949).

GRAHAM, C., *Ideologies of Empire: Nation, Empire, and Victorian Epic Poetry* (Manchester: Manchester University Press, 1998).

GRAINGER, J., *Patriotisms: Britain 1900–1939* (London: Routledge & Kegan Paul, 1986).

GRANT, A. J., and TEMPERLEY, H. W. V., *Europe in the Nineteenth Century: 1789–1914* (London: Longman, 1929).

GREENLEE, J. G., ' "A Succession of Seeleys": The "Old School" Re-examined', *Journal of Imperial History*, 4/3 (1965).

GREENWOOD, C., 'The Relationship between Jus ad Bellum and Jus in Bello', *Review of International Studies*, 9 (1983).

GRIFFIN, R., *Fascism* (Oxford: Oxford University Press, 1995).

—— *International Fascism: Theories, Causes and the New Consensus* (London: Arnold, 1998).

—— *The Nature of Fascism* (London: Routledge, 1993).

GROSSART, J., 'La Politique polonaise de la Révolution Française jusqu'aux traités de Bâle', *Annales historiques de la Révolution Française* (1929, 1930).

GROTIUS, H., *De Jure Belli ac Pacis*, trans. A. Campbell (London: Hyperion Press, 1990).

GRZELONSKI, B. (ed.), *Jefferson–Kosciuszko Correspondence* (Warsaw: Interpress, 1978).

GUELLE, J. DE, *Précis des lois de la guerre: la guerre continentale*, (Paris: G. Pedone-Lauriel, 1881).

GUIBERT-SLEDZIEWSKI, E., 'Pour la patrie: mort héroïque et rédemption', in P. Viallaneix and J. Ehrard, *La Bataille, l'Armée, la Gloire 1745–1871* (Paris: Clermond-Ferrand II, 1985).

GUTTERIDGE, J., 'The Geneva Conventions of 1949', *British Yearbook of International Law*, 26 (1949).

HAGGENMACHER, P., *Grotius et la doctrine de la guerre juste* (Paris: Presses Universitaires de France, 1983).

HAIMAN, M., *Kosciuszko in the American Revolution* (New York: The Kosciuszko Foundation and the Polish Institute, 1943).

—— *Kosciuszko: Leader and Exile* (New York: The Kosciuszko Foundation and the Polish Institute, 1977).

HALE, E. E. Y., *Mazzini and the Secret Societies: The Making of a Myth* (London: Eyre & Spottiswoode, 1956).

HALICZ, E., *Partisan Warfare in 19th Century Poland: The Development of a Concept* (Odense: Odense University Press, 1975).

—— *Polish National Liberation Struggles and the Genesis of the Modern Nation* (Odense: Odense University Press, 1982).

HALL, THADD E., 'The Development of Enlightenment Interest in Eighteenth Century Corsica', *Studies on Voltaire and the Eighteenth Century*, 64 (Oxford: Voltaire Foundation, 1968).

—— *France and the Eighteenth-Century Corsican Question* (New York: New York University Press, 1971).

HALL, W., *A Treatise on International Law* (Oxford: Oxford University Press, 1924).

HAMMER, E., and SALVIN, M., 'The Taking of Hostages in Theory and Practice', *American Journal of International Law*, 38 (1944).

Handbook of the International Red Cross, IV (Geneva: ICRC/IRCS, 1951).

HARRO HARRING, P., *Mémoires sur la Jeune Italie et sur les derniers évènements de Savoie par un témoin oculaire ou mémoires d'un rebelle*, i (Paris: Librairie M. Dérivaux, 1834), ii (Dijon: Imprimerie de Mme. Veuve Brugnot, 1834).

——*Tropical Sketches* (Rio de Janeiro: Instituto Historico e Geográfico Brasileiro, 1965).

HARROLD, C., *Carlyle and German Thought: 1819–1834* (London: Yale University Press, 1934).

HASSNER, P., 'Rousseau and the Theory and Practice of International Relations', in C. Orwin and N. Tarcov (eds.), *The Legacy of Rousseau* (Chicago: University of Chicago Press, 1997).

HAYWARD, J., 'The Official Social Philosophy of the French Third Republic: Léon Bourgeois and Solidarism', *International Review of Social History*, 6 (1961).

HAZAREESINGH, S. K., *From Subject to Citizen: The Second Empire and the Emergence of Modern French Democracy* (Princeton: Princeton University Press, 1998).

HEGEL, G. W. F., *Philosophy of Right*, trans. T. M. Knox (Oxford: Oxford University Press, 1981).

HELLER, M., *La Machine et les rouages: la formation de l'homme soviétique* (Paris: Calmann-Lévy, 1985).

HÉLY, ABBÉ V., *Étude sur le droit de guerre de Grotius* (Paris: Le Clère, 1875).

HERVÉ, G., *Leur patrie* (Paris: Librairie de Propagande Socialiste, 1906).

HERZ, J., *Political Realism and Political Idealism* (Chicago: Chicago University Press, 1951).

HERZEN, A., *My Past and Thoughts: The Memoirs of Alexander Herzen* (Knopf: New York, 1968).

HIGGINS, A., *Non-Combatants and the War* (Oxford: Oxford University Press, 1914).

HIGONNET, P., *Sister Republics: The Origins of French and American Republicanism* (Cambridge, Mass.: Harvard University Press, 1988).

HINSLEY, F. H., *Power and the Pursuit of Peace: Theory and Practice in the History of Relations among States* (Cambridge: Cambridge University Press, 1963).

HIRSCHMAN, A., *The Rhetoric of Reaction: Perversity, Futility, Jeopardy* (Cambridge, Mass.: Harvard University Press, 1991).

HOBBES, T., *Leviathan*, ed. R. Tuck (Cambridge: Cambridge University Press, 1996).

HOBSON, J. A., *The Psychology of Jingoism* (London: Macmillan, 1901).

HOFER, C., *L'Influence de J.-J. Rousseau sur le droit de la guerre* (Geneva: Georg. et Cie., 1916).

HOFFMANN, S., 'Rousseau on War and Peace', *American Political Science Review*, 57 (1963).

—— 'Hedley Bull and His Contribution to International Relations', *International Affairs*, 62 (1986).

—— and FIDLER, D. (eds.), *Rousseau on International Relations* (Oxford: Clarendon Press, 1991).

HOLBORN, H., 'The Prusso-German School: Moltke and the Rise of the German General Staff', in P. Paret, G. Craig, and F. Gilbert (eds.), *The Makers of Modern Strategy* (Princeton: Princeton University Press, 1986).

HOLK, K. VAN, and ROELOFSEN, C. G. (eds)., *Grotius Reader: A Reader for Students of International Law and Legal History* (The Hague: T. M. C. Asser Instituut, 1983).

HOLLAND, H., *Imperium et Libertas: A Study in History and Politics* (London: Edward Arnold, 1901).

HOLLAND, T. E., *Lectures 1874–84* (Oxford: Oxford University Press, 1886).

HOLLS, G. F. W., *The Peace Conference at the Hague and its Bearing on International Law* (New York: Macmillan, 1900).

Hommage à Grotius, ed. F. Rouge (Lausanne: University of Lausanne, 1946).

HORSMAN, R., *Race and Manifest Destiny* (London: Harvard University Press, 1981).

HOURDIN, G., *Lamennais: prophète et combattant de la liberté* (Paris: Perrin, 1982).

HOUSSAYE, H., *La Patrie guerrière* (Paris: Perrin et Cie, 1913).

HOWARD, M., *The Causes of Wars and other Essays* (London: Unwin, 1983).

—— *Clausewitz* (Oxford: Oxford University Press, 1983).

—— 'Empire, Race, and War', in V. Pearl, B. Worden, and H. Lloyd-Jones (eds.), *History and Imagination: Essays in Honour of H. R. Trevor-Roper* (London: Duckworth, 1981).

—— *The Franco-Prussian War: The German Invasion of France 1870–1871* (London: Methuen, 1981).

—— *The Lessons of History* (Oxford: Clarendon Press, 1991).

—— *Soldiers and Governments: Nine Studies in Civilian–Military Relations* (London: Eyre & Spottiswoode, 1957).

—— 'Temperamenta Belli: Can War be Controlled?', in *Restraints on War* (Oxford: Oxford University Press, 1979).

—— *War in European History* (Oxford: Oxford University Press, 1976).

—— *War and the Liberal Conscience* (Oxford: Oxford University Press, 1989).

HOZIER, H., *The Franco-Prussian War: Its Causes, Incidents, and Consequences* (London: MacKenzie, 1876).

HRABER, V., 'Le Rôle de Grotius dans le développement scientifique du droit international', *Revue de droit international et de législation comparée*, 6 (1925).

HULL, W., *The Two Hague Conferences and their Contributions to International Law* (Boston: Ginn & Company, 1908).

HULLIUNG, M., *Citizen Machiavelli* (Princeton: Princeton University Press, 1983).

HURRELL, A., 'Kant and the Kantian Paradigm in International Relations', *Review of International Studies*, 16/3 (1990).

JAEGLÉ, E., *La Guerre est-elle inévitable?* (Paris: Heinrichsen, 1890).

JAURÈS, J., *L'Armée nouvelle* (Paris: J. Rouff, 1911).

JEFFREY, R. (ed.), *Imperialism and Juvenile Literature* (Manchester: Manchester University Press, 1989).

JIMENEZ DE ARACHAGA, E., 'The Grotian Heritage and the Concept of a Just World Order', in The Commemorative Colloquium on International Law and the Grotian Heritage, *International Law and the Grotian Heritage* (The Hague: T. M. C. Asser Instituut, 1985).

JONES, R., 'The English School of International Relations: A Case for Closure', *Review of International Studies*, 7/1 (1989).

JOURDAN, J. B., *Mémoires militaires du Maréchal Jourdan, Guerre d'Espagne* (Paris: Flammarion, 1899).

JUNOD, D., *The Imperilled Red Cross and the Palestine-Eretz Israel Conflict: 1945–1952* (London: Kegan Paul International, 1996).

KALSHOVEN, F., *Belligerent Reprisals* (Leyden: Sijthoff, 1971).

KELLY, C., *Rousseau's Exemplary Life: The 'Confessions' as Political Philosophy* (Ithaca, NY: Cornell University Press, 1987).

KENDLE, J., *The Round Table Movement and the Imperial Union* (Toronto: Toronto University Press, 1975).

KENNEDY, D., 'Primitive Legal Scholarship', *Harvard International Law Journal*, 27 (1986).

KEOHANE, N., *Philosophy and the State in France: The Renaissance to the Enlightenment* (Princeton: Princeton University Press, 1980).

KIENIEWICZ, S., 'La Pensée de Mazzini et le mouvement national slave', *Atti del Convegno sul tema Mazzini e l'Europa* (Roma: Accademia Nazionale dei Lincei, 1974).

KINGSLEY, C., *Charles Kingsley: His Letters and Memories of his Life*, ed. F. Kingsley (London: C. K. Paul, 1877).

—— *The Roman and the Teuton: A Series of Lectures Delivered before the University of Cambridge* (London: Macmillan, 1864).

KLUBER, J., *Droits des gens modernes de l'Europe* (Paris: Guillaumin, 1861).

KNIGHT, W., *The Life and Works of Hugo Grotius* (London: Grotius Society Publications, 1925).

—— 'The Minor Poetry of Hugo Grotius', *Transactions of the Grotius Society*, 13 (1928).

KOOIJMANS, P., 'How to Handle the Grotian Heritage: Grotius and Van Vollenhoven', *Netherlands Journal of International Law*, 81 (1983).

KOSCIUSZKO, T., *Autograph Letters of Tadeusz Kosciuszko in the American Revolution: As well as those by and about him*, ed. M. Budka (Chicago: Polish Museum of America, 1977).

——*Listy, Odezwy, Wspomnienia*, ed. H. Moscicki (Warsaw: Gebethner i Wolff, 1917).

——*Pisma Tadeusza Kosciuszki,* ed. Henryk Moscicki (Warsaw: Pnastowe Zaklady Wydawnictw Szkolnych, 1947).

——*Tadeusz Kosciuszko, jego dezwy I raporta–T.K. His Proclamations and Reports* (Cracow: Nabielak, 1918).

KOSKIENNIEMI, M., *From Apology to Utopia: The Structure of International Legal Argument* (Helsinki: Lakimiesliiton Kustannus, 1989).

KOZLOWSKI, W., 'Kosciuszko et les légions polonaises en France', *Revue historique*, 119, 120 (1915–16).

——'Niemciewicz en Amérique et sa Correspondance inédite avec Jefferson, 1797–1810', *Revue de littérature comparée*, 8 (1928).

KRASNER, S., *International Regimes* (London: Cornell University Press, 1983).

KRYGIER, M., 'Law as Tradition', *Law and Philosophy*, 5 (1986).

KUBALSKI, M., *Mémoires sur l'expédition des réfugiés polonais en Suisse et en Savoie dans les années 1833–4* (Paris: Merrlein Imp. P. Baudoin, 1836).

KUHN, A., 'The Execution of Hostages', *American Journal of International Law*, 36 (1942).

KUKIEL, M. 'Carlo Bianco Conte di Saint Jorioz e il suo trattato', *Teki Historyczne*, 59 (1958).

——'Kosciuszko and the Third Partition of Poland', in W. Reddaway, J. Penson, O. Halecki, R. Dyborski (eds.), *The Cambridge History of Poland* (Cambridge: Cambridge University Press, 1951).

——'Military Aspects of the Polish Insurrection of 1863–4', *Antemurale 1863–1963*, 7–8 (1963).

——'Les Origines de la stratégie et de la tactique des insurrections polonaises au XVIIIe et au XIXe siècle', *Revue internationale d'histoire militaire*, 3 (1952).

KUYPERS, J., *Les Égalitaires en Belgique: Buonarroti et les sociétés secretes d'après des document inédits 1824–1836* (Brussels: Librairie Encyclopédique, 1960).

LACHARRIÈRE, G. LADRIET DE, 'The Controversy Surrounding the Consistency of the Position Adopted by Grotius', in Asser Instituut (ed.), *International Law and the Grotian Heritage* (The Hague: T. Asser Instituut, 1985).

LACORNE, D., *L'Invention de la république: le modèle américain* (Paris: Hachette, 1991).

LAQUEUR, W., *Fascism: A Reader's Guide* (Cambridge: Cambridge University Press, 1976).

——*Guerrilla: A Historical and Critical Study* (London: Weidenfeld & Nicolson, 1977).

LARULOT, *L'Idole Patrie et ses conséquences* (Brochure Datée de la Prison de Valenciennes, 15 May 1907).

LASSUDRIE-DUCHÈNE, G., *Jean-Jacques Rousseau et le droit des gens* (Paris: Imp. Henri Jouve, 1906).

LAUTERPACHT, H., 'The Grotian Tradition in International Law', *British Year-book of International Law*, 23 (1946).

LEDUC-LAFAYETTE, D., *Jean-Jacques Rousseau et le mythe d'antiquité* (Paris: Librairie Philosophique, 1974).

LEE, H., 'Hugo Grotius', *Proceedings of the British Academy*, 16 (1930).

LEHNING, A., 'Buonarroti and His International Secret Societies', *International Review*, 1 (1956).

LEIGH, R. A., 'Jean-Jacques Rousseau and the Myth of Antiquity in the Eighteenth Century', in R. Bolgar (ed.), *Classical Influences on Western Thought A.D. 1650–1870* (Cambridge: Cambridge University Press, 1979).

LESLIE, R. F., *The Age of Transformation* (London: Blandford Press, 1964).

LESNODORSKI, B., 'Rousseau vu de Pologne', *Annales historiques de la Revolution Française*, 34 (1962).

—— *Les Jacobins polonais* (Paris: Presses Universitaires de France, 1975).

—— 'Jean-Jacques Rousseau vu de Pologne', *Voltaire et Rousseau en France et en Pologne*, Actes du Colloque (Warsaw: Éditions de l'Université de Varsovie, 1982).

LETI, G., *Carboneria e massoneria nel Risorgimento italiano* (Bologna: A. Forni, 1966).

LÉVY-BRUHL, L., *L'Allemagne depuis Leibnitz* (Paris: Hachette, 1890).

LEWAK, A., *General M. R. La Fayette o Polsce: listy—mowy—dokumenty* (Warsaw: Gebethner i Wolff, 1934).

LEWALSKI, K., 'Fraternal Politics: Polish and European Radicalism during the Great Emigration', in *Polish Democratic Thought from the Renaissance to the Great Emigration: Essays and Documents* (London: East European Monographs, 1990).

LIDDELL HART, B., *The Ghost of Napoleon* (London: Faber & Faber, 1933).

LIEBER, F., *Miscellaneous Writings* (Philadelphia: Lippincott & Co., 1881).

LIMANOSKI, B., 'Karol Bogumil Stolzman: Steadfast Patriot and Partisan from 1831–1848', in *Szermierze Wolnosci* (Warsaw, 1911).

LINZ, J., 'An Authoritarian Regime: Spain', in Erik Allardt and Stein Rokkan (eds.), *Mass Politics: Studies in Political Sociology* (New York: Free Press, 1970).

LOCKHART, J., *Rhodes* (London: Hodder & Stoughton, 1963).

LOENING, A., 'L'Administration du gouvernement général de l'Alsace durant la guerre de 1870–71', *Revue de droit international et législation Comparée*, 4 (1872).

LUCAS, C., *Les Actes de la Conférence de Bruxelles considérés au double point de vue de la civilisation de la guerre et de la codification graduelle du droit des gens* (Orléans: E. Colas, 1875).

—— *Civilisation de la guerre, observations sur les lois de la guerre et l'arbitrage international* (Paris: Cotillon, 1881).

—— *Compte-rendu sur le 'Traité de droit international public, européen et américain, suivant les progrès de la science et de la pratique contemporaines' par M. Pradier-Fodéré* (Orléans: P. Girardot, 1880).

—— *La Conférence internationale de Bruxelles sur les lois et coutumes de guerre* (Paris: A. Durand, 1874).

—— *Rapport verbal de M. Charles Lucas sur 'Le Droit de la guerre' de M. Der Beer Poortugael* (Orléans: E. Colas, n.d).

—— *Rapport verbal de M. Charles Lucas sur 'Le Précis des lois de la guerre sur terre' par M. le capitaine Guelle* (Orléans: E. Colas, n.d.).

LUKOWSKI, J., *Liberty's Folly: The Polish Lithuanian Commonwealth in the eighteenth century 1697–1795* (London: Routledge, 1991).

LUZIO, A., *Giuseppe Mazzini, carbonaro: nuovi documenti degli archivi di Milano e Turino* (Torino: Fratelli Bocca, 1920).

McCOUBRAY, H., *International Humanitarian Law: The Regulation of Armed Conflict* (Aldershot: Dartmouth Publishing, 1990).

MACHIAVELLI, N., *The Discourses* (London: Penguin, 1985).

MACINTYRE, S., *A Proletarian Science: Marxism in Britain* (Cambridge: Cambridge University Press, 1980).

MACKENZIE, J., 'Heroic Myths of Empire', in id. (ed.), *Popular Imperialism and the Military: 1850–1950* (Manchester: Manchester University Press, 1992).

—— *Propaganda and Empire: The Manipulations of British Public Opinion 1880–1960* (Manchester: Manchester University Press, 1984).

—— *Propaganda and Empire: Imperialism and Popular Culture in Britain*, (Manchester: Manchester University Press, 1984).

MACK SMITH, D., *Mazzini* (London: Yale University Press, 1994).

McLAREN, M., *Corsica Boswell: Paoli, Johnson, and Freedom* (London: Secker & Warburg, 1966).

MAISTRE, J. DE, *Œuvres complètes* (Paris: Vaton Frères, 1870).

—— *St. Petersburg Dialogues*, ed. J. Lively (London: Collier-Macmillan, 1970).

MANENT, P., *An Intellectual History of Liberalism* (Princeton: Princeton University Press, 1994).

MANNFIELD, K., 'Conservative Thought', *Essays on Sociology* (London: Routledge & Kegan Paul, 1953).

MARBOT, Gen., *Mémoires* (Paris: E. Plon Nourrit et Cie., 1880).

MARCHAND, L., *Byron: A Portrait* (London: John Murray, 1971).

MARCHINI, J. P., *Pasquale Paoli: Correspondance, 1755–1769: la Corse, état, nation, histoire* (Nice: Serre, 1985).

MARINI, D. P., 'La Consulte de Caccia et l'élection de Pascal Paoli 1752–1755', *Bulletin de la Société des Sciences Historiques et Naturelles de la Corse* (1913).

MARTENS, F., *La Paix et la guerre* (Paris: A. Rousseau, 1901).

MARTIN, E., *La Gendarmerie française en Espagne et en Portugal* (Paris: Imprimerie-Librairie Léautey, 1898).

MARTIN-FUGIER, A., *La Vie élégante ou la formation du Tout-Paris 1815–1848* (Paris: Fayard, 1990).

MASSON, P., *Une guerre totale 1939–1945: stratégies, moyens, controverses* (Paris: Pluriel, 1990).

MATTINGLY, G., *Renaissance Diplomacy* (Baltimore: Baltimore University Press, 1964).

MAUDE, F., *War and the World's Life* (London: Routledge & Kegan Paul, 1907).

MAURY, F., *Étude sur la vie et les œuvres de Bernardin de St-Pierre* (Paris: Hachette, 1892).

MAVRODES, G., 'Conventions and the Morality of War', *Philosophy and Public Affairs*, 4/2 (1975).

MAZZINI, G., *Lettre à M. Léon Plée sur la question européenne:'L'Europe entière sera libre ou cosaque'* (Geneva: A. Brasset et Cie., 1857).

——*Life and Writings of Mazzini* (London: Smith, Elder, & Co. Cornhill, 1864).

MEINECKE, F., *The Age of Liberation: Germany 1795–1815* (Berkeley and Los Angeles: University of California Press, 1977).

——*Machiavellism: The Doctrine of Raison d'État and its Place in Modern History* (London: Westview, Routledge, 1984)

MELZER, A., *The Natural Goodness of Man: On the System of Rousseau's Thought* (Chicago: University of Chicago Press, 1990).

MÉRIGNHAC, A., *Les Lois de la guerre sur terre* (Paris: Perrin, 1903).

MEYROWITZ, H., 'Le Statut des saboteurs dans le droit de la guerre', *Revue de droit pénal et droit de la guerre*, 5 (1966).

MICHEL, H., *La Seconde Guerre mondiale* (Paris: Presses Universitaires de France, 1972).

MICHELET, J., *France et Français: textes patriotiques* (Paris: Armand Colin, 1893).

——*Légendes démocratiques du nord* (Paris: Presses Universitaires de France, 1968).

MICKIEWICZ, A., *La Tribune des peuples* (Warsaw: Institut National Ossolinski, 1963).

MIDGLEY, E., *The Natural Law Tradition and the Theory of International Relations* (London: Elek, 1975).

MILZA, P., *Les Fascismes* (Paris: Imprimerie Nationale, 1985).

MONTAGNE, J., *Les Avantages du militarisme au point de vue économique et social* (Paris: Berger-Levrault, 1908).

MONTESQUIEU, C., *Œuvres complètes* (Paris: Seuil, 1964).

MOORE, B., *Social Origins of Dictatorship and Democracy* (London: Penguin, 1991).

MORETTI, A., *La Constitution corse de Jean Jacques Rousseau* (Paris: Librairie Recueil Sirey, 1910).

MORGAN, J. (ed.), *The German War Book: Being 'The Usages of War on Land' Issued by the Great General Staff of the German Army* (London: John Murray, 1915).

MORGENSTERN, F., 'The Validity of the Acts of the Belligerent Occupant', *British Yearbook of International Law*, 28 (1951).

MORGENTHAU, H., 'Nationalism', *American Political Science Review*, 16 (1952).

——*In Defence of the National Interest: A Critical Examination of US Foreign Policy* (New York: Knopf, 1951).

——*Politics among Nations* (New York: Knopf, 1973).

——*Scientific Man Versus Power Politics* (Chicago: Chicago University Press, 1946).

MORRIS, W. O'CONNOR, *Fieldmarshall H. Von Moltke* (London: n.p., 1893).

MOUGENOT, R., *Des pratiques de la guerre continentale durant le Premier Empire* (Paris: Librairie Militaire R. Chapelot et Cie., 1903).

MÜLLER, A., *Briefwechsel Zwischen Friedrich Gentz und Adam Heinrich Müller 1800–1829* (Stuttgart: Cottal, 1857).

MURPHY, C., 'The Grotian Vision of World Order', *American Journal of International Law*, 76 (1982).

NAPIER, W., *A Narrative of the Peninsular Campaign 1807–1814* (London: Bickers & Son, 1889).

NARDIN, T. (ed.), *The Ethics of War and Peace: Religious and Secular Perspectives* (Princeton: Princeton University Press, 1996).

——*Law, Morality, and the Relations of States* (New Jersey: Princeton University Press, 1983).

——and MAPEL, D. (eds.), *Traditions of International Ethics* (Cambridge: Cambridge University Press, 1992).

NEGRONI, B., 'Introduction', *Considérations sur le gouvernement de Pologne* (Paris: Flammarion, 1990).

NELKIN, D., 'Disclosing/Invoking Legal Culture: An Introduction', *Social and Legal Studies*, 4 (1995).

NICOLET, C., *L'Idée républicaine en France* (Paris: Gallimard, 1982).

NIEBUHR, R., *The Nature and Destiny of Man: A Christian Interpretation* (New York: Charles Scribner's Sons, 1941).

NIEMCIEWICZ, J., *Notes sur ma captivité à Saint-Pétersbourg: en 1794, 1795 et 1796* (Paris: La Bibliothèque Polonaise, 1843).

NORD, P., *The Republican Moment: Struggles for Democracy in 19th Century France* (Cambridge, Mass.: Harvard University Press, 1995).

NYE, J., and KEOHANE, R., *Power and Interdependence* (Boston: Little Brown, 1989).

OLSZER, K., *For Your Freedom and Ours: Polish Progressive Spirit from the 14th Century to the Present* (New York: New York University Press, 1981).

OMAN, C., *History of the Peninsular War* (Oxford: Clarendon Press, 1902).

ONUF, N., *The Republican Legacy in International Thought* (Cambridge: Cambridge University Press, 1998).

OPPENHEIM, L., *International Law* (London: Longman, 1912).

OUDENDIJK, J., 'Van Vollenhoven's "The Three Stages in the Evolution of the Law of Nations": A Case of Wishful Thinking', *Legal History Review of the Netherlands*, 48 (1980).

PAOLI, P., Letters, *Bulletin de la Société des Sciences Historiques et Naturelles de la Corse*, 95 (1888).

PAPANTONIOU, N., *L'Indépendance grecque dans la faïence française du 19e siècle*, ed. A. Amandry (Athens: Nafplion/Fondation Ethnographique du Peloponnese 1982).

PARET, P., *Clausewitz and the State* (Oxford: Clarendon Press, 1976).

—— 'The Genesis of *On War*', in M. Howard and P. Paret (eds.), *Carl von Clausewitz's On War* (Princeton: Princeton University Press, 1984).

PARQUIN, D.-C., *Souvenirs et campagnes d'un Vieux Soldat de l'Empire 1803–1814* (Paris: Berger-Levraut, 1892).

PASSY, F., *Conférence sur la paix et la guerre* (Paris: Guillaumin, 1867).

PAULSON, S., 'Classic Legal Positivism at Nuremberg', *Philosophy and Public Affairs*, 4/2 (1975).

PEARSON, K., *National Life from the Standpoint of Science* (London: Walter Scott, 1892).

PELISSIER, E., 'Les Libéraux "Patriotes" espagnols devant les contradictions de la Guerre d'Indépendance', in P. Viallaneix and J. Ehrard (eds.), *La Bataille, l'armée, la gloire 1745–1871* (Paris: Clermont-Ferrand II, 1985).

PELLETAN, E., *La Tragédie italienne* (Paris: Pagnerre, 1862).

PELTONEN, M., *Classical Humanism in English Political Thought from 1570 to 1640 with Special Reference to Classical Republicanism* (Helsinki: University of Helsinki, 1992).

PERRY, T., *The Life and Letters of Francis Lieber* (Boston: Osgood, 1882).

PICTET, J., *The Geneva Conventions of 12 August 1949: Commentary*, 4 (Geneva: ICRC, 1960).

PIERI, P., 'Carlo Bianco Conte di Saint Jorioz e il suo Trattato sulla Guerra Partigiana', in *Storia Militare del Risorgimento: Guerre e Insurrezioni*, Biblioteca di Cultura Storica, 71 (Torino: Einaudi, 1962).

PILBEAM, P., *Republicanism in 19th Century France* (London: Macmillan, 1995).

PILLET, A., *Le Droit de la guerre* (Paris: A. Rousseau, 1892).

PILS, F., *Journal de marche du Grenadier Pils 1804–1814* (Paris: P. Ollendorff, 1895).

POCOCK, J., *The Machiavellian Moment: Florentine Political Thought and the Atlantic Republican Tradition* (Princeton: Princeton University Press, 1975).

PRADZYNSKI, I., *Mémoire historique et militaire sur la guerre en Pologne en 1831* (Paris: Nien, 1840).

PRICE, R., 'The Senses of *Virtù* in Machiavelli', *European Studies Review*, 3 (1973).

—— 'The Theme of *Gloria* in Machiavelli', *Renaissance Quarterly*, 30 (1977).

PULICANI, J., 'Le Palais National', *Études corses*, 11 (1978).

RAMBAUD, A., *La Domination française en Allemagne: l'Allemagne sous Napoléon I, 1804–1811* (Paris: Perrin, 1874).

RAWLS, J., in S. Shute and S. Hurley (eds.). *On Human Rights: The Oxford Amnesty Lectures 1993* (New York: Basic Books, 1995).

RAWSON, E., *The Spartan Tradition in European Thought* (Oxford: Clarendon Press, 1991).

REMEC, P., *The Position of the Individual in International Law According to Grotius and Vattel* (The Hague: Martinus Nijhoff, 1960).

RÉMOND, R., *Lamennais et la démocratie* (Paris: Presses Universitaires de France, 1948).

REY, D., 'L'Armée corse 1755–1769', University of Provence, unpublished Master's thesis, 1978.

RICH, P., *Race and Empire in British Politics* (Cambridge: Cambridge University Press, 1990).

RITTER, G., *The Scepter and the Sword: The Problem of Militarism in Germany* (Florida: University of Miami Press, 1969).

ROBERTS, A., 'Land Warfare: From the Hague to Nuremberg', in M. Howard, G. J. Andreopoulos, and M. R. Shulman (eds.), *The Laws of War: Constraints on Warfare in the Western World* (New Haven: Yale University Press, 1994).

—— 'What is a Military Occupation?', *British Journal of International Law*, 55 (1984).

—— and GUELFF, R. (eds.), *Documents on the Laws of War* (Oxford: Clarendon Press, 1989).

ROBERTS, J., *The French Revolution* (Oxford: Oxford University Press, 1978).

ROELOFSEN, C. G., 'Grotius and the "Grotian Heritage" in International Law and International Relations: The Quartercentenary and its Aftermath', *Grotiana*, 11 (1990).

ROLIN, A., *Le Droit moderne de la guerre* (Brussels: Seycourt, 1920).

ROLIN-JACQUEMYNS, G., 'Essai complémentaire sur la Guerre Franco-Allemande dans ses rapports avec le droit international', *Revue de droit international et législation comparée*, 3 (1871).

—— 'Institut de Droit International. Travaux préliminaires à la session de la Haye, 1874–1875', *Revue de droit international et législation comparée* 7 (1875).

ROOSEVELT, G., 'The Role of Rousseau's Writings on War and Peace in the Evolution of the Social Contract', in G. Lafrance (ed.), *Studies on the Social Contract* (Ottawa: Presses de l'Université de Ottawa, 1989).

—— *Reading Rousseau in the Nuclear Age* (Philadelphia: Temple University Press, 1990).

—— 'Rousseau's Fragments on War', *History of Political Thought*, 8 (1987).

ROSAS, A., *The Legal Status of Prisoners of War: A Study in International Humanitarian Law Applicable in Armed Conflicts* (Helsinki: Helsinki Academia Scientiarum Fernica, 1976).

ROSENBERG, J., *Carlyle and the Burden of History* (Oxford: Clarendon Press, 1985).

ROSENBLATT, H., *Rousseau and Geneva: From the First Discourse to the Social Contract 1749–1762* (Cambridge: Cambridge University Press, 1997).

ROTHENBERG, H., 'Moltke, Schlieffen, and the Doctrine of Strategic Envelopment', in P. Paret, G. Craig, and F. Gilbert (eds.), *The Makers of Modern Strategy* (Princeton: Princeton University Press, 1986).

ROUSSEAU, C., *Le Droit de conflit armé* (Paris: A. Pedone, 1983).

ROUSSEAU, JEAN JACQUES, *Correspondance complète*, ed. R. A. Leigh (Geneva: Voltaire Foundation, 1967–95).

——*Œuvres complètes*, ed. B. Gagnebin and M. Raymond (Paris: Pléiades, 1964–96).

RUDE, F., 'La Première Expédition de Savoie', *Revue historique*, 189 (1940).

RUDZKA, W., 'Studies on the Polish Insurrectionary Government in 1863–4', *Antemurale, VII–VIII, 1863–1963* (Rome, 1963).

SAINT-CHAMANS, Gen., *Mémoires 1802–1832* (Paris: E. Plon Nourrit et Cie., 1896).

SCHAMA, S., *Patriots and Liberators: Revolution in the Netherlands 1780–1813* (New York: Knopf, 1977).

SCHER-ZEMBITSKA, J., 'Considérations sur le gouvernement de Pologne', *Conférence sur Rousseau et la Pologne* (Paris: Bibliothèque Polonaise, 1996).

SCHLUTTER, J., *La Poésie de la Guerre de Revanche* (Paris: Heilbronn, 1878).

SCHWARZENBERGER, G., *International Law and Totalitarian Lawlessness* (London: Stevens, 1943).

SCOTT, J., *The Hague Peace Conferences of 1899 and 1907* (Baltimore: Johns Hopkins University Press, 1909).

——(ed.), *Resolutions of the Institute of International Law* (New York: Oxford University Press, 1916).

SEELEY, J., *The Expansion of England: Two Courses of Lectures* (London: Macmillan, 1883).

SEMMEL, B., *Imperialism and Social Reform: English Social Imperial Thought 1895–1914* (London: G. B. Allen & Unwin, 1960).

SHKLAR, J., *Men and Citizens: A Study of Rousseau's Social Theory* (Cambridge: Cambridge University Press, 1969).

SKINNER, Q., *The Foundations of Modern Political Thought* (Cambridge: Cambridge University Press, 1978).

——*Liberty before Liberalism* (Cambridge: Cambridge University Press, 1997).

——*Machiavelli* (Oxford: Oxford University Press, 1981).

——*Reason and Rhetoric in the Philosophy of Hobbes* (Cambridge: Cambridge University Press, 1996).

SKOWRONEK, J., 'Insurrection polonaise de 1830: révolution ou nationalisme?', *Pologne: l'insurrection de 1830–1831 et sa réception en Europe: actes du colloque* (Lille: Université de Lille, 1982).

SKURNOWICZ, J., *Romantic Nationalism and Liberalism: Joachim Lelewel and the Polish National Idea* (New York: Columbia University Press, 1981).

SMITH, M., *Militarism and Statecraft* (New York: Knickerbocker Press, 1918).

SMITH, M. J., *Realist Thought from Weber to Kissinger* (London: Louisiana State University Press, 1986).

SOBIESKI, W., 'Kosciuszko's Early Years (Kosciuszko à Rousseau)', *Rok Polski* (1917).

Société des Études Robespierristes, *Colloque révolution et république, l'exception française* (Paris: IHRF, 1994).

SOULT, N. J., *Mémoires du Maréchal-Général Soult, Duc de Dalmatie* (Paris: N. H. Soult, 1854).

SPAIGHT, J., *War Rights on Land* (London: Macmillan, 1911).

SPENCER, H., *The Principles of Sociology* (London: Williams & Norgate, 1876).

SPERBER, J., *The European Revolutions, 1848–1851* (Cambridge: Cambridge University Press, 1994).

SPERDUTI, G., 'The Heritage of Grotius and the Modern Concept of Law and State', in Asser Instituut (ed.), *International Law and the Grotian Heritage* (The Hague: T. Asser Instituut, 1985).

SPIERS, J., *The Late Victorian Army* (Manchester: Manchester University Press, 1992).

STANLEY, A., *The Life and Correspondence of Thomas Arnold* (London: Minerva, 1881).

STARGARDT, V., *The German Idea of Militarism: Radical and Socialist Critics 1866–1914* (Cambridge: Cambridge University Press, 1994).

STEARN, R., 'G. W. Steevens and the Message of Empire', *Journal of Imperial and Commonwealth History*, 17 (1989).

——'War Correspondents and Colonial War, c.1870–1900', in J. M. MacKenzie (ed.), *Popular Imperialism and the Military: 1850–1950* (Manchester: Manchester University Press, 1992).

STEARNS, P., *The Revolutions of 1848* (London: Weidenfeld & Nicolson, 1974).

STEEVENS, G. W., *Egypt in 1898* (Edinburgh: W. Blackwood & Sons, 1898).

——*With the Conquering Turk: Confessions of a Bashi-bazouk* (London: W. Blackwood & Sons, 1897).

——*With Kitchener to Khartum* (Edinburgh: W. Blackwood & Sons, 1899).

STERNHELL, Z., *La Droite révolutionnaire 1885–1914: les origines françaises du fascisme* (Paris: Seuil, 1978).

——*Ni droite ni gauche* (Paris: Le Seuil, 1983).

STOLZMAN, K., *Partisan Warfare: The Warfare Most Appropriate to Insurgent Nations, Partyzantka czyli wojna dla ludów powstajacych najwalasciwsza*, ed. A. Anusiewicz (Warsaw: Wydawn, Ministerstwa Obrony Narodowej, 1959).

STONE, D., 'Democratic Thought in Eighteenth Century Poland', in M. Biskupski and J. Pula (eds.), *Polish Democratic Thought from the Renaissance to the Great Emigration: Essays and Documents* (London: East European Monographs, 1990).

STONE, J., *Legal Controls of International Conflict: A Treatise on the Dynamics of Disputes and War-Law* (London: Stevens, 1959).

STOWELL, E., 'Military Reprisals and the Sanctions of the Laws of War', *American Journal of International Law*, 36 (1942).

TADASHI, T., 'Grotius's Method: With Special Reference to Prolegomena', in O. Yasuaki (ed.), *A Normative Approach to War: Peace, War, and Justice in Hugo Grotius* (Oxford: Clarendon Press, 1993).

TARLÉ, E., *Napoleon's Invasion of Russia: 1812* (London: George Allen & Unwin, 1942).

TAYLOR, A. J. P., *The Struggle for Mastery in Europe* (Oxford: Oxford University Press, 1971).

TCHERNOFF, I., *Le Parti Républicain au coup d'état et sous le Second Empire* (Paris: Pedone, 1906).

——*Le Parti Républicain sous la monarchie de juillet: formation et évolution de la doctrine républicaine* (Paris: Pedone, 1901).

THIÉBAULT, Général Baron DIEUDONNÉ-ADRIENNE, *Journal des opérations militaires et administratives du Blocus de Gênes* (Paris: J. Corréard, 1846–7).

——*Mémoires* (Paris: E. Plon, Nourrit et Cie., 1893–5).

THORNTON, A., *The Habit of Authority* (London: Allen & Unwin, 1966).

——*The Imperial Idea and Its Enemies: A Study in British Power* (London: Macmillan, 1959).

THRASHER, P. A., *Pasquale Paoli: An Enlightened Hero, 1725–1807* (London: Constable, 1970).

TOMASZEWSKI, M., 'Rousseau, éducation des Polonais', *Rousseau, l'Émile et la Révolution*, Actes du Colloque International de Montmorency 1989 (Paris: Robert Thiéry, 1992).

TREITSCHKE, F., *The Origins of Prussianism: The Teutonic Knight* (London: George Allen & Unwin, 1942).

TUCK, R., 'Peter Haggenmacher, Grotius et la doctrine de la guerre juste', *Grotiana*, 7 (1986).

——'Grotius, Carneades, and Hobbes', *Grotiana*, 4 (1983), 53.

——*Philosophy and Government 1572–1651* (Cambridge: Cambridge University Press, 1993).

TULOUP, F., *Lamennais et son époque: sa vie, son œuvre, son influence, son prophétisme* (Dinan: Impr. Commerciale, 1961).

VAGTS, A., *A History of Militarism* (London: Hollis & Carter, 1959).

VATTEL, E., *The Law of Nations* (Washington: Carnegie Institute, 1916).

VAUGHAN, C., *Studies in the History of Political Philosophy before and after Rousseau* (New York: Russell & Russell, 1960).

VENTURI, F., *Caduta dell'Antico Regime (The End of the Old Regime in Europe), 1776–1789* (Princeton: Princeton University Press, 1991).

——'Il dibattito francese e britannico sulla rivoluzione di Corsica', *Rivista storica italiana*, 86 (1974).

——'Il dibattito in Italia sulla rivoluzione di Corsica', *Rivista storica italiana*, 88 (1976).

——'Pasquale Paoli', in S. Woolf (ed.), *Italy and the Enlightenment: Studies in a Cosmopolitan Century* (New York: New York University Press, 1972).

——*Settecento Riformatore: L'Italia dei Lumi* (Torino: Einaudi, 1969–1987), vol. v.

——*Settecento riformatore (The End of the Old Regime in Europe), 1768–1776* (Princeton: Princeton University Press, 1989).

——*Utopia and Reform in the Enlightenment* (Cambridge: Cambridge University Press, 1971).

VEUTHEY, M., *Guérrillas et droit humanitaire* (Geneva: International Committee of the Red Cross, 1976).

VILLEFRANCHE, J., *Curés et Prussiens* (Paris: Bourg, 1877).

VINCENT, J., 'The Hobbesian Tradition in Twentieth Century International Thought', *Millennium*, 10 (1981).

——'Racial Equality', in H. Bull and A. Watson (eds.), *The Expansion of International Society* (Oxford: Clarendon Press, 1984).

VIROLI, M., *For Love of Country: An Essay on Patriotism and Nationalism* (Oxford: Clarendon Press, 1995).

VIVIÈS, J., 'Boswell, La Corse, et *l'Encyclopédie*' in *Studies on Voltaire and the Eighteenth Century* (Oxford: Voltaire Foundation, 1986).

VOLLENHOVEN, C. VAN, *The Three Stages in the Evolution of the Law of Nations* (The Hague: Martinus Nijhoff, 1919).

VOLTAIRE, *The Complete Works of Voltaire* (Oxford: Taylor Institution, 1987).

VON HARTMANN, J., *Militärische Notwendigkeit und Humanität–Military Necessities and Humanity* (Bonn: Deutsche Rundschau, 1877–8).

VREELAND, H., *Hugo Grotius, the Father of the Modern Science of International Law* (New York: OUP, 1917).

WAHL, J., 'La Bipolarité de Rousseau', *Annales de la Société Jean-Jacques Rousseau*, 33 (1953–5).

WALICKI, A., *The Enlightenment and the Birth of Modern Nationhood: Polish Political Thought from Noble Republicanism to Tadeusz Kosciuszko* (Notre Dame: University of Notre Dame Press, 1989).

——*Legal Philosophies of Russian Liberalism* (Oxford: Clarendon Press, 1987).

WALTZ, K., *Man, The State, and War: A Theoretical Analysis* (New York: Columbia University Press, 1960).

WALZER, M., *Just and Unjust Wars* (New York: Basic Books, 1992).

——*Obligations: Essays on Disobedience, War, and Citizenship* (Cambridge: Harvard University Press, 1970).

——'Political Action: The Problem of Dirty Hands', in M. Cohen et al. (eds.), *War and Moral Responsibility* (Princeton: Princeton University Press, 1974).

WAXEL, P. DE, *L'Armée d'invasion et la population: leurs rapports pendant la Guerre étudiés au point de vue du droit des gens naturel* (Leipzig: Krueger, 1874).

WEBER, E., *My France* (Cambridge, Mass: Harvard University Press, 1991).

WEIDEN, P., *Necessity in International Law* (London: Transactions of the Grotius Society, 1939).

WEILL, G., *Histoire du Parti Républicain en France* (Paris: Alcan, 1900).

WELLS, H. G., *Social Evolution* (London: Macmillan, 1894).

WERNER, K., 'L'Attitude devant la guerre dans l'Allemagne de 1900', in *1914: les psychoses de guerre?* (Rouen: Publications de l'Université de Rouen, 1985).

WHEATON, H., *International Law* (London: G. G. Wilson, 1889).

WIGHT, M., *International Theory: The Three Traditions* (London: Leicester University Press, 1991).

——*System of States* (London: Leicester University Press, 1977).

——'Why is there no international theory?', in H. Butterfield and M. Wight (eds.), *Diplomatic Investigations: Essays on the Theories of International Politics* (London: Allen & Unwin, 1966).

WILKINSON, S., *The University and the Study of War* (Oxford: Clarendon, 1909).

WILLEMS, J. C., 'Grotius and International Law', in F. Elchlepp et al. (eds.) *Hugo Grotius 1583–1983* (Assen: Maastricht Colloquium, 1983).

——'How to Handle Grotian Ambivalence? A Guidance towards some Recent Guides', *Grotiana*, 6 (1985).

WILLIAMS, H., and BOOTH, K., 'Kant: Theorist beyond Limit', in I. Clarke and I. Neumann (eds.), *Classical Theories of International Relations* (London: Macmillan, 1996).

WINCH, P., 'Man and Society in Hobbes and Rousseau', in M. Cranston and R. S. Peters (eds.), *Hobbes and Rousseau: A Collection of Critical Essays* (New York: Doubleday, 1989).

WINDENBERGER, J., *Essai sur le système de politique étrangère de J.-J. Rousseau: la République Confédérative des Petits États* (Paris: A. Picard et Fils, 1899).

WOKLER, R., *Rousseau* (Oxford: Oxford University Press, 1995).

——'Rousseau's Pufendorf: Natural Law and the Foundations of Commercial Society', *History of Political Thought*, 15/3 (1994).

WOOLF, S., *Napoleon's Integration of Europe* (London: Routledge, 1991).

WORMELL, D., *Sir John Seeley and the Uses of History* (Cambridge: Cambridge University Press, 1979).

WRIGHT, J. K., *A Classical Republican in Eighteenth Century France: The Political Thought of Mably* (Stanford, Calif.: Stanford University Press, 1997).

WRIGHT, Lord, 'The Killing of Hostages as a War Crime', *American Journal of International Law*, 25 (1946).

WRIGHT, Q., 'The Law of the Nuremberg Trials', *American Journal of International Law*, 40 (1947).

——'Legal Positivism and the Nuremberg Judgement', *American Journal of International Law*, 42 (1948).

ZURAW, J., 'Tadeusz Kosciuzcko: The Polish Enlightenment Thinker', *Dialectics and Humanism*, 6 (1971).

INDEX

Wilkinson, Spencer 116, 117
will 85, 191, 200, 218
  general 192, 196, 210, 211, 223
Willems, J. C. 130, 133, 134 n., 135 n.,
  139 n.
Winch, P. 186 n.
Windenberger, J. 183, 184–5
Wint, G. 19 n.
Wokler, Robert 182 n., 183 n.
Wolseley, Garnet J., Viscount 102
Woolf, Stuart 23, 43
Wormell, Deborah 112 n.

Wright, Johnson Kent 178 n.

Yasuaki, O. 143 n., 145 n., 152 n., 153 n.
York 115
Young Europe 227, 228, 229, 234, 239
Young Italy 229, 230, 232, 233, 234, 235,
  236
Young Poland 228, 239

Zimmern, Alfred 116
zoology 88
Zuraw, Josef 219 n.